CRS
Wed & reg report.

capital markets.

cross asset feeatures

E C A T. & role in
CRD & BASEL.

December

update knowledge on
CRAS.

national competent
authority.

The Meroni Case

CREDIT RATING AGENCIES
ON THE WATCH LIST

Credit Rating Agencies on the Watch List

Analysis of European Regulation

RAQUEL GARCÍA ALCUBILLA AND
JAVIER RUIZ DEL POZO

OXFORD
UNIVERSITY PRESS

OXFORD
UNIVERSITY PRESS

Great Clarendon Street, Oxford OX2 6DP,
United Kingdom

Oxford University Press is a department of the University of Oxford.
It furthers the University's objective of excellence in research, scholarship,
and education by publishing worldwide. Oxford is a registered trade mark of
Oxford University Press in the UK and in certain other countries

British Library Cataloguing in Publication Data

Data available

Library of Congress Cataloguing in Publication Data

Garcia Alcubilla, Raquel.
Credit rating agencies on the watch list : analysis of European regulation /
Raquel Garcia Alcubilla and Javier Ruiz del Pozo.
p. cm.
ISBN 978-0-19-960886-7 (hbk.)
1. Credit bureaus. 2. Credit bureaus—Government policy—Europe. 3. Credit ratings.
4. Credit ratings—Europe. I. Ruiz del Pozo, Javier. II. Title.
HG3751.5.G37 2012   332.7094—dc23   2012006121

ISBN 978-0-19-960886-7

Printed in Great Britain
on acid-free paper by
MPG Books Group, Bodmin and King's Lynn

For Javi, my enhancement.
For Sofía.

Preface

Ratings are, and have been, highly topical in the financial markets for the past few years as the role of rating agencies in the recent financial crisis has been heavily criticized; and the Euro debt crisis has placed agencies in the spotlight once more. Many academic studies, policy documents, regulatory initiatives, and newspaper articles have been produced on this industry, mostly highlighting the deficiencies of the agencies. We have drawn from this useful and extensive literature and from our experience as supervisors, to produce a book that goes a step forward by providing a comprehensive overview of all the key aspects of ratings and rating agencies.

Our work as rating agencies' experts in the Spanish Securities and Exchange Commission (CNMV) and in ESMA, has allowed us to be directly involved in all the discussions that have taken place in this regulatory sphere since 2003, when the functioning of rating agencies was mostly unknown to the markets and the possibility of regulating them was quite remote.

During these years of non-stop study and frequent journeys to work with our colleges of ESMA and IOSCO, we have had the opportunity to learn about the rating business and the regulatory problems that rating agencies' activities raise. In this learning journey, we have been accompanied by highly qualified professionals from the CNMV, from securities and banking supervisors from all over the world, and from rating agencies. We would like to thank these people for all the shared efforts.

We have done our best to capture in the book all the knowledge we have gained during these years and have tried to anticipate future developments. It has been a challenging task organizing the interesting debates, reports, and regulatory in-itiatives to produce a book that will hopefully be useful for users of ratings, regulators and supervisors, rating agencies, and for anyone interested in having a good insight into what rating agencies do.

This book would not have been possible without the wholehearted and constant support we have received from our 'triple-A' families and friends. Thanks to them, this complicated and time-consuming task has ended up being an enriching and fun experience.

Although we are currently working at the CNMV and have held until recently relevant positions in ESMA, the views expressed in the book are just ours and should not be reported as representing the views either of the CNMV or of ESMA. The book is based exclusively on publicly available information.

Raquel García Alcubilla
Javier Ruiz del Pozo

Contents

List of Tables

List of Abbreviations

ABCP	Asset-backed commercial papers
ABS	Asset-backed securities
AM Best	A.M. Best Company, Inc.
AMF	Autorité des Marchés Financiers
BCBS	Basel Committee on Banking Supervision
CDO	Collateralized debt obligations
CEBS	Committee of European Banking Supervisors
CEIOPS	Committee of European Insurance and Occupational Pensions Supervisors
CEREP	Central Repository
CESR	Committee of European Securities Regulators
CGFS	Committee on the Global Financial System
CMBS	Commercial mortgage-backed securities
CRA	Credit rating agency
CRAs	Credit rating agencies
CRD	Capital Requirement Directives
DBRS	DBRS, Limited
EBA	European Banking Authority
EC	European Commission
ECA	Export credit agencies
ECAI	External Credit Assessment Institution
ECB	European Central Bank
EIOPA	European Insurance and Occupational Pensions Authority
ESMA	European Securities Markets Authority
EU	European Union
Fitch	Fitch Rating, Ltd
FSB	Financial Stability Board (previously FSF—Financial Stability Forum)
G-20	The Group of Twenty Finance Ministers and Central Bank Governors
IMF	International Monetary Fund
IOSCO	International Organization of Securities Commissions
MiFID	Markets in Financial Instruments Directive
Moody's	Moody's Investor Services, Inc.
NRSRO	Nationally Recognized Statistical Rating Organizations
RMBS	Residential mortgage-backed securities

SEC	US Securities and Exchange Commission
S&P	Standard & Poor's Ratings Services
Standard & Poor's	Standard & Poor's Ratings Services
USA	United States of America

Note to the Reader

We have devised a short form for a number of reports, regulatory papers, and rules that are frequently mentioned in the book. The glossary (see pp. 283–5) provides the full reference to these documents and therefore in the text they are just mentioned in their short form.

In those circumstances where an organization has been replaced by another one, we have opted for including in the text the latest name, except in those cases where this replacement could lead to confusion. This has been the case for CESR, that has been transformed into ESMA, CEBS to EBA, CEIOPS to EIOPA, and FSF to FSB. However, bibliographical references are kept using the name of the organization at the time the document was produced.

Finally, when referring to reports we have included a reference to the specific sections, paragraphs and/or pages that are relevant to the issue being discussed in the book. However, we have not done so in relation to those documents that will be changing in the near future as is the case, for example, with some of ESMA's guidance which, according to the amendment of the European Regulation on rating agencies, will have to be revisited shortly.

1

Introduction

1.1 A HISTORY OF RATINGS AND THE ROLE OF RATING AGENCIES

1.1.1 Financial Markets Prior to Rating Agencies

Although nowadays credit rating agencies (CRAs) are a vital element of financial markets, this has not always been the case. In fact, as Professor Richard Sylla[1] accurately explains in his text *An Historical Primer on the Business of Credit Rating*, financial markets functioned well before rating agencies began operating in the USA at the beginning of the twentieth century.

At the start of the seventeenth century, the Dutch Republic, which was at the time the world leading economy, managed to have in place a modern financial system that included a banking system, an incipient central bank, and securities markets. Due to the influence of the Dutch, England also developed its financial market in the last decades of the seventeenth century and the USA, shortly after its independence at the end of the eighteenth century, had in place bond and stock markets in several cities.

Therefore, for several centuries financial markets functioned without CRAs. This was mostly due to the fact that investments during those early stages of securities trading mainly took place in public bonds (in most cases issued to finance wars) and investors trusted the governments as being able to repay their debts. Later on, when the international bond market grew during the nineteenth century in Europe, investment still continued to concentrate mostly on the sovereign debt market and most capital needs were covered by bank loans and share issues.

The situation in the USA was somewhat different, as its economy was of a larger scale than in other countries, but at the same time fragmented due to the federal organization. In the first decades of the nineteenth century, some US states first, and local governments after, issued debt to finance infrastructure projects. But soon the private sector incorporated these projects and an important corporate debt market developed.

The basic need for capital in the USA came in relation to the construction of railroads. Although there was initially some governmental support to create a

---

[1] Sylla, Richard (2002), *An Historical Primer on the Business of Credit Rating.* The New York University Salomon Center Series on Financial Markets and Institutions, Kluwer Academic Publishers.

railway network over the country, most US railroads raised capital as private corporations. At first, these corporations were able to finance themselves with bank loans and share issues as they were located in small regions of the country and local investors had knowledge of the projects. However, after 1850, the expansion of the activities of these companies to far away territories made it more complicated to gather local finance and thus they started issuing bonds. A huge corporate bond market was created, essentially from railroads bonds, that grew as fast as the railroad tracks themselves.

1.1.2 The Predecessors of Rating Agencies

Linked to the expansion of this corporate bond market and to the need of investors to gather information on increasing investment options, three institutions emerged as the predecessors of the credit rating industry.

1.1.2.1 Credit-reporting Agencies

The expanding American business, with transactions increasing in number, amount, and geographical scale, gave rise to a more sophisticated system for gathering information about borrowers. Until then, borrowers and lenders knew each other or had common contacts that could provide recommendation letters. But with the growth of the market, these informal channels became insufficient and a new institution, the credit-reporting agency,[2] appeared to fulfil the new markets need for professional information.

Credit-reporting agencies gathered information on the situation and creditworthiness of companies all over the USA and sold this information to subscribers. These agencies also offered related services, such as analysis of local economic conditions.

As creditors needed such information on companies that were dispersed all over the large territory of the USA, these credit-reporting agencies developed a network (branch) structure. This innovative structure linked local offices into an association trading under a common name. Correspondents sent their reports to local branches, which then forwarded them to the main office.

A well-documented example of the evolution of these agencies is the history of Dun & Bradstreet[3], which starts in 1841 with the creation of the Mercantile Agency as one of the first organizations formed with the sole purpose of providing business information. In 1870, the agency claimed to have 7,000 subscribers, and by the 1880s it estimated 40,000, including the largest companies in the country.[4] In 1962 Dun & Bradstreet acquired Moody's Investors Service, but in 2000 the company spun off its rating activity to create a separate CRA.

---

[2] Olegario, Rowena (2002), *Credit-reporting Agencies: Their Historical Roots, Current Status, and Role in Market Development.* Background document for the World Development Report 2002.

[3] Dun & Bradstreet, *History of Dun & Bradstreet.*

[4] Norris, James D. (1978), *R.G. Dun & Co., 1841–1900: The Development of Credit Reporting in the Nineteenth Century.* Westport, CT: Greenwood Press.

1.1.2.2 Specialized Publications

Together with these credit-reporting agencies, the appearance of a specialized business and financial press was also crucial to improve companies' information that was available for investors. As railroad corporations became the world's first big business, they soon required specialized publications, and by 1832 *The American Railroad Journal* provided thorough information about the industry. When Henry Varnum Poor became its editor in 1849, the journal turned into a publication aimed at investors, as it published systematic information on the ownership of railroads, their assets, liabilities, and earnings. In 1868, Poor[5] and his son published the first annual volume of *Poor's Manual of the Railroads of the United States*, which provided financial and operating statistics covering several years for most of the major American railroads. Through annual updates, the publication allowed investors to chart a company's progress over the years. This manual became the authoritative investors' guide to the state of railroad company finances for several decades and led the way to similar undertakings by others. By 1916 the Poor Company had entered into the bond rating business and in 1941 merged with the Standard Statistics Bureau, which had been publishing an annual volume since 1906 containing corporate news items that focused on industries beyond railroads.

John Moody & Company also started as a specialized publication with the release of *Moody's Manual of Industrial and Miscellaneous Securities* in 1900, the company's founding year.[6] The manual provided information and statistics on shares and bonds of financial institutions, government agencies, manufacturing, mining, utilities, and food companies. Later in 1909, Moody's company evolved into publishing more than a simple collection of information on the property, capitalization, and management of companies; it offered investors an analysis of security values. Moody's company published a book with an analysis and concise conclusion of the relative investment quality of the railroad companies and their outstanding securities. The conclusions were expressed using letter rating symbols adopted from the mercantile and credit rating system that had been used by the credit-reporting firms since the late 1800s. In 1909, *Moody's Analyses of Railroad Investments* described for readers the analytic principles that Moody used to assess a railroad's operations, management, and finance. In 1913, the manual was expanded to include the evaluation of industrial companies and utilities, besides railroads.

Another relevant specialized publisher, the Fitch Publishing Company,[7] was founded in 1913 by John Knowles Fitch. The company published financial statistics through publications such as the *Fitch Bond Book* and the *Fitch Stock and Bond Manual*. In 1924, the Fitch Publishing Company introduced the now familiar 'AAA' to 'D' ratings scale that was accompanied by an in-depth analysis of investment experts.

---

[5] S&P, *Standard and Poor's Company History*.
[6] Moody's, *Moody's History*.
[7] Fitch, *The History of Fitch Ratings*.

1.1.2.3 Investment Bankers

Investment bankers, the financial intermediaries who underwrote, subscribed, and distributed the securities from railroad companies, were also crucial to increasing the amount of information available about these companies. These bankers requested companies to provide all the relevant information in relation to their debt securities and the company itself. By participating in the operation, the banker's reputation was put at stake and, in this sense, the fact that a number of reputed bankers participated in the issuance was considered a certification of the quality of the bonds. This reputation capital, when some conflict-of-interest concerns were raised in relation to the bankers, was somehow transferred to CRAs in the sense that CRAs' participation provided a similar type of comfort to investors.

1.1.3 The Rise of Rating Agencies

CRAs, which evolved as a natural consequence of this need for specialized information based on the three institutions mentioned, were functioning under the 'subscription-paid' model; those investors needing the information would pay for it.

However, in the 1930s there was a change in the situation of CRAs[8] as bank regulators incorporated references in regulations to 'recognized rating manuals'. For the first time, in 1936, a decree prohibited banks from investing in speculative investment securities as determined by 'recognized rating manuals'. In the next decades, insurance regulators also started to include references to ratings and, in 1975, the US Securities and Exchange Commission (SEC) adopted the broker-

dealer net capital rule that used the term 'NRSRO'[9] to classify debt instruments in terms of the amount they would be haircut for regulatory capital purposes, depending on the rating assigned by a NRSRO. Basically two kinds of regulatory requirements were incorporated: rules that restricted the extent to which a firm could hold assets that fell below investment grade and rules that linked capital requirements to the ratings on individual securities, with lower capital charges for high-rated securities.

These rules meant that the 'opinions' given by the CRAs became more and more relevant in financial markets as part of the regulation, and that private judgement on the risks of investments were being outsourced to the CRAs. At this point, CRAs were granted the ability to determine the substantive effect of legal rules.[10]

Among other reasons, this regulatory relevance led to a change in the business models of the CRAs that in the 1970s started charging issuers for the ratings. As CRAs realized that issuers needed their ratings to get their securities in the

---

[8] White, Lawrence J. (2010), Markets: The credit rating agencies. *Journal of Economic Perspectives*, 24 (2).

[9] The SEC then recognized Moody's, S&P, and Fitch as NRSROs.

[10] Partnoy, Frank (1999), The Siskel and Ebert of financial markets? Two thumbs down for the credit rating agencies. *Washington University Law Quarterly*, 77, October.

portfolios of financial institutions, CRAs decided that issuers had to pay for the rating. The stated rationale for this change was based on the belief that issuers should pay for the substantial value objective ratings provided in terms of market access.

In addition, the appearance of high-speed photocopying machines, which eased the possibility of subscribers sharing the rating reports with non-paying investors, and the fact that some CRAs believed that the complexity of the capital markets required a more sophisticated level of staffing and compensation than could be supported only by subscribers fees, led to a definitive change towards the 'issuer-pays' model. This change in model opened the door to potential conflicts of interest.

CRAs expanded quickly from the 1970s to the 1990s. The prosperity of the post-war decades increased the number of potential investors around the world and the breakdown of the Bretton Woods System, allowing for a floating exchange rate regime, opened the international capital flows. More states and private companies issued bonds in domestic and international markets, and financial authorities all over the world began to incorporate agency's ratings in their regulations. CRAs had to rapidly increase their number of analysts and start raising their revenues.

Over the past decades, CRAs have played a very relevant role in the growth of international financial markets. Their ability to produce clear, internationally harmonized indicators of the risk of default was crucial to incentivize investments at an international level as many investors would not have been otherwise capable of assessing the credit risk of those securities on their own. In a sense, ratings helped standardize securities through a simple linear rating scale.

For corporate and sovereign bonds this system proved reasonably reliable and enabled investors to hold a diversified portfolio. However, in structured products markets the role of CRAs goes beyond reducing information asymmetry. These markets needed the quality assurance that ratings provided to non-qualified investors in order to develop. However, the ratings of structured products turned out to be less robust in predicting future developments than traditional ratings.

1.1.4 Role of Rating Agencies

According to the analysis provided by the Bank of England,[11] there are at least three key functions that CRAs perform for the international financial system that are beneficial and that should be retained:

1. CRAs can help mitigate the fundamental information asymmetry in capital markets between investors and firms seeking external financing. This inherent asymmetry may deter some investors from providing financing to firms because of the cost of acquiring the necessary information. A detailed analysis of credit risk would be impractical for most investors to carry out; it might also be inefficient if the investor's stake is small relative to their overall portfolio. A rating from a neutral third party can enable small investors who could not

---

[11] Bank of England (2007), *Financial stability report.* October, Issue No 22.

afford to conduct their own risk assessment to enter the market. As a result, external ratings can help lower the cost of capital. This economic role that CRAs perform is further explained in many papers.[12]

2. Ratings can be a useful mechanism to solve some principal–agent problems. Principals (investors) can attempt to cap the amount of risk that agents (such as pension funds, life insurers, and money market mutual funds) take on their behalf by stating a minimum rating for assets in which to invest or counterparty exposures to take. In addition, access to some financial markets or business models can be restricted to issuers with ratings above a minimum level.

3. Ratings can be used to solve collective action problems between dispersed bond investors. It may not be rational for individual investors to monitor a firm in difficulty. But if the firm continues trading without action being taken, this could reduce recovery values for investors. A credit rating downgrade can act as a clear signal for individual investors to take action, triggering debt restructuring.

However, ratings can also have a negative impact in the economy, as highlighted in the subprime crisis. Rating downgrades can have a systemic impact on the financial markets as they can lead to rating-based triggers with negative effects on the financial system such as the rapid drying up of liquidity.[13] This is even more acute if we take into account the fact that some analyses conclude that rating agencies are pro-cyclical in their assignment of ratings, in the sense that initial ratings and rating changes exhibit excess sensitivity to the business cycle.[14]

1.2 RATING INDUSTRY

1.2.1 Characteristics

When analysing the structure of the CRA industry, many studies have concluded that this market is a natural oligopoly[15] as the nature of the CRA market makes it complicated for new CRAs to succeed and for existing CRAs to expand their business: issuers usually only desire ratings from those CRAs that are respected by investors, and investors tend to respect only those CRAs with a history of accurate and timely ratings. Therefore, new entrants face the challenge of having to develop and demonstrate a track record to acquire the credibility with investors that is necessary to persuade issuers to buy their rating services. In the case of new CRAs,

---

[12] BCBS (August 2000), *Credit ratings and complementary sources of credit quality information.* Working Papers no. 3.

[13] Sy, Amadou N.R., (2009), *The systemic regulation of credit rating agencies and rated markets.* IMF Working Paper 09/129.

[14] Amato, Jeffery D. and Furfine, Craig H. (2003), *Are credit ratings procyclical?* BIS Working Papers No 129.

[15] CESR (March 2005), *Technical advice to the European Commission on possible measures concerning credit rating agencies (Ref. CESR/05-139b).*

investors are normally reluctant to value the ratings of a new entrant as much as those of existing CRAs because new entrants lack historical default rates by which investors can assess their performance. Consequently, issuers may decide not to engage a new entrant for a rating to avoid the risk of investors not relying on the rating of their securities. Without support and interest from investors or issuers, it takes a new company a considerable amount of time for its business to become self-sustaining.

In addition, there are some other natural difficulties that new CRAs face when entering the market. To start with, a new entrant will face high start-up costs and can therefore be perceived to be vulnerable to certain financial pressures that larger CRAs may be insulated against. Investors may fear that the potential conflict of interest to provide a rating favorable for issuers can be higher for a new entrant as, in this case, a single fee-paying issuer may comprise a large portion of its total revenue.

In addition, a new entrant will normally have fewer resources (such as staff, analytical tools, or information technology systems) and less coverage than more established CRAs. Without these resources and coverage, a new CRA may be at a disadvantage vis-à-vis more experienced CRAs, who may be able to hire more staff (and more experienced staff) to analyse large issuers involved in numerous complicated transactions.

Also, new entrants cannot compete much by way of providing more competitive prices, as it is difficult to reduce the cost of providing a rating very far without diminishing the degree of due diligence undertaken and, thus, the quality of the rating that is the main asset CRAs have to gain market share.

Finally, as issuers do not have many incentives to engage new entrants for a rating and to cooperate with them, it is likely that these new entrants will have to base their ratings solely on public information.

In relation to the remuneration model CRAs use, until the 1970s CRAs were paid by subscribers, as mentioned before. However, the 'issuer-pays' system is by far the most dominant remuneration model currently used by CRAs. On average, the revenue generated by the 'issuer-pays' model represents more than two-thirds of total CRA revenues.[16] Under this model, issuers solicit and pay for the ratings of their own securities, while the 'subscription-paid' CRAs generate their revenues by charging subscribers for access to their credit assessments. Consequently, ratings issued by subscription-based CRAs are only available to defined people (the subscribers).

Currently, due to the conflicts of interest that the issuer-pays model entails by its nature, a debate is open on the appropriateness of this remuneration model (see Chapter 5).

1.2.2 Worldwide

Although some studies[17] have calculated that there are around 150 local and international CRAs in the world, the credit rating market is effectively dominated

[16] EC consultation on CRAs, November 2010.
[17] See footnote 12.

by three large agencies that operate globally: Fitch Ratings, Ltd (Fitch), Moody's Investor Services, Inc. (Moody's), and Standard & Poor's Ratings Services (S&P). In fact, the market can be considered a duopoly, since S&P and Moody's have a combined market share, in terms of revenue, of over 80% with Fitch accounting for approximately 14%.[18]

In terms of number of ratings per sector, the level of concentration is even higher. The SEC, when analysing the competition in the industry in its *Annual Report on Nationally Recognized Statistical Rating Organizations* published in January 2011,[19] provided the information included in Table 1.1.

Fitch, Moody's, and S&P issued approximately 97% of all outstanding ratings across all categories reported and the concentration of outstanding ratings for these three CRAs is high across all five categories. However, this concentration varies across the different categories: for instance, Fitch, Moody's, and S&P account for over 99% of all outstanding ratings for government securities, but represent only around 77% in insurance ratings (where AM Best accounts for 22%).

Among the three largest CRAs, concentration is not consistent across rating classes. For example, for ratings on financial institutions, Fitch and Moody's each issued substantially more ratings than S&P, whilst S&P is clearly dominant in sovereign ratings and ABS.

Another indicative factor that is analysed by the SEC in its report refers to the number of credit analysts reported by the agencies: the three largest CRAs employ 3,150 credit analysts, which amounts to approximately 90% of the total number of analysts working for all of the registered NRSROs.

These global CRAs are active in many jurisdictions. Accordingly, they have established subsidiaries in a number of countries that operate as companies set up according to local corporate laws. Additionally, the parent company—based in the USA for the bigger groups—or some of its subsidiaries conduct rating activities in

Table 1.1. Number of ratings per NRSRO

NRSRO	Financial institutions	Insurance companies	Corporate issuers	Asset-backed securities	Government, municipal & sovereign	Total ratings
A.M. Best	3	5,364	2,246	54	0	7,667
DBRS	16,630	120	5,350	8,430	12,400	42,930
EJR	82	45	853	14	13	1,007
Fitch	72,311	4,599	12,613	69,515	352,697	511,735
JCR	156	31	518	64	53	822
LACE	17,263	60	1,000	0	61	18,384
Moody's	76,801	5,455	31,008	106,337	862,240	1,081,841
R&I	100	30	543	186	123	982
Realpoint	0	0	0	8,856	0	8,856
S&P	52,500	8,600	41,400	124,600	1,004,500	1,231,600
TOTAL	235,846	24,304	95,531	318,056	2,232,087	2,905,824

[18] EC impact assessment CRA Regulation.
[19] SEC (January 2011), *Annual report on Nationally Recognized Statistical Rating Organizations*.

additional jurisdictions through branches. But even if a CRA does not have branches a
physical presence in one country, it may rate companies domiciled in that country subsidiaries
or instruments issued by those companies.

Typically, the global rating groups are organized along business lines (such as
corporates, public finance, financial institutions, and structured finance). An
international manager is responsible for each of those global functions and they
are normally supported by regional managers (that would manage, for instance,
the corresponding EU business lines). The business divisions operate through
different subsidiaries and branches. Some of the core service functions (such as
methodologies development and review, compliance, business strategy, finance,
legal, information technology, and human resources) operate globally or region-
ally, providing the relevant services to all the different legal entities across the
group and reporting to the manager of the function in the relevant region or in
some cases to the global manager (who might be based in the US parent
company).

Despite the common features described above, each of the big CRAs has its own
specific organizational structure that is adapted as market and regulation evolves.
A summary of the key aspects of the groups' organizations of the three main CRAs
is provided in the AMF's *2009 Report on Rating Agencies* published in July 2010.

Fitch is dual-headquartered in New York and London and is 60% owned by
Fimalac, a French company, and 40% by Hearst Corporation. In addition to Fitch
Ratings, the Fitch Group also includes Fitch Solutions, a distribution channel for
Fitch Ratings products and a provider of data, analytics, and related services. The
Fitch Group also includes Algorithmics, a world provider of enterprise risk
management solutions.

Moody's Investor Services Inc. is owned by Moody's Corporation (listed in New
York Stock Exchange—NYSE), which is also the parent company of Moody's
Analytics, which encompasses Moody's non-ratings businesses (risk management
software for financial institutions, quantitative credit analysis tools, economic
research and data services, data and analytical tools for the structured finance
market, and training). Therefore, Moody's Investor Services Inc. specializes solely
in rating activities.

S&P is owned by the American publisher McGraw-Hill, a NYSE listed company
that has other businesses in publishing and education. Besides providing credit
ratings, S&P is also a supplier of databases (such as stock market indices). Until 1
January 2009 S&P was a division of The McGraw-Hill Companies, Inc. In 2009 a
wholly owned subsidiary, Standard & Poor's Financial Services LLC, was created
as a limited company incorporated in Delaware, and the McGraw-Hill Companies, Inc. transferred all the US assets of its Standard & Poor's division to the new
company that is now in charge of the main part of S&P's activities in the USA.
Outside the USA, S&P carries on its rating business through subsidiaries,
branches, or divisions of McGraw-Hill, depending on local regulatory and tax
environments. The McGraw-Hill parent company provides a number of shared
services to all divisions of the group, such as IT, accounting, marketing, human
resources, and legal services.

The rest of the market is occupied by smaller CRAs that differ in size and that
normally operate in specific market niches, either in terms of sectors and/or
geographic specialization. Among these smaller agencies, some of them are well

established regional agencies that intend to develop an international presence[20] but most of them have a minor impact on the global financial markets.

Although it is almost impossible to identify all the CRAs that operate around the world, as in many countries CRAs are not registered and there is no common definition of what a credit rating agency is, an indicative list of some of the CRAs that operate around the world can be found on the website of DefaultRisk.com.

1.2.3 Europe

In Europe, the industry structure replicates the global market situation, with the market being controlled mainly by the big three CRAs. In the EC impact assessment CRA Regulation published in November 2008, the EC provided a summary

of the organization of these three CRAs at EU level (see Annex 9.4). Moreover, in the EC impact assessment CRA II, the EC identified the following subsidiaries of the main CRAs: *branches —*

- S&P with subsidiaries in France, Germany, Italy, Spain, Sweden, and UK.
- Moody's with subsidiaries in Cyprus, Czech Republic, France, Germany, Italy, Spain, and UK.
- Fitch with subsidiaries in France, Germany, Italy, Poland, Spain, and UK.

However, since this information was published, and partly due to the Regulation entering into force, these three groups have undertaken certain restructuring that will probably continue for some time. For example, S&P has transformed its subsidiaries in Germany, Spain, and Sweden into branches.

Besides these big agencies, in Europe a number of distinctly smaller CRAs operate with a clear focus on specific industry sectors (such as insurance industry) or financial market segments (for example, municipal bonds), thus responding to specialized market needs. Altogether, around 23 CRAs are established in the EU. The EC impact assessment CRA II incorporated the following list of CRAs established in the EU in 2009:

New CRA II

- Coface (with subsidiaries in France, Belgium, Luxembourg, UK).
- DBRS (to be established, UK).
- Creditreform (Austria).
- Kreditschutzverband von 1870 (Austria).
- Bulgarian Credit Rating Agency (Bulgaria).
- National Credit Rating Agency (Bulgaria).
- Global Ratings (Bulgaria).
- Capital Intelligence Limited (Cyprus).
- Euler Hermes Rating (Germany).
- ASSEKURATA (Germany).
- URA Rating Agentur AG (Germany).
- Prof. Dr Schneck Rating (Germany).

---

[20] DBRS in Canada and USA and Japan Credit Rating Agency, Ltd and Rating and Investment Information, Inc. in Japan.

- Creditreform Rating AG (Germany).
- RS Rating Services AG (Germany).
- MAR-Rating GmbH (Germany).
- Lince Spa (Italy).
- Capp&CAPP Srl (Italy).
- Companhia Portuguesa de Rating (Portugal).
- European Rating Agency (Slovakia).
- ECRAI (Slovakia).
- AM Best (UK).

In the report that ESMA published in December 2010,[21] although no details are provided on individual CRAs, further information on the number of CRAs operating in the EU can be extracted from the data provided in relation to the number of applications for registration.

In particular, between 7 June and 7 September 2010, 23 applications were received for registration and one application for certification (from a Japanese agency). While most of these applications were for individual CRAs, four of them referred to groups of CRAs that cover several subsidiaries (although not mentioned in the report, it can be inferred that these are from Fitch, Moody's, S&P, and Coface). Consequently, in total 45 legal entities applied for registration in the EU during that period of time.

According to the report, the breakdown per country is as follows: the country with the most CRAs established is Germany with a total of ten, then Italy and UK with six, France with four (and one for certification), Spain and Poland with three, Portugal, Bulgaria and Cyprus with two, and Belgium, Czech Republic, Greece, Netherlands, and Slovakia with one.

As discussed in Section 2.1.5, the fact that the European market is dominated by only three CRAs is an issue of concern for the EC. Time will tell whether the different ideas that are now being discussed in international fora, such as those suggested by the EC consultation on CRAs November 2010, finally lead to specific proposals and if the current oligopolistic structure is altered or not.

1.3 USE OF RATINGS

The relevance of CRAs in financial markets is directly proportional to the use market participants make of the ratings these entities issue. As discussed previously, history has shown that the use of ratings has varied significantly across different periods of time. Initially, they played a significant role in the marketing of debt instruments to investors, but over time they were also included in various regulations. This section will cover and explain the different uses of ratings in financial markets.

---

[21] CESR (December 2010), *Annual report according to Article 21 of Regulation (EC) 1060/2009 on credit rating agencies (Ref. CESR/10-1424).*

1.3.1 Use by Market Participants

1.3.1.1 Investors

Ratings are used by short- and long-term investors throughout the world because they provide a common benchmark to measure the credit risk of securities. Ratings allow for a reliable comparison of credit risk across a wide range of investment opportunities available worldwide. There are other methods to assess the creditworthiness of a security, such as the use of yield spreads and price volatility, but these other methods are not as simple and stable as ratings. Moreover, ratings are easily available and offer information on track record performance, which has normally proved that, in many cases, ratings are a reliable indicator to assess the likelihood that a security will default.

In addition, there are investors that have to comply with regulatory requirements or with their own internal investment guidelines who sometimes also make references to ratings.

1.3.1.2 Issuers

Ratings are requested by issuers mainly because investors use them. Therefore, issuers seek ratings because they help them to place their securities in the markets at a lower cost. Ratings are disclosed in promotional materials distributed in connection with the issue of a security as a way to ease the selling process.

Ratings are also used to help price securities that are traded in the secondary markets. Several studies confirm that liquidity is enhanced and pricing is more favourable when a security has at least one rating.

In addition, ratings are also incorporated in loan agreements, derivative financial transactions, and other counterparty arrangements. They are often incorporated in collateral arrangements that govern the collateral supplied to counterparties in the securities markets.

Also, ratings are used in the interbank market by financial institutions judging the creditworthiness of other banks with which they engage in business.

1.3.1.3 Financial Analysts

Together with their own independent research, financial analysts (especially fixed income analysts) are frequent users of ratings. In most cases, analysts use ratings to identify securities which they consider to have a different risk exposure than the rating reflects, securities that are traded in the market at prices and spreads that seem inconsistent with the rating.

1.3.1.4 Intermediaries

Financial intermediaries have incorporated ratings into their risk management policies. As discussed previously, counterparty eligibility and collateral posting requirements are frequently based on ratings.

1.3.2 Use in Private Contracts

Ratings are used in financial contracts in many different ways, the most frequent use being the inclusion of 'rating triggers' in contracts. Rating triggers are contractual provisions that give counterparties and lenders the right to terminate the credit availability, accelerate credit obligations, or have the borrower post collateral in the event of specified rating actions, such as if the rating of the borrower's securities falls below a certain level.

Lenders are willing to pay for triggers by accepting lower spreads or coupons as rating triggers protect them against credit deterioration and asymmetric information problems. On the other side, borrowers are willing to include such triggers because without them lenders would probably demand a higher initial spread on debt contracts.

Therefore, rating triggers attempt to offer protection to investors but, due to the way in which they work, these triggers can precipitate a liquidity crisis and even contribute to extreme events such as bankruptcies, as was the case, for example, in the Enron bankruptcy. In the case of Enron, the use of credit ratings as 'triggers' in trading and other financial agreements gave counterparties the right to demand cash collateral, and lenders the right to demand repayment of outstanding loans, once Enron's credit rating declined to certain levels. As a result, the existence of ratings triggers contributed to an increase in Enron's financial difficulties.

Following Enron and other high-profile bankruptcies, rating triggers received considerable attention and several studies were produced at an international level to analyse the negative consequences of the use of ratings in private contracts.[22]

In general, a rating trigger provides creditors and counterparties with certain rights in the event of a borrower's credit rating falling to, or below, a specified level. The rights given to the creditors usually vary from an increase in the nominal coupon to a put option.

Not all rating triggers are alike and the consequences if they are activated vary substantially.[23] Some are relatively harmless, such as those that incrementally increase the interest paid on loans and bonds in line with rating downgrades. However, some, like the accelerating clauses,[24] might have significant potential negative impact on the issuer. In this case, contractual rating triggers can contribute to 'credit cliff' situations ('credit cliff' is market jargon for a situation in which dire consequences, such as compounding credit deterioration, possibly leading to default, may be expected should certain risk scenarios materialize) and they can seriously escalate liquidity problems in firms faced with a deteriorating financial outlook. Rating triggers and other covenants, particularly when combined, can contribute to the development of such credit cliffs and may speed up the pace at which the cost of capital increases due to credit deterioration. This is especially the

---

[22] See footnote 15.

[23] González, Fernando, Haas, François, Johannes, Ronald, Persson, Mattias, Toledo, Liliana, Violi, Roberto, Wieland, Martin, and Zins, Carmen (June 2004), *Market dynamics associated with credit ratings, a literature review*. Occasional Paper Series, n.º 16, ECB.

[24] Acceleration clauses are used in bond contracts, in bank loan agreements, and in back-up credit lines. For example, for a bond initially issued for a long period, the triggering of the clause may result in an acceleration of repayments, or even early termination of credit.

case in situations where multiple triggers are set off simultaneously, or when the triggering of one clause leads to an accumulation of negative consequences.

The possible negative aspects of rating triggers have been exacerbated because analysts and investors have not always taken them fully into account. Moreover, it has proved difficult to obtain a comprehensive picture of the size of the contingent liability of triggers, despite the fact that this information is crucial for investors, analysts, and rating agencies in order to fully understand the risks attached to a specific issue or issuer.

In this sense, in 2002 Moody's undertook a comprehensive review of rating triggers in the US and European contracts[25] and concluded that there was a widespread use of these triggers, most often in the mid-to-low investment grade category, but that their reporting was unsystematic. This lack of transparency led to little awareness in the market about the possible negative effects of rating triggers.

The importance of disclosing rating triggers was also highlighted in the 2004 European Parliament's *Resolution on the role and methods of rating agencies*.[26] The European Parliament considered 'an obligation of ratings users, whether in the private or in the public domain, to use ratings with proper regard for the stability of financial markets, especially by disclosing any rating triggers included in loan agreements or face the sanction of such clauses being declared null and void'.

Transparency and disclosure are important features that could help mitigate some of the negative aspects of rating triggers as they could increase the awareness of the situation in the market and promote a longer-term view on the part of market participants.

The analysis included the paper entitled *Market dynamics associated with credit ratings, a literature review*:[27]

> the present context of incomplete transparency and disclosure of rating triggers may be seen as impacting on the price discovery mechanism of fixed income products (and, by extension, equities) as it results in an additional risk premium associated with this "rating trigger" uncertainty. This in turn may lead to a higher cost of capital and higher yields than would have been the case under a more transparent framework. Thus, the "benefits" of these clauses are not fully exploited. However, if rating triggers were systematically disclosed from their inception, this information would be priced in from the start in bond issues (and stocks) and the number of triggers used in debt issues of any single borrower would probably be more limited. Moreover, it could also be argued that the expected benefits (for issuers) from these devices would prove illusory, as the relative prices of the various debt instruments of an issuer/borrower and its equity price would adjust to reflect the existence of rating triggers in some debt instruments, and that the benefits (in terms of favourable financing conditions) stemming from trigger-carrying instruments would be offset by deteriorating financing conditions (and increased volatility) for 'unprotected' instruments. It is, of course, unlikely that all rating triggers could be disclosed, since there are private

[25] Moody's (July 2002), *Moody's analysis of US corporate rating triggers heightens need for increased disclosure*, special comment and Moody's (September 2002), *Rating triggers in Europe: Limited awareness but widely used among corporate issuers*, special comment.

[26] European Parliament (January 2004), *Resolution on the role and methods of rating agencies (2003/2081(INI))*.

[27] See footnote 23.

placements and bank loan agreements with embedded options. Still, greater transparency should have both direct and indirect positive effects on credit markets.

Efforts have been made in this area, notably under pressure from rating agencies, to encourage a more systematic disclosure of rating triggers and to renegotiate and smooth out the most dangerous ones. However, despite the European Parliament's message in 2004, and the studies mentioned highlighting the risks, the EU CRA Regulation has not tackled the need to impose mandatory disclosure of rating triggers (concerning companies with securities admitted to trading on regulated markets) and the issue was not discussed during the negotiations of the Regulation, as it was not even mentioned in the EC proposal.

Therefore, currently there are no specific rules in the EU for systematic disclosure of these triggers. Nevertheless, there are two regulatory areas that have an impact on disclosure of these covenants, although they leave a significant degree of discretion as to whether triggers need to be disclosed.

Under the general provisions of the international accounting standards (IAS 1) there is an obligation to disclose material triggers, but material in this context means not only that the contingent obligation is large, but that it potentially has a significant bearing on the company's financial situation. Additionally, IFRS 7 specifically requires companies to provide disclosures about any breaches of loan agreement terms during the reporting period if those breaches permitted the lender to demand accelerated repayment (unless the breaches were remedied, or the terms of the loan were renegotiated, on or before the end of the reporting period).

European legislation on prospectuses also has some provisions that could be understood as requiring the disclosure of material rating triggers in prospectuses. In particular, the Prospectus Regulation requires issuers to provide, amongst other things, the following information in share prospectuses:

- information concerning the issuer's capital resources (both short- and long-term);
- information on the borrowing requirements and funding structure of the issuer; and
- information regarding any restrictions on the use of capital resources that have materially affected, or could materially affect, directly or indirectly, the issuer's operations.

This provision could be understood as requiring the disclosure of material rating triggers. In this sense, *CESR's recommendations for the consistent implementation of the European Commission's Regulation on Prospectuses nº 809/2004 (Ref. CESR/ 05-054b)* recommends the application of the above-mentioned provision of the Commission's Regulation in the following way:

> Where the issuer has entered into covenants with lenders which could have material effect of restricting the use of credit facilities, and relevant negotiations with the lenders on the operation of these covenants are taking place, this fact should be discussed. Where a breach of covenant has occurred or is expected to occur, the prospectus should give information on how the issuer intends to remedy the situation.

According to this recommendation, rating triggers falling under the notion of 'covenants' should be disclosed in prospectuses for public offers or admission to trading of shares.

1.3.3 Use in Regulation

An aspect that worries regulators is the potential negative consequences that the use of ratings in regulation[28] could have had during the crisis that started in 2007, as some considered that these references in the legislation might have contributed to an undue reliance on ratings by market participants.

In this respect, the FSB, in its *Report on enhancing market and institutional resilience* published in April 2008 at the request of the G7 Ministers and Central Bank Governors, concluded, among other things, that the reference to ratings in a variety of regulatory and supervisory frameworks may have contributed to the tendency of investors to over-rely on the ratings.

In addition, the FSB recommended that 'authorities should check that the roles that they have assigned to ratings in regulations and supervisory rules are consistent with the objectives of having investors make independent judgment of risks and perform their own due diligence, and that they do not induce uncritical reliance on credit ratings as a substitute for that independent evaluation'.

Consequently, in its report, the FSB requested the Joint Forum[29] to conduct a stocktaking of the uses of external credit ratings by its member authorities in the banking, securities, and insurance sectors. To implement the FSB's request, the Joint Forum circulated to its members[30] a questionnaire to gather information regarding the use of credit ratings in legislation (statutes), regulations (rules), and/or supervisory policies (guidance) affecting, or generated by, public authorities.

According to the findings of the Joint Forum,[31] credit ratings are generally used in legislation to: determine capital requirements; identify or classify assets, usually in the context of eligible investments or permissible asset concentrations; provide a credible evaluation of the credit risk associated with assets purchased as part of a securitization offering or a covered bond offering; determine disclosure requirements; and to determine prospectus eligibility.

The determination of capital requirements of banks and investment firms is the most common application of ratings in regulation. Regulation uses ratings for the purpose of determining regulatory capital, generally as a means of mapping credit risks to capital charges or risk weights.

Under the Basel II Framework, external ratings are used for the purpose of enhancing the risk sensitivity of the framework, for example, by being incorporated into assessments of the credit quality of an exposure or creditworthiness of a counterparty and thus the imposition of capital requirements.

The different uses of external ratings generally correspond to the probability of default treatments under the standardized approaches, and to situations where the

---

[28] Regulation in this context should be understood in a broad sense including legislation (statutes), regulations (rules), and supervisory policies (guidance).

[29] The Joint Forum was established in 1996 by the Basel Committee on Banking Supervision (BCBS), the International Organization of Securities Commissions (IOSCO), and the International Association of Insurance Supervisors (IAIS) to deal with issues common to the banking, securities, and insurance sectors, including the regulation of financial conglomerates.

[30] The stocktaking was done among 26 agencies representing 12 jurisdictions (Australia, Belgium, Canada, France, Germany, Italy, Japan, Netherlands, Spain, Switzerland, United Kingdom, and the USA).

[31] Joint Forum (June 2009), *Stocktaking on the use of credit ratings.*

use of internally generated ratings is impossible or difficult given, for instance, the lack of statistical data for securitized products. In most cases, the external ratings that can be used for the purpose of determining regulatory capital are limited to those provided by rating agencies recognized by national supervisors as External Credit Assessment Institutions (ECAIs).

All members of the EU have transposed the CRD, which implements the Basel II framework for both banks and investment firms. Within the EU, the decision as to whether or not to recognize an ECAI is within each national authority's discretion, although the 'joint assessment process' set forth in EBA's guidelines on ECAIs is designed to achieve a consistent approach among EU Member States (see Section 3.5.3).

In the USA, which features the most widespread use of credit ratings in regulation that establishes capital requirements in the securities and banking sectors, the use of credit ratings for capital purposes is almost exclusively restricted to those issued by CRAs designated as NRSROs through the US SEC's registration process.

A second frequent use of ratings in regulations is in the context of asset categorization. In the banking and securities sectors, ratings are used, for example, for the designation of permissible investments and/or required investments for mutual funds and for the establishment of, and exceptions to, investment concentration limits for particular types of assets. In the EU, Commission Directive 2007/16/EC,[32] which clarifies certain definitions used in the UCITS Directives,[33] contains in Articles 6 and 10 two specific references to credit ratings relating to money market instruments.

In regulations on securitizations and covered bond offerings credit ratings are also generally used by requiring that these securities are rated by one or more credit rating agencies, especially when they are sold to retail (non-professional) investors.

Regulations dealing with issuers' disclosure requirements also refer to credit ratings by setting requirements to rated entities to disclose their ratings (and when such ratings are changed). In this sense, the EU Prospectus Regulation requires entities preparing a prospectus for debt instruments to disclose the credit ratings assigned to an issuer or its debt securities at the request or with the cooperation of the issuer in the rating process.

Prospectus eligibility is another area where regulations make use of ratings; for example, certain types of prospectuses, such as 'short-form' prospectuses, include an investment grade rating as one of the criteria for eligibility to use the simplified or short form.

Other uses of ratings in regulations highlighted in the report of the Joint Forum include allowing the use of external credit ratings as an input for an entity's own internal ratings.

---

[32] Directive 2007/16/EC of the European Parliament and of the Council of 19 March 2007 implementing Council Directive 85/611/EEC on the coordination of laws, regulations and administrative provisions relating to undertakings for collective investment in transferable securities (UCITS) as regards the clarification of certain definitions, OJ L 79/11, 20.3.2007.

[33] Directive 2009/65/EC of the European Parliament and of the Council of 13 July 2009 on the coordination of laws, regulations and administrative provisions relating to undertakings for collective investment in transferable securities (UCITS), OJ L 302/32, 17.11.2009.

internal ratings; use of ratings for the purpose of stress tests to gauge credit risk; the segregation/custody of customer funds; permissible activities of banks; soundness assessments for banks; as proxies for non-credit forms of risk, such as liquidity; and the for designation of eligible collateral.

After this stocktaking exercise by the Joint Forum and in response to the G-20 recommendations to review the use of ratings in the regulatory and supervisory framework, the FSB created a working group on Reducing Official Sector Reliance on CRA Ratings to develop high-level principles for use by authorities in reducing their reliance on ratings. Section 2.2.5 will discuss the main initiatives undertaken to reduce reliance on CRAs ratings.

1.4 RATING PROCESS

Depending on the CRA and the methodologies used, the processes used by CRAs to reach the final rating vary widely. Some CRAs follow a process whereby analysts form an assessment based on quantitative and qualitative indicators and then report this assessment to a rating committee that decides on a final rating. Other CRAs use mainly quantitative models, where the assessment process is more mechanical in nature and based on statistical analysis of an issuer's financial disclosures to arrive at a rating.

Despite the various approaches that CRAs may take in rating issuers, the largest international CRAs tend to follow similar rating procedures for similar types of instruments. The following description covers the main steps in the rating process that is broadly followed by these agencies for most types of instruments (corporates, financial institutions, insurance companies, sovereigns, etc.). However, due to the specific nature of structured finance there are some differences in the rating process for these instruments that are explained at the end of this section.

The time needed for this process varies, depending on the complexity of the task and its urgency. As a general rule, the process takes one to two months.

1.4.1 Rating Process for Traditional Ratings

1.4.1.1 *Initiation of the Rating*

The rating process typically begins with a rating request from an issuer (see Section 3.8.5 for explanations on unsolicited ratings). The issuer and the CRA sign a contract to govern the main aspects of the rating relationship: information to be provided by the issuer, confidentiality agreement, public or private nature of the rating, fees, and so on.

This file is then sent to the head of the relevant team of analysts, who assigns a team to prepare the rating. In particular, one analyst, the lead analyst, is given the responsibility of preparing the rating file and, normally, a second analyst is also appointed to serve as the backup analyst of the rating. Before starting the analytical process, most CRAs have procedures to check that the analysts assigned at this stage (as well as those that will compose the rating committee) are not conflicted.

To this end, analysts involved in a rating are required to certify that they are not subject to a prohibited conflict of interest.

1.4.1.2 *Sources of Information and Interaction with the Issuer*

The lead analyst begins the credit analysis by gathering all the relevant information about the issuer or obligation. Analysts always use public information about the company (for example, annual reports) and about its sector (sector analyses), which is normally supplemented with information generated by the agency (internal databases or reports examining the current macroeconomic and financial market conditions) or from third party sources, such as macroeconomic and sector-specific data, to which the CRA subscribes.

Moreover, issuers frequently provide CRAs with non-public information, such as internal management reports, forecasts, or strategic orientations, and a meeting with the management is normally undertaken as part of the credit rating process. In these meetings analysts discuss with the management key factors such as strategic and financial plans and projections to develop their assessment of the management and corporate strategy. In cases where the rating is not requested by issuers, they might not participate in the rating process and, therefore, the information used to prepare the rating is normally limited to publicly available information (see Section 3.8.5 for an elaboration on ratings where the issuer does not participate).

As will be discussed in Section 3.8.4, CRAs insist on the fact that they do not and cannot perform an audit of the information they use or receive from the issuer. Although they have processes in place to ensure, to a certain extent, that the information and data they use is from reliable sources and of sufficient quality, they do not verify or independently validate the information.

1.4.1.3 *Analysis*

Once the relevant information has been gathered, the analyst assesses the creditworthiness of the issuer or security in accordance with the relevant methodologies. The CRAs' approach covers three main areas:[34] analysis of operational aspects, such as an assessment of how dependent a company is on a business sector (or on a particular product or service) and overall economic trends; analysis of financial and accounting ratios; and analysis of the company's financial structure and strategy.

In most CRAs, the analytical process typically encompasses an assessment of qualitative parameters, as well as quantitative analysis. The factors that are usually deemed to be relevant depend on the issuer or obligation being rated. For determining a corporate rating some of the relevant factors are the following:

- Quantitative factors: turnover, level of sales, growth rate, earnings ratio, profitability ratio, coverage ratio, capitalization rate, disposable cash flow, cash flow ratio, liquidity ratio, industry-specific key indicator ratios, off-balance sheet adjustments, variations in working capital, capital spending

---

[34] AMF (January 2008), *2007 Report on rating agencies: credit rating of corporate issuers.*

Table 1.2. Business risk/financial risk

Business risk profile	Financial risk profile				
	Minimal	Modest	Intermediate	Aggressive	Highly leveraged
Excellent	AAA	AA	A	BBB	BB
Strong	AA	A	A −	BBB −	BB −
Satisfactory	A	BBB +	BBB	BB +	B +
Weak	BBB	BBB −	BB +	BB −	B
Vulnerable	BB	B +	B +	B	B −

Table 1.3. Financial risk indicative ratios

	Funds from operations/debt (%)	Total debt/capital (%)
Minimal	Over 60	Over 25
Modest	45–60	25–35
Intermediate	30–45	35–45
Aggressive	15–30	45–55
Highly leveraged	Under 15	Under 55

(maintaining current level and changes), non-recurring items, financing flows, including dividends, foreign exchange effects, and accounting effects.

- Qualitative factors: industry sector, main markets, market position, range of businesses, geographical diversity, commercial strategy, company size, barriers to entry, competitive advantages, growth opportunities, financial policy, management quality, financial structure and structural aspects, cash analysis, debt maturity analysis, analysis of the key characteristics of a security, third party guarantors, legal structure, ownership structure, corporate governance, and regulatory framework.

CRAs normally assign indicative weights to the factors reviewed in the rating process. They also prepare matrices to compare the business risk profile and the financial profile to come up with the rating. A sample of such a matrix is provided in Tables 1.2 and 1.3, as included in Annex III of AMF's *2007 Report on rating agencies: credit rating of corporate issuers* published in January 2008.

The analytical team works with the CRA's legal function to ensure that legal risks relevant to the rating analysis are identified. Also, input from other analytical groups might be sought when deemed relevant, for example from the team responsible for the rating of a counterparty to the transaction being analysed.

The lead analyst, after undertaking all this analytical work, drafts a report that is strictly for internal use with a rating recommendation. This report is sent to the rating committee for analysis, discussion, and final rating decision.

1.4.1.4 Rating Committee

The rating committee is at the core of all the rating process as ratings, in the main CRAs, are not determined by an individual analyst but are decided by the vote of a rating committee.

Rating committees are set for each individual rating and the composition is designed to ensure that the committee has the necessary knowledge and experience to consider and, where necessary, challenge a rating recommendation for a specific type of issuer or security. Moreover, the composition of rating committees is also designed to promote consistency across sectors and regions. Therefore, the committee usually includes specialists located in different countries and, when making the rating decision, the committee considers international comparisons to ensure the consistency of ratings worldwide.

The committee is normally composed of a chair who acts as moderator and should be a senior officer, the lead analyst, who presents the report with his/her recommendation, and other analysts with sufficient experience in the sector or instrument being rated (including the backup analyst). In addition, some CRAs also incorporate junior analysts for training purposes (and normally without voting rights).

The rating committee may meet face to face, by email, by videoconference, or by conference call. Rating committee meetings are conducted so as to allow interactive participation of all the members. The chair has a key role in promoting open discussions, ensuring that all the relevant information is taken into account, moderating the debate so that all pertinent critical issues are considered, and ensuring that the appropriate methodologies have been followed. During the course of the discussions within the rating committee, the lead analyst might revise its original recommendation before the voting process takes place. The committees' decisions are made by a majority vote or by consensus, depending on the agency.

Rating committee materials and records with the names of the voting analysts, the outcome of the vote, and the key criteria and assumptions that have lead to the final decision, are retained.

Most CRAs have an internal appeal process that can be exercised after a decision has been taken by the rating committee and before it is notified to the issuer. Normally, any analyst from the agency, participating or not in the rating committee, has the right to request a reconsideration of a rating decision when it has a basis for doubting the decision (for example, due to misapplication of methodologies, insufficient information, conflicts of interest). An internal appeal can give raise to the convocation of a new rating committee that can decide to change the prior decision.

1.4.1.5 Notification to the Issuer, Appeals, and Publication of the Rating

Once the rating committee has reached a decision, the analyst usually provides the issuer (not other external parties) with the report and/or the draft press release so that the issuer can review it for factual verification and, to the extent that the rating is to be made public, ensure that the CRA does not disclose any confidential information. This opportunity for issuers to check the rating in advance is only intended to correct factual errors and/or prevent the disclosure of confidential information and is not envisaged as a control mechanism for issuers of the rating decision.

However, in some cases, CRAs may grant the request of an issuer to appeal the rating if meaningful new information is presented. This is only feasible if the issuer has material new information that may alter its risk profile or outlook and thus influence its rating. In this event, the rating committee is reconvened to assess the new information and consider the impact on the rating decision.

Usually, the time between the notification to the issuer and publication of the rating is quite short, as CRAs consider this a guarantee to prevent leaks and the best way to give the market the benefit of the information as quickly as possible.

After comments are received from the issuer and any appropriate changes made, the CRAs post press releases and rating reports on their websites so that the ratings are accessible to everyone free of charge, but typically the reports are freely available for a limited time only and, after that, they may be consulted only by paying subscribers.

Sometimes, CRAs assign and publish preliminary ratings. Preliminary ratings are determined on the basis of information that is subject to finalization. The CRA will convert the preliminary rating into a final one once it has received the finalized information from the rated entity.

Once the rating has been issued, the CRA will generally continue to monitor the issuer and/or its securities on an ongoing, albeit less intensive, level and continue to meet with senior management on a periodic basis.

1.4.1.6 Monitoring of Ratings

The main CRAs maintain surveillance of their outstanding ratings on an ongoing basis. Surveillance is normally performed by the same analytical teams that prepared the initial ratings and, in general, the monitoring is carried out applying the same principles that were used for the determination of the initial rating.

The monitoring team would typically schedule periodic meetings with the management of the rated entity in order to gather information about the issuer's operations, trends, estimates, and all other areas relevant to the credit analysis. This confidential information would supplement the disclosures that the rated entity might make publicly available following applicable legislation (such as prospectuses, financial statements, market abuse disclosures, etc.).

In addition, analysts will incorporate in the monitoring analysis macroeconomic forecasts produced by the internal department in charge of monitoring the economy and markets. Another relevant source for monitoring is the portfolio review. CRAs periodically conduct these portfolio reviews whereby they assess the credit quality of all the issuers within a sector, so analysts are enabled to check the consistency of the credit quality of the rated entity with that of its competitors.

Finally, analysts will normally look at other sources of information such as market prices where available, research from other institutions, or credit ratings issued by other CRAs.

When the monitoring team believes that the outstanding rating should be reconsidered it puts the rating on the watch list and convenes a rating committee in order to decide on the proposed recommendation. The same process designed for the issuance of the initial rating will be followed for the rating change or any other rating action (for example, regarding adoption of the final decision, notification to the issuer, publication, retention of files, etc.).

1.4.1.7 Rating Withdrawals

Rating agencies have internal policies that provide guidance to their analysts regarding the reasons to withdraw an outstanding rating and the procedure to follow in order to determine the withdrawal.

CRAs do not withdraw ratings simply in response to a request from the rated entity. However, if the rated entity terminates the contract with the CRA, the agency might not be able to obtain the information required to support the rating through public sources only. In these circumstances, a credit rating committee should be held to consider the possibility of withdrawing the rating.

In fact, a lack of or inadequate information to maintain the rating should lead the CRA to withdraw the rating. Other reasons for withdrawing ratings are:

- the rated entity no longer exists (for example, due to bankruptcy, reorganization, or liquidation);
- the rated obligation is no longer outstanding (because the debt matures, is fully repaid before maturity, or is restructured);
- for structured finance transactions, only a minimum amount of the issue or tranche remains outstanding;
- an actual or potential conflict of interest is identified for an existing rating (for example, the CRA finds out that the lead analyst that recommended the rating owned financial instruments of the rated entity—Annex I.B.3 of the CRAs Regulation); and
- the rated entity declines payment of the rating fees.

In any event, at the time of the withdrawal, the outstanding rating must reflect the CRA's current opinion about the creditworthiness of the rated instrument or entity. Therefore, under no circumstances should an entity's request to withdraw a rating avoid an imminent downgrade. If necessary, the CRA should modify the rating prior to the withdrawal.

CRAs' internal procedures will normally require that the withdrawal of the rating is assigned by a rating committee, although there may be cases where a rating committee is not considered necessary (for example, where the rated instrument has matured).

Finally, CRAs should disclose the withdrawal of the rating in the same way in which the rating was released (through a public announcement if the rating was publicly available or via communication to subscribers if the rating was distributed by subscription).

1.4.2 Rating Process for Structured Finance Instruments

1.4.2.1 Determination of the Initial Rating

Although the general rating process is essentially the same for structured finance and traditional ratings, as summarized in Table 1.4, there are some important features that differentiate between both types of ratings.[35]

---

[35] CGFS (January 2005), *The role of ratings in structured finance: issues and implications.*

As will be explained under Section 3.3, structured finance consists of the pooling of assets and the subsequent sale to investors of tranched claims on the cash-flows backed by these pools,[36] usually through a special-purpose vehicle (SPV). The two main characteristics of structured finance products are the pooling of assets and the tranching process that is designed to create seniority ordering among the different tranches of securities. Senior classes of securities are designed in order to be immune, to a certain extent, from default losses, which are initially borne by riskier (equity and mezzanine) tranches. This segmentation enables the product to appeal to investors with different risk profiles.

These characteristics imply a high level of complexity, as the tranching process consists of legally organizing the distribution of cash flows from the asset pool to different tranche investors. Therefore, CRAs need to understand not only the default risk embodied in the collateral pool but also other non-default risks arising from the transaction's structure. They need to have sufficient insight into the legal structure and the specific provisions of the transaction that organize the different seniority levels of the tranches.

Consequently, the ratings of structured finance are more complex and time-consuming. In addition, the rating of structured finance instruments differs from the rating of traditional instruments by the greater flexibility to adapt the features of the transaction in order to achieve the rating level desired for each tranche of the structure. As opposed to traditional ratings, the rating of a structured finance transaction is a target, not the outcome, of the rating process.

Arrangers use CRAs' models to structure the deal and subsequently go through an iterative process with the CRA, with the ultimate goal to maximize the size of the tranches with the highest rating or minimize the cost/quality of assets used to reach a high-rating tranche, or minimize the level of credit protection needed for a certain tranche.

This process implies that the rating of structured finance instruments has a pronounced ex ante nature, which contrasts with traditional bond ratings, for which pre-rating feedback to issuers and targeted ratings play a more limited role, given that corporates tend to be unable to significantly adjust their credit characteristics prior to bond issuance.

In structured finance, ratings are more model-based and usually the quantitative analysis has more weight than the qualitative part of the process. This aspect is also reflected in the monitoring process of structured finance instruments where surveillance normally consists of monitoring and interpreting delinquency and loss performance, measuring levels of credit enhancement, and applying quantitative techniques.

1.4.2.2 Monitoring of Structured Finance Ratings

Contrary to the surveillance of corporate and public finance ratings, the monitoring of structured finance ratings is normally conducted by dedicated teams, different to those that produce the initial rating (and sometimes located in different countries). This is because the review of structured finance ratings is more model-based than the review of the other types of ratings. And also the

---

[36] See footnote 35.

principles applied by the monitoring team differ from those employed by the team responsible for the initial rating. Whilst the rating process focuses on the evaluation of the probabilities of default and potential losses for the asset pool during the life span of the security, the monitoring staff employ models to assess whether the performance of the assets conforms to expectations and to compare potential losses with the credit enhancement of the securities. If, for example, the evaluation shows that the credit support available is not commensurate with the outstanding rating, the CRA will have to take a rating action. The data related to the performance of the collateral is supplied by the issuers or arrangers that requested the rating or by third party data providers.

In addition to the performance of the pool underlying the rated transaction, a supplementary tool for the monitoring teams is the portfolio review. As discussed above for companies or financial institutions, the objective is also to ensure consistency of ratings within the same asset class.

Table 1.4. Structured finance versus traditional credit ratings: commonalities and differences

Issue	Structured finance	Traditional
Rating process	Basically identical: analyst review, credit committee	Basically identical: analyst review, credit committee
Rating concept	Identical rating basis: expected loss or default probability	Identical rating basis: expected loss or default probability. Expected loss may be a reasonable proxy for credit risk
	Tranching can create securities with same expected loss, but very different unexpected loss properties	
Structural features	More complex—extensive analysis of moving parts required	Structural features, such as bond covenants, exist—but analysis is less extensive
Credit risk analysis	Controlled environment enables more model-based, quantitative analysis of asset pool; emphasis on the relatively easily definable cash flow generated by the underlying asset pool; known maturity	More limited scope for quantitative analysis of overall balance sheet/ franchise; emphasis on the cash flow generated by the obligor's ongoing business activities (issuing entity is going concern)
Conflicts of interest	Exist in both cases between originators, investors, third parties—more transparent, easier to control, requires structural mitigants	Exist in both cases between shareholders, different debt holders, management—more difficult to control (covenants)
Nature of rating	Pronounced ex ante nature (targeted ratings, iterative process, rating issued at inception); more model-based; greater flexibility to adjust structural factors	Ex post, though with ex ante elements (pre-rating feedback, issuer first rated in mid-life); more judgemental; limited issuer ability to adjust credit characteristics
Performance	More stable on average, but larger changes—significant instability of particular asset classes	Benchmark for structured finance ratings via expected loss/probability of default mapping

The procedure for reconsideration of the rating is the same as is followed for its initial determination. Normally the lead analyst involved in the initial rating action participates in this process. A rating committee is convened and the agreed rating action then communicated to the issuer and published afterwards.

2

Financial Crisis:
Global Regulatory Reaction

2.1 DEFICIENCIES IN THE RATING INDUSTRY

2.1.1 Introduction

The attention that supervisors, regulators, and market participants have devoted to the activity of CRAs has frequently been directly linked to situations of financial crisis. CRAs jumped into the international debate during the summer of 1997 when they were unable to anticipate the difficulties of the Asian economies, and were again in the spotlight at the beginning of this century when they failed to predict the collapses of huge companies in the USA and the EU (Enron, Worldcom, Parmalat).

The crisis that originated in the US residential subprime mortgage market during the summer of 2007, and extended rapidly to other sectors of the financial markets, led to a serious reflection about the role that CRAs perform in the financial markets and, more extensively, in the financial stability of the world's economy. In this context, many studies have been produced at different instances to analyse the deficiencies in the functioning of the CRAs during the crisis. Most of these analyses have mainly pointed out problems in the context of ratings of structured finance products. However, these studies have also detected structural deficiencies linked to the business model and to the internal processes of CRAs.

The Financial Stability Board in is report of April 2008[1] summarized the main sources of concern in relation to the poor performance of the CRAs in the area of structured finance products: 'weaknesses in rating models and methodologies; inadequate due diligence of the quality of the collateral pools underlying rated securities; insufficient transparency about the assumptions, criteria and methodologies used in rating structured products; insufficient information provision about the meaning and risk characteristics of structured finance ratings; and insufficient attention to conflicts of interest in the rating process'.

According to the EC impact assessment CRA Regulation, the main weaknesses of the rating industry can be grouped into the three broad areas that will be analysed in the next sections: failures in the integrity of the CRAs (mainly in relation to conflicts

---

[1] FSF (April 2008), *Report on enhancing market and institutional resilience*. The FSF published an update on implementation of its report in April 2009.

of interest); unsatisfactory quality of methodologies and ratings; and lack of transparency of the CRAs.

2.1.2 Failures in Integrity

The main conflict of interest that the major CRAs face derives from the business model they follow. The 'issuer-pays' model that replaced the 'subscription-paid' model in the 1970s, implies that the CRAs following the new model face a permanent tension. A CRA's interest in providing ratings that accurately reflect the probability of default of an issuer conflicts with its interest in satisfying the issuer from whom it receives its revenue and who wishes for the highest rating to reduce its borrowing costs. In fact, the SEC staff's examinations of certain CRAs in 2008 found out that the analysts appeared to be aware, when rating an issuer, of the firm's business interest in securing the rating, and that CRAs did not appear to take steps to prevent the possibility that considerations of market share and other business interests could influence ratings.

The risk of undue influence of the issuer (or originator) would increase in the case that the CRA offered additionally advisory or consultancy services (for example, providing proposals or recommendations regarding the design of a structured finance instrument). The conflict can be compounded in these cases when these non-rating services give rise to significant, high-margin revenues from a rated client. A CRA has a clear incentive to provide favourable ratings to the issuer in order not to risk the revenues it receives from it for these non-rating services. Equally, the provision of ancillary services may give rise to similar situations, as in the case of advisory services when the ancillary service relationship prevails over the rigour and independence of the rating process. According to the EU CRA Regulation, ancillary services comprise market forecasts, estimates of economic trends, pricing analysis, and other general data analysis, as well as related distribution services.

Another aspect that can compromise the independence of ratings is the existence of conflicts that affect rating analysts. Among others, situations when independence can be undermined are when analysts' compensation is linked to the ratings they prepare, when analysts own securities of the rated entity, when they accept gifts, or when they have expectations of having professional activity with rated entities after leaving their job in the CRA.

An inappropriate practice that was detected during the crisis and that is linked to the need of CRAs to attract or retain clients is 'rating shopping'. Issuers or arrangers of a potential structured product inquire of several CRAs for their preliminary rating assessment and finally hire the CRA that offers the best rating. This is likely to lead to ratings inflation and lack of methodological rigour as CRAs, aware of this practice, could have an incentive to offer high ratings to attract clients.

2.1.3 Failures in Reliability

The analysis of the activity of the CRAs during the crisis also raised serious doubts over their capacity to reflect, adequately and in timely fashion, on the rating of structured products, the worsening conditions in the market, and of the underlying assets.

This inappropriate performance has been linked, to a great extent, to the lack of adequate methodologies and to the use of hypotheses that did not reflect reality accurately enough. In particular, it was detected that having only limited historical data in the area of certain structured products (such as those linked to subprime lending) led to the inability of CRAs to assess how a pool of assets would respond to given economic scenarios. It was also noticed that CRAs lacked sound macro-economic models to help them envisage the possibility of a global crisis and understand the impact that this scenario would have on their ratings. The agencies underestimated the correlations in the defaults that could occur in the event of a wide market downturn.

[margin handwritten note: inability to respond to certain economic scenarios.]

However, not only CRAs have been pointed at for a lack of diligence when using inadequate information or data to base their ratings on. In some cases, it was also detected that there was irresponsibility, and even cases of fraud, on the side of other market participants. Originators were, in some instances, not diligent enough when controlling the quality of the information they provided to the CRAs and these, in turn, did not take sufficient measures to ensure the quality of the data received, which had an impact on the quality of the ratings. In its study *The impact of poor underwriting practices and fraud in subprime rmbs performance,*[2] published in November 2007, Fitch Ratings concluded that absence of disciplined underwriting allowed for an increase in defaults through the use of inaccurate data or fraud. This report provided an analysis of a sample of loans which underperformed significantly compared to expectations based on each loan's disclosed risk attributes. This analysis showed a significant number of irregularities. Among other issues, 66% of the mortgage files contained occupancy fraud, 51% contained irregularities related to property value or other loan condi- — tions, 44% stated a questionable income or employment, and 10% indicated signature fraud. Less than 5,000 cases of mortgage loan fraud were reported before 2002, while 2004 and 2005 showed 18,391 and 25,989 cases of fraud, respectively.

The difficulties experienced with structured finance ratings demonstrated that CRAs were not attaching sufficient importance to monitoring the performance of the ratings issued. CRAs were not vigilant enough and did not downgrade ratings in a timely manner when the first signs of deterioration in the situation started to become apparent. The CRAs concentrated more in the issuance of new ratings and did not devote sufficient resources to the surveillance. Moreover, according to the SEC staff's examinations, surveillance processes appeared to be less robust than the initial rating processes and there was poor documentation of the surveil-lance conducted. Understaffing and the low qualifications of the surveillance teams, and the insufficient frequency of the monitoring reviews of the ratings, in many cases of a superficial nature, significantly affected the quality of ratings. This lack of good monitoring led to situations in which market participants relied on ratings that were already outdated and that did not reflect the real credit risk of an issuer.

In addition, inconsistencies were also found in how CRAs dealt with ratings issued in the past, if the methodology or key assumptions they were based on had

---

[2] Fitch, (November 2007), *The impact of poor underwriting practices and fraud in subprime RMBS performance.*

been altered. In some cases, when an agency upgraded or downgraded the rating of a specific issue due to a change in the methodology, the agency would not concurrently adjust the ratings assigned to similar products on the basis of such a methodology. Therefore, issuers and investors had difficulties in understanding the changes in the ratings. In this sense, SEC's staff examinations revealed that some CRAs were effectively using different methodologies and models for producing initial ratings and for ensuing surveillance activity.

Finally, and especially in the area of structured finance, the crisis highlighted the lack of sufficient qualified human resources on the side of CRAs, that complicated even more the issuance of high-quality ratings. There was a substantial increase in the number and complexity of structured finance products and CRAs struggled to adapt to the increased deal volume and complexity, with staffing increases that did not appear to match the growth in business volume.

2.1.4 Failures in Transparency

The lack of adequate information about the characteristics and limitations of the ratings, especially of structured products, and the fact that the CRAs did not provide sufficient information on critical model assumptions, was pointed out as one of the main problems detected. In this sense, the SEC staff's examinations highlighted that, in some instances, relevant rating criteria were not fully disclosed. All this information is crucial so that investors can correctly understand the real meaning and value of the ratings. Moreover, information on ratings was not always provided with sufficient clarity.

In addition, some people argued that the use of the same rating scale for structured and traditional ratings caused many investors to be confused as to the risk profile of the instruments involved. These investors, typically less familiar with securitization products, drew simple comparisons with traditional debt, rated according to the same scales.

Finally, the fact that there was no comparable information on CRAs' performance available in the market was also highlighted as a deficiency. CRAs occasionally published rating transition and default studies. These reports—done separately for structured finance and traditional debt—track rating activity for debt instruments over a certain period and usually include a review of upgrades/downgrades and defaults by rating category for each of the main subsectors (for example, for structured finance it could be ABS, RMBS, CMBS, and CDOs). Therefore, these reports are potentially a good basis for assessing CRAs' sound judgement in attributing ratings over the years. However, the fact that CRAs differed in their approaches to collecting relevant data and presenting them to the public did not facilitate comparison between CRAs' performance.

2.1.5 Lack of Competition

Many studies have pointed to the limited scope of competition among CRAs as another failure of the CRAs' industry that has contributed to accentuate the problems mentioned in the previous sections. Some academic researchers consider that innovations in the ratings industry have often 'been initiated by the smaller rating firms [Fitch and its legacy firms], with the larger two [Moody's and S&P] then following'.[3] And, in general, most commentators to the SEC's and EC's consultations on CRAs have mentioned the oligopolistic structure existing in the market as something that could have contributed to the incorrect functioning of the rating industry.

In this sense, the European Securities Market Expert group (ESME), in its report to the European Commission on CRAs published in June 2008,[4] concluded that the oligopolistic structure could have contributed negatively to the quality and integrity of the rating process. ESME argued that, although it was not possible to demonstrate that having more competitors would definitely have materially altered what happened during the crisis, competition, by allowing a greater diversity of thinking and opinion, would have at least opened up the possibility that the underlying flaws and issues in the subprime market would have been identified in a more coherent and timely manner and accordingly communicated to the market.

This problem is compounded by allegations of unfair practices that main CRAs could have been using to avoid new entrants or smaller CRAs gaining a market share. This is the case in the so-called 'notching' that is the practice of lowering or threatening to lower a credit rating on a structured product unless the agency also rates the underlying securities or assets on which the structured product is based. This was expressly criticized by Fitch in the SEC hearings that took place in November 2002 in the aftermath of Enron.[5] Fitch complained that:

> Moody's and S&P are a dual monopoly, each possessing separate monopoly power in a market that has grown to demand two ratings. Each engages in practices designed to perpetuate its market dominance and extend it to otherwise competitive markets such as structured finance. As we have publicly stated for more than a year, through their discriminatory practice known as 'notching', Moody's and S&P are successfully altering competition in the commercial and residential mortgage-backed securities market by leveraging their monopoly position in other markets.

A detailed analysis of this anti-competitive practice is provided in Section 3.8.4.

However, there are also some studies that shed doubts as to whether increased competition would be beneficial for rating industry.[6] In this respect, a paper published in September 2010 by Bo Becker and Todd Milbourn[7] provides an interesting analysis on how Moody's and S&P responded to the rapid growth of the then upstart Fitch, in the corporate ratings in the early 1990s. The paper concludes that 'competition most likely weakens reputational incentives for

[3] White, Lawrence J. (2001), *The credit rating industry: an industrial organization analysis.* Paper presented at a conference at the Stern School of Business.
[4] European Securities Markets Expert Group (2008), *Report to the European Commission on the role of credit rating agencies.*
[5] Fitch, (November 2002), *Fitch's Views Provided on SEC Hearings on the Current Role and Function of Credit Rating Agencies in the Operation of the Securities Markets.*
[6] Bongaerts, Dion, Cremers, K.J.Martijn and Goetzmann, William N. (2009), *Multiple ratings and credit spreads.* NBER Working Paper Series 15331.
[7] Becker, Bo and Milbourn, Todd (September 2010), *How did increased competition affect credit ratings?* NBER Working Paper Series 16404.

providing quality in the ratings industry, and thereby undermines quality. The reputational mechanism appears to work best at modest levels of competition.'

The EC impact assessment CRA Regulation also analysed briefly the lack of competition in the market. It concluded that a legislative proposal could be indirectly beneficial for competition as for small CRAs registration would act as public recognition of their rating capability for the whole market, thus facilitating them to overcome the barriers to entry of the oligopolistic rating business.

CRA Regulation, Article 39, also expressed the need to analyse the lack of competition in the market and mandated the EC to submit, by 7 December 2012, to the European Parliament and the Council a report assessing, among other issues, the impact of the Regulation on the level of concentration in the credit rating market.

The EC consultation on CRAs in November 2010 dealt, among other issues, with possible alternatives to enhance competition. Unfortunately, the paper published by the EC does not provide a thorough analysis of the problems derived from the lack of competition and does not develop in detail the proposals put forward, which are just broadly outlined in the document. In the consultation paper, the EC puts forward four possible options to explore:

- Entrust the ECB or national central banks with the task of issuing ratings to be used for regulatory purposes by European financial institutions. The idea would be to explore whether central banks 'could build up sufficient knowledge and capacity to produce the relevant in-house credit rating services which could be developed to compete with external credit rating agencies'.

- Encourage the creation of new CRAs at a national level as public or private entities, even providing state aid for small and medium-sized CRAs.

- Set up a new independent European CRA in a public or private structure.

- Promote the establishment of a European network of small and medium-sized CRAs with the objective of 'sharing best practices and resources, building expert knowledge and enhancing the quality of ratings'.

2.2 GLOBAL INITIATIVES

2.2.1 Introduction

The market failures identified in Section 2.1 were not speedily addressed due to the lack of direct supervision and enforcement in many countries and to the insufficient powers granted to the authorities in other jurisdictions where some form of supervision existed. As can been inferred from the multiple initiatives at global and country level described in this section, the self-regulatory system was not considered sufficient to ensure that CRAs correctly performed their role.

As a result, in the USA, public authorities, market participants, and academics considered the need to strengthen the legislative and supervisory frameworks on CRAs. But most international financial centres, including the EU, lacked at that time a system of public oversight and regulation of CRAs; therefore, they had to evaluate the need to introduce such a regime.

This section describes how an international consensus was forged on the need to regulate the operations of the CRAs and on the main principles upon which the oversight regimes across the world should be based. Three international fora have led the discussions that brought about the international agreement: the G-20, the Financial Stability Board, and IOSCO.

2.2.2 G-20

In the past couple of years the G-20 has incorporated CRAs into the regulatory agenda of governments and institutions all over the world. In November 2008, the Finance Ministers and Central Bank Governors of the G-20 mentioned CRAs for the first time in the final communiqué of the São Paulo meeting to expressly include them among the 'systemically important institutions' that should be subject to a proper oversight. A week later, in the Washington summit, the G-20 leaders outlined two action points, for immediate action by 31 March 2009, with respect to CRAs, namely:

- Regulators should take steps to ensure that credit rating agencies meet the highest standards of the international organization of securities regulators and that they avoid conflicts of interest, provide greater disclosure to investors and to issuers, and differentiate ratings for complex products. This will help ensure that credit rating agencies have the right incentives and appropriate monitoring to enable them to perform their important roles in providing unbiased information and assessments to markets.

- IOSCO should review credit rating agencies' adoption of the standards and mechanisms for monitoring compliance.

In addition, in this communiqué, as a medium-term action, the G-20 already mentions that CRAs 'that provide public ratings should be registered'.

This agreement was further developed in the G-20 leaders' public announcement of April 2009 which stated:

We have agreed on more effective oversight of the activities of Credit Rating Agencies, as they are essential market participants. In particular, we have agreed that:
- all Credit Rating Agencies whose ratings are used for regulatory purposes should be subject to a regulatory oversight regime that includes registration. The regulatory oversight regime should be established by end 2009 and should be consistent with the IOSCO Code of Conduct Fundamentals. IOSCO should coordinate full compliance;
- national authorities will enforce compliance and require changes to a rating agency's practices and procedures for managing conflicts of interest and assuring the transparency and quality of the rating process. In particular, Credit Rating Agencies should differentiate ratings for structured products and provide full disclosure of their ratings track record and the information and assumptions that underpin the ratings process. The oversight framework should be consistent across

jurisdictions with appropriate sharing of information between national authorities including through IOSCO; and,

- the Basel Committee should take forward its review on the role of external ratings in prudential regulation and determine whether there are any adverse incentives that need to be addressed.

Since the declaration of April 2009, the G-20 has reiterated in all its communiqués the idea that to make the financial system more resilient it is necessary, among other actions, to implement a regulatory monitoring of the CRAs. Besides this, the G-20 has called on CRAs to increase transparency, improve their quality, and avoid conflicts of interest, and on national supervisors to continue to focus on these issues in conducting their oversight.

In addition, the G-20, in its Toronto Summit in June 2010, insisted on the need to work on reducing the reliance on external ratings. The summit declaration stated the following:

> We committed to reduce reliance on external ratings in rules and regulations. We acknowledged the work underway at the BCBS to address adverse incentives arising from the use of external ratings in the regulatory capital framework, and at the FSB to develop general principles to reduce authorities' and financial institutions' reliance on external ratings. We called on them to report to our Finance Ministers and Central Bank Governors in October 2010.

In the Seoul Summit, which took place in November 2010, the G-20 leaders firmly recommitted to work in an internationally consistent and non-discriminatory manner to strengthen regulation and supervision on CRAs. In addition, they endorsed the FSB's principles on reducing reliance on external credit ratings and declared that 'standard setters, market participants, supervisors and central banks should not rely mechanistically on external credit ratings'.

Finally, at the meeting of Finance Ministers and Central Bank Governors that took place in Paris in February 2011 there was a reiteration of the commitment to implement in an 'internationally consistent and non-discriminatory way' the FSB's recommendations on reducing reliance on CRAs' ratings.

2.2.3 Financial Stability Board

The first initiative of global relevance undertaken due to the financial crisis was the request, in October 2007, of the G7 Ministers and Central Bank Governors to the Financial Stability Forum, now the Financial Stability Board, to analyse the causes and weaknesses underlying the market turmoil and to make recommendations to increase market and institutional resilience for the future.

This request ended with the publication in April 2008 of a report[8] where the FSB proposed concrete actions to enhance the resilience of the global system that concentrated on the following areas: strengthened prudential oversight of capital, liquidity, and risk management; enhancing transparency and valuation; strengthening the authorities' responsiveness to risks; robust arrangements for dealing

---

[8] See footnote 1.

with stress in the financial system; and changes in the role and uses of credit ratings.

In relation to CRAs, the report highlighted the relevance of the role played by CRAs in evaluating information on structured financial products and the reliance placed on their ratings by investors. To address the weaknesses detected during the crisis, the FSB made some recommendations, based substantially on the inputs of IOSCO and the Committee of Global Financial System.[9] As summarized in the EC impact assessment CRA Regulation, the FSB suggests that CRAs should:

- implement the revised IOSCO Code to manage conflicts of interest;
- improve the quality of the rating process with periodic reviews of methodologies and models undertaken by an independent function;
- separate consulting and rating activities;
- have adequate resources in the initial rating and in the review function;
- differentiate ratings on structured products from traditional ones (different scales or additional symbols);
- expand the initial and ongoing information (assumptions, volatility of the rating, and limitation of analysis due to insufficient data or untested models); and
- enhance their review of the quality of the data input and of the due diligence performed on underlying assets by originators, arrangers, and issuers involved in structured products.

In addition, the FSB recommends that investors should address their over-reliance on ratings (investors' due diligence) and that regulators should review their use of ratings in the regulatory and supervisory framework (in order to avoid inducement to uncritical reliance on ratings).

In October 2008 and in April 2009, the FSB published follow-up reports reviewing progress in the implementation of the recommendations, and describing the work underway by national authorities and international bodies, as well as parallel initiatives in the private sector complementing official action.

In April 2009, the G-20 leaders agreed in the London summit that the 'Financial Stability Forum should be expanded, given a broadened mandate to promote financial stability, and re-established with a stronger institutional basis and enhanced capacity as the Financial Stability Board (FSB)'.

Responding to its new role of coordinating and monitoring progress in strengthening financial regulation, the FSB has prepared, prior to each G-20 summit, reports that provide an overview of the progress made in implementing the G-20 recommendations. In the context of these periodic reviews, the FSB has undertaken the task of monitoring closely the steps taken by national and regional

---

[9] In July 2008, the CGFS published a paper entitled *Ratings in structured finance: what went wrong and what can be done to address shortcomings?* that explored ways to improve the credibility of ratings of structured finance products and provided a number of recommendations to address the weaknesses identified. This report was produced at the request of the FSF to update the report that the CGFS had published in January 2005 analysing the role of ratings in structured finance—*The role of ratings in structured finance: issues and implications.*

authorities to lessen undue reliance on ratings in rules and regulations. In addition, as a way to assist this work, the FSB published in October 2010 some high-level principles for use by authorities in reducing their reliance on ratings (see Section 2.2.5).

2.2.4 IOSCO

The work undertaken by securities supervisors in the context of IOSCO has been crucial to establish a set of principles that are accepted worldwide by regulators, supervisors, CRAs, and market participants. These principles have orientated the best practices in the sector since they were published and have been reinforced by the G-20 declarations that have endorsed them as the benchmark for all regulations.[10]

2.2.4.1 IOSCO Principles

In September 2003, IOSCO Principles were published for securities regulators, ratings agencies, and market participants with the aim of improving how CRAs operated and how the ratings were used by market participants. The final goal of these principles was to try to improve investor protection, and the fairness, efficiency, and transparency of the securities markets and reduce systemic risk.

When developing the principles, IOSCO acknowledged that CRAs were regulated and operated differently in each jurisdiction. Therefore, the principles were drafted as broad high-level objectives so they could be applied in any country and for any type of CRA, regardless of its size or business model. Also, IOSCO allowed each jurisdiction to decide on the best way to give effect to the principles, without aiming to impose or endorse any particular regulatory approach jurisdictions could take regarding CRAs: legislation; regulation imposed by non-government statutory regulators; industry codes; or internal rating agency policies and procedures.

IOSCO principles are organized following four main objectives, each subdivided into more specific principles.

Quality and Integrity of the Rating Process

The first principle deals with the quality and integrity of the rating process and states that 'CRAs should endeavour to issue opinions that help reduce the asymmetry of information among borrowers, lenders and other market participants'.

This principle encapsulates the ultimate reason for the existence of CRAs. The value of ratings in financial markets lies in the analysis underlying the rating being sufficiently thorough to provide investors with the information they need when making investment decisions. There is information that investors cannot have access to and information that is publicly available but difficult to analyse and summarize. Information asymmetries among the issuers and investors directly

---

[10] In February 2011, IOSCO published its *Report on regulatory implementation of the statement of principles regarding the activities of credit rating agencies in the different jurisdictions*, concluding that IOSCO's Principles are embedded into the CRAs legislation of the main jurisdictions.

relate to the cost of capital that issuers must pay. Therefore, CRAs, if they operate in an adequate way, perform a very relevant role in the good functioning of the financial markets.

In the long term, CRAs that fail to provide clear and useful ratings—that fail to reduce the asymmetry of information between investors and issuers—will likely fail in their business. In the short term, however, a respected CRA that fails to maintain high standards of quality and integrity in its rating will provide investors with a false measurement of the risk of certain securities, thus contributing to making the market less transparent.

Independence and Conflicts of Interest

According to the second principle:

> CRA ratings decisions should be independent and free from political or economic pressures and from conflicts of interest arising due to the CRA's ownership structure, business or financial activities, or the financial interests of the CRA's employees. CRAs should, as far as possible, avoid activities, procedures or relationships that may compromise or appear to compromise the independence and objectivity of the credit rating operations.

The value that investors give to ratings depends, to a large extent, on their confidence that these opinions are not inappropriately influenced by factors unrelated to a credit assessment. Conflicts of interest or factors that reduce a CRA's analytical independence can undermine investor confidence in the ratings. Moreover, if conflicts of interest or the lack of independence are widespread, this can harm the overall investor confidence in the transparency and integrity of a market.

Transparency and Timeliness of Ratings Disclosure

The third principle deals with issues relating to transparency and timeliness of ratings disclosure: 'CRAs should make disclosure and transparency an objective in their rating activities'. It is crucial for the good functioning of the markets that rating agencies have procedures in place that ensure that ratings are disclosed in a timely manner and explained.

For ratings to be useful for investors they must be disclosed in a timely manner. This requirement, which has been included in most of the legislations dealing with CRAs, is not easy to interpret in practice. Actually, due to recent downgrades of sovereign debts in EU countries, concerns have been raised in relation to the moment when CRAs decide to publish a rating (see Section 3.8.5).

Moreover, transparency in the rating process is also key to a good understanding of the meaning of ratings by market participants. CRAs should provide investors and issuers with sufficient information about the procedures, methodologies, and assumptions that result in a credit rating so they can understand how a rating was produced and arrived at.

This transparency is beneficial for investors, as they are given information to help assess the quality of a rating for the purposes of their decision-making process; but also for issuers, as they are reassured of the fairness and objectivity of the rating process and encouraged to provide CRAs with the information they need for forming their opinions.

Confidential Information

The fourth principle states that 'CRAs should maintain in confidence all non-public information communicated to them by any issuer, or its agents, under the terms of a confidentiality agreement or otherwise under a mutual understanding that the information is shared confidentially'.

Issuers have a greater understanding of their credit situation and of the risks related to the securities they offer than investors have. This information asymmetry raises the cost of capital for issuers, as investors insist on being compensated for the uncertainty this asymmetry causes. CRAs help to lower the cost of capital for issuers by reducing these information asymmetries by analysing publicly available information but also non-public information that issuers share with them (directly asking the issuer questions about its operations, management, and financial situation). However, issuers may be reluctant to share with CRAs non-public but potentially relevant information if issuers are concerned that the information will not remain confidential or will be used in a manner other than that relating to a credit rating.

This principle is designed to encourage issuers' cooperation with CRAs by promoting procedures and mechanisms to protect non-public information from premature disclosure or use in ways unrelated to a CRA's rating activities.

2.2.4.2 IOSCO Code

IOSCO Code December 2004

In December 2004, IOSCO released the CRA Code of Conduct Fundamentals as a result of a project that involved IOSCO members, CRAs, representatives of the BCBS, the International Association of Insurance Supervisors, issuers, and the public at large. This project was undertaken at the request of market participants, including some CRAs, who, following the publication of the IOSCO Principles, suggested that it would be useful for IOSCO to develop a more detailed code of conduct providing guidance on how the Principles could be implemented in practice.

The IOSCO Code offers a set of practical measures that serve as a guide to implement the Principles and provides guidance upon which individual CRA codes of conduct must be based, leaving flexibility for each CRA to adopt the measures in the way it considers best, depending on its specific operational, legal, and market circumstances. In fact, as the Principles, the Code is intended to be useful for all types of CRAs regardless of the business model they use. The Code does not indicate a preference for one business model over another, nor are the measures included designed to be used only by large global CRAs.

The measures in the IOSCO Code were not intended to be all-inclusive. In fact, when publishing the Code, IOSCO recommended CRAs and regulators to consider whether or not additional measures could be necessary to properly implement the Principles in a specific jurisdiction, and announced the possibility of a future review of the Code in light of experience.

In 2004, the international regulatory community was happy with the prevalent self-regulating system of the sector. Therefore, the enforcement mechanism of the

Code was left open for the different jurisdictions to decide on, as in the case of the Principles.

Moreover, the Code included a requirement for CRAs to publish their codes of conduct and to describe how the provisions of their codes were consistent with the provisions of the IOSCO Code ('comply or explain' approach). Therefore, whilst CRAs were free to not include or alter specific provisions of the IOSCO Code, if they did so, they should explain where their own codes differ from the IOSCO Code and how these variances nonetheless address the underlying objectives that the IOSCO Code provisions seek to address. In this way, market participants could decide whether the CRAs' variations from the IOSCO Code made sense, and react accordingly.

When approving the Code, IOSCO highlighted that the Code did not address the obligations issuers have of cooperating with and providing accurate and complete information to the marketplace and the CRAs they request to provide ratings. However, even if the Code refers only to CRAs's obligations, IOSCO recognized that issuers had an equally important duty to contribute to the transparency of the financial markets.

Revised IOSCO Code (May 2008)

In February 2007, IOSCO published a paper[11] with its assessment of the degree to which CRAs had adopted codes that reflected the provisions of the IOSCO Code. The outcome of this review was that many CRAs had adopted and published their own codes of conduct based on and consistent with the IOSCO Code. In particular, the main CRAs had implemented the IOSCO Code extensively and where they departed from IOSCO's provisions they provided explanations of those variations. However, IOSCO identified specific areas where there was still room for improvement, for example, on provision 3.9 related to unsolicited ratings.

In March 2007, the FSB requested IOSCO to explore whether there were any outstanding issues relating to the role of CRAs in structured finance. Following this request, IOSCO decided to study the activities of CRAs in the rating of structured finance products and whether any amendments should be made to the IOSCO Code to reflect the specificities of ratings of those instruments.

In March 2008, IOSCO published a consultation paper[12] followed by its final report released in May 2008.[13] The report included an analysis of the role that CRAs have in capital markets, describing the differences between ratings of corporate issuers and ratings of structured finance products. The main conclusion of the report was that CRAs had played a critical role during the subprime crisis and that this role had raised a number of possible regulatory issues, some of which should be addressed in the IOSCO Code provisions.

Consequently, in May 2008 IOSCO published a revised version of the IOSCO Code incorporating significant amendments in order to strengthen the provisions in relation to the rating of structured finance products. Among others, the revised

---

[11] IOSCO (February 2007), *Review of implementation of the IOSCO fundamentals of a code of conduct for credit rating agencies. Consultation report.*
[12] IOSCO (March 2008), *Consultation report. The role of credit rating agencies in structured finance markets.*
[13] IOSCO (May 2008), *The role of credit rating agencies in structured finance markets. Final report.*

recommendation re:

(Sfp)

Code introduced the following measures: to prohibit CRA's analysts from making recommendations on the design of structured finance products that the CRA rates; to establish new products review functions to consider the feasibility of providing ratings for a type of structure materially different from previous structures rated; to publish historical information about the performance of rating opinions, where possible, standardized to assist investors in drawing performance comparisons between different CRAs; and to differentiate ratings of structured finance products from other ratings, preferably through different rating symbols.

Although initially addressed to CRAs, as mentioned previously, the IOSCO Code has also been used by legislators of all jurisdictions as the basis on which to build their oversight regimes. The recently agreed Basel III Framework has confirmed the IOSCO Code as the international benchmark for CRAs' rules of conduct. According to the Basel III text, national supervisors should refer to the IOSCO Code when determining ECAI eligibility. An elaboration of the IOSCO provisions will follow in Section 3.8, when analysing how such measures have been incorporated into the EU CRA Regulation.

External Credit Assessment Institution

2.2.4.3 IOSCO's Oversight on Rating Agencies

After the publication of the revised Code, as IOSCO was drawing lessons from the financial meltdown, it decided to start exploring possible ways through which its members could work together for the effective monitoring of the compliance of CRAs with the Code.

IOSCO clearly opted to enhance international coordination as a way to address the issues that had contributed to the failures in the structured finance market. In this sense, in a statement published in September 2008, IOSCO's members publicly encouraged legislators to consider the IOSCO Code as a regulatory global consensus that should be taken into account when preparing legislation on CRAs in order to avoid fragmentation of regulations that would contribute to create an unlevel paying field in the sector and complicate supervisory cooperation.

As a step forward in this international cooperation, IOSCO committed to work towards developing mechanisms by which national regulators could coordinate their monitoring of CRAs with the substance of the Code and to set the conditions of information exchange and cooperation among its members.

In addition, IOSCO agreed on the need to increase the interaction between CRAs and supervisors and decided to examine the possibility of developing an international monitoring body with a similar structure and purpose to the auditing standards oversight body (the Public Interest Oversight Board). This body would discuss issues with CRAs and, in this way, advance the expectations of the international regulatory community.

Following the path announced in September 2008, in March 2009 IOSCO published a report[14] analysing the extent to which CRAs around the world had incorporated the IOSCO Code provisions into their codes of conduct. This report, which followed the same methodology as the work undertaken in February 2007,

---

[14] IOSCO (March 2009), *A review of implementation of the IOSCO code of conduct fundamentals for credit rating agencies.*

showed that in relation to the 2007 review, a larger proportion of the CRAs examined were aware of the IOSCO Code and had taken steps to incorporate its provisions into their codes of conduct, including the new provisions related to ratings of structured finance instruments that were added in May 2008. In particular, the report concluded in relation to the main CRAs, Fitch, Moody's, and S&P, that they had substantially implemented the revisions of the IOSCO Code.

Together with this report, IOSCO published a note[15] to update market participants on its work on CRAs and to inform them that a new permanent IOSCO CRA standing committee was going to be established to reflect in the structure of the organization the relevance of CRAs' related work. The new standing committee would be in charge of regularly discussing, evaluating, and considering regulatory and policy initiatives vis-à-vis CRA activities and monitoring and would seek cross-border regulatory consensus. Besides this, the committee would serve as a forum for regular interaction between regulators and CRAs.

Basically, IOSCO work was initially focused on trying to find adequate means to enhance international cooperation to avoid duplicative or inefficient requirements in the different jurisdictions.

In addition, and although the enforcement of the rules would be done at a national level, IOSCO members considered it necessary to cooperate in the monitoring and surveillance of CRAs' operations. Sharing information among them would give supervisors a better insight into the activities of the CRAs in other jurisdictions and this would help regulators to monitor best the CRAs' activities in their own jurisdictions. IOSCO discussed the possible forms in which cooperation for CRAs that operate in multiple jurisdictions could take place in practice, and concluded with two non-exclusive options: a college of supervisors and a series of bilateral cooperation arrangements.

Finally, in the area of supervision of globally active CRAs, IOSCO developed a confidential examination module to be used, as appropriate, by those IOSCO members that regulate and inspect CRAs. The aim of setting this module was to help create a common understanding of the types of information that regulators around the world could find useful when inspecting a CRA against regulatory requirements based on the IOSCO Code. This common model could also help to enhance the sharing of information, as it would give IOSCO members some comfort on the type of information they may request from another competent authority.

2.2.5 Over-reliance on Ratings

The excessive reliance of investors on ratings has widely been considered one of the triggers of the most recent crisis in financial markets. Numerous studies[16] conclude that 'rating crisis show that ratings increase systemic risk and may be

---

[15] IOSCO (March 2009), *Note on international cooperation in oversight of credit rating agencies.*

[16] Sy, Amadou N. R., (2009), *The systemic regulation of credit rating agencies and rated markets.* IMF Working Paper 09/129 and Cantor, Richard, and Mann, C. (2009), *Are Corporate Bond Ratings Procyclical?*

pro-cyclical, helping fuel investments in "good times" and accelerating market losses in "bad times"'.

CRAs can increase systemic risk through unanticipated and abrupt downgrades. Such ratings actions can lead to large market losses, fire sales, and liquidity shortages and have knock-on effects on a number of systemically important market participants. These problems may be compounded by the fact that, as rating downgrades are pro-cyclical, a first round of downgrades can lead to further downgrades. The recent sovereign debt crisis has been an example of where downgrades have led to a mechanistic reaction by many market participants that sold at the same time, increasing market volatility and causing a self-sustaining downward spiral of the price of the debt instruments that can have serious negative effects for financial stability. In particular, the specific impact of ratings in the sovereign debt market has been thoroughly analysed in Chapter 3 of the IMF *Global financial stability report* published in October 2010.[17] This paper recommends reducing the negative cliff effects in prices and spreads that rating changes imply by amending regulations that hardwire buy-or-sell decisions to ratings.

Therefore, over-reliance on ratings has become a concern for the international regulatory community, which has, since the subprime crisis, started to reconsider the existing ties between rating and financial stability. Efforts in this respect are mainly concentrated on two areas: requirements on financial firms to undertake their own due diligence and internal risk management instead of relying mechanistically on external ratings; and reconsideration of references to ratings in the regulatory framework in light of their potential to implicitly be regarded as a public endorsement of ratings, and thus their potential to influence behaviour in an undesirable way.

2.2.5.1 *Global Initiatives. FSB Principles*

Already in its report of April 2008, the FSB noted that 'some institutional investors have relied too heavily on ratings in their investment guidelines and choices, in some cases fully substituting ratings for independent risk assessment and due diligence. Some also relied exclusively on ratings for valuation purposes. The over-reliance on ratings was particularly acute in the case of structured finance products.'

Moreover, the FSB considered that references to ratings in various regulatory and supervisory frameworks both at the international and at the national level 'may have played a role in encouraging investors' over-reliance on ratings, by discouraging some investors from paying close attention to what the ratings actually mean'.

Consequently, the FSB recommended authorities to review whether their regulations and/or supervisory policies unintentionally gave credit ratings an official seal of approval that further discouraged investors from making independent judgement of risks and performing their own due diligence.

To analyse the extent of the use of ratings in the banking, securities, and insurance sectors, the FSB requested the Joint Forum to conduct a stocktaking

---

[17] IMF (October 2010), *Global financial stability report: sovereigns, funding, and systemic liquidity.*

exercise among its members. As discussed before, in June 2009 the Joint Forum published an extensive report that has been useful in facilitating authorities' and policymakers' assessment of the use and reliance on credit ratings.

The G-20, in its Toronto Summit in June 2010, insisted on the need to work on reducing the reliance on external ratings and acknowledged the work underway at the FSB to develop general principles to reduce authorities' and financial institutions' reliance on external ratings. Moreover, the G-20 leaders requested the FSB to report on this issue to the Finance Ministers and Central Bank Governors in October 2010.

To comply with this request on 27 October 2010 the FSB published its *Principles for reducing reliance on credit rating agency ratings*,[18] which were endorsed by the G-20 members in November 2010. According to the FSB, the goal of the principles is to reduce mechanistic reliance on ratings and to incentivize improvements in independent credit risk assessment and due diligence capacity. In fact the principles, as explained below, aim to catalyse a significant change in existing practices, as they intend to reduce in the medium term the key role that ratings play in financial markets nowadays.

Authorities to Assess Reference to Ratings in Regulations

The first principle deals with the objective of reducing reliance on CRAs ratings in standards, laws, and regulations and requests standard setters and authorities to assess references to CRAs ratings in regulations and, wherever possible, remove them or replace them with suitable alternative standards of creditworthiness.

Under this principle, the FSB encourages standard setters and authorities to develop transition plans and timetables to enable the removal or replacement of references to CRAs ratings wherever it is possible for them to be safely introduced.

Firms to Make their Own Credit Assessments

The second FSB principle states that 'banks, market participants and institutional investors should be expected to make their own credit assessments, and not rely solely or mechanistically on CRA ratings'. Consequently, the FSB requires that the design of regulations and other official sector actions should support this principle.

When publishing this principle, the FSB also recognized that CRAs play an important role and that their ratings can appropriately be used as input to firms' own judgement as part of internal credit assessment processes. Moreover, the FSB acknowledged that CRAs can provide economies of scale in analysing credit on behalf of smaller and less sophisticated investors, and that ratings can be used as an external comparator by all investors in their own internal assessments. Therefore, the FSB considers that the principles in this area should recognize these useful functions and should differentiate according to size and sophistication of firm, according to the asset class of instruments concerned (for example, sovereign, corporate, or structured), and according to the materiality of the relevant exposures.

---

[18] FSB (October 2010), *Principles for reducing reliance on CRA ratings*.

However, the principles make clear that any use of CRAs' ratings by a firm does not lessen its own responsibility to ensure that its credit exposures are based on sound assessments.

Specific Principles

The FSB's document also highlights more specific principles to apply these two basic principles to particular areas of financial market activity. In this context, its third principle covers central bank operations, prudential supervision of banks, internal limits and investment policies of investment managers and institutional investors, private sector margin agreements, and disclosures by issuers of securities.

CENTRAL BANK OPERATIONS. The FSB states that 'central banks should reach their own credit judgements on the financial instruments that they will accept in market operations, both as collateral and as outright purchases, and their policies should avoid mechanistic approaches that could lead to unnecessarily abrupt and large changes in the eligibility of financial instruments and the level of haircuts that may exacerbate cliff effects'.

PRUDENTIAL SUPERVISION OF BANKS. The FSB highlights that 'banks must not mechanistically rely on CRA ratings for assessing the creditworthiness of assets. This implies that banks should have the capability to conduct their own assessment of the creditworthiness of, as well as other risks relating to, the financial instruments they are exposed to and should satisfy supervisors of that capability.'

In order to provide market discipline, banks should publicly disclose information about their credit assessment approach, and the proportion of their portfolio (or of particular asset classes) for which they have not conducted an internal credit assessment. The FSB suggest that this could be required, for instance, through the third pillar of the Basel II Framework.

> Banks using the standardized Basel II approach currently have minimum capital requirements based on CRAs' ratings. The FSB considers that, as long as some banks continue to have capital requirements based on CRAs' ratings, supervisory processes should be put in place to check the understanding of the appropriate uses and limitations of CRAs' ratings by these banks' risk managers. In its recommendations, the FSB takes into account the different size and sophistication of banks.

INVESTMENT POLICIES OF INVESTMENT MANAGERS AND INSTITUTIONAL INVESTORS. The FSB underscores that investment managers and institutional investors must not mechanistically rely on CRAs ratings for assessing the creditworthiness of assets. While references to CRAs ratings in internal limits, credit policies, and mandates can play a useful role as benchmarks for the transparency of credit policies, they should not substitute investment managers' own independent credit judgements.

The FSB considers that this principle has to apply across the full range of investment managers and of institutional investors, including money market funds, pension funds, collective investment schemes (such as mutual funds and investment companies), insurance companies, and securities firms. Moreover, it should apply to all sizes and levels of sophistication of investment managers and institutional investors.

PRIVATE SECTOR MARGIN AGREEMENTS. The FSB also considers that market participants and central counter-parties should not use changes in CRAs' ratings of counter-parties or of collateral assets as automatic triggers for large, discrete collateral calls in margin agreements on derivatives and securities financing transactions. Furthermore, supervisors should not allow CRAs' rating triggers to be used as a factor that reduces regulatory capital requirements.

DISCLOSURES BY ISSUERS OF SECURITIES. The FSB highlights the need for an improved disclosure regime by issuers to facilitate investors, mainly institutional ones, conducting their own assessment of the creditworthiness of the financial products they invest in.

With this objective in mind, the FSB considers that issuers of securities should disclose comprehensive and timely information and, in case of publicly traded securities, this should be a public disclosure.

In addition, it requires standard setters and authorities to review whether any references to CRAs' ratings in standards, laws, and regulations relating to disclosure requirements are providing unintended incentives for investors to rely excessively on CRAs' ratings and, if appropriate, remove or amend these requirements.

The publication of the FSB's principles, and the endorsement by the G-20 members, has been a relevant step in the path to reduce over-reliance on CRAs' ratings. The FSB has asked standard setters and regulators to consider the next steps that could be taken to translate the principles into more specific policy actions to remove or replace reliance on CRAs' ratings in laws and regulations, taking into account the particular circumstances of products, market participants, and jurisdictions. The SEC has already proposed means to remove or reduce references to CRAs in rules (see Appendix 4).

The FSB undertook to report to future G-20 meetings on the progress in translating the principles into more specific policy actions and of the planned medium-term timetable and milestones, based on information collected from standard-setting bodies and national and regional regulators.

2.2.5.2 European Initiatives

In July 2008, the Commission's Services published, together with its consultation on a proposal to regulate CRAs, a consultation document on policy options to address the problem of excessive reliance on ratings.[19] In this document, the EC identified the references made to ratings in existing EU legislation at the time and looked at possible approaches to the issue of excessive reliance on ratings. The three proposals that the EC envisaged, in a non-mutually exclusive way, were the following:

---

[19] EC (2008), *Consultation document on policy options to address the problem of excessive reliance on ratings.*

- Require regulated and sophisticated investors to rely more on own risk analysis, especially for (relatively) large investments.
- Require that all published ratings include 'health-warnings' informing on the specific risks associated with investments in the rated assets.
- Examine the regulatory references to CRAs' ratings and revisit them as necessary.

After consultation, the EC did not undertake any specific action in this area. However, the Regulation of CRAs includes references to the need to avoid the risk of over-reliance on ratings. In this respect, Recital 10 states that 'the users of credit ratings should not rely blindly on credit ratings but should take utmost care to perform own analysis and conduct appropriate due diligence at all times regarding their reliance on such credit ratings'.

In addition, Article 39.1 of the CRA Regulation required the EC to submit, by 7 December 2012, a report to the European Parliament and to the Council with its assessment of the application of the Regulation, including, among other aspects, 'an assessment of the reliance on credit ratings in the Community'.

To fulfil this request and in view of the international initiatives in this area, mainly those of the FSB, the EC consultation on CRAs November 2010 proposed, among other things, some possible initiatives to reduce over-reliance on external ratings. The consultation concentrates on three areas where external ratings are widely used by market participants and where there is a potential risk of over-reliance. For each of these areas, the EC analyses the uses and possible risks and suggests, through questions, possible policy options to reduce reliance:

- The use of external credit ratings for the calculation of certain regulatory limits and capital requirements for financial institutions (according to the CRD).
- The use by financial firms of external ratings for internal (credit/market) risk management purposes.
- The reference to external ratings in investment policies and mandates of portfolio and asset managers.

In addition to the uses of ratings mentioned above, the document provides, in an annex, a brief overview of other references to external ratings in EU financial legislation that the EC considers to be of less relevance.

3

Analysis of the EU Credit Rating Agencies Regulation

3.1 BACKGROUND

As discussed in the paragraphs below, EU legislators have been considering the possibility of regulating CRAs for a number of years. However, the decisive impetus that propelled the EU into action was the international consensus on the need to regulate CRAs' operations that was reached by the G-20 leaders at the April 2009 summit.

The first milestone was the European Parliament's Resolution[1] adopted in February 2004 with its views on the role and methods of credit rating agencies. This resolution accepted the positive role of CRAs in the financial markets but also highlighted certain problematic issues that warranted further action to ensure the CRAs performed their role in a responsible way.

In fact, the Resolution mentioned all the main aspects that have been focusing the regulatory discussions on CRAs over the past few years and called for an analysis of the convenience of setting a registration regime for CRAs in the EU, requesting the EC to submit by 31 July 2005 its assessment of the need for appropriate legislative proposals to deal with CRAs.

3.1.1 European Commission's Communication

In order to prepare its report to the European Parliament, the EC requested ESMA to provide its views regarding the possible options for regulating the activities of CRAs. In its advice to the EC published in March 2005,[2] ESMA proposed not regulating CRAs at the European level but for the time being adopting a system of self-regulation, with a monitoring of the degree to which CRAs applied the voluntary rules set out in the IOSCO Code.

Following ESMA's advice, the Commission decided not to present new legislative proposals in the area of CRAs, considering that the existing financial services

---

[1] European Parliament (January 2004), *Resolution on role and methods of rating agencies (2003/2081(INI))*.

[2] CESR (March 2005), *Technical advice to the European Commission on possible measures concerning credit rating agencies (Ref. CESR/05-139b)*.

directives applicable to CRAs would provide an answer to all the major issues of concern raised by the European Parliament.

In this context, in January 2006 the Commission published its Communication[3] that concluded that various financial services directives (basically measures included in the Market Abuse Directive and the Capital Requirements Directive), combined with self-regulation by the CRAs on the basis of the IOSCO Code could provide a satisfactory answer to the major issues of concern in relation to CRAs. However, the Communication, as suggested by ESMA, indicated that the EC might consider putting forward legislative action if it became clear that compliance with EU rules or IOSCO's Code was unsatisfactory or if new circumstances were to arise—including market failure or significant changes in the way CRAs were regulated in other parts of the world. In addition, the Commission asked ESMA to monitor compliance with the IOSCO Code and report back on an annual basis.

3.1.2 ESMA's Reports on Rating Agencies

Following the EC's mandate, ESMA established a voluntary framework by which CRAs who wished to join in the process would report annually to ESMA on their degree of compliance with the IOSCO Code. DBRS, Fitch, Moody's, and S&P decided to adhere to ESMA's proposal.

In January 2007, ESMA published its first report for the EC,[4] concluding that agencies complied to a large extent with the IOSCO Code but also indicating certain areas where relevant deviations existed that were common to the four agencies reviewed. In particular, CRAs did not fully comply with the IOSCO Code when it came to unsolicited ratings and ancillary services. These areas, together with the structured finance area, were decided on to be further investigated in the next review.

In May 2007, the EC requested of ESMA a second report specifically asking whether the recent events in financial markets made it advisable to modify the decision taken in 2006 not to regulate CRAs.

In an attempt to avert regulation, and also in response to calls by authorities (such as ESMA) and market participants, a group of CRAs (the big three plus A.M. Best Company, Inc. and DBRS Limited) began working together in October 2007 on initiatives to enhance confidence in the credit rating process, particularly with respect to structured finance securities. In December 2007 they circulated a discussion paper[5] with certain proposals regarding the enhancement of the independence, quality, and transparency of credit ratings. A summary of this joint paper, as well as a list of the main individual initiatives undertaken by the main CRAs, is provided in the EC impact assessment CRA Regulation (pages 86–88 and pages 98–99).

---

[3] EC (March 2006), *Communication by the Commission on Credit Rating Agencies (2006/C 59/02), OJ C59, 11.3.2006*: p. 2.

[4] CESR (December 2006), *Report to the European Commission on the compliance of credit rating agencies with the IOSCO Code (Ref. CESR/06-545)*.

[5] *Discussion paper about measures to enhance the independence, quality and transparency of credit ratings*.

ESMA published its advice to the EC[6] in May 2008, and it was in line with the subsequent report of the European Securities Markets Expert Group (ESME), released in June 2008.[7] ESMA's proposal consisted of strengthening the self-regulation system by creating an international body composed of market participants designated by regulators, which would have a twofold function: establishing a set of rules for conduct in line with those set out in the IOSCO Code, and supervising compliance with it. ESMA proposed that the creation of this body should be coordinated with regulators of other international markets or, if this was not possible, adopted in the European Union.

In March 2009, following the request of the EC, ESMA published its third report on CRAs' compliance with IOSCO Code.[8] This report provided further analysis of the progress made by EU-based CRAs towards implementing the updated IOSCO Code.

ESMA's overall conclusion with respect to the codes of conduct of the global CRAs (S&P, Moody's, Fitch, DBRS, and AM Best) was that they were broadly compliant with the IOSCO Code.

With respect to the other 19 EU CRAs analysed, ESMA identified that about a third had not adopted any code of conduct and, among those that had adopted and published codes the large majority were broadly compliant with the 2004 IOSCO Code but had not adopted the 2008 amendments to the IOSCO Code.

3.1.3 European Commission's Regulation Proposal

As discussed previously, Europe had been debating the need to set up a registration and supervisory regime for the CRAs for several years. The consensus reached among participants in securities markets and supervisors as to the deficiencies in the activities of agencies, was not so strong as that when discussing what the most appropriate solution would be to the problems. In fact, a number of key market participants were in favour of self-regulation, on the basis of the international standards agreed by IOSCO in 2004.

However, the deficiencies identified in recent years in the activity of CRAs highlighted the shortcomings of the self-regulation system which existed in Europe and other jurisdictions. European governments consequently considered that it was necessary to establish an effective public supervision of agencies and, therefore, the EC decided to propose the introduction of legislation on CRAs in the EU.

On 8 July 2008, EU finance ministers agreed in relation to CRAs on 'the principle of European regulations guaranteeing supervision of these agencies in the EU through registration. The Council asked the Commission to present it with

---

[6] CESR (May 2008), *Second Report to the European Commission on the compliance of credit rating agencies with the IOSCO Code and the role of credit rating agencies in structured finance (Ref. CESR/08-277).*

[7] European Securities Markets Expert Group (June 2008), *Report to the European Commission on the role of credit rating agencies.*

[8] CESR (May 2009), *Report on compliance of EU-based credit rating agencies with the 2008 IOSCO Code of Conduct (Ref. CESR/09-417).*

specific proposals for implementing a European mechanism for registering credit rating agencies'.

Consequently, on 31 July 2008, the EC published a consultation paper proposing the adoption of a set of rules introducing substantive requirements that CRAs would need to respect for the authorization and exercise of their rating activity in the EU.[9] The consultation document also included authorization, supervision, and enforcement provisions. In particular, it proposed two options for an EU monitoring of CRAs: a first option was to reinforce ESMA's role in order to enhance cooperation between national regulators. The second option combined the establishment of a European agency (either ESMA or a new agency) for the EU-wide registration of CRAs and the reliance on national regulators for the supervision of CRAs' activities.

It was clear that, beyond technical considerations and the doubts expressed during the consultation period, the EC had taken the political decision to move towards a strong CRAs regulatory regime, and that there was a political will to have legislation in place in a very short period of time to meet the deadline agreed at G-20 level. Therefore, a tight timetable was set to allow the EU Council and the EU Parliament to agree on the rules before the Parliament's elections in June 2009.

The EC published its formal proposal to regulate CRAs on 12 November 2008.[10] The EC published an impact assessment accompanying the proposal, proposing four policy options:

- Self-regulation that could be based on the IOSCO Code, on an industry 'white paper'[11] or on initiatives by individual CRAs.

- A voluntary European code of conduct for CRAs developed by the industry based on the 'comply or explain' principle, together with a monitoring body that would check compliance with the code.

- A Commission's Recommendation setting standards that CRAs would have to comply with to operate in the EU but without an enforcement mechanism.

- EU legislation introducing a registration procedure and substantive requirements.

The EC's conclusion, after discussing the pros and cons that the different options had for achieving the objectives set, was that legislation was the best alternative.

Negotiations of the Regulation at Council and European Parliament level took place at an extremely swift pace. The whole legislative process took one year, and by 17 November 2009 the Regulation was published in the European *Official Journal*.

---

[9] EC (July 2008), *Consultation document on a proposal for a Directive/Regulation of the European Parliament and of the Council on Credit Rating Agencies.*

[10] EC (November 2008), *European Commission's proposal for a Regulation of the European Parliament and of the Council on credit rating agencies (COM(2008) 704 final) (SEC 2008) 2745) {SEC(2008) 2746}).*

[11] In January 2008 the five main CRAs jointly addressed a White Paper to regulators with twelve proposals to improve the IOSCO Code in relation to the independence, quality, and transparency of credit ratings.

3.2 SUPERVISORY STRUCTURE

Regarding the supervisory structure for CRAs, the EU has been moving very quickly. This section will provide a brief overview of the different stages since the approval of the EU Regulation in November 2009, which set up a system of colleges of supervisors until the centralization of supervision in ESMA once the new European financial supervision system was in place.

3.2.1 Colleges of Supervisors

During the debate that took place in the negotiation process of the CRA Regulation different registration and supervision models were analysed. In simplified terms, the options that were placed on the table (from lesser to greater degree of harmonization) were: supervision by the home Member State, combined supervision by several countries (through colleges of supervisors) under the coordination of ESMA, and supervision by a newly created European agency.[12]

Finding a solution acceptable for everyone in the short period of time during which the negotiations took place involved considerable efforts on the part of the Member States and European Parliament. The different positions during negotiations ended with a very complex compromise: a mixed system in which supervision and registration decisions had to be discussed by several institutions (college of supervisors and ESMA) prior to their adoption by the competent authority of the home Member State.

The main harmonizing force during the legislative process was the European Parliament. Although the Parliament was not able, at that time, to impose the creation of a European agency for the supervision of CRAs, it forced the inclusion of a clause that labelled the Regulation model as temporary. Thus, Recital 51 expressly mentioned that the supervisory architecture provided in the Regulation should not be considered the long-term solution and considered that reforms of broad scope would be necessary in the supervisory model, taking into account the conclusions of the Larosière Report.

In essence, the Regulation formally attributed registration and supervision of agencies to the competent authorities of the home Member States (those where the agency has its registered office). Nevertheless, in order to enable all authorities to have the possibility of participating in this registration and supervision, the Regulation required that any decisions adopted by the home competent authority were previously agreed by a college of supervisors. The colleges would be composed, on an obligatory basis, by all authorities where the agency had a registered office (a subsidiary, for example). In addition, the competent authorities of the countries in which the agency had a branch or in which the ratings of that agency were either in widespread use or might have a significant impact, could voluntarily decide to become members of the college. If members of the college did not reach agreement on a decision, the Regulation imposed the intervention of ESMA.

---

[12] Garcia Alcubilla, Raquel and Ruiz del Pozo, Javier (2008), Credit rating agencies: the debate on future European legislation. *CNMV Bulletin, Quarter III.*

Therefore, the weight of supervision was attributed to the colleges, although for legal reasons final decisions regarding registration and supervision were to be taken by the home authority in accordance with its administrative law.

In addition, the Regulation conferred on ESMA an important task of coordinating supervision of the different colleges and competent authorities with the aim of ensuring consistency among different competent authorities.

3.2.1.1 *The Operation of Colleges Between 7 June 2010 and 30 June 2011*

Colleges set up by European supervisors were in charge of the registration and supervision of EU CRAs from June 2010 until July 2011. Therefore, the applications for registration from existing CRAs that were operating in the EU when the CRA Regulation became effective were handled by these colleges. Among those applicants were the EU subsidiaries of the major international CRAs (see Section 1.2.3).

In December 2010 ESMA published some details about the registration process of the EU CRAs that were operating when the Regulation came into force and therefore had to apply for registration by 7 September 2010 at the latest.[13]

According to ESMA's report, ESMA received 23 applications for registration and 1 application for certification from a Japanese agency. Most of the applicants (19) were individual CRAs (mainly focused on rating local corporate entities) and 4 applications were received from EU groups. In total, the CRAs members of groups and the individual CRAs added up to a total of 45 legal entities that had applied for registration in the EU by 7 September 2010.

EU competent authorities formed six colleges of supervisors: four colleges for the four groups and two additional colleges for the two individual CRAs whose ratings, according to ESMA's report, were deemed as having cross-border relevance. The other applications were handled exclusively by the home competent authority of the applicant (or, in other words, by a college composed of just one member).

Although the composition of the colleges was not published by ESMA, the EC impact assessment CRA Regulation II included a table with the EC's estimation of the expected size of supervisory colleges.

The authorities composing the colleges were obliged to cooperate, to exchange the information necessary to carry out their duties, to transmit under certain conditions confidential information to other authorities, and to select a facilitator responsible for coordinating the activities of the college.

An important question that was not resolved in the Regulation was the procedure that colleges should follow to take decisions (such as type of quorum and majorities required, or votes of each member). However, the Regulation did provide, although in a confusing way, that the decision to register an agency required unanimity of members of the college (if there was no unanimity the competent authorities should refuse registration). With respect to other decisions (withdrawal of registration or other penalties, supervisory measures, etc.), if there

---

[13] CESR (December 2010), *Annual report according to Article 21 of Regulation (EC) 1060/2009 on Credit Rating Agencies (Ref. CESR/10-1424).*

was no agreement between the members of the college, and after ESMA had given its opinion, the competent authorities should decide—explaining the reasons for their decision and the diverging positions.

In the event of disagreement between members of the college regarding registration and supervision actions, the Regulation provided for an appeal process to ESMA. For all other issues, it was left to ESMA to agree on the organizational aspects of the colleges. In June 2010 ESMA published its guidelines on the functioning of colleges (ESMA's guidance on registration).

In its report published in December 2010,[14] ESMA included a first and very preliminary assessment of the functioning of the colleges of competent authorities, concluding that 'the operation of these frameworks has revealed some difficulties mainly linked to the problem of ensuring consistency, in terms of analyses and conclusions, across colleges'. However, the key difficulty the colleges had to overcome was one of resources. The CRA Regulation posed a challenge for national authorities that had to develop expertise in an area that up to then had not been in their remit of competences, and had to set up functions in charge of registration and supervision of CRAs in a very short time frame. This effort was even greater taking into account that supervisors already knew that these functions would have to be partly dismantled only a few months later when ESMA took over all supervisory activities over CRAs in July 2011.

3.2.2 ESMA

The subprime crisis highlighted the need to set a more efficient and integrated supervisory framework in Europe. The new European System of Financial Supervisors, in place since 1 January 2011, was established to bring together the actors of financial supervision at a national level and at the level of the EU. The ESFS is composed of the supervisory authorities of the Member States and four new bodies: ESMA, EBA, EIOPA, and ESRB (see Appendix 1 for further details on the ESFS).

ESMA has been established as the European authority in charge of securities markets with a specific governance structure and the necessary resources to fulfil its objectives (see Appendix 2 for further details on ESMA). Among other competences, as explained below, ESMA has been entrusted with direct supervisory powers over CRAs.

3.2.2.1 *Registration and Supervision of CRAs*

Following the establishment of ESMA, and taking into account the fact that credit ratings are used throughout the EU and that rating services are not linked to particular territories, the EU legislators decided that it was no longer appropriate to maintain the traditional distinction between the home competent authority and the other competent authorities and the use of supervisory coordination by colleges.

---

[14] See footnote 13.

In addition to all the powers and competences granted to EBA and EIOPA, ESMA was entrusted with direct supervisory powers over CRAs registered in the EU. This agreement was reflected in Recital 5 of ESMA Regulation and developed in depth in the amendment to the CRA Regulation adopted in 2011 (CRA Regulation II).

Basically, the amendment conferred on ESMA all competences and duties related to the registration and supervision of EU CRAs as of the 1 July 2011. Consequently, the powers that had been given to the competent authorities of the Member States by the CRA Regulation were terminated on that date. In particular, ESMA is responsible for registration of CRAs with submitted applications after 7 September 2010 and day-to-day supervision of all CRAs.

In order to carry out its duties efficiently ESMA was given all the necessary powers to carry out an effective supervision over CRAs and is in the position to require CRAs and other persons involved in rating activities to provide all necessary information; examine any records, data, procedures and any other relevant material, including records of telephone and data traffic; interview or summon and hear a person; and carry out on-site inspections at the premises of CRAs (see Section 3.7).

In the case of an infringement committed by a CRA, ESMA is empowered to take a range of supervisory measures, including requiring the CRA to bring the infringement to an end, suspending the use of ratings for regulatory purposes, temporarily prohibiting the CRAs from issuing ratings and, as a last resort, withdrawing the registration when the CRA has seriously or repeatedly infringed provisions in the CRA Regulation. In addition, it can adopt the decision to impose a fine or a periodic penalty payment.

3.2.2.2 Fees on CRAs

According to Article 19 of the CRA Regulation, ESMA shall charge fees to the CRAs. The fees levied should cover the costs of registration and supervision of CRAs, including the costs that competent authorities may incur when performing delegated tasks. Article 19 also requires the EC to adopt a regulation on fees following two principles: the fees collected shall fully cover ESMA's expenditure necessary for its supervisory activities; and the amount of the fees charged to individual CRAs shall be proportionate to the turnover of the CRA concerned.

The principle of proportionality to the turnover of the CRA tries to ensure that the mechanism takes into account the size of the supervised entities, avoiding over-charging the small ones. It is important that the EC ensures that a common definition of 'turnover' is used by all CRAs and that manipulation of the figures is avoided.

In May 2011, ESMA published its advice to assist the EC in formulating the regulation on fees referred to in Article 19.[15] In its advice, ESMA envisages a fee for the task of processing the application for registration, another for application for certification, and even two supervisory fees: one for on-going supervision of registered CRAs, and another for supervision of certified CRAs.

---

[15] ESMA (May 2011), *Technical advice to the Commission on Fees for CRAs (Ref. ESMA/2011/144).*

Finally, it is relevant to note that the Regulation does not set any mechanism to enforce the payment of fees (there are neither penalties nor supervisory measures envisaged in case of failure to pay fees).

3.2.2.3 *Cooperation with National Competent Authorities*

One of the lessons of the recent financial crisis has been the need to reinforce cooperation between the different supervisors. Therefore, in ESMA Regulation and in the CRA Regulation, EU legislators insisted on the relevance of ensuring an appropriate system of cooperation between all the actors participating in the new supervisory framework and inter-sectoral levels.

The ESMA Regulation summarizes this idea with a clear mandate in Article 2.4 for authorities to 'cooperate with trust and full mutual respect, in particular in ensuring the flow of appropriate and reliable information between them'. In addition, Article 26 of the CRA Regulation further insists on this obligation to cooperate with a straightforward mandate: 'ESMA, EBA, EIOPA, the competent authorities and the sectoral competent authorities shall cooperate where it is necessary for the purposes of this Regulation and for those of the relevant sectoral legislation'. This general principle has to be completed with the guidelines that ESMA shall issue on cooperation and delegation of tasks, according to Article 21.

The cooperation among the different authorities is mainly articulated by the means described below.

3.2.2.4 *Exchange of Information*

Article 27 requires ESMA, the national competent authorities, and the sectoral competent authorities to supply each other, without undue delay, the information required for the purposes of carrying out their duties under the Regulation and under the relevant sectoral legislation.

According to Article 32.2, all the information that under the Regulation is acquired by, or exchanged between, ESMA, the national competent authorities, the sectoral competent authorities, and other authorities and bodies referred to below is considered confidential information. However, it will not be considered confidential information if the authority or body concerned 'states at the time of communication that such information may be disclosed or where such disclosure is necessary for legal proceedings'.

Even if the information is confidential, the Regulation allows ESMA to communicate the information, if relevant for the performance of their tasks, to a limited number of authorities or bodies: 'the central banks, the European System of Central Banks and the European Central Bank, in their capacity as monetary authorities, the European Systematic Risk Board and, where appropriate, to other public authorities responsible for overseeing payment and settlement systems'. And the Regulation expects such authorities or bodies to communicate to ESMA information that it may need to carry out its duties under the Regulation.

3.2.2.5 Delegation of tasks

As recognized in Recital 39 of ESMA Regulation, 'the delegation of tasks can be a useful instrument in the functioning of the network of supervisors in order to reduce the duplication of tasks, to foster cooperation and thereby streamline the supervisory process, as well as to reduce the burden imposed on financial market participants'.

The main principle that should govern delegation is that of allocating supervisory competence to the supervisor who is best placed to take action in the subject matter. In this respect, a reallocation of responsibilities can be appropriate, for example, 'for reasons of economies of scale or scope, of coherence in group supervision, and of optimal use of technical expertise among national supervisory authorities'.

The CRA Regulation, in its Recital 15, also envisages the possibility of ESMA delegating 'specific supervisory tasks to the competent authority of a Member State, for instance where a supervisory task requires knowledge and experience with respect to local conditions, which are more easily available at national level. Possible tasks that may be delegated include the carrying out of specific investigatory tasks and on-site inspections'.

For example, it could be argued that for the supervision of local CRAs that only operate in one Member State it would be more efficient for ESMA to delegate to the national competent authorities, as they would have the necessary language skills and understanding of local conditions. Also, delegation to national authorities of specific supervisory tasks regarding the subsidiaries or branches of the major CRAs located in their territories might be more efficient than a centralization of all the tasks at ESMA's level.

The main aspects of the delegation of tasks from ESMA to national competent authorities are dealt with in Article 30 of the Regulation. However, details will be further developed in the guidelines that ESMA is required to publish according to Article 21.2.(a).

According to the Regulation, possible tasks that may be delegated include the power to carry out information requests and to conduct investigations and on-site inspections (see Section 3.7). However, Article 30.4 sets some limits on delegation: main 'supervisory responsibilities according to this Regulation, including registration decisions, final assessments and follow-up decisions concerning infringements, shall not be delegated'.

It is relevant to highlight that according to the CRA Regulation (Recital 6), ESMA is exclusively responsible for the registration and supervision of CRAs in the EU and, therefore, where ESMA has delegated specific tasks to competent authorities, ESMA will continue to be legally responsible. The delegation of tasks does not affect in any case the responsibility of ESMA and it will always retain the unlimited ability to conduct and oversee the delegated activity. Consequently, delegations of tasks cannot be considered as permanent. In fact, ESMA has to review its decision to delegate a specific task at appropriate intervals and delegation may be revoked at any time.

3.2.2.6 Notifications and Suspension Requests

The Regulation envisages the possibility and obligation for competent authorities to inform ESMA of possible breaches and even request ESMA to assess the need for supervisory actions. In fact, Article 31 envisages two situations, depending on the seriousness of the breaches.

First, a general duty of competent authorities to notify, 'in as specific a manner as possible', to ESMA any acts contrary to the Regulation that are being, or have been, carried out in the EU (not only in its territory). Moreover, when giving notice, if it believes it is appropriate for investigatory purposes, the competent authority may also suggest ESMA assess the need to use its supervisory powers towards the CRA involved in these acts. In these circumstances, ESMA shall take appropriate action and shall inform the notifying competent authority of the outcome and, to the extent possible, of any significant interim developments.

Second, in addition to the duty to notify, where the notifying competent authority considers that a registered CRA, whose ratings are used in its territory, is committing infringements that 'are sufficiently serious and persistent to have a significant impact on the protection of investors or on the stability of the financial system' of its territory, it may request ESMA to suspend the use for regulatory purposes of the ratings of the CRAs concerned and even to examine the need to withdraw registration of a CRA (see Section 3.6.4).

Based on the information provided by the competent authority and on the necessary further investigation, if ESMA considers that the request is justified, 'it shall take the appropriate measures to resolve the issue'. However, where according to ESMA the request is not justified, it will inform the notifying competent authority in writing, setting out the reasons for not taking supervisory actions.

3.2.2.7 *Cooperation with Authorities from Third Countries*

As discussed previously, CRAs operate in a global environment and cooperation with authorities of third countries is necessary for ESMA to be able to perform its duties efficiently, especially taking into consideration that the three main CRAs, which account for almost all the EU market, are global entities.

The change in the supervisory structure, from colleges to ESMA's centralized supervision, has resulted in a significant change in the relations with third countries' authorities. Now ESMA has the exclusive power to conclude cooperation agreements on information exchange with competent authorities of third countries. However, Recital 6 clarifies that 'to the extent that competent authorities participate in the decision making process within ESMA or when executing tasks on behalf of ESMA, they should be covered by these cooperation agreements'.

According to Article 34, ESMA may conclude cooperation agreements on exchange of information with the competent authorities of third countries for the performance of their respective tasks. However, these agreements are only possible if the information disclosed is subject to guarantees of professional secrecy which are at least equivalent to those set out in the Regulation (Article 32). The common EU rules on data protection[16] will apply in the situations where ESMA is to transfer personal data to a third country authority.

---

[16] Regulation (EC) No 45/2001 of the European Parliament and of the Council of 18 December 2000 on the protection of individuals with regard to the processing of personal data by the Community institutions and bodies and on the free movement of such data (*Official Journal* L 8, 12.01.2001: pp. 1–22).

The Regulation also rules, in Article 35, what ESMA can do with the information it receives, stipulating that 'ESMA may disclose the information received from supervisory authorities of third countries only if ESMA or the competent authority has obtained the express agreement of the supervisory authority that has transmitted the information and, where applicable, the information is disclosed only for the purposes for which that supervisory authority gave its agreement or where such disclosure is necessary for legal proceedings'.

Finally, in addition to the general cooperation arrangements to exchange information with third countries, ESMA will have to develop specific cooperation arrangements with the relevant competent authorities of the CRAs established in third countries that want their ratings to be used for regulatory purposes in the EU (see Section 4.5). These arrangements have to include not only mechanisms for exchange of information but also procedures for the coordination of supervisory activities.

At a global level, IOSCO provides supervisors with a multilateral forum that enables them to share information regularly as to the rules and approaches they adopt in implementing the IOSCO Code of Conduct and in regulating CRAs generally.

3.3 DEFINITIONS AND CONCEPTS

The CRA Regulation introduces for the first time Community legislation on CRAs and this has meant incorporating a series of terms into Community law which until now were only used by the market. At a global level, securities supervisors grouped in IOSCO had agreed on and had set out various concepts in the IOSCO Code, such as those of 'rating agency' and 'rating'. Despite the voluntary nature of the IOSCO Code, these definitions meant a certain international standardization, which has been taken into account by European legislators, with certain adaptations. The main definitions set out in the Regulation that are relevant for the proper understanding of the EU rules are explained below.

3.3.1 Credit Rating and Rating Category

3.3.1.1 Credit Rating

According to Article 3.1.(a) of the CRA Regulation a 'credit rating' means an opinion regarding the creditworthiness of an entity, a debt or financial obligation, debt security, preferred share or other financial instrument, or of an issuer of such a debt or financial obligation, debt security, preferred share or other financial instrument, issued using an established and defined ranking system of rating categories'.

Basically, ratings are predictive opinions on one characteristic of an entity: its likelihood to repay debt in a timely manner. As it is not possible to foresee the future it is important to stress that ratings are just opinions and opinions exclusively about the credit risk of debt instruments and obligors. Therefore, ratings are neither indicators of the price of the rated instrument in the markets nor measures of its liquidity. They cannot either, as discussed further down in this section, be considered as recommendations to buy or sell securities.

Another key feature of the ratings is that they are opinions about the relative credit risk of one rated bond versus the credit risk of another bond rated by the same CRA. This means, as explained below, that ratings indicate the relative classification of credit risk according to the CRA's rating scale, with the probability of default increasing with each downward step on the scale. In other words, a holder of a bond rated B by a CRA is more likely to incur in a loss than an investor in a bond rated AAA by the same CRA.

3.3.1.2 Rating Category

Article 3.1.(h) of the Regulation states that a 'rating category' means a rating symbol, such as a letter or numerical symbol which might be accompanied by appending identifying characters, used in a credit rating to provide a relative measure of risk to distinguish the different risk characteristics of the types of rated entities, issuers and financial instruments or other assets'.

CRAs rank securities and issuers on a relative scale. For example, Fitch and S&P use AAA, AA, A, BBB, BB, and so on, while Moody's goes with Aaa, Aa, A, Baa, Ba, and so on. CRAs also use modifiers (such as '+' or '–'; '1, 2, or 3') appended to the rating categories in order to denote relative status within the major rating categories. The combination of a category (for example 'A') and a modifier (such as '+') constitutes a 'notch' in the rating scale (for instance 'A +'). A change of a rating means assigning a credit rating a different notch in the rating scale.

Categories do not reflect absolute measures of risk, only that securities classified in a higher category have higher quality than those in the categories below. However, in practice, market participants tend to assign each rating category a certain absolute value delinked to its relative position in the table of ratings categories. And, to a certain extent, this is also the case with banking supervisors that assign, under the standardized approach of the CRD, a specific risk weight to each category.

Table 3.1 shows the rating categories of Moody's and S&P as included in ESMA's consultation on CEREP.

CRAs differ not only in their definition of each rating category, but also in their methodologies and models employed to arrive at the rating. For example, some of them base their ratings principally on default probability, whilst others use the concept of expected loss (which incorporates expected recovery in the event of default). To make matters even more complicated for investors, CRAs' definitions

Table 3.1. Rating categories S&P and Moody's

	Rating categories			Rating modifiers
	Investment grade	Speculative grade	Default	
S&P	AAA, AA, A, BBB	BB, B, CCC, CC	R, SD, D	+ or –
Moody's	Aaa, Aa, A, Baa	Ba, B, Caa, Ca, C	D, LD	1, 2, or 3

of default also differ, in some cases considerably. The SEC proposed rules for NRSROs in May 2011 offered as standard definition of default the following: 'if the obligor failed to timely pay principal or interest due according to the terms of an obligation, or the issuer of the security or money market instrument failed to timely pay principal or interest due according to the terms of the security or money market instrument'. However, in addition, it allows NRSROs to use their own definitions of default. ESMA was also aware of the multiple definitions of default used by CRAs when building the central repository that makes available historical performance data of the registered CRAs. To make the performance and default statistics comparable among CRAs, ESMA's guidelines on CEREP provided a common standard for reporting defaults (see Section 3.8.6).

3.3.1.3 CRA's Actions that can be Construed as a Credit Rating

Once a rating has been assigned for the first time, a CRA might take a number of different actions as a consequence of the monitoring of the rating. There is no definition of 'rating action' in the CRA Regulation. Therefore, it is important to determine which of those actions would fall under the broader definition of credit rating and hence should be subject to the same requirements, such as due processes and methodologies, presentation, record keeping, or endorsement.

The typical CRA's actions are the following:

- Issuance of a rating: this is the initial formulation of a rating (including a preliminary rating[17]), when it is assigned to a debt instrument or an issuer for the first time. A rating is issued when the issuing CRA distributes it, either by publication or by distribution to subscribers. In fact, according to Article 4.2 of the CRA Regulation, 'a credit rating agency established in the Community and registered in accordance with this Regulation shall be deemed to have issued a credit rating when the credit rating has been published on the credit rating agency's website or by other means or distributed by subscription and presented and disclosed in accordance with the obligations of Article 10'.

- Change of an outstanding rating: the CRA decides either to move the rating upwards on the rating scale—an upgrade—or to do the opposite—a downgrade.

- Confirmation (or affirmation) of an outstanding rating: following a due process, the CRA concludes that the outstanding rating is in line with the CRA's views of the issuer's creditworthiness and therefore no change takes place.

- Withdrawal of a rating: this will happen when the instrument matures but also in other circumstances such as those mentioned in Section 1.4.1.

[17] According to the SEC proposed rules for NRSROs of May 2011, the term 'preliminary rating' includes any rating, any range of ratings or any other indication of a rating published prior to the assignment of an initial rating for a new issuance. Preliminary ratings are normally issued on structured finance transactions before the final documents and legal opinions are provided to the CRA.

Issuance of ratings, changes, and confirmations of outstanding ratings are all opinions about the creditworthiness of an entity or an obligation. Therefore, in principle, it seems reasonable that similar requirements apply to all these actions, albeit with some adjustments when necessary. For example, the amount and type of information necessary for the assignment of the rating and for its monitoring is not the same. The monitoring task will be based, in principle, in part on the work already done at the time of the issuance. Nevertheless, a downgrade that results from that surveillance should follow the same procedure established for the assignment of the initial rating (recommendation by the lead analyst, rating committee, communication to the issuer before publication, etc.).

The usual CRAs' procedures for issuing and withdrawing ratings are described in Section 1.4.1.

Regarding withdrawals, it seems that the CRA should follow the same rules and procedures applicable to the issuance of ratings, except where the withdrawal would not constitute material information for investors—for example, when the rated instrument has matured or the rated company has ceased to exist. But if the instrument is still outstanding, a withdrawal of the rating—implying that the CRA ceases to monitor it—is a significant action that can be comparable to a change of the rating.

Changes and confirmations of an existing rating are the outcomes of surveillance processes. These might be ad hoc reviews (triggered, for example, by a major market event, a deviation from an expected trend, or the release of new information), or the regular annual review required by Article 8.5 of the Regulation. Rating changes can have a significant impact on the price of the rated instruments. In order to avoid market volatility, CRAs warn market participants ahead of a possible change, by placing a rating under review (putting ratings on watch, in the CRAs' terminology). However, CRAs might change ratings without having previously placed them on the watch list.

3.3.1.4 Rating Statuses

The statuses below are used by CRAs to indicate the likelihood of a rating change and, in most cases, the direction of the future change. But as such they are not opinions about the creditworthiness of an obligor or of a specific financial obligation. Therefore, in principle, the CRA would not need to follow the same rules and procedures applicable to the issuance of a rating or to the change of an existing one (for example, placements of ratings on the watch list or the assignment of a certain outlook do not need to be reported to ESMA's central repository as rating actions or communicated to the entity 12 hours before their adoption).

Notwithstanding, given the significant impact on the markets watch and outlook actions may have, it seems reasonable that CRAs apply to these actions the same procedures for publication and handling of confidential information they have established for rating actions. This point has been raised in the European Parliament resolution on CRAs issued in June 2011.[18]

---

[18] European Parliament (June 2011), *Resolution on credit rating agencies: future perspectives.*

Ratings on Watch

Ratings are placed on a CRA's watch list when the agency is going to undertake a review for a possible change in the short term. These reviews are triggered when events or deviations from an expected trend occur and the CRA needs to gather additional information in order to evaluate the impact of the new circumstances. Typically, a CRA may put an issuer on the watch list in case it is undertaking a business combination or when its performance deviates from expectations. The watch list action may also be originated by the CRA itself, for example when an error in a rating is discovered. Interestingly, there is in the Regulation a case where CRAs are specifically obliged to put ratings on watch. Article 8.6 of the Regulation stipulates that when methodologies, models, or key rating assumptions are changed, the affected ratings will be placed under observation until the CRA has completed their review. Once the rating has been put on the watch list, the likelihood of the rating being raised or lowered in a short period of time should be substantial; otherwise, this status would not meet its objective and the marketplace would be confused. After receiving the necessary information to undertake the review, the CRA determines whether the rating should be changed within a short time frame, typically around three months. It can also conclude that there is no need to change the rating, which would lead the CRA to confirm the rating.

[handwritten margin note: is a likelihood of change in rating]

Ratings Outlook

An outlook is the CRA's opinion about the likely direction of a rating over the medium term. Outlooks can be positive, negative, or stable, indicating that the rating may be raised, lowered, or not likely to change. Whilst the likelihood of a change after the outlook period is lower than in the case of watch listings, there must be a certain potential for change when the outlook reflects a positive or a negative trend—however, many outlooks are simply stable. Another difference between both types of statuses is the time frames for the review—reviews of ratings on watch are shorter. The average period for outlooks would normally depend on the type of rating grade; normally investment grade ratings take longer to review than speculative ratings (see Table 3.1).

[handwritten margin note: likelihood of change over all period at level less than WATCH]

3.3.1.5 *Opinions that are not Credit Ratings*

Credit ratings issued by CRAs are just one of the sources of credit analysis available to market participants. There is a great variety of investment firms and broker dealers that provide analytical or evaluative assessments of issuers whose instruments are admitted to trading, for example at the time an issuer is making an offer of its securities in order to assist investors in their investment decisions. Article 3.2 of the Regulation provides a list of opinions or reports concerning financial instruments or obligors that are not credit ratings:

- Recommendations within the meaning of Article 1(3) of Commission Directive 2003/125/EC.[19] This concept includes research or other information

---

[19] Commission Directive 2003/125/EC of 22 December 2003 implementing Directive 2003/6/EC of the European Parliament and of the Council as regards the fair presentation of investment recommendations and the disclosure of conflicts of interest (*Official Journal* L 339, 24.12.2003: pp. 73–7).

recommending or suggesting an investment strategy concerning financial instruments or issuers of financial instruments and that are intended for distribution channels or for the public.

- Investment research as defined in Article 24(1) of Directive 2006/73/EC[20] and other forms of general recommendation, such as 'buy', 'sell' or 'hold', relating to transactions in financial instruments or to financial obligations.

- Opinions about the value of a financial instrument or a financial obligation.

Clearly these opinions are not captured by the CRA Regulation as they do not meet the definition of a credit rating and are subject to their own specific rules.

Finally, other opinions about the creditworthiness of an issuer that are not credit ratings are credit scores. Section 3.4.2 provides an analysis of this type of assessments.

3.3.1.6 Types of Credit Ratings

CRAs issue a wide range of credit ratings. All of them are forward-looking opinions about the creditworthiness of an issuer or a financial obligation, but they incorporate different features in the CRA's assessment in order to cater for different market needs. Each CRA uses its own terminology to name those ratings and obviously its own methodology.

The most common types of ratings are explained in this section. However, there are also many specific types that do not fall in the categories discussed below. Among the myriad of specific types of ratings, ESMA's Q&A has included a question about one of them that has posed difficulties as to whether it should be considered a credit rating for the purposes of the Regulation: the so-called 'financial strength ratings'. ESMA concluded that, according to the widespread definitions used in the market, these financial strength ratings appear to fall under the definition of a credit rating. However, ESMA advised CRAs to examine the exact nature of the ratings in question and compare this to the definition of a credit rating in the Regulation (this answer would be applicable to any kind of opinion issued by CRAs, should doubts arise regarding its categorization as a credit rating).

Issuer Ratings and Financial Instruments Ratings

An issuer rating is an opinion about an obligor's capacity to repay its financial obligations. When assessing an entity's overall creditworthiness, CRAs do not take into consideration the terms and conditions of any specific financial obligation. In addition, they do not consider the support from guarantors, insurers, or other providers of credit enhancement on a specific financial obligation.

In contrast, financial instrument ratings are opinions about the capacity of an issuer to repay all sums due according to the terms and conditions of the rated

---

[20] Commission Directive 2006/73/EC of 10 August 2006 implementing Directive 2004/39/EC of the European Parliament and of the Council as regards organisational requirements and operating conditions for investment firms and defined terms for the purposes of that Directive (*Official Journal* L 241, 2.9.2006: pp. 26–58).

instrument. Therefore, these ratings do take into account all the characteristics of the obligation and any form of credit enhancement.

LONG- AND SHORT-TERM RATINGS. Major CRAs use two different nomenclatures depending on the maturity of the rated instrument. Ratings on obligations having an original maturity of one year or more are categorized as long-term ratings; ratings on short-term debt instruments (either assigned to programmes or to individual instruments) are classified as short-term ratings.

ESMA's guidelines on CEREP require CRAs to report issuer ratings as long-term ratings (in the context of corporate ratings). If an issuer rating is not available, CRAs should report instead the long-term unsecured debt rating.

PUBLIC AND PRIVATE RATINGS. Ratings can also be classified according to their availability to third parties—other than the person that requested the CRA to issue the rating and the CRA itself. Private ratings are provided exclusively to the person that solicited the rating and are outside the scope of the Regulation (see Section 3.4.2). Public ratings would be those that the CRA releases for disclosure on a non-selective basis either to the public at large or to the clients that have subscribed to its services.

Solicited and Unsolicited Ratings

According to Recital 21 of the CRA Regulation, an unsolicited rating is 'a credit rating not initiated at the request of the issuer or rated entity'. Conversely, a credit rating would be 'solicited' if an issuer or its authorized agent requests it. This distinction is important because unsolicited ratings are subject to additional disclosures: the CRA has to designate them as such in the credit rating announcement and has to state whether the issuer participated in the rating process (see Section 3.8.5).

Types of Ratings According to the Issuer's Industry or to the Asset Class

There are multiple options for categorizing ratings according to the issuer's industry or the different types of assets, and CRAs do not always use the same categories. In order to provide some degree of harmonization, ESMA has defined three broad rating categories for CEREP reporting: corporate, structured finance, and sovereign/public finance, and each category has been broken down into further detailed segments (see Section 3.8.6).

3.3.2 Credit Rating Activities and Ancillary Services

3.3.2.1 *Credit Rating Activities*

Article 3.1.(o) of the Regulation defines credit rating activities as 'data and information analysis and the evaluation, approval, issuing and review of credit ratings'. Credit rating activities refer to the core business of a CRA, therefore including all activities directly related to the preparation, issuance, and surveillance of credit ratings. The definition of the Regulation should also encompass the development, approval, and review of rating methodologies, including the development of the qualitative and quantitative models embedded in those methodologies.

Major CRAs typically engage in other activities that are different to credit rating activities. These can be divided into two categories: ancillary services and other activities (see Section 3.8.2).

3.3.2.2 Ancillary Services

The Regulation provides in Annex I, Section B.4 a list of ancillary services that are not part of the credit rating activities: they comprise market forecasts, estimates of economic trends, pricing analysis, and other general data analysis, as well as related distribution services.

Ancillary services are permitted by the Regulation as long as their provision does not create potential conflicts of interests with the issuing of credit ratings. Section 3.8.2 analyses in more detail the requirements imposed by the Regulation that aim at ensuring that CRAs adequately manage any potential conflicts of interest and provide sufficient information to the marketplace about the extent of these activities.

As mentioned above, there might be other permissible services or businesses that are neither rating activities nor ancillary services. These other non-rating services could potentially create a conflict of interest, as in the case of ancillary services. The Regulation does not have any specific rules concerning the other non-rating activities, thus the general rules on independence and avoidance of conflicts of interest would apply (Article 6.1 of the Regulation and Annex I.B.1) and the CRA would be expected to appropriately manage the potential risks of conflicts (ESMA's Q&A). Additionally, ESMA's guidance on registration requires CRAs to indicate in their confidential applications if they provide these other services.

3.3.3 Credit Rating Agency and Group of Rating Agencies

3.3.3.1 Credit Rating Agency

Article 3.1.(b) of the Regulation provides the definition of a credit rating agency: 'credit rating agency means a legal person whose occupation includes the issuing of credit ratings on a professional basis'.

The Regulation defines CRAs as individual entities. One entity that has been established according to the law of a Member State and issues ratings on a professional basis is considered a credit rating agency. This implies that the global CRAs that have set up subsidiaries in the EU will own as many CRAs as subsidiaries incorporated in EU jurisdictions.

All the requirements imposed by the Regulation have to be complied with by each individual entity—the subsidiary—that forms part of the group (see Section 3.4.1). This approach differs markedly from that of the CRD as understood by banking authorities when recognizing and supervising CRAs eligible as ECAIs for the purposes of the CRD (see Section 3.5.3).

The fact that the Regulation stipulates compliance at subsidiary level and does not allow group-level compliance with the different requirements imposed on CRAs has led global CRAs to adopt certain strategies that enable them to continue operating in the way they used to do without breaching the provisions of the Regulation. For example, local subsidiaries may be transformed into branches of another CRA that keeps its status as a legal person, in order to avoid requirements at subsidiary level; central functions can still be provided by the parent company to the different subsidiaries through outsourcing arrangements; and CRAs can also make use of the limited exemptions for small entities provided by the Regulation.

3.3.3.2 *Group of Rating Agencies*

According to Article 3.1.(m) of the CRA Regulation:

> Group of credit rating agencies means a group of undertakings established in the Community consisting of a parent undertaking and its subsidiaries within the meaning of Articles 1 and 2 of Directive 83/349/EEC as well as undertakings linked to each other by a relationship within the meaning of Article 12(1) of Directive 83/349/EEC and whose occupation includes the issuing of credit ratings. For the purposes of Article 4(3)(a), a group of credit rating agencies shall also include credit rating agencies established in third countries.

This provision refers to the Seventh Council Directive on consolidated accounts. A group of EU CRAs is composed by the EU undertakings—falling under the definition of credit rating agency—that are required to draw up consolidated accounts according to the law of a Member State. This means the parent company and the subsidiaries it consolidates, as well as jointly controlled entities. Nevertheless, in this latter case it might not always be easy to interpret how the notion of group of CRAs would apply.[21]

It is worth noting that a group for the purposes of registration does not include CRAs established in third countries. The approach of the Regulation contrasts with that of the US rules, which allow an applicant to include in its registration its separate legal entities established in different countries.

Notwithstanding, the Regulation clarifies that for the purposes of endorsement a group of CRAs shall also include CRAs established in third countries.

In relation to groups, but also when dealing with the definition of 'related third party', the Regulation incorporates a definition of 'control' by reference to the Seventh Council Directive on consolidated accounts: 'control means the relationship between a parent undertaking and a subsidiary, as described in Article 1 of Council Directive 83/349/EEC of 13 June 1983 on consolidated accounts or a close link between any natural or legal person and an undertaking'.

---

[21] If two parties set up a joint venture in order to undertake rating activities they will be jointly controlling the corporation they set up (the CRA). And these two parties (the venturers) will recognize in their respective financial statements only their respective interests in the jointly controlled CRA. Therefore, according to national law, the CRA subject to the joint venture arrangement would be proportionately consolidated in the accounts of the two venturers.

3.3.4 Persons Involved in Rating Activities

The definition of the senior management of the agency is provided in Section 3.8.1. The definitions regarding the analytical staff of the CRA are analysed below.

3.3.4.1 Person Approving the Rating

In the absence of a definition in the Regulation, this has been provided by ESMA's Q&A:

> Persons approving credit ratings are individuals who provide the formal sign-off of credit ratings for publication, and all other related authorizing actions taken after the elaboration of the rating, prior to the publication of the rating. They may be a committee Chair/member and/or senior management of a CRA or another individual carrying out such function. ESMA does not intend to dictate how CRAs should operate in this respect and will therefore consider any proposal put forward by CRAs as part of their application for registration.

There must always be a person designated responsible for the approval of a rating action. In addition to clearing the publication of the rating, the person approving it will normally have the important function of authorizing the record relating to the rating action approved. Following ESMA's Q&A, this person does not necessarily need to be the Committee's Chair.

3.3.4.2 Lead Rating Analyst

According to Article 3.1.(e) of the Regulation, lead rating analyst 'means a person with primary responsibility for elaborating a credit rating or for communicating with the issuer with respect to a particular credit rating or, generally, with respect to the credit rating of a financial instrument issued by that issuer and, where relevant, for preparing recommendations to the rating committee in relation to such rating'.

The Regulation recognizes the pivotal role played by the lead analyst in the development of a credit rating. There must always be a lead rating analyst responsible for a rating action who has to be identified in the rating report or announcement accompanying the publication of the rating (see Section 1.4).

3.3.4.3 Rating Analyst

A rating analyst is a person who is not the lead analyst or the person approving the ratings and who, according to Article 3.1.(d), 'performs analytical functions that are necessary for issuing a credit rating'. Typically, backup analysts provide support to the lead analysts, although it is not necessary that a 'secondary' analyst is always appointed for the determination of a rating action.

It is important to note that the Regulation uses in many cases the term 'rating analyst' as encompassing all the analytical staff involved in rating activities, therefore covering also employees acting in their capacity as lead rating analysts.

3.3.4.4 *Other Natural Persons*

A number of provisions in the Regulation refer to natural persons who are directly involved in credit rating activities. ESMA has clarified that the aim of this expression is that some of the measures on conflicts of interest capture, in addition to persons approving the ratings, lead analysts, and analysts, other individuals that 'influence the determination of the rating and have a relationship with the issuer and related parties'. This means that support and other staff that assist in preparing presentations for rating committees or entering information on a rating into internal systems prior to publication, would not be considered directly involved in credit rating activities 'as long as they were not making rating decisions and are not in contact with the issuer' (ESMA's Q&A).

3.3.5 Rated Entities and Rated Instruments

3.3.5.1 *Rated Entity*

The definition of 'rated entity' included in the Regulation clarifies that it is the 'legal person whose creditworthiness is explicitly or implicitly rated in the credit rating'. Any entity being rated will fall under this definition 'whether or not it has solicited that credit rating and whether or not it has provided information for that credit rating'. This clarification is made to ensure that unsolicited ratings and ratings issued without collaboration of the entity fall under the scope of the Regulation.

In addition, the Regulation defines the term 'related third party' because several provisions of the Regulation on conflicts of interest give the same treatment to the rated entity and to related third parties, for example when dealing with rotation requirements (Annex I.C.8) or with prohibitions to issue credit ratings (Annex I.B.3a).

3.3.5.2 *Related Third Party*

According to Article 3.1.(i) of the Regulation 'related third party' means 'the originator, arranger, sponsor, servicer or any other party that interacts with a credit rating agency on behalf of a rated entity, including any person directly or indirectly linked to that rated entity by control'. There are therefore three categories of related third parties.

The first would encompass some of the functions that are performed by different entities within a securitization transaction that, according to IOSCO,[22] can be defined as follows:

- Originator: the entity that creates the receivables, loans, or other financial assets that will be included in the asset pool.
- Arranger: the entity that organizes and arranges a securitization transaction, but does not sell or transfer the assets to the issuing entity.
- Sponsor: the entity that organizes and arranges a securitization transaction by selling or transferring assets to the issuing entity.

---

[22] IOSCO (April 2010), *Disclosure Principles for Public Offerings and Listings of Asset-backed Securities.*

- Servicer: the entity responsible for the administrative management or collection for the pool assets, or for making allocations or distributions to holders of the asset-backed securities.

The second category of related third parties would include any person that communicates with the CRA on behalf of, and on the authority of, the rated entity.

Finally, the Regulation also considers as a related person any person directly or indirectly linked to the rated entity by control; the term control is in turn defined in Article 3.1.(j). This means any person directly or indirectly controlling, controlled by, or under common control with the CRA.

3.3.5.3 *Financial Instrument and Structured Finance Instrument*

The definition of 'financial instrument' included in the Regulation refers to the instruments listed in Section C of Annex I to the MiFID Directive.

For defining 'structured finance instruments' the Regulation also refers to previous EU legislation. In fact, Article 3.1.(l) of the Regulation considers that a structured finance instrument means a financial instrument or other assets resulting from a securitization transaction or scheme referred to in Article 4.36 of the CRD. According to this Directive:

> Securitisation means a transaction or scheme, whereby the credit risk associated with an exposure or pool of exposures is tranched, having the following characteristics:
>
> (a) payments in the transaction or scheme are dependent upon the performance of the exposure or pool of exposures; and
>
> (b) the subordination of tranches determines the distribution of losses during the ongoing life of the transaction or scheme.

According to the CGFS,[23] structured finance 'involves the pooling of assets and the subsequent sale to investors of claims on the cash flows backed by these pools. Typically, several classes (or "tranches") of securities are issued, each with distinct risk-return profiles. In addition, the underlying collateral asset pool is usually legally separated from the balance sheet of the transaction's originator.' Therefore, structured finance has three characteristics: pooling of assets, tranching of securities, and de-linking from the originator of the assets. IOSCO's definition of structured finance products is also based on these three elements.[24]

The critical feature of the CRD's definition is the tranching of the securities. This element, for the purposes of the CRA Regulation, would distinguish structured finance instruments from pass-through instruments issued out of traditional securitizations (which have in common with structured finance the pooling and the de-linking features).

However, the interpretation of the structured finance definition is not clear-cut. There are a number of complex instruments that are not easy to categorize and there is a clear risk that each CRA comes to its own different conclusions as to whether a particular product is a structured finance instrument or not. The issue is

---

[23] CGFS (January 2005), *The role of ratings in structured finance: issues and implications.*

[24] IOSCO (July 2010) *Transparency of structured finance products, final report.*

far from being just a theoretical one. For example, the rules on presentation of ratings are more stringent regarding structured finance products.

It would be very useful if ESMA issued guidelines regarding the range and type of products which may be considered to be structured finance products for the purposes of this Regulation. This would provide clarity to the market and ensure a harmonized approach.

3.3.6 Other Definitions

3.3.6.1 Regulatory Purposes

The use for 'regulatory purposes' is the use of credit ratings for the specific purpose of complying with Community law, as implemented by the national legislation of the Member States. As discussed in Section 3.5, this is a key notion in the Regulation.

3.3.6.2 Home Member State

'Home Member State' is the State in which the credit rating agency has its registered office. The location of the registered office in the European Union of a rating agency (parent or subsidiary) was, before the CRA Regulation II, the criterion used to allocate the competent authority which was to be responsible for registering and supervising it. After the centralization of competences in ESMA this definition is no longer crucial, although it has remained in the Regulation because it is included in the transitional provisions.

3.3.6.3 Competent Authorities

'Competent authorities' are the authorities designated by each Member State in accordance with the Regulation. Article 22 requested Members States to designate by 7 June 2010 a competent authority for the purpose of this Regulation that had to be 'adequately staffed, with regard to capacity and expertise', in order to be able to apply the Regulation. Member States have designated their national securities supervisors, that are all members of ESMA, for this task (in some cases, they are integrated supervisors dealing not only with securities markets but also with banking and/or insurance supervision).

3.3.6.4 Sectoral Competent Authorities

'Sectoral competent authorities' are the national competent authorities designated under the relevant EU sectoral legislation for the supervision of credit institutions, investment firms, insurance undertakings, assurance undertakings, reinsurance undertakings, undertakings for collective investment in transferable securities (UCITS), institutions for occupational retirement provision, and alternative investment funds.

3.3.6.5 *Sectoral Legislation*

The term 'sectoral legislation' comprises the EU legislative acts referred to in the areas mentioned in the definition of sectoral competent authorities.

3.4 SCOPE

3.4.1 Ratings under the Scope

3.4.1.1 *Introduction*

Determining the scope of application of a monitoring regime on rating agencies is a complex question as there is a great variety of CRAs, with different business models and territorial impact, and many different uses of ratings.

In fact, the different monitoring systems that are emerging across the world as a result of the subprime crisis that started in 2007 are providing different solutions to this issue, although they can be reduced to the two following approaches.

The first considers CRAs as direct subjects of the legislation and establishes a regulatory system which affects all agencies. Consequently, any entity that falls within the definition laid down by the legislation would have to comply with it, irrespective of the use made of its ratings by market participants. This is the alternative followed by the EU CRA Regulation for EU CRAs.

The second option considers CRAs as indirect subjects of the legislation and regulates the use made of ratings by market participants. In this case, the agencies are indirectly subject to regulation, since they would have to comply with the requirements laid down by legislation in order for their ratings to be used by market participants. This is the system adopted by the US legislator where CRAs are not required to register simply because they engage in the activity of issuing credit ratings, but they apply to become NRSROs so that their ratings can be used for regulatory purposes.

The European model will probably give rise to a higher number of supervised agencies than the US model, since all agencies big and small will have to apply for registration even if their ratings are not used for regulatory purposes. Also, small agencies have an incentive to be registered by a public authority as a way of obtaining a seal of respectability that might help them to expand their business.

The advantage of the US system is that it allows the supervisor to concentrate resources on supervising the entities that actually matter for market participants. However, the EU scope might be better in terms of promoting new entrants to the market—as long as they are able to comply with the strict and detailed requirements. Contrary to the US regime, applicants for registration in the EU do not need to prove a track record of three years in the rating business.

3.4.1.2 *The Scope in the EU CRA Regulation*

The EU Regulation provides two different ways of determining its scope of application, one for rating agencies with registered office in the EU and another for agencies domiciled in third countries (which is similar to the US approach).

European Agencies

Article 2.1 of the Regulation delimits its scope: 'the Regulation applies to credit ratings issued by credit rating agencies registered in the Community and which are disclosed publicly or distributed by subscription'.

Therefore, any CRA that freely publishes its ratings (or distributes them to subscribers) will be required to register. Article 2.1 must be read in combination with Article 14.1 that requires a CRA to apply for registration for the purposes of Article 2.1 'provided that it is a legal person established in the Community'.

Regulators interpret the Regulation as requiring all CRAs established in the Community to register before starting their rating activities, although this is not clearly stated in the text. Neither Article 14.1 nor Article 2.1 imposes a clear requirement of registration before issuing ratings. EU legislators could have used the amendment of the Regulation passed in 2011 to clarify the interaction between these articles and state in a clear way that all entities conducting rating activities in the EU are required to register irrespective of the use made of their ratings.

However, the fact that the CRA Regulation II considers a breach of the Regulation in Annex III, item 54, when 'the credit rating agency, where it is a legal person established in the Union, infringes Article 14 (1) by not applying for registration for the purposes of Article 2 (1)', supports the interpretation made by regulators.

Thus, the Regulation establishes a reserve of activity. The activity of issuing ratings is reserved in the EU exclusively to entities which are registered as agencies in accordance with the Regulation. This means that legal persons established in the EU that issue ratings are subject to the Regulation and are obliged to register with ESMA.

Therefore, under the EU Regulation, the determination of which entities would be subject to the legislation depends solely on the definitions of rating agency and credit rating.

This gives rise to important difficulties for setting the scope as it is not always easy in practice to interpret the definition of credit rating and, in particular, to delineate the boundaries between credit ratings and scores (see Section 3.4.2).

In addition, another practical difficulty related to the scope of the EU Regulation is that it is complicated to apply a territorial principle to determine the agencies which are subject to European legislation. This problem is theoretically solved by Article 14.1 that stipulates that only those CRAs that are companies incorporated in the EU according to the laws of a Member State are required to register.

However, this system creates a problem for the global CRAs that is not very easy to solve. The big CRAs are used to operating on a global basis serving the markets internationally, irrespective of where any subsidiary, analyst, or issuer is located; in fact, they have their principal business centres and many central functions outside the EU (see Section 1.2).

Before the EU Regulation entered into force, market participants were interested only in knowing which of those global brands had produced the rating. The markets, therefore, did not care much about which subsidiaries or branches within the group were involved in its development.

Now the global rating groups have to determine which of their companies has actually issued the rating. If the rating is issued by one of their subsidiaries established in the EU then it will be subject to the Regulation (due to the combination of Articles 2.1 and 14.1). Conversely, if the rating is issued by an entity not incorporated in the EU (for example, the US parent company) then the rating is out of the scope of the Regulation. Additionally, even within the EU it is necessary to determine which of the EU subsidiaries of a group of CRAs has issued a rating in order to be deemed legally responsible for the rating (and to apply to that legal entity subsequent supervisory measures and sanctions, if necessary).

CRAs operating in the US do not face this problem as registration is voluntary and CRAs, if they wish, may include their foreign subsidiaries in their application for NRSRO registration; this is what all the global CRAs have done (NRSRO status is granted to the group—the parent company and its overseas affiliates). This implies that any credit rating issued by a credit rating subsidiary within the group that has been registered will be considered a credit rating issued by the registered group (the registered NRSRO).

In the EU it is, therefore, essential to determine the issuing entity (especially in the case of CRAs' groups). To deal with this aspect, which is unclear in the text of the Regulation, ESMA consulted market participants on different alternatives[25] and finally concluded that the issuing entity is the registered CRA that employs the lead analyst. This option, chosen by ESMA because it was 'simple and easily applicable', was the alternative favoured by the CRAs, as it gives them some leeway to determine where the rating is issued.

However, the lead analyst criterion is not exempt from drawbacks. Deciding something as important as the issuing entity just on the basis of where someone is physically located seems arbitrary, not only because the type of work performed by an analyst can be done anywhere but also because the issuance of a rating is not the work of a single person but the combined work of a number of people in the CRA and a decision of the rating committee.

In addition, the determination of where a lead analyst sits is not clear-cut as it could either be the entity (subsidiary) that has legally hired the analyst or the entity where they are physically working.

Moreover, the lead analyst criterion could pose the risk of circumvention of the Regulation, if the CRA decides to move the location of the analyst for spurious reasons. ESMA already envisaged this possibility and in its guidance on registration expressly included as general principle that 'CRAs should not shift a lead rating analyst to another CRA in order to circumvent the Regulation'.

This is particularly risky if the EU CRA shifts its lead analysts to other offices within the group that are located outside the EU to avoid falling under the scope of the EU Regulation. To deal with this issue, in the context of the endorsement regime, ESMA's Q&A clarifies that 'rating activity should not be moved outside the EU as a means of circumventing the EU requirements'. Furthermore, according to ESMA it is 'unlikely that it would be acceptable that the rating activity

---

[25] CESR (October 2009), *Consultation paper, Guidance on registration process, functioning of colleges, mediation protocol, information set out in Annex II, information set for the application for certification and for the assessment of CRAs systemic importance (Ref. CESR/09-955).*

relating to an issuer or security that had traditionally been carried out by analysts based in the EU could be moved without an objective reason'.

ESMA's Q&A seems to contradict to a certain extent the guidance on location of ratings via the lead analyst criterion. The language of the Q&A suggests that EU companies should be rated by EU CRAs (that is, by the EU subsidiaries of the CRAs' global group). So ESMA could be worried about a situation in which a CRA justifies rating the bonds of an EU company in the New York office because the lead analyst that used to cover such company happened to relocate to the USA a few months before.

It seems that ESMA is comfortable with the CRAs applying the lead analyst criterion within the EU (as it would not matter much in which Member State the rating is issued) but is concerned with the possibility of CRAs using the criterion to circumvent the EU Regulation. It is still not very clear how this will be applied in practice by the CRAs and supervised by ESMA.

Agencies from Third Countries

As we have seen above, legal persons established in the EU who issue ratings are subject to the Regulation and are obliged to register in the EU. On the other hand, agencies of third countries (that is, countries which are not members of the EU), will only be subject to the EU monitoring regime insofar as their ratings are used for regulatory purposes by supervised entities in the EU. In other words, these agencies do not need to be registered in order to issue ratings in the EU, but these ratings may not be used for regulatory purposes by EU financial institutions.

Consequently, in this case the direct subjects of the Regulation are the EU banks and other financial institutions (those in Article 4.1 of the Regulation) to the extent that they wish to use ratings issued by agencies of third countries for regulatory purposes (they may not do so if these agencies are not subject to the Regulation). Agencies are therefore indirect subjects, since they are only affected by the Regulation to the extent that their ratings are used for regulatory purposes.

For example, the rating by a CRA incorporated in the EU of a bond issued by an EU company would be unlawful if the agency has not been previously registered in accordance with the Regulation (even if the said rating is not used for regulatory purposes by any European supervised entity). However, the same bond may be rated by a non-Community agency without being subject to the Regulation (although in this case European supervised institutions may not use this rating for regulatory purposes).

What the Regulation in fact establishes is an incentive for agencies of third countries to submit themselves to the legislation of the European Union, since European institutions will thus be able to use their ratings for regulatory purposes. Furthermore, it constitutes an incentive for EU issuers to commission their ratings solely to agencies subject to the Regulation, since their placement is thereby facilitated amongst supervised entities. For example, credit institutions which use the standardized method for calculating their own regulatory capital will be interested only in ratings issued by a registered CRA.

Chapter 4 provides an explanation of the two procedures which the Regulation has established in order to permit European institutions to use the ratings issued by agencies domiciled in third countries for regulatory purposes.

3.4.2 Ratings and Credit Scores Outside the Scope

3.4.2.1 Private Ratings

In some instances, CRAs issue ratings that are not intended for public distribution. It seems that these types of ratings represent just a small proportion of all ratings produced by CRAs but they perform an important function in financial markets. Typically, a company may solicit a confidential opinion on how a planned transaction (such as an acquisition or a capital restructuring) would affect its outstanding credit rating under different scenarios provided by the entity.

Also, a borrower might request a private credit rating in order to pass it on to certain third parties. These parties would vary depending on the purpose of the rating. A company needing refinancing might need to get the new loan rated before the banks agree to grant it. A monoline insurer asked to insure a bond issue might also demand a rating from the issuer before granting the protection.

According to Article 2.2.(a), the Regulation does not apply to 'private credit ratings produced pursuant to an individual order and provided exclusively to the person who placed the order and which are not intended for public disclosure or distribution by subscription'.

Although this is a relevant provision to determine the scope of the Regulation, ESMA has not issued any guidance about it. The following paragraphs analyse the conditions CRAs have to comply with in order for their private ratings to be outside of the Regulation, taking into account the three cumulative elements in the definition provided by Article 2.2.(a).

First, the Regulation requires that the rating is issued 'pursuant to an individual order'. As the CRA must have been contracted to issue the rating, this requirement excludes unsolicited ratings from the definition. Actually, it would make little sense for a CRA to assign an unsolicited credit rating just in order to keep it for itself.

Second, the private rating must be 'provided exclusively to the person who placed the order'. This condition raises doubts of interpretation. It is clear that the CRA is banned from passing the rating on to any person other than the one that requested the rating, but the wording of the Regulation allows the rated issuer to provide the rating to third parties. The subject that performs the action of the verb 'provide' in Article 2.2.(a) is the CRA that formulated the rating. Therefore, the fact that the rated company provides it to a third party—as in the cases mentioned above—should not be an obstacle for that rating to be considered as private, as long as the rating is not subsequently published or distributed by subscription.

This is the approach adopted by the EC in relation to the ratings produced by central banks. As discussed further in this section, ratings issued by central banks are excluded from the scope of the Regulation provided that these ratings fulfil several conditions; one of these conditions is that the ratings are not disclosed to the public. The EC has considered that the Banque de France meets this requirement even if its ratings are accessible to certain categories of actors listed in the Banque de France's code of conduct (among them are credit institutions that have access to a special database).[26]

---

[26] EC Decision of 18 June 2010 exempting the Banque de France from the application of Regulation (EC) No 1060/2009 of the European Parliament and of the Council on credit rating agencies (2010/342/EU).

However, rated entities have to be aware of the restrictions imposed by the Market Abuse Directive in case they have securities admitted to trading on a regulated market. If the issuer has disclosed inside information to the CRA for the preparation of the private rating, disclosure of the rating to a third party should comply with the conditions and prohibitions imposed on the issuer and on the recipient of the information.

For example, for some structured finance transactions CRAs only make public the rating assigned to the senior tranches. However, the rating on the junior tranche that first absorbs losses might constitute information that—if known—would affect the price in the market of the more senior securities—therefore amounting to inside information; if some investors had access to this information the requirement imposed on the issuer by the Market Abuse Directive to publish the inside information would be triggered.

Third, the Regulation requires that the ratings 'are not intended for public disclosure or distribution by subscription'. This requirement follows the logic of the two previous ones. As the rating is issued only for use by the person who asked for it, there is no point in publishing the rating or in distributing it to subscribers. Furthermore, the Regulation considers that a rating that is available to the public should not be categorized as a private rating because in this case there is a need to protect investors—the overall objective of the Regulation as set out in Article 1—and therefore all the requirements of the Regulation should be complied with. For these reasons, a recipient of a private rating could share it with a limited number of third parties only on a strictly confidential basis.

Private ratings issued by CRAs having ECAI status may not be used by credit institutions for the purpose of determining their regulatory capital under the standardized approach. This conclusion can be extracted from several provisions in the CRD. In particular, the CRD requires competent authorities to verify that individual credit assessments are accessible at equivalent terms at least to all credit institutions having a legitimate interest in these individual credit assessments. Regarding the calculation of securitized exposures, the CRD stipulates that credit institutions may use the credit assessments of CRAs recognized as ECAIs only when, among other conditions, the credit assessments are available publicly to the market. Furthermore, credit assessments that are made available only to a limited number of entities shall not be considered to be publicly available.

Normally, private ratings are issued as point-in-time ratings that are valid only at the moment they are formulated. In some cases though, the CRA undertakes also to monitor the rating.

3.4.2.2 *Credit Scores, Credit Scoring Systems,* *and Similar Assessments*

Article 2.2.(b) carves out from the Regulation credit scores, credit scoring systems, or similar assessments related to obligations arising from consumer, commercial, or industrial relationships.

The aim of the EU monitoring regime on CRAs is to address a market failure in the rating business. No market failure has been identified in the scoring sector; therefore there is no need to add new requirements and costs to their operations.

In fact, it can be argued that many of these scoring entities are not subject to some of the major problems identified in the rating business, namely the conflict of interest embedded in the issuer-pays model (as they derive their revenues from subscribers) and the subjectivity implicit in the qualitative methodologies used by the agencies. Regarding this last point, whilst the exercise of discretion and judgement by CRA analysts is widely considered a positive feature, the drawback of that discretion is that it adds opacity to the process, making it more difficult to determine whether 'inaccurate' ratings stem from problems with the model or from the exercise of bad judgement by the analyst.

This lack of market failure has been taken into account when EU legislators opted to exclude credit scores from the scope of the Regulation, as reflected in Article 2.2.(b). This article gives rise to two questions that are discussed in the following paragraphs.

Are all Credit Scores Outside the Scope of the Regulation?

The wording of Article 2.2.(b) made regulators wonder whether all credit scores, credit scoring systems, or similar assessments are excluded from the Regulation or only those that arise from consumer, commercial, or industrial relationships. The question is whether some credit scores would be subject to the Regulation whilst others would be out of its scope.

After lengthy discussions, EU supervisors came to the conclusion that there should not be any distinction between scores arising from consumer, commercial, or industrial relationships and other scores. This is because all of them have the same purpose, which is limited to the provision of information to lenders about the credit risk of borrowers—without any impact on capital markets.

Credit scores exist because companies need to know the creditworthiness of the companies they want to do business with. Regulators consider that scores are used by the 'real economy' with marginal or no effect either on financial markets or on investors. Typically, the entities assessed by scoring entities are small and medium-sized companies that are not issuers of securities in the capital markets. Scoring entities do not assess the creditworthiness of structured finance securities, financial institutions, or sovereigns. Therefore, the population they score is very different from that covered by the traditional CRAs, whose assessments have a direct impact on the functioning of capital markets. This rationale seems supported by Recital 7 of the Regulation, which states that 'the principal aim of this Regulation is to protect the stability of financial markets and investors. Credit scores, credit scoring systems and similar assessments related to obligations arising from consumer, commercial or industrial relationships should not fall within the scope of this Regulation.'

To sum up, the approach taken by regulators is that credit scores are assessments on the overall creditworthiness of an entity (and not on a particular obligation arising, for example, from the sale of goods or provision of services) and that all scores should be out of the scope of the Regulation.

What is the Difference between Scores and Credit Ratings?

QUALITATIVE INPUT. ESMA's starting point to distinguish between the two types of assessments is the market definition of scores. In general, people refer to scores *scaes*

as measures of the creditworthiness of an entity that are derived from a model that uses historical default data and statistical methods to assign weights to the inputs factored into the model. The model is fed with public data and the entire process is automatic—without human intervention. This lack of qualitative analysis explains the huge population of entities (small and medium-sized companies), and sometimes also private persons, assessed by scoring entities, as the cost of producing the scores is very low compared to the cost of developing ratings.

Following this notion, ESMA has interpreted that the distinction between credit ratings and scores is based on the different methodologies employed to determine them. ESMA's guidance on registration considers that the process of issuing credit ratings requires qualitative input. In particular, it requires the performance of rating specific analytical functions by a person (the rating analyst) and thus any opinion about the creditworthiness of a company that is based purely on a quantitative model would not be a credit rating and should be considered as a score instead:

> This performance of analytical functions should be understood as a substantial rating specific expert analysis and evaluation of information regarding creditworthiness employing significant professional knowledge, experience and analytical skills that according to the rating process must have an impact on the rating process and the outcome of the rating process. Therefore if no rating analysts are employed to arrive at a specific expression of creditworthiness of a particular entity, debt or financial obligation, debt security, preferred share or other financial instrument, such an expression on creditworthiness is not an opinion within the meaning of the definition of a credit rating, and consequently cannot be deemed to be a credit rating within the meaning of the CRA Regulation. Summarizing and expressing data according to a pre-set statistical system or model alone without any additional substantial rating specific analytical input from a rating analyst in the assessment process does therefore, like the activities listed in the exceptions in Article 2.2. of the Regulation (e.g. private credit ratings, credit scores and others) not require registration according to the Regulation.

For the same reasons, ESMA considers that assessments commonly known as 'non-qualitative ratings' do not fall under the definition of credit ratings for the purposes of the Regulation (ESMA's Q&A).

DRAWBACKS OF ESMA'S INTERPRETATION. Actually, ESMA's approach of considering that purely quantitative models are not sufficient to produce credit ratings as defined in the CRA Regulation could run against one of the key principles of the EU regime, which is that public authorities should not dictate what methodologies CRAs should use. According to Recital 23, the requirement that CRAs should use rating methodologies that are rigorous, systematic, continuous, and subject to validation including any appropriate historical experience and back-testing should not provide grounds for interference with the content of credit ratings and methodologies by the authorities and the Member States. Moreover, Recital 23 emphasizes that these four principles on methodologies should not be applied in such a way as to prevent new CRAs from entering the markets.

In fact, most probably ESMA's interpretation had the effect of preventing some EU scorers from obtaining CRA status—or at least forcing them to change their business models—on the grounds that they do not include any judgmental analysis in their methodologies. However, ESMA's restrictive approach is understandable, as the underlying rating methodology of a CRA is obviously a critical point in assessing the reliability of its ratings. And if scores are not considered suitable for use by credit institutions when calculating their capital requirements (this point is developed later in this section) it might make sense to exclude from the Regulation all assessments based on a pure econometric valuation without incorporating any qualitative judgement.

Perhaps it would have been more appropriate to differentiate scoring entities and CRAs purely on the basis of the different populations of entities assessed by each of them, as explained at the beginning of this section. Although scoring entities provide an extremely valuable function for the economy, their assessments, as they are mainly over smaller entities, do not directly affect capital markets and investors, as underlined by Recital 7.

Finally, it is worth noting that in the USA a pure quantitative model for assessing the creditworthiness of corporates would not per se preclude an entity from obtaining NRSRO status. According to the Credit Rating Reform Act of 2006, the term 'credit rating agency' means any person ... 'employing either a quantitative or qualitative model, or both, to determine credit ratings'.

SCORING ENTITIES' STRATEGIES. Despite ESMA's restrictive interpretation, some scoring entities might be considering the registration according to the Regulation as an opportunity to gain market recognition and thus market share, assuming that registration is going to provide a kind of quality stamp from authorities.[27]

Once EU supervisors clarified that scoring entities may not be registered on a voluntary basis, those that would like to be registered should be considering what changes they need to implement in their policies and procedures in order to fall under the definition of credit rating agency. Thus, some of those EU scoring companies may now be adapting their methodologies in order to include a qualitative element in their processes. The revised methodologies should enable analysts to adjust the quantitative outcome of the model to take into account qualitative inputs. Compliance with ESMA's guidance on this point would imply that the resources needed to provide the required analytical input should be adequate to the volume and complexity of the credit assessments produced.

Also, there might be other scoring entities thinking about keeping their current procedures for issuing scores but setting up a new separate segment devoted to issuing credit ratings. This strategy is perfectly valid and would enable them to get the ratings segment registered and subject to ESMA's supervision as long as they can satisfy the authority that the changes are not purely cosmetic ones with the goal of circumventing Article 2.2.(b) and ESMA's guidance.

Are Scoring Entities Eligible for ECAI Recognition?

Under the standardized approach of the CRD, exposure to small or medium-sized entities not exceeding one million Euros and grouped together with similar exposures are assigned a fixed risk weight of 75%. Therefore, it might not make

---

[27] This is the same approach some small CRAs operating in the EU might be considering.

much sense to recognize external credit assessments of this category of exposures for solvency purposes.

However, scoring entities also assess companies not falling within the small or medium-sized category. Score providers might have an interest in being recognized as ECAIs and their assessments could be of interest for credit institutions using the standardized approach. Notwithstanding, as explained below, legal obstacles might prevent the recognition of scorers as eligible ECAIs.

Article 2.3 of the Regulation requires CRAs wishing to be recognized as ECAIs to be previously registered under the Regulation unless they only issue the credit ratings referred to in paragraph 2 of said article (those excluded from the Regulation). It can be argued that this provision is not applicable to scoring entities because the language of Article 2.3 only refers to 'credit rating agencies' and not to scoring companies.

Nevertheless, prudential supervisors have analysed whether scoring entities are banned from applying for ECAI recognition on the basis of their exclusion from the scope of the Regulation and therefore the impossibility of them being registered (even on a voluntary basis).[28] Banking supervisors came to the conclusion that entities producing only credit scores should not be recognized as ECAIs. If entities that produce only credit scores could be recognized as ECAIs without going through the registration process under the Regulation, there would be an uneven playing field between ECAIs that are registered CRAs and ECAIs that are only scoring entities not registered in accordance with the Regulation.

Also, while it makes sense that small and medium-sized credit institutions use credit ratings under the standardized approach of the CRD, as these ratings will have probably been produced using more information than that available to the credit institution, it does not make sense that credit institutions use external credit scores, given that these scores would have been normally produced with less information than that available to the credit institution.

However, nothing in the CRD precludes scoring entities from being recognized as ECAIs. Banking supervisors might not be able to turn down applications for ECAI recognition solely on the grounds that the applicant is a scoring entity. This is why EBA has advised the European Commission to amend the CRD in order to clarify that an ECAI has to be registered in accordance with the Regulation as a precondition for being recognized as an eligible ECAI for capital requirement purposes.[29] According to EBA, if the proposed amendment is implemented, entities which may not register under the Regulation (notably entities only producing credit scores) will not be eligible to apply for ECAI recognition, the only possible exception being central banks.

There might be cases where a registered CRA produces both credit ratings and scores (the latter being out of the scope of the CRA Regulation). In these cases, EBA considers that the registered CRA may apply for ECAI recognition but only its credit ratings would be valid for regulatory use.

---

[28] CEBS (October 2010), *Consultation paper CP43 on CEBS's advice to the European Commission on the non-eligibility of entities producing only credit scores for ECAI recognition.*

[29] CEBS (December 2010), *Advice to the European Commission on the non-eligibility of entities only producing credit scores for ECAI recognition.*

In any case, as the borderline between rating agencies and scoring entities might be blurred in some cases, coordination during the registration process between ESMA and the banking authorities is essential. Whilst the final decision on who can be registered under the CRA Regulation is up to ESMA, prudential supervisors should feed appropriately into the decision-making process.

3.4.2.3 *Credit Ratings Produced by Export Credit Agencies*

Article 2.2.(c) of the Regulation excludes from its scope the credit ratings produced by export credit agencies (ECAs) in accordance with point 1.3 of Part 1 of Annex VI to the CRD. The following paragraphs are based on the description of ECAs provided by the BCBS. (for further information, refer to the BCBS 2000 report on credit ratings and other sources of credit analysis.)[30]

International trade has specific risks that are difficult to assess and assume by exporters. This is why all major economies have set up official programmes that assist exporting companies with the goal of making their export terms competitive. These publicly sponsored agencies provide insurance against export credit risks. However, there is a risk that the credit and insurance terms provided by an export credit agency do not reflect market conditions if they seek to improve the competitiveness of its exporters vis-à-vis exporters from other countries. In this case, the assistance provided by the official schemes may become subsidization.

Countries wishing to eliminate subsidies in this area signed off the OECD Arrangement.[31] The Arrangement was issued in 1978 and has been updated several times. In essence, it sets minimum premium rates for insurance against country risk. The minimum premium rates must reflect the risk covered; therefore they are based on a classification of countries into eight categories of risk.

Export credit agencies participating in the OECD Arrangement must assess the risk of lack of payment by the foreign buyer of the exported goods or services according to the OECD classification method. This methodology has an econometric model embedded and also factors in qualitative elements.

The ratings issued by export credit agencies are outside the scope of the Regulation only when issued in accordance with the CRD. This Directive limits the use of ECAs' credit assessments to exposures to central governments and central banks. Institutions are allowed to use ECAs' ratings to calculate the risk weight of their exposures to central governments and central banks if one of the following conditions is met:

- the ratings are consensus risk scores from export credit agencies participating in the OECD Arrangement; or

- the export credit agency publishes its credit assessments, and subscribes to the OECD agreed methodology, and the credit assessment is associated with one of the eight minimum export insurance premiums that the OECD agreed methodology establishes.

---

[30] BCBS (August 2000), *Credit ratings and complementary sources of credit quality information.* Working Papers no. 3.
[31] OECD, *Arrangement on Guidelines for Officially Supported Export Credits.*

Thus if neither of these two conditions are met, the ECAs' credit ratings will be inside the scope of the CRA Regulation.

It has not been deemed necessary to set up a recognition process for ECA equivalent to that required for ECAIs. EBA's guidelines on ECAIs have clarified that banking authorities shall simply ask the institutions that wish to use an export credit agency's credit assessments to demonstrate that one of the above conditions is met.

3.4.2.4 *Credit Ratings Produced by Central Banks*

Traditionally, central banks have been an additional source of credit assessments. The above-mentioned BCBS's report on credit ratings and complementary sources of credit quality information has been used to summarize the tasks they perform in this area. Typically, they collect and operate databases containing information on the private banks' credit exposures (credit databases) and on the credit quality of the counterparties to which those banks are exposed (financial statements databases).

Credit Databases

The input to the databases on credit exposures is the information that banks are required to supply to the central bank. In this respect, the source of information for central banks' assessments of these exposures is clearly different than that of the rating agencies. Whilst central banks obtain compulsory information from the creditors (the credit institutions they supervise), CRAs get the information from the borrowers.

The types of credit instruments reported to central banks vary from country to country. Normally, reporting categories include loans, credit lines, and guarantees. The reported borrowers also differ, but according to the BCBS, European databases would typically cover more than 75% of the assets held by the banking sector.

Financial Statements Databases

Contrary to the credit exposures reported to the credit databases, the information reported to the financial statements databases is generally in the public domain. Also the number of reporting entities is completely different. Credit databases are built with the information submitted by a limited number of banks, whilst financial statements databases are fed with the accounts of all companies and entities subject to financial reporting.

Purpose and Users of Central Banks' Databases

Central banks operate these databases for different purposes. These include determining eligibility of claims in the central banks' refinancing arrangements, prudential supervision, and research. The rating methodologies employed by the central banks for determining a credit rating vary depending on the purposes of the database. Some central banks use predominantly quantitative models, whilst others also perform a qualitative assessment.

The users of the central banks' ratings are the central banks themselves, the supervised credit institutions, and the entities that report to the financial statement databases as they receive the ratings assigned to them by the central bank.

Conditions to be Exempt from the Regulation

The CRA Regulation sets out a number of conditions that central banks have to fulfil if they want their ratings not to be subject to the Regulation. They are out of the scope if they:

- are not paid for by the rated entity;
- are not disclosed to the public;
- are issued in accordance with the principles, standards, and procedures which ensure the adequate integrity and independence of credit rating activities as provided for by the Regulation; and
- do not relate to financial instruments issued by the respective central banks' Member States.

The Regulation delegates to the European Commission the power to decide that a central bank falls within the scope of Article 2.2.(d) and that its credit ratings are therefore exempt from the application of the Regulation. The request for an exemption must be submitted by a Member State. The list of exempted central banks is published on the website of the European Commission. Up to now, the only central bank that has been granted such exemption is the Banque de France.[32]

3.5 USE OF RATINGS FOR REGULATORY PURPOSES

3.5.1 Introduction

EU-regulated entities may use ratings for regulatory purposes only if those ratings are issued by a CRA registered in accordance with the CRA Regulation. According to Article 3.1.(g), the term 'regulatory purposes' means 'the use of credit ratings for the specific purpose of complying with Community law, as implemented by the national legislation of the Member States'. This article refers only to Community law but national legislation might also impose a use of ratings not envisaged in EU legislation. In these cases, it would be logical that the required ratings should be issued in accordance with the CRA Regulation. Otherwise, Member States could create a parallel supervisory regime for the ratings issued solely to comply with local rules and it seems that this would be at odds with the principles of the Regulation.

Article 4.1 of the Regulation provides the list of regulated entities subject to the above-mentioned restriction:

> Credit institutions as defined in Directive 2006/48/EC, investment firms as defined in Directive 2004/39/EC, insurance undertakings subject to the First Council Directive 73/239/EEC of 24 July 1973 on the coordination of laws, regulations and administrative provisions relating to the take-up and pursuit of the business of direct insurance other than life assurance (*), assurance undertakings as defined in Directive 2002/83/EC of the European Parliament and of the Council of 5 November 2002 concerning

---

[32] See footnote 26.

life assurance (**), reinsurance undertakings as defined in Directive 2005/68/EC of the European Parliament and the Council of 16 November 2005 on reinsurance (***), UCITS as defined in Directive 2009/65/EC of the European Parliament and the Council of 13 July 2009 on the coordination of laws, regulations and administrative provisions relating to undertakings for collective investment in transferable securities (UCITS) (****), institutions for occupational retirement provision as defined in Directive 2003/41/EC and alternative investment funds may use credit ratings for regulatory purposes only if they are issued by credit rating agencies established in the Union and registered in accordance with this Regulation.

Although the Regulation does not consider contracting a rating relating to the issuer or its securities as a use for regulatory purposes, the second subparagraph of Article 4.1 imposes an obligation on issuers or offerors to state, in the prospectuses which are published by reason of public offerings of securities or their admission to trading on a regulated market, whether the rating has been issued by a registered or unregistered entity:

> Where a prospectus published under Directive 2003/71/EC and Regulation (EC) No 809/2004 contains a reference to a credit rating or credit ratings, the issuer, offeror, or person asking for admission to trading on a regulated market shall ensure that the prospectus also includes clear and prominent information stating whether or not such credit ratings are issued by a credit rating agency established in the Community and registered under this Regulation.

The Prospectus Regulation requires retail prospectuses to include any 'credit ratings assigned to an issuer or its debt securities at the request or with the cooperation of the issuer in the rating process'. In case an issuer voluntarily includes other references to ratings in its prospectus, it should also provide the information required by the CRA Regulation on the agency (question 76 of ESMA's frequently asked questions on prospectuses—ESMA/2011/85).

Recitals 4 and 5 clarify that the CRA Regulation does not impose any other obligations in connection with offers of securities or their admission to trading. In particular, it does not oblige investors to invest only in securities for which a prospectus has been published and which are rated under the Regulation. In addition, the Regulation does not require issuers, offerors, or persons seeking admission to trading on a regulated market to obtain credit ratings for securities that are subject to the requirement to publish a prospectus under the Prospectus Directive.

In the USA, the Dodd–Frank Act eliminates CRAs' shield from lawsuits when underwriters include their assessments in documents used to sell debt. On this basis, some CRAs have declined to consent to the inclusion of their ratings in prospectuses and registration statements because of an increased risk of being sued. Although CRAs' ratings (at least those issued by CRAs paid by issuers) are anyway accessible to investors via their websites, this move could make issues of some bonds more difficult (see Section 5.4).

The legal framework for the insurance and reinsurance sector, which consists of a number of different directives and is usually referred to in the market as 'Solvency I', does not include references to external ratings. This is because there is no explicit credit risk charge for the solvency margin. This regime has been recently amended by the so-called 'Solvency II framework directive'[33] which introduced some risk-orientated solvency requirements for insurance and reinsurance undertakings. According to Solvency II, capital requirements are determined either by a standard formula or, subject to the authorities' approval, by the entity's internal model. The standard formula has yet to be developed, but according to the current discussions it is possible that external ratings could be incorporated in its design.

The rest of this section focuses on the two key regulatory uses of ratings in the EU: use by EU financial institutions for calculation of capital requirements and use by the European Central Bank to determine eligible collateral for their operations.

3.5.2 Basel and Capital Requirements Directive

3.5.2.1 Introduction

The CRD is the European implementation of the Basel II framework and the use of ratings for capital requirement calculations in the CRD is fully consistent with the international rules. For a good understanding of the use of ratings under the CRD, it is worthwhile briefly analyzing the relevant aspects of the Basel accord, upon which the CRD is based. The Joint Forum report on the use of ratings,[34] published in June 2009, provides a good overview of the use of external credit ratings under Basel II, explaining the main elements that are summarized below.

The Basel II Framework consists of a set of standards for establishing minimum capital requirements for banking organizations. It was prepared by the BCBS that developed the first standard in 1988.[35]

The overarching goal of the Basel II Framework is to promote the adequate capitalization of banks and to encourage improvements in risk management, thereby strengthening the stability of the financial system. This goal is promoted through the introduction of 'three pillars':

- minimum capital requirements;
- supervisory review of banks' internal assessments of their overall risks; and
- market discipline, which sets out the public disclosures that banks must make.

As part of the global initiatives to strengthen the financial regulatory system that have been endorsed by the FSB and the G-20 leaders, the BCBS has undertaken a comprehensive reform package to address the lessons learnt from the financial crisis. The text of this reform, known as the Basel III Framework, was issued by the BCBS in December 2010. Basel III complements the Basel II and Basel I frameworks but does not replace them; in particular, it does not change the fundamentals of the

---

[33] Directive 2009/138/EC of the European Parliament and of the Council of 25 of November 2009 on the taking-up and pursuit of the business of Insurance and Reinsurance (*Official Journal* L 335, 17.12.2009: pp. 1–155).

[34] The Joint Forum (June 2009), *Stocktaking on the use of credit ratings*.

[35] BCBS (July 1988). *International convergence of capital measurement and capital standards* (so-called Basel Capital Accord).

use of ratings under Basel II. The new framework will take effect from the beginning of 2013 and will have beeen progressively phased in by 2019.

3.5.2.2 Use under Basel II Framework

Under the Basel II Framework, there are references to external credit ratings under pillars one and three. The main use of external credit ratings can be found in the first pillar (minimum capital requirements). In particular, external credit ratings are primarily used for the calculation of capital charges for credit risk. The use of ratings permits the differentiation of exposures in a risk-sensitive manner and the setting of capital charges accordingly. Basel II establishes two ways of determining regulatory capital requirements: the internal and the standardized approaches.

In the internal approach, financial institutions use internally produced credit rating models to determine the risk weights of their exposures. External ratings are only used under this approach for the calculation of capital charges of securitization exposures, and there is also some marginal use, for example, to validate the internal models.

External ratings are mainly used under the standardized approach, which allows institutions to calculate the risk weights of their exposures to the corporate, sovereign, and banking classes. The risk weights applied to these exposures are differentiated according to the external rating (or credit assessment, in the language of the Basel accord) assigned to each exposure. The Basel II framework provides tables that attribute different risk weights to each rating grade issued by a recognized external credit assessment institution (ECAI). For example, for corporate exposures, a triple A rating means a 20% risk weight, an A rating a 50% risk weight, and so on.

There are also references to ratings in the credit ratings mitigation rules of the first pillar. These rules define how credit protections (such as collateral, guarantees, or credit derivatives) can be recognized. They refer to external ratings in order to identify an eligible credit protection provider (for example, a guarantor must have a certain rating) and adjust the extent of the recognition of the protection (such as the haircuts to 'the collateral proportionate to the rating of its issuer).

The first pillar also contains references to external ratings under the market risk and operational risk rules. With respect to market risk measurement, the main use is for the calculation of the specific risk capital charges arising from debt positions under the standardized approach. Similarly to the credit risk rules, different risk weights are applied to the trading book debt exposures, depending on the issuer's ratings. With operational risk, the risk mitigation techniques use external ratings in the same way as the risk mitigation techniques under the credit risk rules (the protection provider must have a rating above a certain threshold).

Finally, pillar three on market discipline requires institutions to provide some qualitative disclosures regarding the use of ECAIs and export credit agencies (ECAs). In the context of credit risk, institutions have to disclose the names of the ECAIs and ECAs used, the types of exposure for which each agency is used, and the alignment of different agencies' scales with risk buckets.

3.5.3 ECAIs Recognition Process under the CRD

3.5.3.1 Introduction

As the European transposition of Basel II, the CRD allows institutions to use external assessments to determine the risk weight of their exposures, provided that the entities that produce these assessments have been recognized as eligible for that purpose by the EU banking authorities. The entities that issue external credit assessments and that have been determined by the banking authorities to meet the eligibility requirements set out in the CRD are then called ECAIs.[36] As stated by the EBA's guidelines on ECAIs, the ECAI recognition for capital purposes does not constitute a form of regulation of ECAIs or a form of licensing of rating agencies to do business in the EU.

Given the critical role that the CRD attributes to external ratings in the determination of risk weights, and the lack of regulation in Europe on CRAs at the time of the adoption of the CRD, EU legislators considered that it was necessary to establish a process of recognition of these entities by the banking authorities (Recital 34a of the CRD).

Now a legal framework of authorization and monitoring of CRAs has been established, but the recent CRA Regulation has not replaced the CRD's processes of recognition and supervision of ECAIs. EU legislators could have established a single registration and monitoring system that would have allowed banking, insurance, and securities supervisors to leverage off one another's supervisory efforts. Instead, Article 2.3 of the CRA Regulation requires CRAs to register under the Regulation as a pre-condition for being recognized as an ECAI in accordance with the CRD: 'a credit rating agency shall apply for registration under this Regulation as a condition for being recognized as an External Credit Assessment Institution (ECAI) in accordance with Part 2 of Annex VI to Directive 2006/48/EC, unless it only issues the credit ratings referred to in paragraph 2'.

The ratings referred to in paragraph 2 of Article 2 are those that are outside the scope of the CRA Regulation (and therefore an entity that only issues those ratings is not obliged to register under the Regulation). Registration is a necessary condition, although not sufficient, for a CRA to be recognized as an ECAI. As examined in this section, EU banking authorities are responsible for the recognition of an entity as an ECAI.

However, EU legislators acknowledged the duplication existing between the CRD and the CRA Regulation and decided to amend the CRD in order to ensure consistency between the two frameworks. The changes to the CRD have been effected through the CRD II. Member States were required to transpose the Directive into national legislation by 31 October 2010 and to apply the national provisions from 31 December 2010.

In particular, the CRD II has modified Articles 81.2 and 97.2 of the CRD in order to avoid duplication of work and reduce the burden of the recognition process where an ECAI is registered as a CRA at Community level. In this case, 'the competent authorities shall consider the requirements of objectivity,

---

[36] The Directive does not provide a definition of the term 'ECAI'.

independence, ongoing review and transparency with respect to its assessment methodology to be satisfied'.

This means that the only criteria that should be assessed in the ECAI's initial recognition process and ongoing review are the technical criteria on 'credibility and market acceptance' and 'transparency and disclosure' with respect to their individual credit assessments. The remaining technical criteria are assessed during the registration process under the CRA Regulation and are considered to be satisfied for the purposes of the ECAIs' recognition process.

For those entities that produce credit ratings which do not fall under the CRA Regulation, in accordance with its Article 2.2, the entire set of CRD's eligibility criteria and EBA's guidelines on ECAIs applies.

In addition, Recital 23 of the CRD II invited EBA to review its guidelines on the recognition of ECAIs that were published on 20 January 2006 in order to fulfil the above-mentioned objectives of reducing the level of overlap between the two rules. In this context, on 30 November 2010 EBA published its revised guidelines. The overview of the ECAIs' recognition process and mapping of their credit assessments provided below is based on these guidelines.

3.5.3.2 Responsibility for ECAI's Recognition

Article 81.1 of the CRD stipulates that 'an external credit assessment may be used to determine the risk weight of an exposure in accordance with Article 80 only if the ECAI which provides it has been recognized as eligible for those purposes by the competent authorities'.

According to EBA's guidelines on ECAIs, the responsibility for deciding whether an ECAI should be recognized as eligible lies with the competent authority of the country where the institution that intends to use that ECAI's credit assessment is authorized and supervised. This means that, for example, a Spanish bank may use only the assessments of ECAIs that have been recognized by the Spanish competent authority according to the CRD.

Recognition of an ECAI by a competent authority is granted exclusively for the purpose of the calculation of regulatory capital requirements using the standardized approach or the securitization ratings-based approach under the CRD. In fact, competent authorities should proceed with an application for recognition only when they are satisfied that at least one institution within their jurisdiction intends to use the ECAI's credit assessments for risk weighting purposes. This approach contrasts with that of the CRA Regulation, whereby a CRA can be registered as long as it complies with all the Regulation's requirements, even if authorities do not have evidence regarding the actual use of its ratings in the market.

3.5.3.3 The Application

The recognition process is initiated when the competent authority receives an application for recognition. Competent authorities can accept applications from ECAIs and/or institutions that intend to use the ECAIs' credit assessments. In practice, according to the information published by EBA, applications have been submitted by the ECAIs themselves in most cases.

In case of groups of CRAs that have subsidiaries in several Member States, the CRD does not specify who should be the applicant and, therefore, whether recognition by a competent authority applies to the subsidiary located in the jurisdiction where the competent authority is based or to the whole group.

According to EBA, the central question for deciding whether to grant recognition at the level of the group or at the level of the subsidiary is whether each grade within the ECAI's scale means the same regardless of the geographical location where the rating is issued. If the ECAI's group can demonstrate that each of the subsidiaries for which it seeks recognition adhere to the same standards and procedures set at the group's level, then recognition may be given at the level of the group.

EU banking authorities have opted for the sensible approach of recognizing ECAIs at group level. EBA does not clarify whether its notion of group refers to the worldwide group or to the EU group. But in practice banking authorities do not care whether the ratings issued by the major global ECAIs that are used by EU institutions are issued in Europe or in a third country. So, in fact, the ECAI recognition system is allowing recognition at worldwide group level as long as competent authorities are satisfied that the same standards are consistently implemented in all their subsidiaries. This flexible approach contrasts with the rigid system of the CRA Regulation, where registration and ongoing requirements apply at subsidiary level in the EU and recognition of ratings issued by the parent company or subsidiaries located in third countries is subject to a set of different and complex requirements (see Chapter 4).

Regarding the content of the application, EBA has developed a 'common basis application pack', which sets out the minimum information to be provided by applicants (attached as Annex I to EBA's guidelines). The objective of the common pack is to promote a consistent approach by individual competent authorities. Nevertheless, although the assessment of the applicant's eligibility should be based on the information provided in the agreed pack, EBA notes that competent authorities can ask for the additional information necessary to address any country specific issues.

ECAIs must indicate in the application for which market segment (public finance, commercial entities, and/or structured finance) recognition is being sought and whether it is sought for risk weighting of securitization positions. Competent authorities undertake a separate assessment for each of those market segments.

Application in more than one Member State: Lack of Passport and Joint Assessment

One of the drawbacks of the ECAI recognition system is that a decision of recognition by a competent authority is only effective for the institutions authorized in the authority's jurisdiction. In other words, there is no passport within the EU for decisions of recognition. This contrasts with the approach of the CRA Regulation, which stipulates that the registration of a CRA by ESMA shall be effective for the entire territory of the EU.

Under the CRD, a CRA has to apply in all the 27 Member States if it wishes its ratings to be used by any European credit institution regardless of where it is based. This means that there will be applications for recognition of the same ECAI or group of ECAIs in several Member States (for example, from the global ECAIs, whose ratings are of widespread use by EU banks).

In the event of filings in several Member States, EBA recommends[37] that competent authorities carry out a single joint process for reviewing the applications, with the goal of avoiding duplication of work on the part of the authorities and reducing the burden for applicants. The authorities involved will appoint a 'facilitator' whose role consists of coordinating and producing the joint assessment report taking into account the consensus reached among the supervisors involved.

The joint process should lead to a common view on the ECAI's eligibility and on the mapping of its credit assessments to the CRD's credit quality steps. Then each competent authority should make its own decision on the basis of the joint assessment. However, EBA acknowledges that the joint assessment does not preclude supervisors from asking for the additional information necessary to address any country-specific issues and from undertaking any additional assessment they might deem appropriate.

In addition to the possibility of following a joint process, the CRD allows what is called indirect recognition, where the competent authority that recognizes the ECAI does not conduct its own assessment (as would be the case in the direct recognition system) and relies instead on the assessment and recognition previously granted by another authority (Article 81.3).

Review of the Application and Publication of the Decision

Competent authorities will analyse the application submitted and the information provided to support it and will base their recognition decisions on an assessment of the technical criteria laid down in the CRD regarding the ECAI's methodologies (objectivity, independence, ongoing review, and transparency), where applicable, and the credibility and transparency of its credit assessments.

The way in which the decision is communicated to the applicant will be determined in accordance with the relevant national law. As these decisions are obviously of interest to banks and investment firms, Article 81.4 of the CRD requires competent authorities to make publicly available a list of eligible ECAIs and an explanation of the recognition process. EBA has clarified that the list of eligible ECAIs should be accompanied by the mapping carried out by the competent authority and the recognition process should include information on how the recognition process was initiated, whether a joint process has been carried out, and the market segments for which recognition has been sought. In addition, EBA publishes on its website this information regarding the ECAIs recognized by EU authorities.

The Technical Criteria

Competent authorities' decisions on ECAIs' eligibility for the standardized approach will be based on the technical criteria laid down in Article 81.2 of the CRD: 'competent authorities shall recognize an ECAI as eligible for the purposes of

---

[37] EBA's guidelines have developed a detailed explanation of what is a joint assessment and how it works.

Article 80 only if they are satisfied that its assessment methodology complies with the requirements of objectivity, independence, ongoing review and transparency, and that the resulting credit assessments meet the requirements of credibility and transparency. For those purposes, the competent authorities shall take into account the technical criteria set out in Annex VI, Part 2.'

Similarly, according to Article 97.2, the eligibility criteria for the use of ECAI's ratings in the determination of the risk weight of a securitization position are those laid down in Article 81, taking into account the technical criteria in Annex VI, Part 2. In addition, the ECAI must demonstrate ability in the area of securitization which may be evidenced by a strong market acceptance. Article 97.5 further indicates that the credit assessments shall comply with the principles of credibility and transparency as elaborated in Annex IX, Part 3 of the CRD.

EBA sets out some general principles that competent authorities should follow when undertaking their assessments of the applicants' eligibility. There are a couple of these principles that should be highlighted. First, while admitting that a recognition regime might create barriers to entry in the market for external credit assessments, EBA clearly states that competent authorities' primary objective is the prudential need to identify which ECAIs are eligible for risk weighting purposes. In other words, EBA wants players that are capable of producing robust credit assessments, even if the requirements imposed in order to select them might impinge on the level of competition in the sector.

Second, EBA introduces some flexibility in the assessment process by recommending supervisors to take a differentiated approach to assessing how individual ECAIs satisfy the CRD's recognition criteria, given the different business models existing in the market. Accordingly, authorities may place different weights on the various criteria for different ECAIs—subject to them complying with all these CRD's requirements.

As discussed earlier in this section, following the adoption of the CRA Regulation, CRD II amended both Articles 81.2 and 97.2 to stipulate that where an ECAI has been registered in accordance with the CRA Regulation, the competent authorities shall consider the requirements of objectivity, independence, ongoing review, and transparency with respect to the assessment methodology to be satisfied.

The CRD's criteria on methodologies will be analysed in detail in Section 3.8.4, which deals with the Regulation's requirements on methodologies. The discussion below will focus on the only criteria that should be assessed under the CRD for CRAs which are registered under the CRA Regulation: 'credibility and market acceptance' and 'transparency and disclosure' with respect to the applicant's individual credit assessments.

CREDIBILITY AND MARKET ACCEPTANCE OF THE INDIVIDUAL CREDIT ASSESSMENTS. This requirement is included in Article 81.2 for the standardized approach and in Article 97.2 for calculation of the risk weight of securitization exposures.

Regarding the standardized approach, the CRD obliges competent authorities to 'verify that ECAIs' individual credit assessments are recognized in the market as credible and reliable by the users of such credit assessments'. The same paragraph further specifies that competent authorities shall assess credibility according to the following indicative factors: Market share of the ECAI; revenues generated by the

ECAI, and more in general financial resources of the ECAI; whether there is any pricing on the basis of the rating; and at least two credit institutions use the ECAI's individual credit assessment for bond issuing and/or assessing credit risks.

EBA has added two more indicators. The first is evidence that a large number of institutions plan to use the applicant's credit assessments. This could alleviate the difficulties that new entrants might face to meet the CRD's factors at the time of the application, as EBA does not require that the institutions are currently using the applicant's ratings.

The second was added to EBA's guidelines on ECAIs in November 2010 and concerns the number of years of experience of the ECAI. EBA requires that ECAIs have five years of experience in issuing ratings for each market segment in which recognition is sought. The aim of this requirement is to allow markets and competent authorities to assess a minimum set of historical data on the performance of the ratings. Alternatively, EBA allows a shorter period of experience where the ECAI can provide a sufficiently broad database.

Neither market acceptance nor a track record in issuing ratings is required by the CRA Regulation. In fact, these requirements might represent a strong barrier to entry for new players, thereby reducing the spectrum of external ratings available to supervised institutions. Banking supervisors have other measures to assess compliance with the market acceptance requirement and to ensure an appropriate level of quality of ECAIs' ratings. For example, as explained below, authorities can always conduct a very conservative mapping in cases where the ECAI does not have a sufficient number of years of default data (meaning that exposures having the highest rating by an inexperienced ECAI would be assigned a higher risk weight than exposures for which an experienced ECAI has issued the highest rating). This approach would guarantee that appropriate levels of capital are required, depending on the different ECAIs used, whilst at the same time ensuring a fear treatment for all the applicants.

Finally, from a legal point of view, and as discussed above, the CRD sets out a list of indicative factors that competent authorities might take into account when assessing whether the requirement of credibility and market acceptance is fulfilled. But the CRD has not set any binding criterion for competent authorities that would force them to turn down an application in case the ECAI does not meet it. Therefore, it seems that the absolute criterion of five years of experience should not be understood as restricting supervisors' ability to apply the factors cited in the Directive according to the circumstances of the case or to use additional factors.

TRANSPARENCY AND DISCLOSURE OF INDIVIDUAL CREDIT ASSESSMENTS. The principle of transparency of the individual credit assessments issued by eligible ECAIs is included in Articles 81.2 (standardized approach) and 97.5 (securitization ratings based approach) of the CRD and are further elaborated in Annexes VI and IX, respectively.

Regarding the standardized approach, the CRD obliges competent authorities to 'verify that individual credit assessments are accessible at equivalent terms at least to all credit institutions having a legitimate interest in these individual credit assessments. In particular, competent authorities shall verify that individual credit assessments are available to non-domestic parties on equivalent terms as to domestic credit institutions having a legitimate interest in these individual credit assessments'.

Concerning the securitization framework, the CRD prescribes that 'the credit assessments shall be available publicly to the market. Credit assessments are considered to be publicly available only if they have been published in a publicly accessible forum and they are included in the ECAI's transition matrix. Credit assessments that are made available only to a limited number of entities shall not be considered to be publicly available.'

The above provisions of the CRD have not been amended following the adoption of the CRA Regulation. Therefore, eligible ECAIs have to demonstrate to prudential supervisors that they fulfil the requirements on transparency and disclosure of individual credit assessments.

Nevertheless, EBA did amend its guidelines when the Regulation on CRAs came into force to state that for ECAIs registered under the CRA Regulation, 'the fulfilment of the criterion on transparency and disclosure of individual credit assessments can be assumed by the competent authority'.

It is clear that Annex VI of the CRD does not require eligible ECAIs to publish their ratings if they operate under a subscription-based model. It is sufficient for an ECAI to demonstrate that all institutions having a legitimate interest in its credit assessments have equal and timely access to them. EBA understands that all institutions using the standardized approach and the securitization ratings-based approach to calculate their regulatory capital requirements have a legitimate interest in knowing the credit assessments of the ECAI they are using. Undue discrimination could happen according to EBA if, for instance, the subscriber-based ECAI charges different prices to users that are under the same economic circumstances.

Regarding the securitization framework, the language used by the CRD on transparency of individual credit assessments is different and could be understood as requiring ECAIs operating under the subscriber-pays model to publish their ratings. However, EBA considers that disclosure on a non-discriminatory basis is also sufficient to comply with the Directive in the case of securitization.

The authority under the CRA Regulation, ESMA, will verify that all individual credit assessments are disclosed by any registered CRA (irrespective of their business model) on a non-selective basis and in a timely manner; in addition CRAs will have to comply with all the detailed requirements on presentation of ratings set out in Annex I.D of the CRA Regulation (see Section 3.8.5).

Ongoing Review of Eligibility

Competent authorities have to assess whether recognized ECAIs continue to meet the criteria that led to their initial recognition and they can withdraw the recognition of any eligible ECAI that ceases to fulfil the criteria.

To this effect, the CRD requires supervisors to take the necessary measures to be promptly informed by ECAIs of any material changes in the methodology they use for assigning credit assessments. EBA has clarified that a material change is any modification in methodology that could change a significant proportion of credit assessments in a given market segment. In addition, EBA recommends

Table 3.2. CRD risk weights of exposures to corporates under the standardized approach

Credit quality step	1	2	3	4	5	6
Risk weight	20%	50%	100%	100%	150%	150%

competent authorities to undertake an in-depth analysis of each ECAI's eligibility every five years.

3.5.3.4 Mapping Process under CRD

Mapping in the ECAI framework of the CRD is a process by which competent authorities assign the different credit assessments of eligible ECAIs according to their scales (such as Aaa, Aa, A, Baa, etc. for Moody's) to the credit quality steps of the CRD (1, 2, 3, 4, etc.).

Table 3.2 (table 6 in Annex VI of the CRD), which determines the risk weights of exposures to corporates under the standardized approach, illustrates how institutions have to apply the authorities' mapping.

For example, if an institution has an exposure to a senior bond rated Aaa by Moody's, the bank will have to know to what credit quality step in the CRD a rating of Aaa by Moody's is associated. The mapping conducted by banking supervisors assigns the quality step 1 to a rating of Aaa issued by Moody's. Therefore the risk weight of the exposure will be 20%.

It is important to note that the mapping process is different from the assessment by authorities of the ECAI's compliance with the eligibility criteria and should not lead to the imposition of additional eligibility requirements.

The mapping is the responsibility of the competent authorities—although authorities may rely on the mapping previously carried out by another—and EBA recommends competent authorities follow the guidance provided by the Basel II Framework (Annex two).

As stated in EBA's guidelines, competent authorities conduct annual reviews of the initial mappings in order to decide whether they need to be updated or changed. To this aim, ECAIs have to submit annually their default rates and the data related to the mapping of securitization positions.

When determining with which of the credit quality steps the relevant credit assessments of an eligible ECAI are to be associated, competent authorities shall apply the principles of objectivity and consistency established by Articles 82.1 and 98.1 of the CRD and the technical criteria laid down in Annex VI, Part 2 for the standardized approach and Annex IX for securitization positions (see Appendix 3 for details on the mapping factors under CRD).

3.5.3.5 Possible Future Review of the Recognition and Mapping Processes

As discussed previously, in addition to changing its guidelines where necessary to reflect the amendments to the CRD as a result of the CRA Regulation, EBA also used the CRD II to introduce limited adjustments to its understanding of the

Directive requirements on 'credibility and market acceptance' and 'transparency and disclosure' with respect to the individual credit assessments.

It could be argued that the adoption of the CRA Regulation should have also led EBA to modify its guidelines with the aim of strengthening the cooperation between ESMA and the banking authorities. However, EBA adopted the cautious approach of waiting until the current regulatory uncertainties disappear.

As analysed further in this book, the CRA Regulation was revised in 2011 in order to transfer the powers on registration and ongoing supervision from national authorities to ESMA. As far as the ECAI recognition is concerned, it is still unclear who will be responsible for the recognition of ECAIs in the future. The Commission Services Staff proposed in several working documents published for consultation in July 2009 and February 2010[38] in the context of the proposed review of the CRD, that responsibility for conducting the evaluation process and the mapping of the credit assessments where an ECAI seeks recognition in more than one Member State was assigned to EBA, following a similar approach to that of the CRA Regulation. It is therefore likely that EBA will only consider possible changes to its guidelines once it is clear which authorities will be responsible in the future for the recognition process and mapping of ECAIs.

Apart from a possible move towards more centralized recognition and mapping processes, none of the proposals for CRD III[39] and for CRD IV (published on 20 July 2011) would significantly change the ECAI recognition process or the use of ratings under the CRD, besides some measures to reduce to the extent possible reliance by credit institutions on external credit ratings. In addition, the EC consultation on CRAs of November 2010 contains proposals to address the over-reliance on credit ratings that, if endorsed by the EU Council and Parliament, could lead to further amendments in the CRD.

3.5.3.6 *Rules of CRD on use of ECAIs' Credit Assessments*

Standardized Approach and Securitization Framework

Below are enumerated the key CRD's rules about how institutions should use ECAI's credit assessments for the determination of risk weights. These rules aim to ensure that banks and investment firms employ ECAI's assessments in an objective and consistent manner, avoiding cherry-picking the most favourable ratings available.

STANDARDIZED APPROACH (ANNEX VI, PART 3).

- Institutions may nominate one or more eligible ECAIs for the calculation of their regulatory capital.
- If a credit institution uses the assessments of the ECAI for a certain class of items, it must use those credit assessments consistently for all exposures belonging to that class.

---

[38] EC (July 2009), *Commission Services Staff working document: Possible further changes to the capital requirements directive and EC (February 2010), Commission Services Staff working document: Possible further changes to the capital requirements directive.*

[39] EC (July 2009), *Proposal for a Directive of the European Parliament and of the Council amending Directives 2006/48/EC and 2006/49/EC as regards capital requirements for the trading book and for resecuritisations, and the supervisory review of remuneration policies.*

- The assessments must be used in a continuous and consistent way over time.
- Credit institutions can only use ECAIs' credit assessments that take into account all amounts both in principal and in interest owed to them.
- If only one credit assessment is available, that assessment shall be used to determine the risk weight of the rated item. If there are two assessments available and they correspond to different risk weights for the rated item, the higher risk weight shall be assigned. If more than two assessments are available for an item, the institution will use the two assessments generating the two lowest risk weights; if the two lowest risk weights are different, the higher risk weight shall be assigned; if the two lowest risk weights are the same, that risk weight shall be assigned.

SECURITIZATION FRAMEWORK (ANNEX IX, PART 3).

- Institutions may nominate one or more eligible ECAIs for the calculation of their risk-weighted exposure amounts.
- The ECAIs' credit assessments must be used consistently.
- A credit institution may not use an ECAI's credit assessment for its positions in some tranches and another ECAI's assessment for its positions in other tranches within the same structure that may or may not be rated by the first ECAI.
- Where a position has two credit assessments, the institution shall pick the less favourable one. Where a position has more than two credit assessments, the two most favourable shall be used; if the two most favourable assessments are different, the least favourable of the two shall be used.
- Finally, CRD II requires competent authorities to take the necessary measures to ensure that an ECAI explains publicly how the performance of the pool of assets affects its credit assessments.

Internal Ratings Based Approach

As already discussed, there is a limited use of external ratings under the internal ratings-based approach. In some cases, credit institutions incorporate external ratings as an input to their internal models or as a means of validating these internal models. More importantly, banks often lack sufficient empirical experience to make predictions on further performance. Therefore, they have to use default frequencies from ECAIs when estimating probability of default.

However, it seems that this use would not qualify as use for regulatory purposes in the context of the CRA Regulation. The Regulation defines 'regulatory purposes' as the use of credit ratings for the specific purpose of complying with Community law, as implemented by the national legislation of the Member States. Different from the standardized approach and the securitization framework, the provisions of the internal ratings-based approach do not contain any references to external ratings. Therefore, if credit institutions use external ratings, for instance as benchmarks in their internal models, this is not required by Community legislation and, therefore, Article 4 of the CRA Regulation does not cover this use. This has a practical consequence: credit institutions could use ratings issued by a CRA incorporated in a jurisdiction outside the EU for this purpose without the need for following the endorsement or certification process (see Chapter 4).

Finally, it is worth noting that Annex VII, part 4, item 18 of the CRD stipulates that 'if a credit institution uses an external rating as a primary factor determining an internal rating assignment, the credit institution shall ensure that it considers other relevant information'. This provision has been included to avoid credit institutions using as internal ratings solely external ratings that might not fulfil the requirements set out under the standardized approach or the approach applicable for securitizations. Therefore, external ratings can be used as a primary factor for determining an internal rating but have to be complemented by other relevant information.

3.5.4 Eligibility as Collateral by European Central Bank

In order to achieve its objectives, the Eurosystem[40] has at its disposal a set of monetary policy instruments; it conducts open market operations, offers standing facilities, and requires credit institutions to hold minimum reserves on accounts with the Eurosystem.

The Eurosystem uses market operations for the purposes of steering interest rates, managing the liquidity situation in the market, and signalling the stance of monetary policy. Among the market operations conducted by the Eurosystem, the most important are reverse transactions that may be executed either in the form of repurchase agreements (where the ownership of the asset is transferred to the creditor, while the parties agree to reverse the transaction through a re-transfer of the asset to the debtor at a future point in time) or as collateralized loans (an enforceable security interest is provided over the assets but, assuming fulfillment of the debt obligation, the ownership of the asset is retained by the debtor). Other market operations conducted by the Eurosystem are the buying or selling of eligible assets outright on the market.

Standing facilities provide and absorb overnight liquidity, signal the general stance of monetary policy, and bound overnight market interest rates. The standing facilities of the Eurosystem are the marginal lending facility (used by credit institutions to obtain overnight liquidity against eligible assets and provided either in the form of overnight repurchase agreements or as overnight collateralized loans) and the deposit facility (used by counterparties to make overnight deposits with national central banks). These facilities are administered in a decentralized manner by the national central banks.

All Eurosystem liquidity-providing operations are based on underlying assets provided either in the form of the transfer of ownership of assets or in the form of a pledge, an assignment, or a charge granted over relevant assets. The underlying assets have to fulfil certain criteria in order to be eligible for the Eurosystem's operations and they have to satisfy a high credit standard. In the assessment of the credit standard of the assets, the Eurosystem takes into account credit assessment information from several sources, among others the assessment of an ECAI. The ECAIs accepted by the ECB are listed on its website.

---

[40] The Eurosystem, according to Guideline ECB/2000/7, denotes those components of the European System of Central Banks that carry out its basic tasks: the European Central Bank (ECB) and the national central banks of those European Union Member States which have adopted the Euro as their single currency. The primary objective of the Eurosystem is to maintain price stability. Without prejudice to its main objective, the Eurosystem supports the general economic policies in the EU.

The ECB's guideline 2000/7 contains detailed requirements regarding the disclosures that ECAIs must make public if the rated securities are to be eligible:

> With regard to the ECAI source, the assessment must be based on a public rating. The Eurosystem reserves the right to request any clarification that it considers necessary. For asset-backed securities, ratings must be explained in a publicly available credit rating report, namely a detailed pre-sale or new issue report, including, inter alia, a comprehensive analysis of structural and legal aspects, a detailed collateral pool assessment, an analysis of the transaction participants, as well as an analysis of any other relevant particularities of a transaction. Moreover ECAIs must publish regular surveillance reports for asset-backed securities. The publication of these reports should be in line with the frequency and timing of coupon payments. These reports should at least contain an update of the key transaction data (e.g. composition of the collateral pool, transaction participants, capital structure), as well as performance data.

The ECB's required disclosures—adopted in October 2010—differ from those imposed on CRAs by the CRA Regulation regarding structured finance instruments. In particular, the Regulation requires CRAs to periodically review their outstanding ratings—at least annually—but does not oblige them to issue periodic surveillance reports for asset-backed securities. An elaboration of the Regulation's rules on presentation of ratings will follow in Section 3.8.5.

The Eurosystem's credit quality threshold is defined in terms of a 'single A' credit assessment (this means a minimum long-term rating of 'A-' by Fitch and S&P, or 'A3' by Moody's, or 'AL' by DBRS). The Eurosystem considers a probability of default of 0.10% as equivalent to a 'single A' credit assessment, subject to regular review.

With regard to asset-backed securities, the Eurosystem credit quality threshold is defined in terms of a 'triple A' credit assessment (this means 'AAA' by Fitch, S&P, and DBRS, or 'Aaa' by Moody's) at issuance. Over the lifetime of the asset-backed security, the Eurosystem's minimum threshold of 'single A' must be retained.

The ECB's guideline establishes the above-mentioned high credit standards for marketable assets on the basis of the following set of criteria:

- For asset-backed securities the Eurosystem requires at least two credit assessments from any accepted ECAIs for the issue. To determine the eligibility of these securities, the 'second-best rule' is applied, which means that not only the best, but also the second-best available ECAI credit assessment must comply with the credit quality threshold for asset-backed securities. Based on this rule, the Eurosystem requires for both credit assessments an 'AAA'/'Aaa' level at issuance and a 'single A' level over the life of the security in order for the securities to be eligible.

- In the absence of a credit assessment of the issuer from an acceptable ECAI, high credit standards are established on the basis of guarantees provided by financially sound guarantors.

Finally, it is relevant to mention that the ECB is considering loan-by-loan information requirements for asset-backed securities in the Eurosystem collateral framework. This would mean that for RMBS and some other asset classes, standardized data would be collected and made available to the market. Loan-by-loan information is currently provided to the CRAs that are hired to rate the products and to conduct the subsequent monitoring of their performance. Therefore, the ECB's proposal would put CRAs and other market participants to some extent on an equal footing as regards information on the underlying assets for certain structured finance products.

The aim of the ECB's initiative is to increase transparency levels in the securitization markets regarding the underlying assets. The enhanced transparency should have a beneficial effect in the market, as it will help rating agencies to conduct their credit risk assessments and investors to comply with their due diligence obligations (as required by Article 122(a) of the CRD).

The ECB's proposal will have a second positive effect of assisting with valuations of asset-backed securities and with price formation. The ECB considers that investors, directly or through third parties, will be able to process the loan-level information in order to build their own cash-flow models of the transactions for valuation purposes. This measure could also have an impact on the liquidity of the EU asset-backed securities markets, as increased transparency on the underlying assets could contribute to restore investors' confidence.

In December 2009, the ECB launched a public consultation on this initiative and received very strong support from market participants. In light of the positive feedback, the ECB announced in April 2010 that the Eurosystem was going to commence the preparatory work for the establishment of loan-level information. The ECB's project team worked to develop loan-level data templates and the key elements of the initiative and on 16 December 2010 the ECB announced the establishment of loan-by-loan information requirements. The requirements will apply to existing and newly issued ABSs and the ECB intends to introduce them in the 18 months following the December 2010 announcement, first to RMBSs and then gradually to other asset classes, such as CMBSs and small and medium-sized enterprise transactions.

3.6 REGISTRATION PROCESS AND REQUIREMENTS

3.6.1 Rating Agencies Operating in Europe in 2010

The registration procedure envisaged in the CRA Regulation conferred on competent authorities designated by Member States the power to register and supervise CRAs. This system was revamped by the amendment introduced in 2011 (CRA Regulation II), which transferred all competences and duties regarding registration and supervision of CRAs to ESMA with effect from 1 July 2011 (see Section 3.7). However a transitional measure included in Article 40a of the Regulation stipulated that applications for registration received by competent authorities by 7 September 2010 should be handled by those competent authorities and therefore the registration or refusal decision should be taken by them (in coordination with other members of the relevant college).

Therefore, colleges of competent authorities were responsible for the registration process of the existing CRAs, including the EU subsidiaries of the major CRAs. At the time of writing, only five CRAs had been registered (Euler Hermes Rating GmbH, Feri EuroRating Services AG, Creditreform Rating AG, PSR Rating

GmbH, and Bulgarian Credit Rating Agency AD) and one had been certified (Japan Credit Rating Agency Ltd), according to the list of registered agencies published on the website of the EC.

ESMA's guidance on registration issued in June 2010 set guidelines on some procedural aspects of the registration process and also on the information CRAs had to include in their applications according to Annex II of the Regulation. This guidance, frequently cited in the following paragraphs and in Section 3.8 on substantive requirements, will be partially superseded by the regulatory technical standards on the information to be provided by a CRA in its application for registration that the EC will issue according to the amended Article 21 of the Regulation. However, it can be expected that this formal process of transforming former guidance into regulatory technical standards (as required by the Regulation) will not change substantially the provisions in the guidance.

The remainder of this section describes the new registration process as amended in 2011 by the CRA Regulation II.

3.6.2 Scope for Registration

According to Article 14.1 of the Regulation 'a credit rating agency shall apply for registration for the purposes of Article 2 (1) provided that it is a legal person established in the Community'.

The registration of a CRA will enable ESMA to verify that the applicant complies with all the requirements set out in the Regulation at the point of registration and thereafter to conduct regular examinations to ensure compliance on an ongoing basis. ESMA's monitoring should contribute to improving the integrity of registered CRAs, the quality of their ratings, and their accountability to investors.

It is important to highlight that EU legislators, even in the previous supervisory system of national competent authorities, opted for requiring a single registration for each CRA. Thus, they avoided replicating the traditional home-host and passporting system that is envisaged in many of the EU rules dealing with securities markets (for example, Prospectus Directive).

Consequently, Article 14.2 of the Regulation provides that the registration of a CRA shall be effective for the entire territory of the EU once the registration decision adopted by ESMA has taken effect. Therefore, a decision by ESMA is valid in all EU Member States. Once a CRA has been registered, its ratings are in compliance with Community law without any need for additional administrative procedures in any Member State.

3.6.3 Registration Process

3.6.3.1 Introduction

Paragraphs 4 and 5 of Article 14 stipulate that:

> Without prejudice to Articles 16 or 17, ESMA shall register the credit rating agency if
> it concludes from the examination of the application that the credit rating agency

complies with the conditions for the issuing of credit ratings set out in this Regulation, taking into consideration Articles 4 and 6.

ESMA shall not impose requirements regarding registration which are not provided for in this Regulation.

These paragraphs aim to provide an objective and transparent process to apply for registration and establish a maximum harmonization regime that protects CRAs against the risk of different approaches by EU supervisors (that were in charge of the registration process and supervision before ESMA took them over) and now shields them from the risk of possible arbitrary requests from ESMA.

3.6.3.2 Application for Registration

According to Article 15.1 of the Regulation, 'the credit rating agency shall submit an application for registration to ESMA. The application shall contain information on the matters set out in Annex II'.

Purpose

The purpose of the application is to provide ESMA with the relevant information to determine whether an applicant should be granted registration, in accordance with Article 14.4.

To this end, in addition to the disclosures required by Annex II, ESMA expects applicants to provide accompanying explanations on how they meet each requirement as set out in the Regulation. Furthermore, ESMA retains the ability to ask for any information submitted to be verified in a manner directed by it (ESMA's guidance on registration).

In the USA, the application serves additionally to provide information about a CRA to users of credit ratings. To achieve this goal, CRAs registered as NRSROs must make an important part of the application publicly available within 10 working days after registration is granted. The EU approach is different; as pointed out by ESMA in its guidance on registration, the information submitted as part of an application for registration will only be used by ESMA to discharge its responsibilities and shall remain confidential.

Nevertheless, the Regulation requires CRAs to disclose to the public some of their policies and internal processes, achieving to some extent, although in a less straightforward way, the same goal as the US legislation (see Section 3.8.6).

Form

Although neither the CRA Regulation nor ESMA's guidance prescribes a form for the application or a mandatory order of the items, it would be desirable that the documents submitted followed the structure laid down in Section VIII of ESMA's guidance on registration, as this would greatly facilitate the processing of the application by supervisors. If applicants do not follow this order, they should at least submit a cross-reference list of all the documents evidencing compliance with the Regulation against the relevant requirements in the order set out in ESMA's guidance. Regarding the format of the application, ESMA considers that applications should be submitted electronically, to speed the processing of the applications.

General guidelines about the information to be submitted by applicants

The information that applicants have to submit for registration is listed in Annex II of the CRA Regulation and includes the following items:

1. Full name of the credit rating agency, address of the registered office within the Community.
2. Name and contact details of a contact person and of the compliance officer.
3. Legal status.
4. Class of credit ratings for which the credit rating agency is applying to be registered.
5. Ownership structure.
6. Organizational structure and corporate governance.
7. Financial resources to perform credit rating activities.
8. Staffing of credit rating agency and its expertise.
9. Information regarding subsidiaries of the credit rating agency.
10. Description of the procedures and methodologies used to issue and review credit ratings.
11. Policies and procedures to identify, manage, and disclose any conflicts of interest.
12. Information regarding rating analysts.
13. Compensation and performance evaluation arrangements.
14. Services other than credit rating activities, which the credit rating agency intends to provide.
15. Programme of operations, including indications of where the main business activities are expected to be carried out, branches to be established, and setting out the type of business envisaged.
16. Documents and detailed information relating to the expected use of endorsement.
17. Documents and detailed information relating to the expected outsourcing arrangements, including information on entities assuming outsourcing functions.

ESMA's guidance provides details on the above requirements with the aim of helping applicants understand what specific disclosures should be included under each of the items. Full details regarding the information that ESMA would expect to receive as part of an application for registration can be consulted in Section VIII of ESMA's guidance on registration. In addition, commentary on the detailed information to be submitted by applicants is included in Section 3.8 when analysing each relevant substantive requirement of the Regulation.

Besides the detailed guidance on each item, ESMA included in the guidance on registration some general remarks that are applicable across different areas of the application. First, where an applicant does not submit specific information required in the guidance, a clear explanation for the omission should be provided. This should include how compliance with the relevant requirement is otherwise being met and evidenced. Second, the submission of the information required by ESMA's guidance does not preclude further information requests or on-site inspections by ESMA. ESMA might request interviews with any employee of the applicant during the registration process (such as senior management or compliance officer).

Finally, ESMA's guidance on registration requires applicants to provide a number of policies and procedures. This means the submission of the relevant policy documentation (a mere description of a policy is not sufficient). In addition, the policies and procedures must indicate the persons responsible for their approval and maintenance; how compliance will be enforced and monitored and the persons responsible for this; the measures undertaken in the event of a breach; and the procedures, if any, for reporting to ESMA a material breach of the Regulation.

Applications from Groups of CRAs

According to Article 15.2 of the Regulation, where a group of CRAs applies for registration, the members of the group shall mandate one of their members to submit all the applications to ESMA on behalf of the group. The mandated CRA shall provide the information required for each member of the group (see Section 3.3.3 for the definition of 'group of rating agencies').

The mandated CRA shall provide just one submission for the whole group containing a breakdown of Annex II disclosures by each CRA member of the group. The submission shall clearly set out the different applicants and the information related to each member of the group should not be mixed up with the information related to the other members.

Accordingly, the application pack for groups must include a formal application for each of the applicants, a general part including all the disclosures that are common to all the CRAs belonging to the group, and separate sections with the specific disclosures for each of the applicants (ESMA's guidance on registration).

Finally, where the applicant conducts, either directly or through subsidiaries, non-rating activities (ancillary or other services) it has to provide information on those non-rating activities only when specifically required by ESMA's guidance. For example, applicants have to provide the revenue generated over the past three years by the ancillary services and by the non-rating activities as a proportion of total revenue (irrespective of whether the ancillary and non-rating business is performed directly by the applicant or by any of its subsidiaries).

Language of the Application and of the Disclosures Imposed on CRAs

According to Article 15.3 of the Regulation,

> A credit rating agency shall submit its application in any of the official languages of the institutions of the Union. The provisions of Regulation No 1 of 15 April 1958 determining the languages to be used by the European Economic Community (*) shall apply *mutatis mutandis* to any other communication between ESMA and the credit rating agencies and their staff.

The above-mentioned Regulation establishes that the official languages and the working languages of the institutions of the EU are Bulgarian, Czech, Danish,

Dutch, English, Estonian, Finnish, French, German, Greek, Hungarian, Irish, Italian, Latvian, Lithuanian, Maltese, Polish, Portuguese, Romanian, Slovak, Slovenian, Spanish, and Swedish.

Also according to this Regulation, documents which a person subject to the jurisdiction of a Member State sends to institutions of the Community may be drafted in any of the official languages selected by the sender. The reply shall be drafted in the same language. Documents which an institution of the Community sends to a person subject to the jurisdiction of a Member State shall be drafted in the language of such State.

Therefore, CRAs may choose the language of the Member State where they are incorporated not only for drawing up their applications for registration, but also for all interaction with ESMA during the registration process.

The Regulation does not clearly establish a language regime for the disclosures registered CRAs have to make public (for example, rating announcements or disclosures about their policies and internal processes). However, following the rationale of the language regime set for the application of registration and considering the last sentence of Article 15.3, it can be interpreted that CRAs can use any of the official languages of the institutions of the Union to comply with the disclosure and presentation requirements imposed by the Regulation (Annex I Sections D and E).

This is an odd outcome, taking into account the rationale for entrusting ESMA with the supervision of rating activities in the EU (the pan-European structure and impact of the credit rating activities, as stated in Recital 23 of the CRA Regulation II) and the precedents in Community legislation; for example, the Prospectus Directive requires for cross-border public offers of securities a prospectus drawn up in a language customary in the sphere of international finance. Although not explicitly mentioned in the EU Directives for political reasons, this language is widely understood to be English.

Prior to the CRA Regulation II, ESMA discussed the language regime and in its guidelines on CEREP it required CRAs to submit any qualitative information in 'a language customary in the sphere of international finance'. More explicitly, ESMA's guidance on registration stated that CRAs should submit information to the central repository only in English. However, for the rest of disclosure requirements, ESMA's guidance on registration considered that local CRAs established only in one Member State could publish and provide the information exclusively in their local language. Both sets of guidelines, issued in June 2010, predate Article 15.3 of the Regulation, introduced by the CRA Regulation II. Therefore, any ESMA provision requiring English as the only acceptable language should be considered repealed by the CRA Regulation II. Global CRAs use English for all their communications. However, the language regime established in the Regulation can make a positive difference for small local CRAs but, at the same time, will complicate ESMA's work and investors' (at least professional ones) understanding of the information published by the CRAs that do not choose English.

Calendar

The Regulation does not define the term 'working day' and does not refer to a relevant calendar to use for the purpose of the Regulation. The guidelines issued by ESMA before ESMA was granted exclusive powers on CRAs recommended as the best option the calendar defined by the European Central Bank for the operation of the TARGET system (Guideline of the ECB of 26 April 2007—ECB/2007/2). Had ESMA not issued that guidance, different calendars—those of the different competent authorities—would have coexisted for the registration of the CRAs that existed when CRA Regulation entered into force. Once ESMA became the sole authority responsible for the registration and ongoing supervision of CRAs it could be argued that the relevant calendar to count the different deadlines set in the Regulation should be that of the Member State where ESMA sits (France). Nonetheless, the TARGET calendar should be the applicable one unless ESMA's new draft regulatory technical standards provide another interpretation of the term 'working day' that supersedes ESMA's guidance on registration.

3.6.3.3 ESMA's Analysis of Completeness of the Application

The Regulation envisages a first step in the application process that is the assessment of completeness of the application by ESMA. Article 15.4 stipulates that 'within 20 working days of receipt of the application, ESMA shall assess whether the application is complete'.

The completeness check should focus exclusively on identifying whether all the items of information required by Annex II of the Regulation have been included in the application and should not entail an analysis of the content of the information supplied (according to ESMA's guidance on registration).

If after the 20-day period of examining completeness, ESMA concludes that there are obvious pieces of information that the applicant has not provided, the authority shall set a deadline by which the applicant must provide the missing information. In setting the deadline, the guidance on registration indicates that ESMA will take into consideration the amount and type of information being requested. Normally a time frame of up to 20 working days should be sufficient. This time frame will start from receipt by the CRA of the notification from ESMA.

Once the applicant submits the additional information requested, ESMA will assess whether the response contains the required information. The Regulation does not prescribe a time period for this review. Following ESMA's guidance, it seems appropriate to consider that a new period for assessment of completeness commences and, therefore, ESMA would have an additional period of up to a maximum of 20 working days since the day of receipt of the additional information—ESMA's guidance reference to 25 days should be understood now as 20 days following the amendment introduced by the CRA Regulation II.

3.6.3.4 ESMA's Examination of Compliance with the Regulation

Once the examination of completeness of the application has taken place and the completeness has been notified to the applicant, ESMA has to examine the documents and information received. At this stage, ESMA has to do an in-depth analysis of the content of the information supplied to determine whether or not the CRA (and each of the CRAs in cases of groups) complies with all the requirements set in the Regulation. This might entail seeking clarification over the information provided, requesting the amendment of the submitted policies, or requiring information or the creation of new policies or procedures to meet the requirements of the Regulation.

As the time limits set by the Regulation for ESMA to adopt a final decision are quite tight, it is necessary for ESMA to receive a complete initial application before the time periods begin to run. It seems that the SEC is in a better position than ESMA as its time frames are longer. In fact, the time period the SEC has to decide whether to grant or deny an initial application for registration is 90 days after the date on which the application form for registration is deemed to be complete and properly executed—or a longer period if the applicant consents.

ESMA has less time to decide whether to grant or refuse registration. According to Articles 16 and 17 of the Regulation, after examining all the information, ESMA must adopt a fully reasoned registration or refusal decision within 45 working days (55 working days in case of applications of a group) from the date it notifies the applicant that the application is complete. The decision adopted by ESMA on the registration or refusal 'shall take effect on the fifth working day following its adoption'.

ESMA is entitled to extend this period by 15 working days, up to 60 days (70 days in case of applications of a group of CRAs), in particular if the applicant, or any of them in the case of a group, envisages endorsing credit ratings, using outsourcing, or requests exemption from compliance with certain requirements in accordance with Article 6.3. Examination of compliance in case endorsement or exemptions are envisaged will certainly require significant extra time. This is less clear regarding outsourcing, especially where the outsourcing arrangements refer to unimportant operational functions. Finally, although the Regulation only mentions these three examples, ESMA could prolong the period in other circumstances that might justify an extended period.

ESMA's Q&A has considered how the refusal of a small office exemption (Article 6.3) would affect the timetable for registration. If, for example, the exemption in relation to the compliance function is turned down, the applicant will need time to set up such a function and have it operational by the time registration is granted. ESMA examined some options to give applicants sufficient time to implement the requirement, such as extending the timetable for registration or granting registration conditional on the implementation of the compliance function within a certain deadline established for the CRA.

However, ESMA concluded that it could provide the applicant more time to establish the required function only if the refusal is decided during the completeness period. If the time allotted in Article 15.4 has expired, ESMA considers that there is no further possibility for providing a CRA with additional time.

Given the purpose of the completeness assessment, it seems unlikely that ESMA could reach the conclusion that the request for an exemption should be denied during the completeness period. But at least informal input to the applicant about their request should be desirable. Otherwise the CRA would be in a risky position in the event that the exemption was denied during the examination phase.

In order to address this risk, CRAs also suggested to ESMA a possible system of pre-approval for certain issues (not only for exemptions, but also governance or rotation requirements) prior to the receipt of the formal application. ESMA ruled out in its Q&A any form of official pre-approval, although it accepted the possibility of providing informal comments to any CRA's proposal prior to the submission of the application.

3.6.4 Withdrawal of Registration

There are several circumstances where ESMA has to withdraw the registration of a CRA. In particular, Article 20 of the Regulation deals with four situations where a CRA will cease to be registered. Regarding certified CRAs, this article 'shall apply *mutatis mutandis* to certified credit rating agencies and to credit ratings issued by them' (Article 5.8). Withdrawal proceedings may be triggered not only by ESMA but also by national competent authorities—and by the CRA itself in case of voluntary withdrawal. A national competent authority may be aware that a CRA whose ratings are used in its territory is under any of the cases for withdrawal laid down in Article 20. The Regulation provides this national authority with the possibility of requesting ESMA to examine whether the conditions for the withdrawal of the registration (or certification) are met. If ESMA decides not to withdraw the registration (or certification) of the CRA concerned, it shall provide full reasons.

The immediate consequence of ESMA's decision to withdraw a registration or a certification of a CRA, for any reason, is that the CRA will have to stop its rating activity immediately, as it will not be able to operate in the EU without being registered or certified. According to Article 20.3 'the decision on the withdrawal of registration shall take immediate effect throughout the Union'. However, the Regulation envisages a transitional period in Article 24.4 to avoid the possible negative impact on EU entities using for regulatory purposes the ratings issued by a CRA whose registration or certification is being withdrawn. The Regulation stipulates that the ratings of these entities may continue to be used for regulatory purposes during a period not exceeding ten working days (from the date that the withdrawal decision is made public) if there are ratings from other registered CRAs available or three months if that is not the case (see Section 3.7).

3.6.4.1 Voluntary Withdrawal

The first situation envisaged in Article 20 is the voluntary withdrawal when a CRA expressly renounces the registration. So far, ESMA has not developed a process that CRAs have to follow to request the voluntary withdrawal of registration. The US rules also envisage the possibility of a voluntary withdrawal and request that the NRSRO submit a written notice of the withdrawal to the SEC, using a specific form. The withdrawal from registration will become effective 45 calendar days after the notice is provided to the SEC upon the terms and conditions that the SEC may establish as necessary in the public interest or for the protection of investors.

3.6.4.2 Withdrawal due to Inactivity of the CRA

The second case for the withdrawal of registration is when a CRA 'has provided no credit ratings for the preceding six months'. Although the wording of the provision refers to ratings provided, it should be interpreted as complete inactivity of the registered agency. Therefore, if a CRA does not provide new ratings but keeps monitoring existing ones, it would not, in principle, make sense to withdraw the registration, as the rationale behind this provision is to avoid having as registered CRAs entities that no longer operate as such. However, the drafting of the provision seems to be quite strict by setting a six-month period. The US legislation also allows the SEC to withdraw registration as NRSRO when it finds out that the entity 'is no longer in existence or has ceased to do business as a credit rating agency' but does not set a specific time period.

Article 20 does not regulate the procedure ESMA should follow for deciding a withdrawal of registration. As this decision would put a CRA out of business, ESMA considered in its guidance on registration that it is important to provide CRAs 'with sufficient notification of withdrawal proceedings being initiated, with the possibility to provide additional evidence and information and with an appropriate mechanism for challenging the decision to withdraw its registration'. As discussed below, withdrawal decisions adopted as a supervisory measure must follow the procedural rules laid down in Article 23e.

3.6.4.3 *Withdrawal due to Supervisory Measures*

Article 20 also envisages withdrawal of registration when the CRA has 'obtained the registration by making false statements or by any other irregular means'; in these circumstances, registration should not have been granted in the first place so the withdrawal of the registration is the immediate consequence. In addition, ESMA shall withdraw registration of a CRA if it 'no longer meets the conditions under which it was registered'. As explained before, all the conditions that are examined at the moment of registration have to be fulfilled on an ongoing basis. Should this not be the case, the CRA can no longer be registered.

Actually, the last two cases of withdrawal of registration should be construed as supervisory measures that should be adopted by ESMA according to Article 24— they would amount to a breach of the Regulation. This means that the withdrawal decision should be taken in accordance with the procedural rules set out in Article 23e (see Section 3.7).

3.6.5 Notification and Publication

According to Article 18, once ESMA makes a decision on registration, refusal to register, or withdrawal of registration of a CRA, it has to communicate such a decision to interested parties.

First, ESMA shall notify its decision to the CRA concerned within five working days of the adoption of such decision. When ESMA refuses to register or withdraws the registration of a CRA 'it shall provide full reasons in its decision'. Regarding certified CRAs, ESMA's guidance on registration considers that, although not expressly mentioned, the provisions in Article 18 on notification of the decisions on registration, refusal, and withdrawal would also apply to certification of CRAs.

In addition, ESMA has to communicate its decision to the European Commission, EBA, EIOPA, the national competent authorities, and the sectoral competent authorities.

Finally, the Regulation also considers it necessary that users of ratings are aware of ESMA's decisions. Therefore, it requires ESMA to publish on its website a list of CRAs registered in accordance with the Regulation that shall be updated within five working days following the adoption of a decision to register or withdraw a registration. Moreover, the EC shall publish that updated list in the Official Journal of the European Union within 30 days following such an update. Article

18.3 only obliges ESMA to publish the list of registered CRAs; therefore, decisions to refuse an application for registration do not have to be published (although ESMA could decide to do so).

Market participants will know the CRAs that are registered through ESMA's website. The time frame for including a new registered CRA in ESMA's list (within five working days from the adoption of the decision) has been aligned with the moment when such decision takes effect, that is on the fifth working day following its adoption (Articles 16.4 and 17.4). Consequently, market participants will be informed in a timely manner.

Regarding the publication of withdrawal decisions, it is noteworthy that withdrawals constituting supervisory measures are to be published within ten days (according to Article 24.5) whilst the rest of withdrawals must be published within five days from the date the decision is adopted. In any case, the transitional period for the use of the ratings of the CRA concerned—envisaged in order to give some time for EU entities to stop using for regulatory purposes the ratings of the CRA whose registration has been withdrawn—will start counting down from the date ESMA updates the list of registered CRAs on its website.

3.6.6 Material Changes to Initial Conditions

Article 14.3 of the Regulation prescribes that a registered CRA 'shall comply at all times with the conditions for initial registration'. A CRA must demonstrate that it is compliant with the Regulation at the point of application in order for the registration to be granted and thereafter on an ongoing basis. To facilitate ESMA's ongoing supervision, the second subparagraph of Article 14.3 obliges the CRAs to notify ESMA, without undue delay, 'of any material changes to the conditions for initial registration, including any opening or closing of a branch within the Union'. In addition, an infringement is envisaged if the CRA does not notify (or does not do so in a timely manner) any material changes (Annex III, II, item 6).

US rules require NRSROs to provide the SEC with an annual certification attesting that the information submitted in the application form continues to be accurate, and providing a list of material changes to the information or documents in the application that occurred during the previous calendar year. The EU Regulation does not contain such a periodic requirement. Instead, registered CRAs are obliged to notify of any material changes to the conditions for initial registration as soon as the change happens.

What is a Material Change?

The key issue is to determine what a 'material change' is. ESMA's guidance on registration considers that a material change is any change that may affect the substantive information submitted in the application and, in any event, all changes that may affect compliance with the requirements of the CRA Regulation. Besides the 'opening and closing of branches' already envisaged in Article 14.3, Recital 52 of the Regulation provides two additional examples: significant changes in the endorsement regime, and in the outsourcing arrangements. In addition, according to ESMA, material changes to the following circumstances, among others, could fall under Article 14.3:

MATERIAL CHANGES (non-exh)

- Legal form, including business combinations.
- Type of business activities.
- Class and type of credit ratings.
- Ownership structure: acquisition or disposal of holdings above 10% known to the agency.
- Administrative and/or supervisory board; compliance and review function.
- Procedures and methodologies used to issue and review credit ratings.
- Financial resources.

Procedure with ESMA

The Regulation requires CRAs to notify 'material changes' instead of proposed changes, suggesting that prior authorization of the changes by ESMA is not required. This approach, however, would not always make sense. In practice, there are different types of material changes. Some of them relate to the normal business life of the CRA, such as the opening of a branch or a change in the ownership structure. While it is important that supervisors are aware of these developments in order to understand the business, a vetting procedure does not seem necessary. Nevertheless, it would be prudent to consult with ESMA before implementing changes that could affect compliance with the requirements of the Regulation.

PRIOR PROCEDURE OF APPROVAL

However, there are other cases where a prior procedure of approval seems necessary. Where the registered CRA wants to start issuing ratings of a new class or type or wishes to endorse ratings from another third country CRA not envisaged in the initial application, ESMA should follow the same procedure as designed for the initial registration. Only this procedure will enable the authority to be satisfied that the requirements set out in Article 4.3 are complied with regarding endorsement or that the CRA has the appropriate resources, methodologies, and processes to issue a new class or type of ratings.

ESMA stated in its guidance on registration that it is currently analysing what procedure ESMA should carry out in the case of notifications of material changes to the conditions for initial registration. However, at the time of writing, ESMA has not published any guidance on this issue; it would be desirable for ESMA to do so as soon as possible as this lack of clarity about the procedure it follows when receiving notifications of material changes gives rise to a risk of inconsistencies and uneven treatment to different CRAs.

How will changes be vetted CRA?

3.7 SUPERVISION AND ENFORCEMENT

3.7.1 Introduction

3.7.1.1 Background

An essential element of the CRA Regulation was the introduction of an external monitoring regime whereby CRAs were to be supervised in the EU for the first time. The CRA Regulation introduced a system of supervision based on colleges of competent authorities of the Member States, which gave the possibility to all concerned competent authorities of participating in the process of supervision of CRAs; nevertheless, due to legal reasons the final decision was always taken by the competent authority of the home Member State. National competent authorities of the different Member States were invested with the necessary supervisory and investigatory powers. In addition, the Regulation envisaged a set of supervisory measures that competent authorities could take when a registered CRA breached the provisions of the Regulation and requested Member States to lay down the rules on penalties applicable to infringements of the Regulation.

However, this college-based supervision was already envisaged as temporary (see Section 3.2). The CRA Regulation II was mainly designed to change this structure and concentrate the supervisory powers over CRAs in ESMA.

3.7.1.2 EC Proposal on CRA Regulation II

In June 2010, the EC published a proposal to amend the CRA Regulation (EC proposal CRA Regulation II) with the aim of 'securing effective supervision of CRAs in the EU; streamlining the supervisory architecture for the CRA industry and ensuring legal certainty for CRAs and market participants'. To meet these objectives the EC impact assessment CRA Regulation II compared the consequences of maintaining the supervisory framework as provided by the CRA Regulation (substituting references to CESR by references to ESMA) versus changing to a system of a centralized monitoring of CRAs in the EU.

Under the option that ESMA would assume general competence in matters relating to ongoing supervision of registered CRAs, the EC distinguished two alternative scenarios: ESMA's authority would be limited to the supervision of groups of CRAs with a legal presence in more than one Member State; or ESMA would be the sole supervisor of all EU-based CRAs.

The EC concluded that the best alternative to fulfil the objectives mentioned above was to set a framework in which ESMA assumed exclusive supervisory powers over all CRAs in the EU, and therefore it should be entrusted with appropriate authority to investigate breaches of the legislation.

Moreover, an effective sanctioning regime had to be introduced to ensure an effective supervision. But the question remained as to how to articulate the sanctioning regime. In any case, it would be within the remit of ESMA to determine whether a CRA had breached the provisions of the Regulation; but once an infringement had been determined, there were three possible alternatives. The decision on imposing a fine could be taken by the national competent authority of the Member State in which the CRA was established, by ESMA, or by the European Commission.

After disregarding the first alternative because of the risk of creating an unlevel playing field within the EU, the EC opted for the third, arguing that the option to entrust ESMA with sanctioning powers 'could raise some concerns of consistency with the Community acquis and notably the jurisprudence of the Court of Justice of the European Union in the Meroni case'.

As explained by the EC impact assessment CRA Regulation II, according to the Meroni case:[41]

> agencies/authorities may not be delegated the power to take decisions which require difficult choices in reconciling various objectives laid down in the Treaty amounting to the execution of actual economic policy. On the other hand, clearly defined executive powers can be delegated to an agency including powers, that involve the need to interpret Community law provisions to determine their application and which leave the authority a certain margin of appreciation in applying these rules.

Therefore, according to the principles underlying this case, a delegation of powers would be permissible where it involves clearly defined executive powers, the exercise of which can be subject to strict review in the light of objective criteria determined by the delegating authority. However, a delegation of powers would not be permissible where it involves a discretionary power, implying a wide margin of discretion which, according to the use that is made of it, may make possible the execution of actual economic policy (economic policy is to be understood as an EU policy).

In particular, the main concerns raised were in relation to giving ESMA the power to impose fines or periodic penalty payments. It was understood that this power is an exercise of a discretionary power as it entails discretion as to whether or not to impose a fine or a periodic penalty payment on a CRA and discretion as to what the level of the pecuniary sanction should be.

In view of the jurisprudence of the Court of Justice of the European Union, the EC opted for a middle point option. Therefore, the EC proposal CRA Regulation II entrusted ESMA with exclusive monitoring powers over CRAs and granted ESMA powers to request information, to launch investigations, and perform on-site inspections, but entrusted the EC, on a recommendation from ESMA, with pecuniary sanctioning powers.

3.7.1.3 Negotiations at the European Council and Parliament

During the negotiations of the CRA Regulation II, the split of sanctioning powers between ESMA and the EC was heavily criticized because it established a system that undermined ESMA as single regulatory authority and created confusion and regulatory uncertainty for CRAs.

The strong support for giving ESMA the full panoply of supervisory authority brought substantial modifications to the EC's proposal to entrust ESMA with sanctioning powers but complying with the *Meroni Case* requirements. Therefore, the main amendments made during the negotiations were aimed at limiting as much as possible the discretion that ESMA would have when setting fines.

Consequently, the following safeguards were included in the Regulation:

- a list of infringements of the provisions of the CRA Regulation that can be enforced by fines when the CRA acts intentionally or negligently;

[41] Judgment of the Court of 13 June 1958.—*Meroni & Co., Industrie Metallurgiche, SpA v High Authority of the European Coal and Steel Community.*—Case 9–56. The *Meroni Case* has been endorsed in several occasions by the Community judicature (Joint Cases T-369/94 and T-85/95, Case C-301/02, Joint Cases C-154/04 and C-155/04).

- minimum and maximum amounts of fines for each breach, taking into account the gravity of the infringement committed and the effect on the ratings issued by the CRA;
- objective parameters (aggravating and mitigating factors) to be taken into account by ESMA in determining the amount of the fine;
- procedural rules for taking supervisory actions and imposing fines;
- a requirement for ESMA to fully respect the principle of proportionality and fundamental rights when exercising sanctioning powers; and
- the review of ESMA's decisions on fines and periodic penalty payments by the Court of Justice of the European Union.

The following sections will analyse the supervisory structure set out in the CRA Regulation II.

3.7.2 Supervision by ESMA

3.7.2.1 Ongoing Supervision

ESMA is entrusted with the supervision of the activities of the registered CRAs in the EU. As explained in ESMA's guidance on enforcement, this duty covers not only investigatory activities, but also any practices and activities that ESMA may undertake to monitor CRAs on an ongoing basis. Where the ongoing monitoring discovers potential breaches of the Regulation, further investigation will be required, the scope of which will depend on the specific nature of the potential breach.

Normally, national authorities in charge of the monitoring of the securities market adopt a risk-based approach to supervision. This means that the supervised entities are assessed and classified according to the impact an infringement would have on the markets and also according to the probability of occurrence of significant breaches. On the basis of this risk categorization, authorities determine the assessment cycle in which compliance by the supervised entity with the requirements is assessed. Article 40a.6 of the Regulation (as amended by CRA Regulation II) requires ESMA to conduct by July 2014 'at least one verification of all credit rating agencies falling under its supervisory competences'.

According to national securities supervisors' usual practice, ESMA's ongoing supervision should typically include desk-based periodic reviews and more intrusive inspections. ESMA's sources of information to conduct its supervision would normally be the following:

- information provided by CRAs in their application for registration and any subsequent notifications of material changes to the conditions for initial registration;
- lists of clients and ratings to be provided annually by CRAs (Annex I.E.II.2);
- records that CRAs are required to maintain according to the Regulation;
- information provided by market participants or national competent authorities; and
- periodic information required by ESMA and ad hoc requests.

Regarding the last item, ESMA will typically require CRAs to provide a set of standard information and data as part of ongoing supervision. Some information will be required on a regular basis and other information will be required on an ad hoc basis if significant issues arise or in the case of any potential breach of the Regulation. In particular, ESMA's guidance on enforcement distinguished the following types of data that would be requested on a periodic basis:

- operational data: ratings updates (including withdrawals), new issuances, outcome of methodologies reviews, internal control reviews, financial data, information on staff turnover, data on changes of location of lead analysts, and outsourcing arrangements; and

- compliance data: updated work plan, identification and mitigation of potential and actual conflicts of interests or breaches of the Regulation, compliance reports, internal audit or risk reports produced by the CRA, and board minutes, where relevant.

In addition, as part of the ongoing supervision, ESMA will organize regular and ad hoc meetings with key staff (chairman; independent directors of the administrative/supervisory board; senior management; compliance chief officer, etc.) to have a good understanding of how each CRA operates and to gain insight into the areas that may present risks.

Article 21.4.(e) of the CRA Regulation requires ESMA, by seven months after the entry into force of the Regulation, to prepare draft regulatory technical standards for endorsement by the Commission on 'the content and format of ratings data periodic reporting to be requested from the credit rating agencies for the ongoing supervision by ESMA'. Therefore, on these aspects, ESMA will soon be revising prior guidance published by CESR.

Finally, it is worth noting that Article 22a of the Regulation expressly requests ESMA to examine regularly one requirement: the back-testing of methodologies included in Article 8.3 (see Section 3.8.4). It is questionable why the Regulation has singled out this requirement. Peculiar provisions in Community legislation like this one are usually the result of an odd compromise between EU legislators. In this case, it probably reflects the tension between those wanting ESMA to pass judgement on the accuracy of CRAs' methodologies and those who want the authority to simply verify that CRAs have robust processes in place to produce their methodologies and that they apply them consistently.

3.7.2.2 Scope

A key element in the supervisory structure is the determination of the scope of ESMA's monitoring activity, the understanding of 'scope' being the persons that are subject to the supervisory powers of the authority. This means that the persons included in the scope might be subject to ESMA's investigations. To this end, these persons must, for example, submit to on-site inspections or to requests for information. They can also be summoned to ESMA's premises for oral or written explanations on the matter being investigated. Failure to provide the information required might lead ESMA to impose periodic penalty payments—and fines if the information provided is misleading or incorrect—on the relevant entities or individuals.

Entities and Persons in the Scope

The CRA Regulation has included a very broad scope for ESMA's powers to ensure that ESMA can perform its duties appropriately. According to Article 23b.1, ESMA can exercise its supervisory powers over 'credit rating agencies, persons involved in credit rating activities, rated entities and related third parties, third parties to whom the credit rating agencies have outsourced operational functions or activities and persons otherwise closely and substantially related or connected to credit rating agencies or credit rating activities'.

Recital 13 of CRA Regulation II further clarifies that the latter group of persons covers, for instance, 'staff of a credit rating agency who are not directly involved in rating activities but who, due to their function within the credit rating agency, may hold important information on a specific case. Firms which have provided services to the credit rating agency may also fall into that category.'

As discussed in the remainder of this section, the power to request information, initiate investigations, or undertake on-site inspections can be exercised over all the persons included in the scope. However, the sanctioning regime is mainly envisaged just for CRAs, except in the case of periodic penalties payments that can also be applied on other persons under the scope to oblige them to submit to a request of information, an investigation, or an on-site inspection decided by ESMA.

Entities out of the Scope: Users of Ratings

The entities using the credit ratings are not subject to ESMA's powers. According to Article 25a, 'sectoral competent authorities shall be responsible for the supervision and enforcement of Article 4(1) in accordance with the relevant sectoral legislation'. This means that, as explained in Recital 9 of CRA Regulation II, ESMA is not responsible for the monitoring of the users of credit ratings. Users of ratings should be supervised by 'competent authorities designated under the relevant sectoral legislation for the supervision of the credit institutions, investment firms, insurance undertakings, assurance undertakings, reinsurance undertakings, undertakings for collective investment in transferable securities (UCITS), institutions for occupational retirement provision and alternative investment funds'.

Moreover, according to Article 36 of the Regulation, 'Member States shall lay down the rules on penalties applicable to the infringements of Article 4(1) and shall take all measures necessary to ensure that they are implemented. The penalties provided for shall be effective, proportionate and dissuasive.' In addition, 'Member States shall ensure that the sectoral competent authority disclose to the public every penalty that has been imposed for infringements of Article 4(1), unless such disclosure would seriously jeopardize the financial markets or cause disproportionate damage to the parties involved.'

3.7.2.3 Powers

In order to carry out its duties under the Regulation, ESMA is empowered with all the necessary supervisory and investigatory functions that are exercised in relation to all the persons included in the scope, as explained before. In particular, the Regulation distinguishes in separate articles three broad areas: requests for information (Article 23b), investigations (Article 23c), and on-site inspections (Article 23d).

Request for Information: Simple Request and Formal Request

ESMA (or any ESMA official) may use its power to require information and documents from the persons under the scope of its powers to support both its supervisory and its enforcement functions. This can be done in an informal way, by simple requests, or in a formal way, following a decision. In both cases, to ensure adequate cooperation, ESMA shall forward a copy of the request for information to the competent authority of the Member State in whose territory the person concerned by the request for information is situated (Article 23b.5).

The Regulation indicates the minimum content that the requests have to contain to ensure that the recipients understand the authority's reasons and legal basis: refer to Article 23b of the Regulation as the legal basis of the request; state its purpose; specify what information is required; and set a time limit within which the information is to be provided. In relation to the latter, as delays in the provision of information can have a significant impact on the efficient progression of an investigation, persons requested are expected to respond to information requests in a timely manner to appropriate deadlines.

SIMPLE REQUEST. If ESMA asks for the information by simple request, the person from whom this information is requested is not obliged to provide it. However, in the case of a voluntary reply to the request, the information should be made available without delay and the information provided should not be incorrect or misleading.[42] In these cases, the request has to make clear to the person from whom the information is requested that 'that there is no obligation to provide the information but that any reply to the request for information must not be incorrect or misleading'. In addition, the request will indicate the possible fine that can be imposed in the event that the answers to questions asked are incorrect or misleading. From the above-mentioned requirements, it can be inferred that the request must be in written form (including electronic communications).

FORMAL REQUEST. In cases of formal requests, the letter should also indicate the periodic penalty payments envisaged where the recipient does not answer within the requested time frame or where the answer is incomplete, and the possible fine that can be imposed in the event that the answers to questions asked are incorrect or misleading. Finally, it should indicate the right to appeal the decision before ESMA's Board of Appeal and to have the decision reviewed by the Court of Justice of the European Union.

---

[42] Recital 13 CRA Regulation II.

General Investigations

Article 23c empowers ESMA's officials and other persons authorized by ESMA to conduct all necessary investigations of persons under the scope of its supervisory powers. In particular, the following powers are expressly included in the Regulation:

- examine, and take or obtain certified copies of or extracts from, any records, data, procedures, and any other material relevant to the execution of its tasks, irrespective of the medium on which they are stored. The Regulation is drafted in a very broad way so as to allow ESMA to examine all types of materials as long as they are relevant to the investigation being carried out. This can be understood as including the right to examine any written, printed, or typed matter in the possession, custody or control of the entity or individual; any electronically stored information; and any other data stored in any medium from which information can be retrieved, obtained, or manipulated;

- summon and ask any person under the scope of ESMA's supervisory powers, or their representatives, or their staff, for oral or written explanations on facts or documents related to the subject matter and purpose of the inspection and record the answers;

- interview any other natural or legal person who consents to be interviewed for the purpose of collecting information relating to the subject matter of an investigation; and

- request records of telephone and data traffic; under this power, ESMA will be authorized to obtain information that will normally include name, address, telephone connection records, or records of session times and durations, and telephone number or other subscriber number or identity. The requirement of telephone and data traffic records is a sensitive aspect that in some EU countries is directly linked to fundamental rights issues. Therefore, in case authorization from a judicial authority is necessary according to national rules, the Regulation stipulates that ESMA should apply for such authorization (even as a precautionary measure).

On-site Inspections

Normally, ESMA will conduct its examinations through desk reviews and interviews at ESMA's premises. Nevertheless, where necessary to carry out its supervisory functions, the Regulation provides for ESMA to be able to conduct all necessary on-site inspections at the business premises of the legal persons included in the scope of ESMA's powers. Therefore, ESMA's officials and other persons authorized by ESMA 'may enter any business premises and land of the legal persons subject to an investigation decision adopted by ESMA' and shall have all the powers mentioned before for general investigations. In addition, in the context of an on-site inspection, 'they shall also have the power to seal any business premises and books or records for the period of, and to the extent necessary for, the inspection'.

In situations where a person opposes an inspection, as on-site inspections will take place in the territory of the Member State where the entity's premises are located, the Regulation imposes on the competent authority of the Member State concerned the obligation to afford ESMA's officials 'the necessary assistance, requesting, where appropriate, the assistance of the police or of an equivalent enforcement authority, so as to enable them to conduct their on-site inspection'.

If the on-site inspection or the assistance of an enforcement authority requires authorization from a judicial authority according to national rules, such authorization shall be applied for (even as a precautionary measure).

Common Provisions to General Investigations and On-site Inspections

DECISION TO INITIATE AN INVESTIGATION OR ON-SITE INSPECTION. The Regulation contains very detailed rules on the way ESMA should carry out its ongoing supervision. As supervisory activity might lead to the opening of infringement proceedings—when the authority suspects there is a possible breach—EU legislators wanted to ensure that ESMA follows appropriate procedures.

Ongoing supervisory decisions—for example, asking for specific information to evaluate compliance under the annual work plan, reviewing the periodic information submitted by CRAs, or planning of meetings with them—should be made by working-level supervisory staff.

However, decisions to initiate investigations or on-site inspections should be made by one of ESMA's decision-making bodies, as part of the supervisory work plan that will be approved annually. The only decision-making body empowered to approve the annual supervisory work plan—or decisions on whether there has been a breach of the Regulation, supervisory measures, the levying of fines, or periodic penalty payments—is according to ESMA Regulation the Board of Supervisors. Notwithstanding, the Board of Supervisors may delegate specific tasks to internal committees or panels, to the Management Board, or to the Chairperson.

In order for ESMA's officials and other persons authorized by ESMA to start an investigation or inspection and exercise the powers mentioned above, it is necessary to have a written authorization specifying the subject matter and purpose of the investigation or inspection. The authorization shall indicate the possible periodic penalty payments and/or fines (Articles 23c.2 and 23d.3).

As already indicated, the persons under the scope of ESMA's supervisory powers are required to submit to investigations and inspections. The decision to launch an investigation or inspection shall specify the matter and purpose of the action, the possible periodic penalty payments in case of infringements, the legal remedies available under ESMA Regulation (possibility to appeal against the decision to the Board of Appeal according to Article 60 of ESMA Regulation), and the right to have the decision reviewed by the Court of Justice of the European Union. In cases of on-site inspections, it should also indicate the date on which the inspection will begin. However, ESMA may carry out the on-site inspection without prior announcement 'where the proper conduct and efficiency of the inspection so require' (Article 23d.1).

AUTHORIZATION FROM JUDICIAL AUTHORITY. There might be situations arising in the context of a general investigation or an on-site inspection where, according to national rules, an authorization from a judicial authority is warranted. In these circumstances, to avoid excessive interference from national judges, the Regulation clarifies that the national judicial authority shall neither review the necessity for the investigation or inspection nor demand to be provided with the information in ESMA's file, as the lawfulness of ESMA's decision is only subject to review by the Court of Justice of the EU.

However, the national courts can 'control that the ESMA decision is authentic and that the coercive measures envisaged are neither arbitrary nor excessive' having regard to the subject matter of the investigations or inspections. When performing this control, the national judicial authority can request ESMA for detailed explanations that may, in particular, relate to the grounds ESMA has for suspecting that an infringement has taken place, to the seriousness of the suspected infringement, and to the nature of the involvement of the persons subject to the coercive measures.

COOPERATION WITH NATIONAL COMPETENT AUTHORITIES. The Regulation also envisages the need for ESMA to communicate and cooperate with the national competent authority of the Member State in whose territory the investigation or inspection is to be carried out.

In the case of an on-site inspection, ESMA shall take the decision to initiate it after consulting the national competent authority. This consultation gives the possibility of the national authority providing its opinion to ESMA in relation to the convenience of the inspection and serves as an initial contact to ease further cooperation. However, it is ESMA who has the final decision on conducting or not the inspection. In the case of general investigations, prior consultation with the national authority is not necessary, although ESMA might decide to consult to facilitate a possible future involvement of the national authority.

In good time before the investigation or inspection starts, ESMA shall inform the competent authority of the investigation or inspection and of the identity of the authorized persons.

In addition, ESMA might request officials (and authorized or appointed persons) of the national competent authority to assist those authorized persons in carrying out their duties and even request officials of the national competent authority to attend the investigations or the on-site inspections. When requested, national competent authorities should assist ESMA.

Finally, ESMA may also require national authorities to carry out specific investigatory tasks and on-site inspections on its behalf. To this end, national competent authorities (and their staff) shall enjoy the same powers as ESMA (and its officials).

3.7.3 Infringements

The text of the CRA Regulation adopted in September 2009 referred to 'infringements of the provisions of this Regulation' in a generic way but did not contain a specific list of infringements. It was up to each Member State to determine the penalties applicable for the infringements of the provisions and thus the determination of the sanctions for each specific breach was left at national level.

However, in the amendment of the Regulation, Annex III was added to include a detailed list of all possible infringements of the Regulation. This Annex, contrary to the rest of the annexes in the Regulation, may not, according to Article 37, be amended by the EC by means of delegated acts.

As explained previously, it was necessary to include, one by one, all the possible breaches of the provisions of the Regulation to respect the requirements deriving from the *Meroni Case*. Moreover, a careful assessment of the nature of each individual infringement was needed to determine the respective fining level and avoid an open discretionary power for ESMA. As the understanding of the *Meroni Case* required a quasi-automatic imposition of fines, the Regulation had to include a list of all the offences worded in a clear way and limiting the degree of ESMA's subjective judgement.

Consequently, Annex III lists a total of 73 infringements of the Regulation, dividing them into three broad categories: 54 infringements related to conflicts of interest, organizational, or operational requirements; 8 infringements related to obstacles to the supervisory activities; and 11 infringements related to disclosure provisions.

Among the list of infringements, there are some where the CRA is required to ensure the behaviour of individuals. For example, a CRA will breach the Regulation if it does not ensure that a rating analyst does not take up a key management position with the rated entity within six months of the credit rating. As CRAs cannot ensure that individuals will not take those actions, it does not seem appropriate to penalize them for actions that are out of their control. These types of breaches could have been drafted in a different way, for example, making the breaches related to a failure of the CRAs to take efforts to educate, monitor, and take dissuasive action against individuals that breach those requirements and report any incidents of concern.

3.7.4 Sanctioning Regime

3.7.4.1 Introduction

The sanctioning regime included in the Regulation is a direct consequence of the need to create an effective system within which ESMA can fully deploy its supervisory powers. In fact, one of the objectives of the CRA Regulation II was to set a full sanctioning regime with sufficiently deterrent and effectively applied sanctions.[43] Obviously, the sanctioning regime of the CRA Regulation involves only the assessment of the individual behaviour of specific CRAs, but does not encompass the assessment of the functioning of the market or the market behaviour of the CRAs.

The effectiveness of a regulatory system depends to a significant extent on maintaining an open and cooperative relationship between the supervisor and the regulated entities. Therefore, ESMA should strive to create a fluent cooperation with CRAs to try to minimize the need for imposing sanctions. However, when ESMA has to use its sanctioning powers, the penalties should be effective, proportionate, and dissuasive to meet the main objectives of any sanctioning regime: have the deterrent effect to keep at bay the risk that CRAs breach the

---

[43] The financial crisis has also spurred other EU initiatives regarding the issue of sanctions. In particular, the EC has published a Communication that considers the need for further convergence of sanctions applied by the Member States in the whole of financial sector legislation.

provisions of the Regulation; ensure that once an offence has been committed, sanctions are strong enough to change the behaviour of the CRA that has committed the infringement and to deter future non-compliance by others; eliminate any financial gain or benefit from non-compliance; and where appropriate, remedy the harm caused by the non-compliance and compel the CRA to restore the situation.

Given the nature of the requirements in the CRA Regulation (organizational, operational, and disclosure requirements) breaches of the Regulation are categorized as administrative offences, as opposed to more serious criminal offences, which would require the involvement of national criminal courts for issuing the sanctions. The administrative nature of the fines and periodic penalty payments imposed by ESMA is expressly mentioned in Article 36d.2 of the Regulation. The Regulation has followed in this aspect the common practice in most Member States that considers breaches of similar types of requirements (such as provisions in MiFID on organizational requirements or conflicts of interests) also as administrative offences.

However, in some cases, the behaviour of persons involved in rating activities may, in addition to infringing the CRA Regulation, amount to a criminal offence (for example, use of inside information) according to the criminal legislation of the Member State where the act is committed. In these situations, ESMA is obliged to refer matters for criminal prosecution to the relevant national authorities and it would be up to these authorities to act accordingly.[44]

In order to build up an effective sanctioning regime, the CRA Regulation provides for a number of enforcement measures in case a CRA infringes provisions of the Regulation, including pecuniary sanctions (fines and periodic penalty payments).

Basically, the sanctions envisaged in the CRA Regulation can be divided into supervisory measures and pecuniary sanctions, which include fines and periodic penalty payments. As explained before, the sanctioning regime is envisaged to be mainly applicable on CRAs. In this respect, supervisory measures and fines can only be imposed over CRAs as only CRAs are the subject of the infringements listed in Annex III of the Regulation. However, periodic penalty payments are also envisaged for other persons (among those included in the scope) to make them supply the information requested by ESMA or submit to an investigation or on-site inspection.

3.7.4.2 Supervisory Measures

Article 24 includes the supervisory measures that ESMA is empowered to take when a CRA has committed an offence. The supervisory measures should be applied by ESMA taking into account the nature and seriousness of the infringement, respecting always the principle of proportionality. In particular, ESMA should take into account the following criteria: the duration and frequency of the infringement; whether the infringement has revealed serious or systemic weaknesses in the undertaking's procedures or in its management systems or

---

[44] EC impact assessment CRA Regulation II.

internal controls; whether financial crime was facilitated, occasioned, or otherwise attributable to the infringement; and whether the infringement has been committed intentionally or negligently.[45]

Supervisory Measures Subject to Transitional Period

As the measures below can have a significant impact on the market, before taking a decision ESMA's Board of Supervisors shall inform EBA and EIOPA. In addition, to avoid market disruption, a transitional period has been set.

WITHDRAWAL OF THE REGISTRATION. This is a last resort measure that is envisaged for the most serious breaches of the Regulation, notably where a CRA has seriously or repeatedly infringed the provisions of Regulation (Recital 25 of CRA Regulation II). The objective of this measure is to help ensure high standards of regulatory conduct by preventing a CRA from continuing to conduct its rating business if it is not a fit and proper entity to perform that activity. Consequently, the withdrawal decision will mean the CRA has to immediately stop its rating activity, as it will not be able to operate in the EU without being registered.

TEMPORARY PROHIBITION TO ISSUE RATINGS. ESMA can decide to temporarily prohibit the CRA from issuing credit ratings, with effect throughout the Union, until the offence has been brought to an end.

SUSPENSION OF THE USE OF RATINGS FOR REGULATORY PURPOSES. ESMA can suspend the use, for regulatory purposes, of the credit ratings issued by the credit rating agency with effect throughout the EU, until the infringement is ceased.

TRANSITIONAL PERIOD. The Regulation sets out in Article 24.4 transitional measures to avoid the possible negative impact on EU entities using for regulatory purposes ratings issued by a CRA that is being subject to a supervisory measure. Consequently the Regulation provides that, following the adoption of one of the above decisions, the ratings may continue to be used for regulatory purposes during a period not exceeding:

- ten working days from the date ESMA's decision is made public if there are ratings of the same financial instrument or entity issued by another CRA registered under the Regulation; or

- three months from the date ESMA's decision is made public if there are no credit ratings of the same financial instrument or entity issued by another CRA registered under the Regulation. This period can be extended, if requested by EBA or EIOPA, by three additional months, but only in exceptional circumstances where there is a risk of market disruption or financial instability.

---

[45] Article 36a.1, when dealing with fines, considers, as an indication of when it can be considered that an infringement has been committed intentionally, 'if ESMA finds objective factors which demonstrate that the credit rating agency or its senior management acted deliberately to commit the infringement'.

Supervisory Measures not Subject to Transitional Period

Besides the three supervisory measures described above, ESMA can also take two other supervisory actions that, because they do not have a direct impact on the use of ratings by EU entities, have effects that are not subject to a transitional period.

REQUIRE THE CREDIT RATING AGENCY TO BRING THE INFRINGEMENT TO AN END. This measure will normally be coupled with the imposition of periodic penalty payments if the CRA does not comply with the order in a given deadline. These combined measures aim at restoring compliance with the Regulation as soon as possible.

ISSUE PUBLIC NOTICES. The publication of notices can be useful when a certain conduct can be adequately addressed by raising public awareness of a bad practice. In a sector like the rating one, where the reputational incentive is quite high, issuing public notices can have an important dissuasive effect.

Notification and Publication of Supervisory Measures

For all supervisory measures, ESMA's Board of Supervisors shall notify the decision to the CRA concerned, and shall also communicate it to the competent authorities and the sectoral competent authorities of the Member States, the Commission, EBA, and EIOPA.

The decision imposing a supervisory measure has to be publicly disclosed on ESMA's website within ten working days from the date when it was adopted. When publicly disclosing the decision, ESMA 'shall also publicly disclose the right for the credit rating agency concerned to appeal the decision, as well as, where relevant, the fact that such an appeal has been lodged, specifying that such an appeal does not have suspensive effect, as well as the possibility for the Board of Appeal to suspend the application of the contested decision'.

3.7.4.3 *Pecuniary Sanctions*

Introduction

The possibility of ESMA imposing pecuniary sanctions is necessary in order to provide a proportionate reaction to individual breaches of the Regulation which do not justify the immediate withdrawal of the registration or any other of the supervisory measures envisaged in the Regulation. However, the fact that ESMA could impose fines and periodic penalty payments was discussed heavily during the negotiations of the Regulation because of the doubts in relation to the *Meroni Case*, as discussed previously.

In the end, an agreement was reached between EU legislators and the Regulation empowers ESMA with the possibility of imposing pecuniary sanctions (fines and periodic penalty payments) but sets a very tight framework where ESMA's discretionary powers are maximally limited. It is noteworthy that ESMA does not retain the amounts coming from pecuniary sanctions; these are allocated to the general budget of the European Union.

To respect the general principle of publicity of sanctions, the Regulation stipulates the obligation of these pecuniary sanctions to be publicly disclosed 'unless such disclosure to the public would seriously jeopardize the financial markets or cause disproportionate damage to the parties involved'.

Fines

Where a CRA has committed, intentionally or negligently, one of the infringements listed in Annex III of the Regulation, ESMA shall adopt a decision imposing a fine in accordance with Article 36a.2.

Bearing in mind the principles underlying the *Meroni Case*, EU legislators included in the Regulation a very detailed system for the imposition of fines where ESMA does not have much room for manoeuvre. In order to fix the amount of the fine related to a specific infringement, ESMA has to follow a two step methodology consisting of the setting of a basic amount for the fine and the adjustment, if necessary, of that basic amount by certain aggravating or mitigating coefficients.

BASIC AMOUNT. The basic amount is established taking into account the type of breach committed. Infringements are divided into nine different groups, according to the level of seriousness of the offence, for which specific maximum and minimum amounts of fines are allocated (Article 36a.2).

The minimum fine set for the less serious infringement (for not retaining records which set out the respective rights and obligations of the CRA and the rated entity) is of 10,000 Euros. The maximum fine that ESMA can impose amounts to 750,000 Euros and is envisaged for breaches of key provisions of the Regulation such as a CRA 'not using rating methodologies that are rigorous, systematic, continuous and subject to validation based on historical experience, including back-testing'.

Although it is not specifically stated, it seems that EU Regulators have considered that infringements related to conflicts of interest and organizational or operational requirements are the most serious ones, since the highest fines are envisaged for the breaches listed under Section I of Annex III. On the other hand, it seems that the less serious ones are those in Section II of Annex III, related to obstacles to the supervisory activities.

In between the minimum and maximum quantities, the specific basic amount is established by taking into account the annual turnover of the preceding business year of the CRA concerned. The Regulation provides, once again, detailed elements for ESMA to decide whether the basic amount of the fines should be at the lower, middle, or higher end of the limits:

> The basic amount shall be at the lower end of the limit for credit rating agencies whose annual turnover is below EUR 10 million, the middle of the limit for the credit rating agencies whose annual turnover is between EUR 10 and 50 million and the higher end of the limit for the credit rating agencies whose annual turnover is higher than EUR 50 million.

ADJUSTMENTS. In order to give the necessary tools to ESMA to decide on a fine which is proportionate to the seriousness of the infringement committed by a CRA, taking into account the circumstances under which the breach has been committed, the Regulation allows for adjustments to be made.

These adjustments are determined by increasing or decreasing the basic amount through the application of the relevant coefficients, linked to the aggravating and mitigating circumstances set out in Annex IV of the Regulation.

The coefficients are applied one by one to the basic amounts. This means that if 'more than one aggravating coefficient is applicable, the difference between the basic amount and the amount resulting from the application of each individual aggravating coefficient shall be added to the basic amount'. In addition, if 'more than one mitigating coefficient is applicable, the difference between the basic amount and the amount resulting from the application of each individual mitigating coefficient shall be subtracted from the basic amount'.

To avoid excessive fines and take into account the different sizes of CRAs, the Regulation stipulates an overall maximum amount of the fine (after the calculation of the basic amount and the adjustments): 'the fine shall not exceed 20% of the annual turnover of the credit rating agency concerned in the preceding business year'.

On the other hand, to ensure the removal of any financial benefit derived directly from the breach, a minimum overall amount has also been included in the Regulation: 'where the credit rating agency has directly or indirectly benefitted financially from the infringement, the fine shall be at least equal to that financial benefit'.

Finally, if the actions committed by a CRA constitute more than one infringement listed in Annex III, only the higher fine calculated in accordance with previous rules and related to one of those breaches will apply.

Periodic Penalties Payments

Periodic penalties are foreseen in situations in which the CRA is compelled by ESMA to act in a specific manner at a given deadline, for instance, to put an end to an infringement, supply information, or submit to an investigation or an on-site inspection.[46] Therefore, if the CRA complies with the order by ESMA within the given deadline, no periodic penalty payment will be imposed, as this penalty has a primarily compelling effect but does not sanction or compensate a breach of a substantive requirement of the Regulation.

According to Article 36b of the Regulation, ESMA can take a decision to impose periodic penalty payments in order to compel CRAs to put an end to an infringement, in accordance with a supervisory measure taken by ESMA.

In addition, periodic penalty payments are envisaged to compel any person under the supervisory scope of ESMA to supply complete information which has been requested by a decision by ESMA; to submit to an investigation and in particular to produce complete records, data, procedures, or any other material required and to complete and correct other information provided in an investigation launched by a decision taken by ESMA; and/or to submit to an on-site inspection ordered by a decision taken by ESMA.

---

[46] As is the case in the Council Regulation (EC) No 1/2003 of 16 December 2002 on the implementation of the rules on competition laid down in Articles 81 and 82 of the treaty (*Official Journal* L1, 4.1.2003: p. 1).

In these circumstances, the periodic penalty payments will be imposed on a daily basis until the person concerned complies with the decision. The payments will be calculated from the date stipulated in the decision imposing the periodic penalty payment and may not be imposed for a period of more than six months following the notification of ESMA's decision.

The penalties are imposed for each day of delay, according to the specific amounts envisaged in Article 36b.3: the amount shall be 3% of the average daily turnover in the preceding business year or, in case of natural persons, 2% of the average daily income in the preceding calendar year.

Enforcement of Pecuniary Sanctions

Another aspect that had to be resolved in relation to pecuniary sanctions was how to enforce them in an efficient way, bearing in mind the need for ESMA to rely to some extent on the national enforcement systems.

To deal with the enforcement of fines and periodic penalty payments, Article 36d.3 stipulates that the enforcement is governed by the rules of the civil procedure in force in the State of the territory in which it is carried out. However, to avoid possible interferences of national enforcing and judicial authorities the Regulation sets a quasi-automatic process:

> The order for its enforcement shall be appended to the decision without other formality than verification of the authenticity of the decision by the national authority which the government of each Member State shall designate for this purpose and shall make known to ESMA and to the Court of Justice of the European Union.
>
> When those formalities have been completed on application by the party concerned, the latter may proceed to enforcement in accordance with the national law, by bringing the matter directly before the competent body.
>
> Enforcement may be suspended only by a decision of the Court of Justice of the European Union. However, the courts of the Member State concerned shall have jurisdiction over complaints that enforcement is being carried out in an irregular manner.

In particular, in relation to the role of the Court of Justice of the European Union, Article 36e clarifies that it has unlimited jurisdiction to review ESMA's decisions on fines or periodic penalty payments and that it may annul, reduce, or increase the fine or periodic penalty payment imposed.

3.7.4.4 Procedural Rules for Taking Supervisory Measures and Imposing Fines and Periodic Penalties

Introduction

When performing its supervisory activity, ESMA might find out facts liable to constitute an infringement according to the Regulation. For these situations, Article 23e describes in quite a detailed way the process that ESMA has to follow to take a supervisory measure or impose a fine.

This article seems to leave out of these procedural rules the adoption of periodic penalty payments (although in paragraphs 7 and 8, periodic penalty payments are referred to). However, many of the steps envisaged in this article would also apply to the imposition of periodic penalty payments. In particular the Regulation states, although in different articles, that the decision to impose a periodic penalty has to be taken by ESMA's Board of Supervisors and that the rights of being heard and of defence of the person subject to a penalty payment are to be guaranteed. It is less clear, though, whether the steps in relation to the investigation phase have to be followed as the imposition of a periodic penalty payment does not require, in general, that there is a breach of the requirements of the Regulation as listed in Annex III.

In any event, this will hopefully be clarified by the EC, as Article 23e.7 requires the EC to adopt by means of delegated acts 'further rules of procedure for the exercise of the power to impose fines or periodic penalty payments, including provisions on rights of defence, temporal provisions, and the collection of fines or periodic penalty payments', and 'shall adopt detailed rules on the limitation periods for the imposition and enforcement of penalties'.

3.7.4.5 Process

The process for taking supervisory measures and imposing fines consists of the steps described below.

Appointment of an Independent Investigation Officer

The process begins with the appointment of an independent investigation officer within ESMA to investigate the matter. This person 'shall not be involved or have been involved in the direct or indirect supervision or registration process of the credit rating agency concerned and shall perform his functions independently from ESMA's Board of Supervisors'.

Investigation

The investigation officer shall investigate the alleged infringements. To do so, the officer shall have access to all documents and information[47] gathered by ESMA in its supervisory activities and will be able to exercise all the powers described above (to request information, to conduct investigations, and to carry out on-site inspections).

Right of being Heard and of Defence

During the investigation, the officer shall give the persons concerned the opportunity of being heard on the matters being investigated and shall take into account their comments. Moreover, the Regulation requires the officer to base the findings only on facts on which the persons concerned have been able to comment. As the process might end in an enforcement action, it is essential that during the investigation the rights of defence of the persons concerned are fully respected.

Submission of the File to ESMA's Board of Supervisors

Upon completion of the investigation, the officer shall submit a complete file with the findings to the Board of Supervisors and, at the same time, notify this fact to

---

[47] Except those subject to legal privilege, according to Article 23a of CRA Regulation.

the persons who are subject to the investigations. These persons are entitled to have access to the file 'subject to the legitimate interest of other persons in the protection of their business secrets'. Therefore, the 'right of access to the file shall not extend to confidential information affecting third parties'.

Before taking any decision, according to Article 25, ESMA's Board of Supervisors shall give the persons who are the subject of the proceedings the opportunity of being heard. In fact, according to the Regulation, the Board can only base its decisions on findings on which the parties concerned have been able to comment. However, in the event that urgent action is needed 'in order to prevent significant and imminent damage to the financial system', it is possible for ESMA's Board of Supervisors to adopt an interim decision and afterwards, as soon as possible after having taken its decision, give the persons concerned the opportunity of being heard. In any event, the rights of defence of the persons concerned shall be fully respected in the proceedings and, as in the phase of investigation, these persons are entitled to have access to ESMA's file—again, subject to the protection of the business secrets of other persons.

Decision of ESMA's Board of Supervisors

On the basis of the file containing the investigation officer's findings, the Board shall deliberate on the main aspects of the investigation. The officer shall neither participate in the deliberations nor intervene in any way in the decision-making process. The Board of Supervisors shall decide if one or more of the infringements listed in Annex III of the Regulation has been committed by the persons who have been subject to the investigations and, in such a case, shall take a supervisory measure in accordance with Article 24 and impose a fine in accordance with Article 36a.

Referring Matters for Criminal Prosecution

Where, in pursuing an investigation or inspection, ESMA finds out that there are serious indications of the possible existence of facts liable to constitute criminal offences, ESMA shall refer the matters for criminal prosecution to the relevant national authorities. Besides, to avoid double sanctioning, the Regulation requires ESMA to 'refrain from imposing fines or periodic penalty payments where a prior acquittal or conviction arising from identical facts, or from facts which are substantially the same, has acquired the force of res judicata as the result of criminal proceedings under national law'.

3.7.4.6 *Appeals of ESMA's Decisions*

To effectively protect the rights of persons affected, and for reasons of procedural economy, where ESMA has decision-making powers, persons affected should be granted a right of appeal on those decisions. The body and process for this appeal has been regulated for all ESMA's decisions, in ESMA Regulation.

Therefore, according to Article 60 of ESMA Regulation (in connection with Article 1.2), any natural or legal person may appeal any decision taken by ESMA in accordance with the CRA Regulation that is of 'direct and individual concern to that person'.

In relation to supervisory measures decided by ESMA, the right of appeal is envisaged in Article 24.5 of the CRA Regulation. Also, in relation to pecuniary sanctions, although not expressly mentioned in the Regulation, affected parties have the right of appeal.

The body in charge of analysing the appeal is the newly created Board of Appeal, which is a joint body of the three European Supervisory Authorities regulated in Articles 58 and 59 of ESMA Regulation. This body has legal expertise to provide expert legal advice on the legality of all the Authorities' exercise of their powers and has to act independently and in the public interest. In fact, the Board of Appeal is composed of six members and six alternates, 'who shall be individuals of a high repute with a proven record of relevant knowledge and professional experience, including supervisory, experience to a sufficiently high level in the fields of banking, insurance, occupational pensions, securities markets or other financial services'.

The decisions of the Board of Appeal are adopted on the basis of a majority of at least four of its six members and where the appealed decision falls within the scope of ESMA's powers, as is the case of decisions on CRAs, the deciding majority shall include at least one of the two members of the Board appointed by ESMA, to ensure a certain degree of expertise in the specific issue under discussion.

Article 60 of ESMA Regulation specifies the process to be followed to appeal a decision taken by ESMA. The main steps of the process are the following:

1. The appeal, together with a statement of grounds, shall be filed in writing at ESMA within two months of the date of notification of the decision to the person concerned, or, in the absence of a notification, of the day on which the decision has been published.

2. The presentation of an appeal does not have suspensive effect. However, in specific cases, the Board of Appeal may, if it considers that circumstances so require, suspend the application of the contested decision.

3. If the appeal is admissible, the Board of Appeal will invite the parties to the appeal proceedings to file observations within specified time limits and to make oral representations if they wish.

4. The Board of Appeal has two months after the appeal has been lodged to decide on the issue. The decision taken by the Board of Appeal shall be reasoned and shall be made public by ESMA.

5. The Board of Appeal may confirm the decision taken by ESMA or remit the case to ESMA. In the latter event, ESMA is bound by the decision of the Board of Appeal and shall adopt an amended decision regarding the case concerned.

6. In any event, all the decisions of the Board of Appeal are subject to appeal before the Court of Justice of the European Union (Article 61 of ESMA Regulation).

It is important to highlight that the timings set for the appeal process are not aligned with those envisaged for the publication of ESMA's decisions on supervisory measures (ten days). Besides, as the presentation of an appeal does not have a suspensive effect, it can be argued that the system included in the CRA Regulation can lead to situations where the rights of a CRA can be seriously undermined. Once a supervisory measure is published, even if an appeal can be presented and eventually succeed, it will cause long-term and possibly irreversible reputational damage to the CRA. Moreover, it could also have a detrimental effect on users of ratings and even have an impact on financial stability. Given the extent of the negative effects of ESMA's decisions, it would have been desirable that the CRA Regulation envisaged some suspensive effect for appealed decisions and that the decisions were not made public until the appeal had been determined.

3.8 SUBSTANTIVE REQUIREMENTS

This section analyses in detail all the substantive requirements that CRAs have to fulfil in order to be registered in the EU. An effort has been made to organize the section in a structured and straightforward way to facilitate such analysis. In addition, when dealing with each specific requirement all the relevant pieces of information, such as guidance from several organizations (ESMA, EBA, IOSCO, etc), related EU legislation and, in some cases, also SEC rules, have been compounded to provide a complete overview of the requirement and a better understanding of the provision included in the CRA Regulation.

3.8.1 Organization and Governance

3.8.1.1 General Structure and Governance

The CRA as a Legal Person—Status of Branches

As discussed in previous sections of the book, the obligation to register in the European Union is imposed on CRAs that are legal persons established in the Community (Articles 2.1 and 14.1 of the CRA Regulation). In order for ESMA to determine whether a CRA falls within the scope of the Regulation, entities applying for registration have to provide the information set out in ESMA's guidance on registration.

This covers details about the legal status of the applicant and evidence of the country of incorporation (such as excerpt from the relevant commercial or court register). Where the CRA is applying as part of a group of CRAs, it has to submit an organizational chart providing information about all the entities and branches within the group, including the ownership details of each entity. This chart will reveal where potential conflicts of interest relating to the business activities of other entities of the group might arise. Where the CRA is not a part of a group of CRAs, it will have to provide an organizational chart with details of its branches.

The Regulation does not apply to CRAs established outside the European Union. Therefore, applicants do not need to provide competent authorities with all the information items laid down in ESMA's guidance on registration regarding members of the group that are established in non-EU countries. Compliance with the requirements of the Regulation has to be demonstrated only in respect of the EU legal entities.

Notwithstanding, there might be areas where applicants are utilizing global functions—operated outside the EU—in order to meet specific requirements of the Regulation. In these cases, applicants will have to make clear how these functions operate within the EU.

It is also worth noting that, as branches are not legal entities, when a non-EU branch of an EU CRA produces ratings, these will be treated as ratings issued by the EU registered CRA; and consequently those ratings will be captured under the CRA Regulation and the oversight by ESMA (ESMA's Q&A). This means that applicants will have to demonstrate that branches of EU CRAs (established either in the EU or in foreign countries) operate according to the standards of the EU-registered CRA.

The fact that the ratings developed in foreign branches of an EU-registered CRA are to be considered for the purposes of the Regulation as the same as all other ratings that EU entity produces in its EU office is extremely important; the legal status of a foreign office of a CRA might determine whether the ratings developed in that office (prepared by a lead analyst based in that office) may be used in the EU for regulatory purposes or not. If the subsidiary of an EU CRA does not meet the endorsement requirements set out in Article 4.3 of the Regulation, the CRA could transform that subsidiary into a branch. This way, the ratings produced by lead analysts based in the foreign branch would be considered as ratings issued by the EU CRA and therefore usable for regulatory purposes in the EU.

Notwithstanding, CRAs will have to ensure that the setting up of these foreign branches does not prejudice the ability of the EU CRA to meet the requirements of the Regulation, and that ESMA is able to effectively supervise all relevant activities performed by the CRA. For example, before establishing branches in foreign countries, CRAs should analyse the legal framework of these jurisdictions, so as to ensure that there are no conflicts of law that could prevent the registered CRA from complying with the CRA Regulation.

Corporate Governance

Recital 28 of the CRA Regulation indicates the overall objective that a CRA should consider when determining its corporate governance arrangements: 'the need to ensure that it issues credit ratings that are independent, objective and of adequate quality'.

Annex I.A of the Regulation sets forth a number of detailed organizational requirements with the aim of ensuring CRAs' independence and the avoidance of conflicts of interest. This principle is specifically included in Annex I.A.2: 'a credit rating agency shall be organized in a way that ensures that its business interest does not impair the independence or accuracy of the credit rating activities'. The CRA should reflect this principle in its organizational structure and manage any possible conflicts with the interests of holders of a significant stake in the shares of the CRA.

Conflicts could arise with the interests of the owners of the CRA. The way these types of conflicts are handled by CRAs should be assessed by ESMA during the registration process. With this objective, the application must include the identity and brief description of business activity of each shareholder of the applicant that owns a stake greater than 10% of the applicant, including the size of its stake or ownership (ESMA's guidance on registration).

In addition, the CRA should set up an internal structure that complies with the conflict-of-interest requirements of the Regulation. Annex I.A.4 requires agencies to 'implement and maintain decision-making procedures and organizational structures which clearly and in a documented manner specify reporting lines and allocate functions and responsibilities'. ESMA's guidance on registration prescribes that CRAs should prove compliance with that provision by submitting to ESMA—as part of the information included in the application—an organizational chart detailing the organizational structure of the CRA; the chart must identify the significant roles and identity of the senior management and senior analysts and should also cover any ancillary services and how these are separated from the rating business.

If the CRA adheres to a recognized corporate governance code of conduct it should indicate this information in its application. In case it deviates from the recognized code, the CRA should provide an explanation for the deviation. And any internal corporate governance policy will have to be included in the application, also according to ESMA's guidance on registration.

The information discussed above is not only relevant for ESMA but also for market participants. The transparency report that a registered CRA has to publish annually must include relevant information about its legal structure and ownership, significant holdings, and composition and operation of its governing bodies. Also, a CRA has to publish its code of conduct and explanations in cases where it deviates from its provisions. This information will enable users of ratings to judge for themselves whether a CRA is organized in a way that ensures the independence, objectivity, and quality of its ratings (see Section 3.8.6).

3.8.1.2 Administrative or Supervisory Board and Senior Management

Board of Directors

Annex I.A.1 of the Regulation requires CRAs to have an administrative or—depending on national legislation—a supervisory board. In general, company law assigns the board of directors full powers for the company's strategy and management but the Regulation does not include details on the tasks the board should perform (instead, these details are provided with respect of the senior management, as indicated below). In addition, as stated in Annex I.A.2, the remit of the board should also include the receipt of reports from the independent directors—where applicable—and from the compliance and review functions.

The application for registration must contain the terms of reference of the CRA's board that will normally include matters such as frequency of meetings, decision-making process, quorum, and reporting. In addition, the application will provide the curriculum vitae of the board's members, including an identification of the independent directors (unless an exemption applies) and, in the case of CRAs that issue ratings of structured finance instruments, identification of the two members of the board who have in-depth knowledge and experience of that market. One of the board's members with this kind of expertise must be independent. ESMA will review the curriculums of the members of the board in order to check that knowledge and also that in general the majority of them have sufficient expertise in financial services.

Senior Management

The notion of senior management in the Regulation is wider than that of the board of the CRA; according to Article 3.1.(n) of the Regulation, it is composed of 'the person or persons who effectively direct the business of the credit rating agency and the member or members of its administrative or supervisory board'.

Members of the senior management shall be of good repute and sufficiently skilled and experienced, and shall ensure the sound and prudent management of the CRA. The 'good repute' should be confirmed by means of an individually signed declaration. The senior management is assigned the specific tasks of ensuring that:

- credit rating activities are independent, including from all political and economic influences or constraints;
- conflicts of interest are properly identified, managed and disclosed; and
- the CRA complies with the remaining requirements of the Regulation.

3.8.1.3 *Independent Members of the Board*

Criteria for Assessment of Independence

The presence of independent directors on the board of a company is widely considered a means of protecting the interests of minority shareholders and of making managers accountable. The Regulation prescribes that at least one-third, but no less than two, of the members of the CRA's board shall be independent members who are not involved in credit rating activities. Annex I of the Regulation does not indicate which criteria non-executive directors should fulfil in order to be regarded as independent, but its Recital 29 refers to the European Commission's Recommendation of 15 February 2005.[48]

The Recommendation considers that 'a director should be considered to be independent only if he is free of any business, family or other relationship, with the company, its controlling shareholder or the management of either, that creates a conflict of interest such as to impair his judgement'. The Recommendation indicates that the determination of what constitutes independence is fundamentally an issue for the board itself to determine. In order to help companies to make this assessment, Annex II of the Recommendation spells out in more detail the profile of independent directors. According to this annex, situations that could compromise independence are current posts as executive director, non-executive director, employee, or auditor of the company or an associated company; significant additional remuneration from the company or an associated company or significant business relationship with any of these; representation of controlling

---

[48] Commission Recommendation 2005/162/EC of 15 February 2005 on the role of non-executive or supervisory directors of listed companies and on the committees of the (supervisory) board (*Official Journal* L 52, 25.2.2005: pp. 51–63).

shareholders; significant links with executive directors of the company; and finally, close family links with executive directors or persons in the above-mentioned situations should be also considered as a factor undermining independence.

ESMA's Q&A has clarified that the independent directors who have been put in place by the CRA should fulfil the above-mentioned EC's criteria. CRAs should obtain information from their independent directors in order to evaluate whether they meet the criteria for independence at the time of appointment and on an ongoing basis.

The US Dodd–Frank Act has also introduced the requirement for NRSROs to have independent directors (see Appendix 4). In order to be considered independent, directors may not, other than in their capacity as members of the board of directors, accept fees from the CRA, or be associated with the CRA or with any affiliated company. Finally, it is worth noting that in the US framework independent directors are disqualified from any deliberation involving a specific rating in which they have a financial interest in the outcome of the rating.

Compensation and Term of Office

The EU Regulation and the Dodd–Frank Act have identical provisions regarding compensation and term of office of the independent directors. Their compensation shall not be linked to the business performance of the CRA and shall be arranged so as to ensure the independence of their judgement. Their term of office shall be for a pre-agreed fixed period not exceeding five years and shall not be renewable. This prohibition of renewing the tenure applies irrespective of the length of the initial tenure (even if the combined length of the initial term and the renewed one would have been less than five years), as clarified by ESMA's Q&A. In case of independent directors already in this role at the time of registration, the maximum five-year term will start from the date of registration—and not from the date of appointment—also following ESMA's Q&A.

Additionally, EU CRAs are prohibited from dismissing independent directors except in cases of misconduct or professional underperformance. This provision of the Regulation aims to ensure that independent directors enjoy a certain stability of tenure, protecting them to some extent against the will of the CRA's executive directors or major shareholders. On the other hand, it would also seem logical that independent directors are removed when new developments mean that they no longer fulfil the independence's criteria.

Tasks

Regarding the functions assigned to independent directors, in addition to the overall responsibility of the board, they have the specific task of monitoring (Annex I.A.2):

- the development of the credit rating policy and of the methodologies used in the rating activities;
- the effectiveness of the internal quality control system in relation to credit rating activities;
- the effectiveness of measures and procedures instituted to ensure that any conflicts of interest are identified, eliminated, or managed and disclosed; and

- the compliance and governance processes, including the efficiency of the review function.

Independent members should confirm to the CRA that they are able to allocate sufficient time to meet the expectations of their role. It also seems appropriate that they commit to inform the CRA before accepting directorships or similar positions with other companies.

Opinions to be Provided to the CRA's Board

The Regulation also stipulates that the opinions of the independent directors on the matters mentioned above 'shall be presented to the board periodically and shall be made available to ESMA on request'. ESMA has not clarified how often these reports should be issued. CRAs will adapt their timing to that of the other internal memos that will feed into the independent directors' opinions (such as the reports issued by the compliance or the internal control functions).

ESMA's Q&A deals with the nature of the independent directors' opinions. Not much is said about the content of the opinion—only that it must discuss the areas of the independent directors' remit—but ESMA indicates that the 'opinions should be based on a thorough and risk-based analysis performed by such members rather than a formulaic or bureaucratic process' and that the opinions 'should lead to appropriate follow-up and subsequent consideration by the board as necessary'.

Finally, ESMA's guidance on registration requires that the last three opinions presented to the board are included in the application for registration. Obviously, this requirement applies only to those CRAs that have independent directors at the time of the application.

Independent Directors Sitting on Several Boards Within the Same Group of CRAs

In order to alleviate the burden of having to appoint independent directors in several subsidiaries, groups of CRAs have considered the possibility of having the same independent members on the boards of the parent company and the different subsidiaries. ESMA's Q&A has clarified that this possibility is allowed by the Regulation. Moreover, ESMA has also indicated that previous work as a non-executive director for the parent company would not be an impediment for considering that director as an independent member in the board of a subsidiary.

3.8.1.4 *Small Office Exemptions*

The EC proposal CRA Regulation did not consider setting a specific regime for smaller CRAs. In fact, the only requirement that was exempted, for CRAs that employed less than 50 employees, was the rotation obligation of analysts.

However, during the negotiations with the EU governments and Parliament, concerns were raised in relation to the excessive burden that the Regulation could imply for smaller CRAs that could, in turn, diminish competition in the market. In addition, the larger CRAs also highlighted the difficulties they could face to comply with all the requirements at subsidiary level and lobbied for the inclusion of certain exemptions for their small offices. In fact, the exemptions are mainly designed for this case, considering that the exempted functions could be provided by other entities within the group. For this reason, the discussion below focuses on the application of the exemptions to small CRAs that belong to a group. Notwithstanding, single CRAs can obviously benefit from the exemptions regime using the same rationale, if they demonstrate that they comply with the objectives of the Regulation by employing different means.

Therefore, Article 6.3 of the CRA Regulation establishes a proportionate regime for CRAs that have fewer than 50 employees. At the request of a CRA, and provided that the CRA complies with the conditions set out in Article 6.3, ESMA is able to exempt it from the obligations laid down by the Regulation as regards independent members of the board, the compliance function, and the rotation mechanism (points 2, 5, and 6 of Annex I.A and Article 7.4). In particular, the CRA must demonstrate that the requirements of the Regulation are not proportionate in view of the nature, scale, and complexity of its business and the nature and range of its issue of credit ratings and that:

- the CRA has fewer than 50 employees;
- the CRA has implemented measures and procedures, in particular internal control mechanisms, reporting arrangements, and measures ensuring independence of rating analysts and persons approving credit ratings, which ensure the effective compliance with the objectives of the Regulation; and
- the size of the CRA is not determined in such a way as to avoid compliance with the requirements of the Regulation by a credit rating agency or a group of CRAs.

ESMA's guidance on registration observes that where an applicant wishes to be exempted from some, or all, of the above-mentioned requirements, the application should contain a detailed description of the relevant requirements from which it is requesting an exemption and the reason why the applicant considers the requirement is not proportionate.

As noted by ESMA's Q&A, the number of employees being less than 50 is not sufficient on its own to be granted an exemption. Applicants have to demonstrate in their application that they have implemented the measures and procedures set forth in Article 6.3.(b). In this respect, the CRA should confirm to ESMA that the group's policies on conflicts of interest and the group's internal control mechanisms are implemented consistently on a global basis and therefore also on the entity to be exempted. Adequate reporting arrangements should ensure the proper flow of information between the exempt subsidiary and the body at the group's level that performs the exempted functions.

The last paragraph of Article 6.3 stipulates that in the case of a group of CRAs, ESMA shall ensure that at least one of the CRAs in the group is not exempted from complying with the requirements. The objective of this provision is that the non-exempt CRA ensures that the objectives of the Regulation are also met regarding the exempt subsidiaries. As discussed above, this is achieved through the core functions performed by the non-exempt CRA that will service the other entities in the group.

Recital 32 of the Regulation requires ESMA to examine in particular the anti-avoidance clause in Article 6.3.(c). A CRA applying for the exemptions should be able to demonstrate that its size has been driven by the business needs of the group and not with the aim of circumventing the requirements of the Regulation. To this effect, the CRA should provide ESMA with the historic numbers of employees, in order to show that the figures have not changed materially in the period preceding the application.

Finally, it is worth noting that the requirements that might be exempted (independent directors, compliance function, rotation) do not apply to branches as they are considered a part of the company that has created them. Therefore, a small office will be treated differently, depending on whether it is a company set up according to national corporate law (a subsidiary) or a branch.

The paragraphs below discuss in more detail each of the three possible exemptions.

Exemption from the Requirement to have Independent Directors

If the group of CRAs has placed independent directors on the board of the parent company, it seems unnecessary to put other (or the same) independent directors in the boards of the small subsidiaries. The independent directors of the parent CRA can perform the tasks set out in Annex I A.2 of the Regulation regarding also the exempt subsidiaries. Actually, for groups of CRAs it is essential to adopt and apply their policies, methodologies, and procedures on a global basis. Therefore, it makes sense that the task of monitoring the implementation of these policies, methodologies, and procedures is carried out by the same independent directors (those placed at the parent CRA). Another means of ensuring compliance by the exempt entity with the objectives of the Regulation is that a controlling function within the group takes on the tasks assigned to the independent directors.

It is important to stress that a CRA may be exempted from the requirement to have independent members on its board, but not from the requirement to have a board of directors (Annex I.A.1). Therefore, all CRAs must have a fully consti-tuted board of directors, established in accordance with the relevant national law. Regarding branches, the roles of the CRA's board will be performed in relation to the CRA and all the branches it has set up.

Exemption from the Requirement to have a Compliance Function

The same considerations regarding the independent directors' exemption would apply to the exemption from the requirement to have a compliance function established at a small subsidiary. The provision of compliance services by another entity within the group (such as the parent company) may justify the exemption where the size and complexity of the operations of the exempt CRA would not warrant a local compliance function. This has been accepted by ESMA's Q&A, according to which a compliance officer located in the parent CRA or in a larger CRA within the group could be charged with all the responsibilities and authority set out in the Regulation regarding the exempt subsidiaries. In addition, automated systems to manage compliance are designed from a global perspective, rather than at the level of the individual subsidiaries. This approach would help groups of CRAs to assess compliance on a global basis, ensuring consistency across the group.

However, when the exemption is granted for compliance purposes if a group's function is used, it is important to note ESMA's Q&A requirements: 'a CRA will need to demonstrate there is appropriate coverage in each office—this may require local staff depending on the size and business conducted in the office. Where staff have a compliance role in an office it should not be combined with another role that may present a conflict with this activity.' Therefore, the group has to ensure that there is someone placed at the exempt CRA providing information and the documents necessary for the compliance function to perform its duties in relation to the exempt entity.

Exemption from the Requirement to Rotate Analysts

The analyst rotation requirements imposed by the Regulation create a problem for small entities. The reduced number of analysts they employ makes it impossible for the CRAs to rotate them, unless they hire additional staff just to comply with the rotation requirements. In the absence of new mandates to rate more products, hiring new staff might cause these small offices to no longer be cost-effective.

Analysts have to combine analytical expertise in their relevant area of work with knowledge of the local language and legal framework. Whilst normally all the analysts employed by the small CRA will speak the local language, not all of them would be interchangeable in terms of analytical skills. An analyst specializing in rating financial institutions might not be best placed to move to the structured finance area. Moving analysts from another subsidiary might not be a solution if they lack the necessary language skills; in addition, this solution might still not be cost-effective for the group.

A rotation mechanism with respect to the persons approving the ratings—such as the chair of the rating committee—combined with the other policies and procedures designed to address potential conflicts of interest and ensure the independence of the ratings seem to be sufficient to fulfil the objectives of the Regulation when analyst rotation is exempted.

Rating opinions are determined by committee, rather than by an individual analyst (see Section 1.4). A robust rating process that encourages a lively debate within rating committees in order to avoid the recommendations of the lead analyst being simply rubber-stamped by the committee can achieve the objectives pursued by the analyst rotation rules.

Another factor that ESMA will take into account when considering this exemption is the level of interaction between the analysts of the CRA and the rated issuer. Small CRAs normally start building their reputations issuing unsolicited ratings which are determined without issuer's participation. If the issuer does not interact with the CRA during the rating process, the risk of interference is obviously very limited. Additionally, the CRA can have procedures in place to ensure that the lack of periodic rotation does not affect the quality of the ratings.

3.8.1.5 *Internal Controls*

General Safeguards, Internal Procedures, and Controls

According to Annex I.A.4 of the Regulation:

> A credit rating agency shall have sound administrative and accounting procedures, internal control mechanisms, effective procedures for risk assessment, and effective control and safeguard arrangements for information processing systems.

Those internal control mechanisms shall be designed to secure compliance with decisions and procedures at all levels of the credit rating agency.

Additionally, point A.10 stipulates that:

A credit rating agency shall monitor and evaluate the adequacy and effectiveness of its systems, internal control mechanisms and arrangements established in accordance with this Regulation and take appropriate measures to address any deficiencies.

ESMA's guidance on registration requires that CRAs applying for registration submit to ESMA a description of the measures in place to ensure sound administrative procedures, and where the applicant has an audit committee or other relevant committees in place (such as remuneration or strategy committees), their terms of reference.

Audit Committee

Having an audit committee is not a requirement of the Regulation nor, in general, of the corporate governance requirements in EU Member States (although in some Member States an audit committee would be required if the CRA's shares were admitted to trading on a regulated market). However, big organizations have audit committees in place, as well as the internal control and risk management functions discussed in the following section. These functions operate normally on a global basis, having purview over all the subsidiaries and branches within the group.

Typically, audit committees have the purpose of assisting the board of directors in fulfilling its oversight responsibilities relating to two broad areas:

- Internal control and reporting systems: this would include the monitoring of the preparation and the integrity of the financial information drawn up on the company and the review of the internal control and risk management systems.

- Audit process: under this role, the audit committee monitors the independence and efficacy of the internal audit function and also the appointment, independence, and performance of the external auditor.

Normally, audit committees are comprised of a number of directors having skills in accounting, auditing, and risk management matters and meeting independence criteria.

Internal Control/Audit Function and Risk Management Function

Similarly to the audit committee, these two functions are not required by the Regulation. Notwithstanding, ESMA expects that at least major CRAs have all these functions in place and therefore requires CRAs to provide certain details in their applications for registration. The description of the internal control and risk management functions would include their organizational charts; role and responsibilities and mechanisms to monitor their effectiveness; number of allocated employees; reporting lines and frequency of reporting; work plan for the next three years; and curriculum vitae of the officers in charge of the functions.

Additionally, ESMA's guidance on registration requires that, where the CRA adheres to a recognized internal control code of conduct, it should indicate, where appropriate, where it deviates from such a code and provide an explanation for any deviation. For example, the Institute of Internal Auditors (IIA) has issued the *International standards for the professional practice of internal auditing (standards)*.

According to these standards, the internal control function 'adds value to the organization (and its stakeholders) when it provides objective and relevant assurance, and contributes to the effectiveness and efficiency of governance, risk management, and control processes'. For example, the responsibility of the control function should be defined in its charter; normally this should include performing periodic reviews regarding the integrity and reliability of financial and operational information, compliance with the controls (processes and policies) developed for the rating process, and the quality of the compliance function. Finally, the IIA also recommends that the internal control function is independent (for example, reporting directly to the board).

Concerning the risk management function, its typical responsibilities include the identification of the main possible events that on occurrence would have a negative impact on the CRA achieving its objectives, the determination of the level of risk the CRA is willing to accept, and the monitoring and mitigation of those risks.

CRA's risk assessment functions should address not only the risks associated with the rating process (or other business lines of the entity) but also the risks related to the horizontal divisions, such as financial, human resources, or information technology.

Compliance Function

In accordance with Annex I.A.5 of the CRA Regulation:

> A credit rating agency shall establish and maintain a permanent and effective compliance function department (compliance function) which operates independently. The compliance function shall monitor and report on compliance of the credit rating agency and its employees with the credit rating agency's obligations under this Regulation.

INDEPENDENCE. A key requirement of the Regulation is that the compliance function operates independently. This means that the compliance officers do not report to, and are not supervised by, the business personnel. The independence of the compliance function must be ensured by its direct reporting to the senior management and to the independent members of the board (last paragraph of point A.6). The reporting lines of the compliance function are relevant in assessing its level of independence from the business managers. This function is required to review the activities overseen by the business managers, so if the compliance officer were to report to the manager of a business line, their ability to review the area overseen by that manager would be seriously jeopardized.

RESPONSIBILITIES. According to Annex I.A points 3 and 5 the compliance function has three main responsibilities:

1. Establish adequate policies and procedures to ensure compliance with its obligations under this Regulation. This task is assigned by the Regulation not specifically to the compliance function but to the CRA as a whole. It is expected, though, that the compliance function is involved in the development of policies and procedures to implement all relevant regulatory requirements and business practices. As an example of these controls, CRAs must establish policies governing the way rating committees operate.

2. Monitor and, on a regular basis, assess the adequacy and effectiveness of the measures and procedures put in place in accordance with Annex I.A.3, and the actions taken to address any deficiencies in the CRA's compliance with its obligations. The compliance function should prepare an annual work plan providing details of the actions to be carried out throughout the forthcoming year in order to monitor adherence to applicable regulatory requirements and the CRA's policies. Monitoring activities would include tasks such as conducting risk-based approach examinations in order to assess the firm's controls, handling of identified breaches of rules or policies, and dealing with regulators (for example, notifying significant compliance issues).

CRAs typically conduct two types of examinations. First, regular reviews evaluate the controls put in place to ensure compliance with the requirements of the Regulation; the appropriate sample size and the frequency of the tests are determined taking into account the likelihood of a failure and the impact it would have upon the CRA's business. Second, CRAs might undertake more focused reviews, due, for example, to an special perceived risk or to a change in legislation; a CRA might carry out a specific examination of the processes established to ensure that analysts are not involved in the negotiation of fees. The outcome of the compliance function's annual review must be published by the CRA as part of its annual transparency report (Annex I.E.III.5).

Finally, it is worth noting here that the Regulation obliges any employee considering that another employee or person associated by the CRA has engaged in illegal conduct to report such information immediately to the compliance function ('whistle-blowing'). The CRA must prohibit any form of retaliation against the employee that reported the suspected wrong-doing (Annex I.C.5).

3. Advise and assist the managers, rating analysts, employees, as well as any other natural person whose services are placed at the disposal or under the control of the credit rating agency or any person directly or indirectly linked to it by control who is responsible for carrying out credit rating activities, to comply with the CRA's obligations under the Regulation. This role would include providing guidance and pro-active and re-active advice to staff and management regarding compliance.

Finally, an essential element of the compliance strategy is the provision of training programmes. Typically, the compliance function provides training to assist new recruits in understanding their obligations and also to the staff in general where regulatory changes or the outcome of compliance monitoring warrants an adjustment to an existing practice.

The role and responsibilities of the compliance function must be described in CRAs' application for registration, along with its organizational chart, its work

work plan for the next three years, and other information that will assist ESMA in evaluating whether this department can properly discharge its duties (ESMA's guidance on registration).

CONDITIONS THE COMPLIANCE FUNCTION HAS TO FULFIL. In addition to independence from the business managers, the Regulation (Annex I.A.6) imposes further conditions on the CRA, in order for the compliance function to discharge its responsibilities properly and independently.

1. The compliance function has to have the necessary authority, resources, expertise, and access to all relevant information. The CRA should periodically assess whether it has adequate personnel devoted to the compliance function; additional resources should be made available where necessary. The staff employed by the compliance function should go through a rigorous recruitment process in order to ensure an appropriate level of skills and experience. In addition, the CRA should provide the compliance's personnel with adequate training. Finally, compliance officers should have access to all the CRA's relevant systems and databases in order to be able to fulfil their duties.

As part of the application for registration, CRAs have to provide ESMA with the number of employees contracted (temporary and permanent) 'allocated to the compliance function and the resource typically dedicated to this function (man hours)'. This information about the persons that assist the compliance officer will enable ESMA to determine whether the applicant devotes the necessary resources to perform its function.

2. A compliance officer should be appointed and made responsible for the compliance function and for any reporting with regard to compliance required by Annex I.A.3. ESMA's guidance on registration requires CRAs to provide in their applications for registration the curriculum vitae of the designated compliance officer. This information about the experience and employment history of the individual in charge of compliance will assist ESMA in evaluating whether the CRA devotes adequate managerial resources to comply with the Regulation and the CRA's procedures and methodologies.

One of the responsibilities of the chief compliance officer is to prepare regular compliance reports for the board, including its independent members. As discussed previously, one of the specific tasks the Regulation assigns to independent directors is the monitoring of the compliance processes. To provide senior management and independent directors with effective oversight, it is important that the compliance function issues periodic reports about the work undertaken— in particular about the results of its monitoring activity—and summarizing also any planned actions as a result of the examinations.

3. The managers, rating analysts, employees, and any other natural person whose services are placed at the disposal or under the control of the credit rating agency, or any person directly or indirectly linked to it by control who is involved in the compliance function, cannot be involved in the performance of credit rating activities they monitor.

Obviously, compliance staff interact with the business lines on a regular basis. For example, in order to identify potential conflicts of interest in securities transactions reported by analysts, in the course of examination programmes, or training sessions. Also, regular contacts with the analytical staff will enable the compliance function to identify and assess risks. However, compliance personnel must not be able to influence ratings. This should be clear in the CRA's rating process manual. The interaction between the compliance function and the analysts must be described by CRAs in their application for registration; this description should include the CRA's whistle-blowing policy.

4. The compensation of the compliance officer should not be linked to the business performance of the credit rating agency and has to be arranged so as to ensure the independence of his or her judgement.

For ESMA to assess compliance with this requirement, applicants have to submit a copy of the compensation and performance evaluation policies and procedures regarding the compliance function. A common practice in the ratings industry is to pay employees the variable part of their salary out of a bonus pool that is determined by the overall performance of the CRA. ESMA's Q&A has clarified that any bonuses awarded to the staff employed by the compliance function must be based on individual merit and therefore should not be linked in any way to such a CRA's performance pool.

PROHIBITION OF CONFLICTS OF INTERESTS. Finally, the last subparagraph of Annex I.A.6 stipulates that 'the compliance officer shall ensure that any conflicts of interest relating to the persons placed at the disposal of the compliance function are properly identified and eliminated'. It is important to note that the Regulation requires the CRA to eliminate any conflicts of interest relating to the personnel employed by the compliance function. Therefore, measures to mitigate the compliance staff's conflicts should not be sufficient according to the Regulation. This contrasts with the treatment of conflicts relating to other employees, which, as prescribed by Annex I.B.1, may be either eliminated or managed and disclosed.

3.8.2 Business Activities and Resources

3.8.2.1 Business Activities

Principal Activities

As already mentioned, the CRA Regulation defines a CRA as a legal person whose occupation includes the issuing of credit ratings on a professional basis. Typically, CRAs' principal activity is the issuance of ratings and other activities directly related to credit ratings. In fact, the Regulation recommends CRAs to focus in their professional activity on the issuing of credit ratings, in order to avoid potential conflicts of interest (Recital 22).

TYPES OF CREDIT RATINGS ISSUED BY THE CRA. In its application for registration, CRAs have to inform about the type of credit ratings they produce according to the classifications defined in ESMA's CEREP: corporate, public/sovereign, and structured finance instruments. The corporate category should contain data and details according to the following industry categories: financial institutions, insurance, and corporate issuers. This information will enable ESMA to understand the CRA's business and assess whether it has sufficient resources to issue the classes of credit ratings it intends to produce according to the application.

In addition to the information about the business lines covered by the CRA, the application will also include details that will enable ESMA to understand the applicant's processes and methodologies for determining ratings: definitions of any rating action and statuses available to the applicant (such as negative watch, for example); rating nomenclatures used for each type of credit rating; proportion of public ratings and private ratings for each asset class; and details of whether the applicant produces solicited or unsolicited ratings (or both).

NUMBER OF YEARS OF EXPERIENCE FOR EACH ASSET CLASS. For each type of credit rating produced by the applicant, the application will have to disclose the number of years of experience the CRA has in producing these ratings. This information will assist ESMA in assessing the CRA's level of experience. However, as CRAs are not required in the EU to make their applications public and they do not have to include this information in the subsequent reports they have to publish according to Annex I.E, users of ratings will not have access to regulated information about CRAs' experience.

The NRSRO form for registration in the USA also elicits information on the approximate number of credit ratings issued in each class by the CRA as of the application date. This information enables the SEC to understand the CRA's coverage with respect to issuers within a particular asset class. In the USA, a condition for an applicant to be registered as an NRSRO is to have been in the business as a CRA for at least the three consecutive years immediately preceding the application. As already explained, this is not the case in the EU, because registration is mandatory before a CRA starts issuing ratings.

This actually means that new CRAs will not be able to provide the required information about the number of years of experience for each asset class. Nevertheless, where applicable, new CRAs might provide useful information about their experience in producing other assessments that are not credit ratings subject to the Regulation (such as scores or private ratings) or, in case of foreign groups, experience gained outside the EU by the non-EU parent company or fellow subsidiaries of the applicant.

Ancillary Services and Other Non-rating Activities

CRAs can also provide other services that, although related to ratings, may be provided independently. Agencies typically produce reports that explain in detail the analysis and assumptions underlying a credit rating; they are able to sell these reports to subscribers because they provide more information than the public releases accompanying the publication of the rating. Other ancillary services related to the rating activities include different types of evaluations or assessments that are produced using the CRA's credit rating analytical methodologies. In addition, CRAs might perform other ancillary activities that are unrelated to the rating business (such as pricing services).

The IOSCO Code does not provide a definition of the term 'ancillary services'. Rather, it requires a CRA to define what it considers, and does not consider, to be an ancillary business and why. The EU Regulation does not define the term either, but Annex I.B.4 does provide a list of services considered as ancillary services: 'a credit rating agency may provide services other than issue of credit ratings (ancillary services). Ancillary services are not part of credit rating activities; they comprise market forecasts, estimates of economic trends, pricing analysis and other general data analysis as well as related distribution services.' The EC impact assessment CRA Regulation cites as examples of ancillary services, pricing analysis for structured finance securities that do not have a liquid market or rating assessment services, where CRAs provide issuers with the likely impact on a rating of hypothetical events.

It is unclear whether the list in the EU Regulation is exhaustive. This uncertainty led CRAs and regulators to question whether CRAs could provide other services (ancillary or not) not included in the list. For this reason, ESMA clarified in its guidance on registration that a CRA can perform non-credit-rating activities different from ancillary services. Therefore, CRAs would be able to provide three categories of services: credit ratings, ancillary services, and other permissible services (this latter category is not expressly contemplated in the Regulation).

Since CRAs are allowed to perform other non-rating activities not captured by the Regulation's list of ancillary services, what really matters is that these other services are identified and any conflict of interest they could create is appropriately managed in a way that satisfies Annex I.B.1 (this provision spells out the overall requirement of identification and appropriate management and disclosure of potential conflicts of interest).

Regulators have a concern with these other non-rating services because they could affect the integrity of ratings. The influence a rated entity might have over a CRA in order to obtain a favourable rating could increase if the CRA provided to that entity other services in addition to credit rating assessments. A CRA may issue a more favourable than warranted rating in order not to lose other business from the rated issuer or to obtain additional business. Multiple relationships between a CRA and a rated entity increase the possibilities for mutual influence, dependency, or pressure.

These risks lead IOSCO to require CRAs to separate, operationally and legally, its credit rating business and analysts from any other businesses that may present a conflict of interest (IOSCO Code, provision 2.5). IOSCO further requires that ancillary services 'which do not necessarily present conflicts of interest with the CRA's rating business have in place procedures and mechanisms designed to minimize the likelihood that conflicts of interest will arise'.

Whilst the language used by the Regulation is less categorical than the IOSCO one, it seems that the approach is the same: only ancillary operations (and other services) that do not create potential conflicts of interests are allowed. According to Recital 6 of the Regulation, 'the performance of ancillary activities should not compromise the independence or integrity of credit rating agencies' credit rating activities'. More clearly, Recital 22 stipulates that CRAs should be able to provide ancillary services 'where this does not create potential conflicts of interest with the issuing of credit ratings'.

The key article of the Regulation regarding the handling of conflicts arising from the provision of ancillary services is the third subparagraph of Annex I.B.4: 'a credit rating agency shall ensure that the provision of ancillary services does not present conflicts of interest with its credit rating activities and shall disclose in the final ratings reports any ancillary services provided for the rated entity or any related third party'. This means that the CRA should either separate legally the ancillary business from the rating business or at least should implement strict firewalls or alternative mechanisms aimed at safeguarding against any potential conflicts of interest. Additionally, investors will be able to learn whether the CRA has provided ancillary services to the rated issuer. They will assess themselves whether this fact might have affected the credit assessment process, although for the information to be meaningful it would be necessary to know the proportion that the fees charged for ancillary services constitute against the total revenue earned by the CRA from the rated entity.

It can also be noted that conflicts of interest might also arise in respect of services provided to customers that are not rated entities. For example, some CRAs have developed pricing services for structured finance securities. Examples of possible conflicts would be the use of information gathered during the rating process for the pricing of the security or the reluctance of the CRA to unfavourably price a security to which it had itself attributed a high rating.

Information on Rating and Ancillary Activities to be Provided to ESMA and to the Public

At the time of registration, applicants have to submit information that will assist ESMA in assessing how CRAs handle any conflicts arising from the provision of ancillary services and other non-rating activities:

DESCRIPTION OF THE TYPES OF BUSINESS. The application must include a description of the type of business CRAs conduct (rating and ancillary) directly or through branches; and where the applicant is planning to conduct any new ancillary activity, it should describe the new activity and the time frame for setting up the new business line. In case the applicant is applying as part of a group of CRAs, it has to describe the type of business conducted by each entity of the group.

ORGANIZATIONAL CHART. The organizational chart detailing the significant roles and the identification of the person responsible for each significant role should cover any ancillary activities and include details on the separation of rating and ancillary business.

BREAKDOWN OF REVENUES. Disclosure on the revenues generated over the past three years should be broken down by rating, ancillary, and other services as a proportion of total revenue (and presented on a fiscal year basis). In the event that the CRA is applying as part of a group of CRAs, the identification of the ancillary and other services and the corresponding revenues have to be provided in respect of the applicant, its parent company, subsidiaries, fellow subsidiaries, and branches.

POLICIES AND PROCEDURES TO MANAGE CONFLICTS OF INTEREST. In particular regarding the management of conflicts of interest, CRAs have to submit the policies and procedures with respect to the identification, disclosure, and mitigation of conflicts arising from the performance of ancillary business and any assessment performed to identify those conflicts. Finally, applicants have to disclose the resources, both human and technical, shared by the rating and ancillary services.

Finally, as soon as practicable after registration, CRAs have to publish a list of the ancillary services they provide (Annex I.E.I.2) and subsequently each year they will have to include in their transparency report the fees received from the non-credit rating business (Annex I.E.III.7). These disclosures are designed to ensure that users of credit ratings are made aware of the potential conflicts of interest that arise from a CRA's business activities. In particular, the breakdown of revenues will help market participants determine whether the non-rating fees the CRA earns from a rated entity are sufficiently high as to call into question the impartiality of the CRA's rating actions with respect to that entity.

Consultancy or Advisory Services

As discussed in the previous paragraphs, the Regulation's general approach to non-rating services is that CRAs are allowed to provide them as long as they identify, manage, and disclose any potential conflicts of interest that may arise from the performance of those activities. There are, however, certain services that are prohibited outright. The rationale is that it would be too difficult for the CRAs to manage them given the risk that they could cause undue influence over the rating process. Recital 22 refers to those prohibited services: 'a credit rating agency should not be allowed to carry out consultancy or advisory services. In particular, a credit rating agency should not make proposals or recommendations regarding the design of a structured finance instrument.'

The prohibition to advise on structured finance has been taken from the similar clause introduced in the IOSCO Code in May 2008. However, whilst the IOSCO Code allows in general CRAs to provide consulting services—provisions 2.5 and 2.8.(a)—the Regulation has gone further, as it prohibits certain types of advisory services across all rating classes. According to Annex I.B.4, 'a credit rating agency shall not provide consultancy or advisory services to the rated entity or a related third party regarding the corporate or legal structure, assets, liabilities or activities of that rated entity or related third party'. In February 2009 the SEC adopted a similar prohibition which will certainly help the global CRAs to develop a consistent practice in the EU and the USA. Nevertheless, in the absence of a definition of advisory activity in the EU Regulation, market participants might have different expectations and CRAs might develop different interpretations of the I.B.4 rule.

To apply the rule to the corporate area, CRAs will have to consider the purpose of the prohibition, which is to address the potential lack of impartiality that could arise when the CRA is requested to rate an issuer after having recommended to it the changes in its corporate structure that would be necessary to achieve a certain rating. It seems, for example, that a CRA would not be able to provide to the rated company a credit assessment of the impact of a potential transaction (such as a merger or assèt purchase) on the company's credit rating if the company's final structure was developed in consultation with the CRA on how to achieve a desired credit rating. The Regulation considers that this sort of advice would impair the objectivity of the CRA's opinion about the creditworthiness of the company.

Regarding the structured finance area, Annex I.B.5 develops the principle included in Recital 22: 'a credit rating agency shall ensure that rating analysts or persons who approve ratings do not make proposals or recommendations, either formally or informally, regarding the design of structured finance instruments on which the credit rating agency is expected to issue a credit rating'. The nature of structured finance implies that there is a more iterative interaction between the CRAs and issuers and arrangers. Whilst this flow of information between the CRA and the issuer or sponsor during the rating process is beneficial, regulators were concerned that CRAs were actually doing more than rating structured finance securities, namely advising issuers on how to design the deals. This is why they decided to modify the IOSCO Code in order to introduce an outright prohibition.

The rationale is the same as in the corporate area: CRAs should not rate their own work. In order to avoid falling under the prohibition, CRAs have to limit themselves to carry out their modelling and assessment of the underlying assets over the structure proposed by the issuer or arranger. As a result of this evaluation, the CRA will indicate the strengths and weaknesses of the structure, asset pool, and credit enhancement levels, as well as provide an indicative rating. Then the issuer or arranger will accept the initial rating proposed or otherwise will be able to change the features of the transaction in order to improve the proposed rating. For example, a CRA would not fall under the prohibition if the analyst of a RMBS transaction informs the issuer or sponsor that the average loan to value ratio of the pool is too high to assign the desired rating given the level of credit enhancement proposed by the sponsor or issuer. On the other hand, the CRA would violate the prohibition under Annex I.B.5 if the analyst recommends how to change the loans in the pool to obtain the desired rating.

In any case, it is clear that drawing the line between legitimate and unlawful communications during the rating process will not always be easy. The SEC has recommended CRAs to mitigate the risk of violating this prohibition by enhancing their disclosures about their rating methodologies.[49]

3.8.2.2 *Human Resources*

Quantity and Quality

According to Annex I.A.8, 'a credit rating shall employ appropriate systems, resources and procedures to ensure continuity and regularity in the performance of its credit rating activities'. This section provides an analysis of the CRA Regulation's requirements on human resources.

One of the concerns raised during the financial crisis was that the level of staffing of CRAs, both in terms of numbers and experience, was inadequate to rate and monitor the structure finance deals that initiated the meltdown in 2007 and 2008 (see Section 2.1). This issue is addressed by Recital 31 of the Regulation: 'a credit rating agency should allocate a sufficient number of employees with

---

[49] SEC, 17 CFR Parts 240 and 249b [Release No. 34-59342; File No. S7-13-08], 9 February 2009.

appropriate knowledge and experience to its credit rating activities. In particular, the credit rating agency should ensure that adequate human and financial resources are allocated to the issuing, monitoring and updating of credit ratings.'

Adequate skills, experience, and number of rating analysts are essential for the high quality of ratings, given the importance of human capital to the CRAs' business model. CRAs have a strong incentive to take on and employ skilled staff as the quality of the assessment of the information available on the rated entity depends on the quality of the analysts. One of the key tasks of the senior management of the CRA is to ensure that its business lines are adequately staffed at all times in order to perform their rating activities.

The main tasks performed by analysts are analysing new deals, monitoring existing transactions, attending and participating in rating committees, developing criteria, and writing research. Normally, analysts devote most of their time to the first two tasks, although this depends on their level of seniority and the economic environment. For example, during the market turmoil CRAs had to shift their focus from analysing new deals to monitoring the transactions that were not performing according to expectations and to reviewing existing criteria. CRAs should be flexible enough to be able to respond to changing circumstances and redeploy resources or recruit new staff from outside the company accordingly. In some cases, CRAs will have to stop analysing new deals while they develop new methodologies.

It should also be noted that just having a better ratio of analysts to transactions does not necessarily mean that a CRA is better staffed than another one with fewer analysts per transaction. Not only the numbers, but also the experience and skills of the analysts and analysts' supervisors must be taken into account. And the quality of the resources that support the analytical staff (such as information technology, macroeconomic research, legal support, or investment in acquisition of data from external providers) is also a key factor for the performance of the CRA's rating activities.

Ultimately, the adequacy of a CRA's human resources is demonstrated by the statistical reports showing its performance. Nevertheless, EU legislators considered it prudent to establish some requirements in this area. Although the Regulation sets out in general very detailed requirements for CRAs, regarding human resources it imposes neither specific educational and professional requirements for analysts nor specific ratios of analysts to transactions. Rather, it establishes the broad principle of Recital 31 about the adequacy of human resources, which is further specified by Article 7.1. According to the latter, 'a credit rating agency shall ensure that rating analysts, its employees and any other natural person whose services are placed at its disposal or under its control and who are directly involved in credit rating activities have appropriate knowledge and experience for the duties assigned'.

This is also the SEC's approach. The US Credit Rating Agency Reform Act of 2006 requires the SEC to grant registration if it finds that the applicant complies with the Act's requirements unless it finds that the CRA does not have adequate financial and managerial resources. In order for the SEC to understand the human resources the CRA devotes to determining credit ratings, applications for registration have to provide the total number of analysts, the total number of analysts' supervisors, a general description of the minimum required qualifications of the analysts (including education and work experience), and a general description of the minimum required qualifications of the analyst supervisors, including education level and work experience. In addition to the information about credit analysts, the application in the USA has to provide organizational information including a chart showing the management structure and senior management reporting lines within the CRA. This information will enable the SEC to assess whether the applicant has adequate managerial resources. In addition, the Dodd–Frank Act requires NRSROs to establish standards of training, experience, and competence for analysts. The SEC proposed rules for NRSROs of May 2011 suggest requiring that at least one individual with at least three or more years experience in performing credit analysis participates in determining a rating.

The application in the EU also provides the following information that will assist ESMA in assessing the quality and quantity of the applicant's personnel responsible for determining and monitoring credit ratings:

- Number of permanent and temporary employees contracted to the applicant and involved in the rating business, including data on length of employment according to the following buckets (over five years, between two and five years, less than two years).

- Number of rating analysts, lead rating analysts, chairs and persons approving ratings. This should include further information on the type of ratings produced or monitored (corporate, public, structured finance); number of years of experience; and area of work (issuance of ratings or monitoring).

The number of employees should be provided on a headcount basis. It is worth noting the required breakdown of analysts by issuance and monitoring. Critics of the CRAs have pointed to the area of ratings surveillance as lacking sufficient resources and in the past ESMA urged CRAs to apply uniformly the principle of adequacy of human resources both to initial credit ratings and monitoring of existing ratings (this is highlighted in paragraph 164 of ESMA's May 2008 report to the European Commission).[50]

CRAs have to provide ESMA with a description of the measures in place to ensure that appropriate resources are employed; rotation policy and detail of the work plan of how it has been implemented; training policies relevant to the rating process, including any type of formal assessment required for the conduct of rating activities; sample templates of employment contracts for rating analysts; procedures for dealing with any complaint made against or by an employee; whistle-blowing policies; measures in place to mitigate the risk of over-reliance on key employees; and any other applicable employment policies and procedures.

Finally, CRAs applying for registration have to submit to ESMA the ratio of analysts to transactions, which is the common benchmark to assess the level of resources devoted to the issuance and monitoring of ratings. It is, however, not a perfect measure due to the differences in the type and depth of analysis required to rate and monitor the different transactions. For example, in the corporate category, the creditworthiness of the issuer primarily determines the credit quality of all the securities it issues, allowing one analyst to rate and monitor many transactions.

---

[50] See footnote 6.

Conversely, in structured finance each deal is unique because each one has a different underlying asset pool, therefore necessitating different analysts.

For these reasons, the application has to include the number of transactions or obligors rated and being monitored per lead rating analyst, broken down by rating category (corporate, public finance, and structured finance). CRAs have to provide the average, top 10%, and bottom 10%.

Compensation

This is another area where concerns were raised in the aftermath of the financial crisis, especially regarding the remuneration criteria for structured finance analysts. If analysts or rating committees' members received compensation dependent on the revenues the CRA earns from the entities they have rated, a conflict would arise as they would have an incentive to determine more optimistic ratings than would have otherwise resulted from an objective assessment.

This is why Article 7.5 of the Regulation stipulates that 'compensation and performance evaluation of rating analysts and persons approving the credit ratings shall not be contingent on the amount of revenue that the credit rating agency derives from the rated entities or related third parties'.

As ESMA pointed out in its Q&A, this article is less strict than the similar provisions concerning the compensation of compliance officers or the independent members of the board, which must be compensated independently of the business performance of the CRA. ESMA has clarified that a different treatment is acceptable and therefore analysts and persons approving the ratings may receive compensation that is dependent on the overall business performance of the CRA—or the performance of the entire group of which the CRA is part—'as long as the overall business performance of the credit rating agency does not rely to a significant extent on the payments received from a rated entity with which the rating analyst interacts with directly on an ongoing basis or in a way that will have a material impact on the independence and quality of the rating process'. However, the CRA will have to ensure that this sort of bonus to analysts and managers does not give rise to conflicts of interest.

This interpretation is in line with the international consensus reflected in provision 2.11.(a) of the IOSCO Code, which stipulates that 'a CRA analyst will not be compensated or evaluated on the basis of the amount of revenue that the CRA derives from issuers that the analyst rates or with which the analyst regularly interacts'.

A CRA has to include in its application for registration the following information that will enable ESMA to assess the applicant's compliance with the requirements concerning the compensation:

- Copy of the compensation and performance evaluation policies and procedures covering all employees involved in the rating business, and especially rating analysts, persons approving ratings, senior management, and the compliance personnel.
- Total remuneration of the above-mentioned employees in the previous business year broken down by the following—in each case the applicant must include a minimum average figure, as well as the top 10% and bottom

10%: base salary versus additional remuneration; employee seniority/rank; and type of credit rating (corporate, public/sovereign, structured finance).

This information on employees' compensation will also assist ESMA in determining whether the applicant has adequate financial resources as required by Annex I.A.8 of the Regulation. ESMA will compare this information with the revenues earned by the applicant for credit rating services to evaluate the CRA's financial condition.

3.8.2.3 Financial Resources

The Regulation does not set out specific requirements concerning the financial resources of the CRA. Only Annex I.A.8 states the general principle that CRAs shall employ appropriate resources to ensure continuity and regularity in the performance of its credit rating activities. ESMA's guidance on registration requires applicants to submit to ESMA the following information: financial statements (on individual as well as consolidated and group of CRAs basis, where applicable) for the past three years and projections, if available, for the next three years; relevant management information and reports; auditor's report; description of the measures in place to ensure sound accounting procedures; and information on revenues.

Financial Statements

The financial statements comprise the balance sheet, the profit and loss account, and the notes on the accounts. The most relevant requirement to assess the financial resources of the applicant is the submission of the individual and, if applicable, the consolidated financial statements. This submission will provide ESMA with information as to the CRA's equity and income; it will also alert ESMA to any possible downward trend that could significantly affect the applicant's financial condition. In addition, where the applicant is a subsidiary of a holding company, ESMA requires the consolidated financial statements of the parent company. This will ensure that ESMA obtains information on the financial strength of the CRA's parent, which is relevant to assess the financial resources of the applicant because the holding company will be in a position to support the CRA. Finally, the financial statements of the applicant must be audited in accordance with the EU accounting Directives.[51]

According to ESMA, all the information required has to be provided only to the extent that it is available. For example, the applicant will not be able to provide financial statements for three years if it was created less than three years ago. Or even if it has been in operation for more than three years, it might happen that not all its annual accounts have been audited in the past (for example, due to small size).

It is less clear what 'if available' means regarding the requirement to submit projections for the next three years. Normally accounting legislation does not

---

[51] Fourth Council Directive of 25 July 1978 on the annual accounts of certain types of companies (78/660/EEC) (*Official Journal* L 222, 14.8.1978: p. 11) and Seventh Council Directive of 13 June 1983 on consolidated accounts (83/349/EEC) (*Official Journal* L 193, 18.7.1983: p. 1).

require companies to produce profit forecasts or estimates. Therefore, it seems that projections will be available only when the CRA has voluntarily produced them for management purposes. In any case, as there is no reference to any rules according to which the projections should have been prepared—for example, requiring verification by an independent accountant or auditor—ESMA should exercise due care when drawing conclusions from such projections when the applicant submits them.

Relevant Management Information and Reports

'Management information' in ESMA's guidance on registration seems to refer to internal information produced by the management of the CRA. This information should be submitted where relevant for ESMA's assessment of the applicant's operations and financial situation. 'Reports' should include the annual report that the company has to produce according to the above-mentioned accounting EU Directives as implemented by national law. This annual report must include at least a fair review of the development and performance of the company's business and of its position, together with a description of the principal risks and uncertainties that it faces. If the reporting company is required to formulate consolidated accounts, the report shall also refer to the entities included in the consolidation.

Information on Revenues

Finally, the information on revenues (broken down by rating, ancillary, and other non-rating services) that must be included in the application, as discussed earlier in this section, will also assist ESMA in determining whether an applicant has adequate financial resources to consistently produce and monitor credit ratings in accordance with their procedures and methodologies and the provisions of the Regulation. The information on revenues will provide additional detail as to the fees generated by different types of services—financial statements alone might not itemize revenues earned from the different segments of the company.

3.8.2.4 *Record-keeping Requirements*

Purpose of the Requirements

The Regulation requires CRAs to make and keep certain records and also to retain other records that they create in the normal course of their business operations. The purpose of the record-keeping requirements is to facilitate ESMA's supervision of CRAs' compliance with the Regulation. ESMA has to examine whether CRAs have appropriately disclosed to the public the methodologies and procedures according to which they determine credit ratings. When conducting investigations, ESMA's officers will use the CRA's records to check whether the agency is adhering in practice to those methodologies and procedures.

Detailed record-keeping requirements ensure consistency among CRAs and facilitate the work of the supervisor's officials when conducting examinations. It is worth noting that the SEC rules on record-keeping are more prescriptive than the European ones. The US rules are more detailed and require more records to be retained. As an example, the SEC requires a record of the rationale for any material difference between the credit rating of a structured finance product implied by a quantitative model and the final credit rating issued or a record of communications from third parties containing complaints about the performance of an analyst. As discussed below, these records are not required in the EU. Another significant difference between both regimes is the time frame for retention of the records—three years after the date the record is created or received in the USA, as opposed to five years in the EU. This might mean that global CRAs end up keeping the records for five years in the USA too.

Although not explicitly required, a CRA is expected to update its records. Once a record is updated with a new element (for example, a new credit rating), the CRA should maintain that element complete in its original form without any alteration.

List of Records in Annex I.B.7

Annex I.B.7 prescribes that 'a credit rating agency shall arrange for adequate records and, where appropriate, audit trails of its credit rating activities to be kept'. And then it enumerates the list of records included in the general rule. The reference to audit trails would mean that CRAs have to generate documents listing all the material files and documents that have been relied upon by the CRA when adopting a rating action and referring to the place where those elements can be retrieved. A discussion of the records included in Annex I.B.7 is provided below.

RATING DECISIONS. According to Annex I.B.7, point (a), for each credit rating decision a CRA has to record 'the identity of the rating analysts participating in the determination of the credit rating, the identity of the persons who have approved the credit rating, information as to whether the credit rating was solicited or unsolicited, and the date on which the credit rating action was taken'. In addition, point (e) of said provision requires the CRA to keep 'the internal records and files, including non-public information and work papers, used to form the basis of the credit rating decision taken'.

This provision requires a CRA to keep for each rating action all the relevant information related to the decision taken: identity of the relevant staff that participated in the formation of the decision, indication whether the rating was solicited or unsolicited, date of the rating action, and all the documents and files that were used as material inputs into the rating decision (in addition to other obvious information not mentioned in the Regulation, such as the identification of the rated entity or the code that identifies the rated instrument).

The record with the identity of the relevant staff that developed the rating action will enable ESMA to contact the persons that formed the credit opinion in the event that it has doubts about a particular rating. Also, identification of those persons will facilitate the monitoring of the rules addressing the handling of material non-public information; although not explicitly required by point (a) of Annex I.B.7, CRAs are also expected to identify in the record any recipients of confidential information for each rating issued (ESMA's guidance on registration).

The Regulation uses the term 'rating analysts' in this provision as encompassing all analytical staff directly involved in the determination of the rating, therefore including primary and secondary analysts (or, according to Article 3 of the Regulation, 'lead rating analysts' and 'rating analysts').

The information as to whether a rating was unsolicited would help ESMA assess if the specific policies and procedures that the CRA has to disclose regarding unsolicited ratings are correctly applied in practice.

The requirement in point (e) should not be understood as requiring the retention of every record that somehow relates to the credit rating process. Only documents or files that form the basis of the rating action or, in other words, that were relied upon in formulating the CRA's opinion, should be kept.

Examples of documents to be retained under this point might be the business plan of the issuer, annual reports, non-public financial statements, loan agreements, prospectuses, notes from meetings or telephone conversations with the issuer, model inputs and outputs, materials presented to the rating committee as part of the lead analyst's recommendation, letter communicating the rating, and so on. Neither the Regulation nor ESMA's guidance clarifies whether public documents should be retained. It seems that they should be part of the record as long as they formed the basis of the rating opinion—taking into account that public documents might not be accessible in the future.

As already indicated, Annex I.B.7 requires CRAs to keep, in addition to records, audit trails of its credit rating activities 'where appropriate'. Interpretation of these words is left to the CRAs. It seems, nevertheless, that an audit trail would not mean that CRAs have to retain draft versions of records, because normally only the final version would be 'used to form the basis of any credit rating decision taken'. However, draft documents that factor into the determination of a credit rating should be maintained.

The retention of all this information will assist ESMA in assessing whether the CRA is applying its procedures and methodologies for determining credit ratings and for handling confidential information.

FEES FROM RATING ENTITIES AND SUBSCRIBERS. Point (b) of Annex I.B.7 requires CRAs to keep the account records relating to fees received from any rated entity or related third party or any user of ratings; in addition, point (c) of the same provision obliges CRAs to retain the account records for each subscriber to the credit ratings or related services.

The language of point (b) is not entirely clear, but it seems to require CRAs to create a record indicating the identification of each person that has paid the CRA for the issuance of a rating; each credit rating issued at that person's request; and the amount paid for each rating. This information will assist ESMA in determining whether the CRA is complying with the rules regarding conflicts of interest. For example, the record will show whether there are persons that have paid the CRA significant fees, therefore giving rise to a potential conflict of interest—as these persons could be in a position to exert undue influence on the CRA.

Regarding clients that have subscribed to the CRA's services, although not explicitly mentioned in point (c), it seems logical that this provision would require the CRA to include in the record the payments received from the subscriber—in addition to the identity of that person—as prescribed by point (b) regarding rated entities. The purpose of this record is to facilitate the supervision by ESMA of the rules on conflicts of interest and also those designed to preserve the confidentiality of material non-public information.

PROCEDURES AND METHODOLOGIES. According to point (d) of Annex I.B.7, a CRA should keep the records documenting the established procedures and methodologies it uses to determine credit ratings.

As required by Article 8.1 and Annex I.E.I.5 of the Regulation, a CRA has to disclose to the public the methodologies, models, and key rating assumptions it uses in its credit rating activities (see Section 3.8.4). In addition, the information to be provided to ESMA in the application for registration must include a description of the CRA's procedures and methodologies used to issue and review credit ratings (Annex II.10). ESMA's guidance on registration has already clarified that the latter should be a 'high level description for each type of credit rating of the range of core models and methodologies used to determine credit ratings'. And it seems that the disclosure to the public of the methodologies used by the CRA to determine credit ratings should also consist of a description of such methodologies, as opposed to the publication of the complete methodologies. What matters is that such a description allows users of ratings to understand how the CRA determines credit ratings. Making the methodologies public would mean a voluminous publication that would not help users of ratings more than a clear description; additionally, publication of methodologies could force CRAs to disclose proprietary information.

Accordingly, the record-keeping provision on procedures and methodologies used to determine ratings should be understood as requiring CRAs to internally document those procedures and methodologies—not just their description. This requirement would permit ESMA to assess whether CRAs are publishing sufficient information about their procedures and methodologies to enable users of ratings to understand how CRAs arrive at them. In addition, it would assist ESMA in supervising whether CRAs are adhering to their procedures and methodologies when assigning ratings.

CREDIT REPORTS. CRAs have to create a record including credit analysis reports, credit assessment reports and private credit rating reports, and internal records, including non-public information and work papers, used to form the basis of the opinions expressed in such reports (Annex I.B.7, point (f)).

CRAs usually sell reports to clients containing detailed information about the analysis undertaken to support a rating opinion (see Section 3.8.2). Private credit ratings are outside the scope of the Regulation because they are only provided to the person that requested the rating; notwithstanding, this article requires CRAs to maintain the information that was used as a material input into the private rating decision.

CRAs might factor confidential information received from the rated entity into those reports. ESMA would be able to review the proper handling of non-public information by examining the retained records.

RECORDS ON COMPLIANCE. Annex I.B.7 in its point (g) also requires CRAs to record the procedures and measures they have implemented to comply with this Regulation. It seems that the Regulation expects the agency to document and maintain all the procedures developed by the compliance function and also the measures adopted to ensure compliance with these procedures and with the Regulation. As an example, CRAs should retain the reports produced by the compliance function for the board in accordance with Annex I.A.6 or the reviews issued by the internal control function. These reports will provide information to ESMA as to whether the CRA is complying with the Regulation and with its own procedures.

COMMUNICATIONS. Finally, the Regulation requires the retention of copies of internal and external communications, including electronic communications, received and sent by the credit rating agency and its employees, which relate to credit rating activities (Annex I.B.7, point (h)). This record might assist ESMA in identifying unlawful practices and compliance deficiencies. It should be noted that the scope of this provision is broader than that of letter (e) and (f) as it requires maintaining a communication that relates to the issuance or monitoring of a rating even if did not contribute to forming the opinion of the CRA. Basically, it means that all communications with the issuer relating to the rating need to be retained.

Other References to Records in the Regulation

In addition to the records required by Annex I.B.7, there are references to records in other parts of the Regulation.

ANTI-COMPETITIVE PRACTICES IN STRUCTURED FINANCE (NOTCHING). The Regulation requires a CRA to record all instances where, in determining the rating of a structured finance instrument, it departs from an existing rating on the underlying assets issued by a competitor (see Section 3.8.4). The CRA has to include in the record the justification for the different assessment (Article 8.4). This record will be useful for ESMA in determining whether the CRA is adhering to its procedures and methodologies for the issuance of structure finance credit ratings and to detect any possible anti-competitive practices.

THREATS TO INDEPENDENCE. The second sentence of paragraph 7 of Annex I.A prescribes that a CRA 'shall arrange for records to be kept of all significant threats to the independence of the credit rating activities, including those to the rules on rating analysts referred to in Section C, as well as the safeguards applied to mitigate those threats'.

This provision requires a CRA to document, for each rating action, the presence or absence of any conflicts of interest regarding the decision taken. If a potential conflict of interest was identified, the CRA should also document the measures applied to mitigate the risk to the CRA's objectivity. For example, a CRA would have to make a record documenting that it has received more than 5% of its annual revenue from the entity being rated and the steps taken to prevent this conflict from impairing the objectivity of its opinions.

The reference in the provision to Section C is somewhat unclear, because this section contains prohibited conflicts which are therefore not manageable. For example, an analyst owning financial instruments of the rated entity may not participate in the determination of the rating. It seems that a negative statement retained in the file of the rating would address the prohibitions under Section C.

Annex I.A.7 supplements some of the retention requirements set out in Annex I.B.7 that also refer to conflicts of interest. For example, as previously discussed, the latter provision requires a CRA to create records relating to the conflicts arising from receiving payments from issuers and subscribers or to those that arise from some ancillary activities.

CRAs have to disclose to the public any actual or potential conflicts of interest according to Annex I.B.1 and Annex I.E.I.1. Also, although not expressly required by Annex II, applicants for registration will provide ESMA with an inventory of potential conflicts of interest (ESMA's guidance on registration). This record-keeping requirement will assist ESMA in examining whether a CRA has adequately disclosed to the public all conflicts that arise from its activities and also whether it has notified ESMA of any material modification to its application regarding the identification of conflicts of interest, in case this was necessary. In addition, ESMA will use these records to review whether the CRA has implemented procedures to manage these conflicts.

TELEPHONE AND DATA TRAFFIC. Article 23c.1.(a) of the Regulation empowers officials of ESMA to 'examine any records, data, procedures and any other material relevant to the execution of its tasks irrespective of the medium on which they are stored'. This power refers to the records that, as discussed in this section, CRAs are required to create and retain, or to maintain according to the record-keeping requirements of the Regulation.

In addition, Article 23c.1.(e) expressly authorizes ESMA to 'require records of telephone and data traffic'. An almost identical provision is included in MiFID and the Market Abuse Directive, with the aim of allowing competent authorities to gather evidence in market abuse investigations. As specifically indicated in Article 23c.6, the objective of this power is to enable ESMA to investigate possible infringements of the Regulation. It seems that the possible infringements would be only those related to abuse of inside information, as CRAs are not required to tape telephone conversations of their employees and include them in the record of each rating. Therefore, the records referred to by Article 23c.1.(e) would be, as in the case of MiFID and the Market Abuse Directive, any existing records of phone numbers dialled from the telephone devices owned by the CRA.

Paragraph 5 of Article 23c stipulates that if a request for records of telephone or data traffic requires authorization from a judicial authority according to national rules, such authorization shall be applied for. Where such authorization is applied for, the national judicial authority shall control the proportionality of the coercive measures envisaged by ESMA, according to paragraph 6 of the same article. Of relevance for the exercise of this power are the E-Privacy Directive[52] and the Data Protection Directive.[53]

Time Period and Manner of Retention

Annex I.B.8 stipulates that:

> Records and audit trails referred to in point 7 shall be kept at the premises of the registered credit rating agency for at least five years and be made available upon request to ESMA.

---

[52] Directive 2002/58/EC of the European Parliament and of the Council of 12 July 2002 concerning the processing of personal data and the protection of privacy in the electronic communications sector (Directive on privacy and electronic communications) (*Official Journal* L 201, 31.07.2002: pp. 37–47).

[53] Directive 95/46/EC of the European Parliament and of the Council of 24 October 1995 on the protection of individuals with regard to the processing of personal data and on the free movement of such data. (*Official Journal* L 281, 23.11.1995: pp. 31–50).

Where the registration of a credit rating agency is withdrawn, the records shall be kept for an additional term of at least three years.

The five-year retention time frame will give ESMA sufficient time to review the files before they are discarded by the CRA. In the case of withdrawal of the registration, the records will have to be retained for an additional period of at least three years.

There is neither manner nor time frame for retention specified with respect to the records not included in Annex I.B.7. In the absence of ESMA's guidance on this point, it seems that CRAs should also keep the records on structured finance and threats to independence for at least five years and in the manner indicated in paragraph 8.

CRAs should maintain records in a manner that allows them to provide the records to ESMA upon request and in a timely manner. The Regulation does not specify the format in which the records must be retained. Consequently, CRAs may keep them as electronic files, hard copies, or any other format. The requirement that the records and audit trails must be kept at the premises of the CRA would suggest that EU legislators were thinking of storage of physical documents. Nonetheless, a group of CRAs will normally keep the documents stored electronically in a system that is managed centrally for the whole group. Analysts or the record retention system scan the documents in printed form and the electronic image is uploaded—along with the records originally generated in electronic form—into the system. This practice should ensure ESMA's timely access to the records if needed—for example, records originating in a foreign branch.

ESMA was asked to confirm that electronic imaging and storage of these documents off-site (that is accessible on-site) complies with the above-mentioned provision of the Regulation. ESMA's Q&A responded affirmatively, clarifying that accessibility is a key condition for this practice to be acceptable and that responsibility for the safety and integrity of the data must remain at the CRA level (the CRA is required to retain the record according to the Regulation).

Regarding physical files, it seems that paragraph 8 would prohibit CRAs using the services of a third party custodian, because in that case the records would not be maintained at the premises of the CRA.

Finally, Annex I.B.9 prescribes a specific time frame for retention of the contract with the rated entity: 'records which set out the respective rights and obligations of the credit rating agency and the rated entity or its related third parties under an agreement to provide credit rating services shall be retained for at least the duration of the relationship with that rated entity or its related third parties'. In the case of private ratings, the recorded contract will enable CRAs to justify to ESMA the lack of publication or distribution of the rating.

Protection of the Records

Annex I.C.3.(a) of the Regulation requires a CRA to ensure that its personnel that are directly involved in credit rating activities and persons closely associated with them take all reasonable measures to protect the records in possession of the CRA from fraud, theft, or misuse. A good practice to ensure that the records are protected is to store them electronically in a central system of record retention with restricted access. Any physical documents should be retained in centralized archives and in a manner that prevents unauthorized access.

Information on Record Keeping to be Provided in the Application for Registration

ESMA's guidance on registration requires applicants to submit their policies and procedures on record-keeping. It is expected that these policies and procedures will cover all the requirements set out in Annex I.B, points 7–9, Article 8.4, Annex I.A.7, Article 23e.1.(e) and indicate which records are kept and for how long. Finally, as discussed above, ESMA requires the procedures to identify recipients of confidential information for each rating issued. All this information is required for ESMA to asses that the applicant is complying with the record retention requirements.

3.8.2.5 Business Continuity

In order to be registered, a CRA must demonstrate to ESMA its ability to ensure the continuity and regularity in the performance of its rating activities. This would mean having policies and procedures in place that would indicate to the staff how to react in the event of the occurrence of a major incident that prevents it from conducting its normal business. Continuity plans will typically detail the key staff that will coordinate the response to the incident, the communications strategy, the key decisions and tasks that need to be performed, and alternative premises.

As part of the application for registration, CRAs will submit to ESMA copies of the above-mentioned procedures including, where applicable, information on their applicability to outsourced service providers. Additionally, applicants will provide information about their continuity planning tests (where applicable), indicating the types of tests conducted and the frequency of testing (ESMA's guidance on registration).

3.8.2.6 Information Systems

CRAs use information systems to support their rating activities and administrative functions and to manage their websites. Annex I.A.8 stipulates that a CRA shall employ appropriate systems 'to ensure continuity and regularity in the performance of its credit rating activities'. In addition, Annex I.A.4 obliges a CRA to have 'effective control and safeguard arrangements for information processing systems'.

In its application for registration, a CRA is required by ESMA to describe its information systems, including any backup systems, and identify the senior manager responsible (guidance on registration). In addition, the application will include a description of the procedures implemented to ensure effective control and safeguard arrangements for the information systems in place, as well as the mechanisms to monitor their effectiveness (such as audits conducted by the internal audit function of the CRA). Finally, ESMA also indicates that the analytical staff should not have permission to access the systems and records documenting the fees charged by the CRA.

3.8.2.7 Outsourcing

Definition and Requirements

Article 9 of the Regulation provides that 'outsourcing of important operational functions shall not be undertaken in such a way as to impair materially the quality of the credit rating agency's internal control and the ability of ESMA to supervise the credit rating agency's compliance with obligations under this Regulation'.

As the CRA Regulation does not define outsourcing, the first question that arises when interpreting this provision is what outsourcing means. As the language in the CRA Regulation has been taken from Article 13.5 of MiFID, it seems appropriate to follow the definition of outsourcing provided by Directive 2006/73/EC (MiFID implementing directive).[54] Accordingly, 'outsourcing' would mean an arrangement of any form between a CRA and a service provider by which that service provider performs a process, a service, or an activity which would otherwise be undertaken by the CRA itself. This definition is consistent with that included in the IOSCO principles on outsourcing. The term would cover a broad range of functions, from relatively tangential activities, such as payroll processing or the security of the firm's premises and personnel, to material tasks, such as the provision of credit rating activities or information technology services. However, purchasing contracts—the acquisition from a vendor of standardized services and goods—would not fall within the definition of outsourcing.

Whilst the use of outsourcing might bring substantial benefits to the outsourcing firms, it also poses a number of challenges, both for those firms and for their supervisors. This is why international regulators have developed a number of principles designed to help firms to manage the risk associated with the use of this strategy. Among them, IOSCO issued in 2005 its *Principles on outsourcing of financial services for market intermediaries*. Subsequently, EBA and EIOPA, drawing from the IOSCO principles, released their own guidelines focusing respectively on the utilization of outsourcing by financial institutions and insurance companies.[55] Regarding the securities area, international good market practices existing before MiFID were codified in Directive 2006/73/EC. This directive sets out the conditions that investment firms have to follow when outsourcing critical or important operational functions or investment services or activities.

ESMA has also issued guidance on outsourcing arrangements used by CRAs through its public Q&A. According to ESMA, if a CRA is relying on outsourcing arrangements it should have a policy covering, as a minimum:

a) The checks that the CRA would conduct when assessing the viability of utilising an outsourcing arrangement for a certain aspect of their business— this should include a consideration of whether using an outsourcing arrangement would breach Article 9 or any other Article of the Regulation; an

---

[54] Article 2.6 of the EC Directive 2006/73/EC of 10 August 2006 implementing Directive 2004/39/EC of the European Parliament and of the Council as regards organisational requirements and operating conditions for investment firms and defined terms for the purposes of that Directive (*Official Journal* L 241, 2.9.2006: pp. 26–58).

[55] IOSCO (2005), *Principles on outsourcing of financial services for market intermediaries*; CEBS (2006), *Guidelines on outsourcing*; CEIOPS (2009), *Advice for level 2 implementing measures on Solvency II: system of governance*.

evaluation of the risks presented to the quality, integrity, and continuity of ratings; the controls that would need to be put in place; and the level at which this would need to be signed-off.

b) The checks that the CRA would perform with regard to potential out-sourcing partners to ensure that they would handle any sensitive data appropriately; are able to perform the role required without putting the quality, integrity, and continuity of ratings at risk; and the level at which the final sign-off for the arrangement would need to be made.

c) The monitoring that the CRA would conduct to ensure that outsourcing arrangements remained appropriate.

In order to put into context the ESMA's guidance on CRAs, it is relevant to consider the key topics on outsourcing that can be drawn from the above-mentioned international guidelines, as set out below.

Materiality

Article 9 of the CRA Regulation only applies to 'important operational functions'. Neither the Regulation nor ESMA's Q&A provide a definition of these functions, so again MiFID implementing measures can help to understand the meaning of Article 9. According to Article 13 of the MiFID implementing directive, an operational function shall be regarded as critical or important[56] if a defect or failure in its performance would materially impair the continuing compliance of an investment firm with the conditions and obligations of its authorization or its other obligations under MiFID, or its financial performance, or the soundness or the continuity of its investment services and activities.

The assessment of what is important is normally subjective and depends on the nature and circumstances of each CRA and the service provider. IOSCO has developed a non-exhaustive list of factors that would help firms when determining the importance of an outsourcing arrangement: financial, reputational, and oper-ational impact on the outsourcing firm of the failure of a service provider to perform; potential impact of outsourcing on the provision of adequate services to an outsourcing firm's customers; potential losses to an outsourcing firm's custom-ers on the failure of a service provider to perform; impact of outsourcing activity on the ability and capacity of the outsourcing firm to conform with regulatory requirements and changes in requirements; cost; affiliation or other relationship between the outsourcing firm and the service provider; regulatory status of the service provider; and degree of difficulty and time required to select an alternative service provider or to bring the business activity in house, if necessary.

Taking into account these IOSCO factors, it seems that the important CRA functions should include all tasks that are fundamental to carry out its core business. Accordingly, important operational functions within a CRA would be its management, the compliance and internal quality control functions, the development and review of rating methodologies, the credit rating activities as

---

[56] 'Critical or important' is a single concept as it seems that there is not any difference between the two terms in the MiFID context. Therefore, this concept would be similar to the expression used in the CRA Regulation, which only refers to 'important' functions.

defined by the Regulation, the provision of ongoing systems maintenance and support, the provision of ongoing software and systems management, and the maintenance of records.

Even if an arrangement has been categorized as an important operational function, CRAs can still outsource the task. Article 9 does not prohibit the outsourcing of important operational functions, but it does set some requirements for this to be possible. Therefore, CRAs should be able to apply Article 9 of the Regulation and ESMA's guidance in a proportionate way, taking into account the circumstances of the case. Nonetheless, it seems that record retention may not be outsourced to third parties because the records must be kept at the premises of the CRA, according to the language of the Regulation (see Section 3.8.2). This exemption could be justified because the records CRAs are required to retain are an essential tool for supervisors when conducting examinations. However, outsourcing of the record retention to another entity of the group should be allowed because it would permit a better management of the retention system for the whole group and enhanced protection of the records.

Regarding non-material activities, there should be no restrictions on their outsourcing, although CRAs could consider the appropriateness of applying the principles set out in ESMA's guidance.

Accountability

The CRA remains fully responsible for discharging all of its obligations under the Regulation in the event of the use of outsourcing arrangements, as stated in Recital 54 of the Regulation. Accordingly, as required by ESMA, prior to entering into an outsourcing arrangement, the CRA should consider whether using an outsourcing agreement would breach any article of the CRA Regulation and should evaluate the risks it could pose to its core business.

Moreover, once it has entered into an outsourcing arrangement, the CRA should retain in-house competence to ensure ongoing compliance with all regulatory requirements, to assess whether the service provider delivers according to contract, and to resume control over the outsourced activity if necessary.

Finally, according to the above-mentioned MiFID implementing directive, the outsourcing must not result in the delegation by senior management of their responsibility. This means that the outsourcing CRA, including its board of directors and senior management, remains fully responsible. Delegation of responsibility would be incompatible with the managers' obligation to run the CRA under their own responsibility.

Supervision of the Outsourced Function by ESMA

The ability of the competent authority to assess and monitor compliance of a CRA with the obligations provided for under the CRA Regulation should not be limited by any outsourcing arrangements entered into by the CRA (Recital 54 of the CRA Regulation). Therefore, Article 23b.1 of the CRA Regulation recognizes that ESMA may use the supervisory and investigatory powers referred to in the article also in relation to third parties to whom the credit rating agencies have outsourced operational functions or activities.

Outsourcing to Affiliates

It is generally recognized that intra-group outsourcing poses a lower level of risk. The MiFID implementing directive stipulates that in these cases the extent to which the firm controls the service provider or has the ability to influence its actions will be taken into account. The outsourcing firm is likely to have a greater familiarity with the service provider's business attributes than in the case of an external provider. These elements will be considered by CRAs when applying ESMA's Q&A to their intra-group outsourcing arrangements. As an example, ESMA explicitly allows the outsourcing of the internal function in charge of the review of methodologies to another entity of the global group (see Section 3.8.4).

Outsourcing Outside the EU

The CRA Regulation does not restrict the ability of CRAs to enter into outsourcing arrangements with providers located in third countries. Accordingly, CRAs should be free to outsource functions within the EU as well as outside the EU. However, CRAs entering into and managing outsourcing agreements that are undertaken outside the EU should take into account additional concerns.

The MiFID implementing directive imposes some limitations to investment firms wishing to outsource the investment service of portfolio management provided to retail clients to a service provider based in a third country. As CRAs' business consists just of issuing opinions, it is doubtful that similar restrictions should be imposed on outsourcing CRAs. Nevertheless, CRAs should ensure that outsourcing outside the EU does not hinder the effective supervision by ESMA. This would mean that the outsourcing CRA ensures supervisory authority access to relevant data regarding the outsourced function held by the service provider. To this end, ESMA may require that the records are maintained in the EU or that the service provider agrees to send the books and records to the EU authorities upon request. At least, as discussed above, the records relating to the outsourced function that the CRA must retain according to the Regulation should be kept at the premises of the CRA or of its parent company, or another entity of its group.

Principles for Outsourcing CRAs

The above-mentioned international guidance on outsourcing in the financial sector and ESMA's Q&A can be summarized as follows:

- The CRA should have a policy that covers all aspects of outsourcing, including intra-group outsourcing, and should conduct suitable due diligence processes in the selection and monitoring of service providers. The CRA should manage the risks associated with its outsourcing arrangements.
- There should be a legally binding written contract (the outsourcing arrangement) between the CRA and each third party service provider; that should include provisions relating to the termination of the contract and appropriate exit strategies.
- The service provider should be obliged to protect confidential information, to take appropriate measures to protect the CRA's software, and to establish

emergency procedures and disaster recovery and contingency plans where this is necessary, having regard to the function outsourced.

- The CRA should inform ESMA about outsourcing of important operational functions[57] and outsourcing should not limit ESMA's ability to supervise compliance with the rules.

More details on these principles can be found in the relevant guidance issued by IOSCO, EBA, and EIOPA.

Application for Registration

According to ESMA's guidance on registration, a CRA has to include the following information in its application for registration in order for ESMA to assess that the applicant's outsourcing arrangements do not impair the quality of its internal control and ESMA's ability to supervise the outsourced activities: policies and procedures with respect to outsourcing; description of the functions being outsourced; description of the entity to which rating activities are outsourced, including its full name and address; description of the outsourcing agreements between the applicant and the service provider; and a copy of any internal or external review of the risks posed by the outsourcing arrangements (where applicable).

3.8.3 Independence and Conflicts of Interest

Recital 26 of the CRA Regulation prescribes that CRAs should establish appropriate internal policies and procedures in order to prevent, identify, eliminate or manage, and disclose any conflicts of interest. Recital 27 adds two other key principles in this area: disclosure of conflicts in a timely manner and record-keeping of all significant threats to the independence of the CRA.

Moreover, Article 6.1 establishes the overarching principle that CRAs should take the necessary measures to ensure that only elements relevant to the credit assessment should be factored into the determination of a credit rating:

> A credit rating agency shall take all necessary steps to ensure that the issuing of a credit rating is not affected by any existing or potential conflict of interest or business relationship involving the credit rating agency issuing the credit rating, its managers, rating analysts, employees, any other natural person whose services are placed at the disposal or under the control of the credit rating agency, or any person directly or indirectly linked to it by control.

Those steps are spelled out in Sections A and B of Annex I, in the form of organizational and operational requirements imposed on CRAs. The objective of the requirements is to preserve the independence of the CRA and avoid conflicts of interest.

---

[57] According to Recital 52 of the CRA Regulation significant changes to the outsourcing arrangements should be considered as material changes to the conditions for initial registration of a CRA.

3.8.3.1 Independence

According to provision 2.1 of the IOSCO Code, 'a CRA should not forbear or refrain from taking a rating action based on the potential effect (economic, political, or otherwise) of the action on the CRA, an issuer, an investor, or other market participant'.

In the EU, according to Annex I.A.1.(a), the senior management of the CRA is the body responsible for adopting the measures that will ensure that 'credit rating activities are independent, including from all political and economic influences or constraints' (see Section 3.8.1). The Regulation does not contain any specific requirements that would give effect to this principle, apart from the detailed requirements on conflicts of interest that are analysed further in this section. This is because the Regulation's safeguards focus on the independence of CRAs vis-à-vis issuers and related parties whose financial instruments are rated.

The EC impact assessment CRA Regulation made clear that:

> Rating opinions and rating methodologies should not be subject to supervisory scrutiny or any form of regulatory influence. In addition, under no circumstances will a competent authority of a Member State be able to take measures against a CRA based on the fact that the CRA issues rating opinions that may be contrary to the interests of the Member State or specific issuers.

The crisis that affected the market confidence on the sovereign debt of several Members of the Euro area starting in 2010 tested CRAs' compliance with provision 2.1 of the IOSCO Code. Successive downgrades of the debt of several EU Member States contributed to the dramatic increase of their borrowing costs, even forcing some of them to request bail-outs from the EU. Moreover, these rating actions had a systemic impact not only on the financial markets of the country subject to the downgrade but also on other countries of the Euro zone. Although CRAs are always criticized for reacting too slowly to macroeconomic and market events, the fact that they took rating actions that had a significant economic and political impact for the Euro area countries is an indication of their independence vis-à-vis political powers.

Provision 2.10 of the IOSCO Code also aims to safeguard the independence of CRAs: 'in instances where rated entities (e.g. governments) have, or are simultaneously pursuing monitoring functions related to the CRA, the CRA should use different employees to conduct its rating actions than those employees involved in its oversight issues'. Although ESMA is independent from EU governments, it would seem prudent for CRAs to observe this principle when ESMA is in the process of conducting an investigation.

3.8.3.2 General Approach on Conflicts of Interest

The approach of the Regulation to the handling of conflicts of interest is set out in Annex I.B.1:

> A credit rating agency shall identify, eliminate or manage and disclose, clearly and prominently, any actual or potential conflicts of interest that may influence the analyses and judgments of its rating analysts, employees, or any other natural person whose services are placed at the disposal or under the control of the credit rating

agency and who are directly involved in the issuing of credit rating and persons approving credit ratings.

In accordance with this provision, a CRA has to take three steps, as discussed below.

Identification of any Actual or Potential Conflict

The CRA will identify the conflicts in the records documenting the rating actions, as discussed in the analysis of record-keeping requirements provided in Section 3.8.2.

The EU CRA Regulation does not include a list of the conflicts of interest a CRA should manage. It just indicates the conflicts that are prohibited and prescribes some policies and procedures to ensure that those that are permitted do not influence the opinions and analysis the CRA makes. The SEC rules do provide such a list of the conflicts that a CRA is prohibited to have unless it manages and discloses the type of conflict identified in the list. The SEC's list covers the types of conflicts that normally arise from the rating business; in addition to those types of conflicts, it includes a catch-all provision for all other additional conflicts that a CRA might include in its application for registration.

The lists of prohibited and permitted conflicts, along with the specific policies and procedures designed to address them, are provided in this section. These two lists have been drawn up on the basis of the EU Regulation, SEC rules, and the IOSCO Code, along with the specific policies and procedures designed to address them.

Elimination or Management of the Conflict

Annex I.A.7 states that 'a credit rating agency shall establish appropriate and effective organizational and administrative arrangements to prevent, identify, eliminate or manage and disclose any conflicts of interest referred to in point 1 of Section B'. Once a conflict is identified, the CRA has to assess whether it is a conflict prohibited by the Regulation or by its internal procedures, or whether the conflict is permitted. In the former case, the CRA has to eliminate the conflict— this means that the rating activity shall not be carried out if the conflict is present. In the latter case, the CRA has to implement policies and procedures to address and manage the conflict.

There are some general policies and procedures that are designed by the Regulation to address all the conflicts that might arise when CRAs conduct their activities. These are some of the organizational requirements imposed by Section A of Annex I, that have been already analysed in the relevant sections of the book: roles of the board of directors and specifically of the independent members of the board; compliance function; record-keeping requirements regarding conflicts of interest; and whistle-blowing policies. In addition, the Regulation imposes other measures aimed at addressing particular conflicts. These are analysed further in this section when discussing the list of possible conflicts.

Disclosure of the Conflict

According to Annex I.E.I.1 of the Regulation, CRAs are obliged to disclose any actual and potential conflicts of interest referred to in Annex I.B.1. This information, along with the other disclosures required by Annex I.E.I, will be published by a CRA on its website as soon as practical after registration is granted. As prescribed by provision 2.7 of the IOSCO Code, these disclosures should be complete, timely, clear, concise, specific, and prominent.

The approach followed in the USA regarding the means and timing for publication of conflicts of interest is somewhat different. As already discussed, in the USA most of the information included by an applicant in its registration form has to be publicly available; therefore market participants will be able to know the conflicts relating to a CRA by means of its public application—that the CRA is required to update. In the EU, the information submitted to ESMA in the application for registration is not made public; rather, CRAs will make their conflicts of interest public after registration, as indicated above. In addition, the press release or report accompanying the publication of a rating should indicate whether there is any particular conflict that could have impaired the objectivity of the rating process and what measures were adopted to handle the conflict (for example, if the rated entity contributes to more than 5% of the CRA's revenues).

The EU framework ensures that users of ratings are made aware of the potential conflicts of interest that arise from a CRA's business activities and that a CRA sets up policies and procedures that will address the conflicts that are not prohibited outright in order to avoid any undue influence on the rating activities. This is also the system adopted by the SEC in the USA, although, as discussed in more detail below, there are some differences between the specific requirements imposed by both regimes.

3.8.3.3 Prohibited Conflicts

EU legislators have considered that there is a number of conflicts that should be prohibited in order to ensure the integrity of ratings and protect investors. These cases would be too difficult to manage given the risk that they could cause undue influence. Therefore, a CRA should refrain from issuing a rating action when it is aware of the presence of any of the situations set out below. However, a conflict could arise or be known only once the rating has already been issued. This circumstance is envisaged in Annex I.B.3, which requires the CRA to immediately disclose the conflict and put the rating on the watch list, in order to determine whether the rating should be modified or withdrawn. Although this course of action is only prescribed for the first set of conflicts described below, it seems logical that a CRA applies the same logic to any existing credit rating that has been issued in breach of any of the prohibitions discussed below.

Issuing a Credit Rating under any of the Circumstances
Laid Down in Annex I.B.3

The Regulation considers that under the circumstances referred to in Annex I.B.3 it would be very difficult for the CRA or the persons indicated to remain impartial. The 'persons referred to in point 1', that are mentioned in the following letters (a) and (c) are those indicated in Annex I.B.1: 'rating analysts, employees, or any other natural person whose services are placed at the disposal or under the control of the credit rating agency and who are directly involved in the issuing of credit rating and persons approving credit ratings'. Annex I.B.3 stipulates that:

> A credit rating agency shall not issue a credit rating in any of the following circumstances, or shall, in the case of an existing credit rating, immediately disclose where the credit rating is potentially affected by the following:
>
> (a) the credit rating agency or persons referred to in point 1, directly or indirectly owns financial instruments of the rated entity or a related third party or has any other direct or indirect ownership interest in that entity or party, other than holdings in diversified collective investment schemes, including managed funds such as pension funds or life insurance;
>
> (b) the credit rating is issued with respect to the rated entity or a related third party directly or indirectly linked to the credit rating agency by control;
>
> (c) a person referred to in point 1 is a member of the administrative or supervisory board of the rated entity or a related third party; or
>
> (d) a rating analyst who participated in determining a credit rating, or a person who approved a credit rating, has had a relationship with the rated entity or a related third party which may cause a conflict of interests.
>
> A credit rating agency shall also immediately assess whether there are grounds for re-rating or withdrawing the existing credit rating.

The prohibition imposed on CRAs by Annex I.B.3 is that they shall not 'issue a credit rating'. However, the prohibition covers any other rating activities with respect to the rated issuer in which a conflicted person participates (for example, the CRA should not have analysts monitoring transactions if they own securities issued by the rated entity).

ESMA's Q&A has clarified the scope of the prohibition under letter (a). It asks whether the rule prohibits any individual specified in the Regulation from trading or owning securities of any rated entity or related third party, even if that individual is not involved in rating the specific entity. ESMA's answer is that the Regulation only prohibits the individuals directly involved in credit rating activities to have a direct financial interest in a rated entity 'within the individual's area of primary analytical responsibility'. Therefore, the Regulation allows employees to own securities issued by a company rated by the CRA, as long as they are not involved in the rating activities with respect to that rated entity.

It should be noted that letter (a) also prohibits the CRA itself from issuing a rating with respect to an entity where the CRA owns financial instruments issued by said entity. Only holdings in diversified collective investment schemes are excluded from the prohibition. The reason for this prohibition is that the objectivity of the CRA could be jeopardized if it has a financial interest in the rated issuer. However, the drafting of the CRA Regulation seems pretty strict, as it does not set any exemption for small holdings or even for government securities that might be held as cash equivalents (as is the case in the SEC proposed rules for NRSROs of May 2011).

Letter (b) should be understood as prohibiting the CRA from rating the securities of its parent company, a company under common control with the CRA, or a company controlled by the CRA. Logically it would also prohibit a CRA from rating its own securities.

Letter (c) prohibits a CRA from assigning a rating if any of the analysts involved is a member of the board of the rated company. Concerning sovereign ratings, this provision should be construed as banning a CRA from issuing a rating where any of the analysts holds a public function in the government or public entity being rated.

The possible conflict prohibited by letter (d), about past relationships between rating analysts or persons approving the rating and the rated entity or related third parties, raises several interpretative issues. First, it does not seem logical to consider that a conflict might arise due to past relationships but not due to current relationships (such as the existing business relationships that might give rise to a permitted conflict, as discussed further in this section). Second, although letter (d) only mentions rating analysts and persons approving the ratings as subjects of the possible conflict, the prohibition should also encompass lead analysts, despite the fact that the terms 'rating analyst' and 'lead rating analyst' are defined separately in Article 3 of the Regulation. Finally, the Regulation gives flexibility to the CRA in determining whether the relationship with the issuer may or may not cause a conflict of interest.

Rating an Obligor or Financial Instrument where the Obligor or Issuer has been Previously Advised by the CRA

This conflict, and the type of consultancy or advisory services that would be captured by Annex I.B.4, first subparagraph and Annex I.B.5, have been analysed in Section 3.8.2. These provisions prohibit this conflict because the Regulation considers that a CRA could not manage it; a CRA would not be impartial rating a structure that has been designed following its advice.

Participation of Employees Directly Involved in Credit Rating Activities in the Negotiation of Fees

According to Article 7.2 of the CRA Regulation, a CRA shall ensure that rating analysts, their employees, and any other natural person whose services are placed at its disposal or under its control and who are directly involved in credit rating activities 'shall not be allowed to initiate or participate in negotiations regarding fees or payments with any rated entity, related third party or any person directly or indirectly linked to the rated entity by control'.

Therefore, this conflict is prohibited. The purpose is to insulate the analytical staff from commercial discussions with the issuer; participation in such negotiations could make analysts more or less favourably disposed towards the issuer and this influence would compromise the impartiality of their analytical judgements. Moreover, the prohibition does not only cover the analytical teams involved in the rating process; as rating activities would also encompass the development and review of methodologies (see Section 3.3.2), the staff working for the review function would also be prohibited from discussing fees with rated entities. If analysts responsible for approving methodologies were allowed to negotiate payments with an issuer, for example, they could have a bias in favour of the rated entity and this would influence their judgement when deciding whether to implement an adjustment to a methodology that could have an adverse impact on the existing ratings assigned to that issuer.

Finally, the language in Article 7.2 (and the similar rule adopted by the SEC) goes beyond provision 2.12 of the IOSCO Code, which restricts the prohibition only to negotiations of fees by the analysts with an issuer that the analyst is rating.

**Assigning or Monitoring a Rating where the Analysts Directly Involved
in the Credit Rating Activities Received Money, Gifts, or Favours
from the Rated Entity or from its Related Third Parties**

The Regulation prohibits this conflict because accepting gifts from the rated issuer
could seriously compromise the impartiality of the analysts directly involved in
the rating process. Moreover, the prohibition has a very wide scope, which conforms to provision 2.15 of the IOSCO Code.

According to Annex I.C.4, rating analysts, employees, as well as any other
natural person whose services are placed at the disposal or under control of the
CRA and who is directly involved in credit rating activities, and persons closely
associated with them 'shall not solicit or accept money, gifts or favours from
anyone with whom the credit rating agency does business'.

This provision means that the analytical staff are not only prohibited from
receiving gifts from the issuers they rate or monitor, but also from any other client
or provider of services to the CRA. In addition, it prohibits also the solicitation of
money, gifts, or favours.

3.8.3.4 Permitted Conflicts

The conflicts set forth below are not prohibited as long as the CRA adopts
adequate measures to ensure that impartiality is maintained in the rating process.

**Receiving Compensation from Rated Entities to Determine
Credit Ratings or from Subscribers**

COMPENSATION FROM RATED ENTITIES. Being paid by rated entities or underwriters to determine credit ratings with respect of the financial instruments they
issue or underwrite has always been one of the conflicts that has drawn more
criticism to CRAs operating under the issuer-pays model. The conflict also
includes being paid by an entity to assign a rating to the entity as an obligor.

The entity that requests a rating obviously has an interest in obtaining the
highest possible rating in the CRA's scale because this will lower the cost of its
financing. Thus it might try to influence the CRA in order to be assigned a more
favourable rating than warranted. The concern is that the CRA might allow this
conflict to influence the rating process, downplaying the financial risks of the
issuer in order to retain the business. In a similar way, the risks taken by an
underwriter paying for the rating of the securities it is going to underwrite will
presumably diminish with an optimistic rating, as prospective investors will be
more likely to be interested in the deal.

Many observers have noted that this conflict of interest is even more acute in
the structured finance area, given the volume of deals, high fees, and limited
number of financial institutions that bring the business to the CRAs, therefore
increasing the risk of client dependency.

COMPENSATION FROM SUBSCRIBERS. Although the issuer-pays model has been
the main focus of concern, the 'subscriber-pays' model is not exempted from
conflicts. Subscribers pay for access to credit ratings detailed reports, research,
models, and other data and analysis developed by the CRA. Where the subscriber

has invested in the rated instruments, it will have an interest in a stable rating. For example, a bank or investment firm calculating their capital according to the standardized approach of the CRD may have to apply a higher haircut if the securities lose their investment grade status as a result of a downgrade. Even subscribers without a direct interest in the rated instruments might be interested in a high rating, such as managers of investment portfolios. Also in this case, the concern is that these types of subscribers might be able to exert undue influence over the CRA or its analysts.

POLICIES AND PROCEDURES TO MANAGE THE CONFLICT. The Regulation considers that the conflict arising from the payments received from rated entities or subscribers should not be prohibited; but rather subject to procedures to manage it. Below are indicated the measures imposed by the Regulation to address the conflict.

1. Publication of the general nature of the CRA's compensation arrangements. This publication required by Annex I.E.I.4 applies to fees set for the assignment of ratings and also to fees for the subscription to other CRA's reports and analyses. Fees for the issuance and monitor of ratings will depend on the complexity of the transaction and the size of the issuer; the objectivity of the CRA would be put at risk if, for example, the amount of the fees charged to a rated entity would depend on the number of ratings assigned to that issuer or the success of the offer of the rated securities. Although transparency about the CRA's range of fees and the way to determine them will not prevent issuers from trying to influence the rating, it will allow market participants to monitor and draw conclusions about the way CRAs charge issuers and subscribers.

2. Publication of 'the names of the rated entities or related third parties from which it receives more than 5% of its annual revenue' (Annex I.B.2). Such entities will be in a position to exert influence on the CRA, therefore the Regulation considers it appropriate to make users of ratings aware of the risk. Actually, the most effective measure a CRA can adopt to mitigate the risk embedded in the issuer-pays model would be to ensure that no particular issuer constitutes a significant portion of the overall CRA's revenue.

The Regulation does not indicate any timing for the disclosure of the entities that contribute to more than 5% of the CRA's revenue; it seems logical to apply to this requirement the same timing as ESMA's guidance on registration prescribes for the public disclosures required under Annex I.E.I. Thus CRAs would have to disclose to the public the list of significant clients as soon as practicable after the CRA is registered by ESMA and subsequently update the disclosure within three months after the end of each financial year. In addition, publications of rating actions on a particular issuer included in the list should mention that the CRA derives more than 5% of its revenue from that issuer.

Regarding the types of clients captured by Annex I.B.2, although the Regulation refers only to 'rated entities or related third parties', it seems that CRAs should also publish the same information with respect to subscribers.

Annex I.B.2 draws from a similar requirement included in provision 2.8.(b) of the IOSCO Code, although the IOSCO's threshold is higher: only the identity of persons that contributed with 10% or more of the CRA's annual revenue needs to be disclosed. The SEC has also gone beyond the IOSCO Code but in a different way: it prohibits a CRA from issuing a rating solicited by a person that was the source of 10% or more of the total net revenue of the CRA during the most recently ended fiscal year. This effectively means prohibiting a CRA from reaching the 10% of its revenue from a single issuer because it if does, the next year it would not be able to issue or monitor ratings on that issuer.

Finally, it is worth noting that according to ESMA's guidance on registration, applicants for registration have to disclose to ESMA a lower threshold of significant clients. At the time of the application CRAs have to submit to the supervisor the identities of the rated entities (based upon legal groupings) or related third parties 'that account for more than 3% in terms of the applicant's revenue (with corresponding percentage) and number of ratings at the applicant and, where appropriate, Group of CRAs level for each type of credit ratings issued'. The same disclosure has to be provided broken down by each related party to the rated issuer in a structured finance transaction that reaches the 3% threshold (sponsor, originator, etc.).

3. Compensation and performance evaluation of analysts and persons approving the ratings should not be contingent on the amount of the revenue that the CRA derives from issuers that the analyst rates or with which the analyst regularly interacts. This measure, incorporated in Article 7.5 of the Regulation, is analysed in Section 3.8.2.

4. Rotation of analysts and persons approving the ratings. Article 7.4 of the Regulation provides that 'a credit rating agency shall establish an appropriate gradual rotation mechanism with regard to the rating analysts and persons approving credit ratings as defined in Annex I.C. That rotation mechanism shall be undertaken in phases on the basis of individuals rather than of a complete team.' CRAs have to disclose to the public their rotation policies in their annual transparency report (Annex I.E.III.6). Regarding the persons subject to the policy, ESMA's Q&A has clarified that the list of persons to which the rotation requirements in Annex I.C.8 apply is exhaustive. For example, 'other persons directly involved in rating activities' are not required to rotate.

The purpose of this provision is to prevent long-term relationships being developed between the analytical staff of the CRA and rated entities, which could compromise the independence of rating analysts and persons approving the ratings (Recital 33 of the Regulation). It is worth noting that Japanese legislation also mandates gradual rotation of key analytical staff; however, this requirement is not contemplated in the SEC rules on conflicts of interest.

Annex I.C.8, points (a), (b), and (c) prescribe that 'the lead rating analysts shall not be involved in credit rating activities related to the same rated entity or its related third parties for a period exceeding four years'; the maximum periods for rating analysts and persons approving credit ratings are, respectively, five and seven years.

After these persons cease in their roles with respect to the rated entity, a cooling-off period of two years starts before they can serve again in rating activities related to that issuer (last paragraph of Annex I.C.8). This means that, for example, those individuals shall not be analysts, lead analysts, produce analysis, or vote in rating committees with respect to the issuer they covered prior to the beginning of the cooling-off period.

The rotation requirements seem to have been designed considering the way CRAs operate in the corporate area. An analytical team is assigned to an issuer and then it is in charge of the ongoing credit rating activities with respect to that issuer. However, regarding structured finance ratings, the same entity does not necessarily have an exclusive lead analyst or analytical team for all the transactions in which it participates as an originator, sponsor, or servicer, and frequently the surveillance of the transaction is transferred at some point from the assignment team to a monitoring team. In addition, in the structured finance area there is a number of different asset classes and different parties to the transactions, which make the design of a rotation policy more complex.

ESMA has dealt with the scope of related third parties in relation to the rotation of structured finance staff in its Q&A. ESMA clarified that any party with whom the analytical staff (including surveillance) 'interacts with directly on an ongoing basis or in a way that will have a material impact on the independence and quality of the rating process will be included in the scope of the related third parties'.

Therefore, for example, the lead analyst and the person that approved the rating of a structured finance deal assigned on 1 December 2011 will have participated in a rating activity in relation to issuer A, originator B, sponsor C, and servicer D, assuming that all these functions in the rated transaction are performed by these different entities. Those two persons will have to rotate respectively on 1 December 2015 and 1 December 2018, with respect to entities A, B, C, and D; notwithstanding, if prior to those dates they complete a cooling-off period of two years in relation, for example, to entity B (that is, they have not taken part in any rating activity with respect to entity B for two years), they will have to rotate on 1 December 2015 and 1 December 2018 only with respect to entities A, C, and D; and the four-or-seven year period that triggers rotation will start counting for entity B only after they are appointed lead analyst or person approving the rating for a new transaction in which entity B is the issuer or a related third party.

Finally, another key issue of interpretation of the rotation requirement that arises in relation to all financial instruments is whether analysts are obliged to rotate even if they do not interact with the rated issuer. According to Recital 33, the Regulation aims at preventing a long-lasting relationship with the rated entities or their related third parties. It is doubtful that a 'relationship' can be developed without any direct analytical communication between the analyst and the rated entity or its related third parties. In practical terms, the question arises, for example, in relation to unsolicited ratings where the issuer does not participate in the rating process; it can be argued that in this case it would not make sense to force analysts and persons approving the ratings to rotate. Another example of lack of interaction might be the surveillance of a structured finance rating.

The language in ESMA's Q&A seems to require interaction for the rotation requirement to be triggered, although the wording might be unintentional, because actually the question is only dealing with rotation with respect to related third parties in structured finance. Annex I.C.8 of the Regulation requires rotation after a number of years of involvement in rating activities irrespective of whether there is interaction with the rated entity or not. Therefore, it seems that the analytical staff have to rotate even if there has not been communication with the issuer. In addition to preventing long-lasting relationships, the Regulation might try to avoid analysts' complacency with their abilities to assess a well-known issuer; a fresh look at the company after a certain period of time can have beneficial effects not only for the quality of the ratings but also for the career development of the analysts.

5. Annual disclosure to ESMA of the lists of the largest 20 clients and of those with a higher growth rate of contribution to the revenues of the CRA (see Section 3.8.6). ESMA will take into account the information submitted in its supervisory activities.

Being Paid by Rated Entities for Ancillary Services or Other Non-rating Services

This conflict has already been described in Section 3.8.2. As discussed in that section, the Regulation falls short of requiring CRAs to legally separate their rating business from any other business activities, as recommended by IOSCO. Instead, Annex I.B.6 considers that operational separation is sufficient to address the potential conflict: 'a credit rating agency shall design its reporting and communication channels so as to ensure the independence of the persons referred to in point 1 from the other activities of the credit rating agency carried out on a commercial basis'. The persons referred to in this provision are the CRA's 'rating analysts, employees, or any other natural person whose services are placed at the disposal or under control of the credit rating agency and who are directly involved in the issuing of credit rating and persons approving credit ratings'.

Some CRAs address the potential conflict related to the provision of ancillary services by not offering ancillary services at all, or at least not providing them to issuers they rate. Where the CRA does provide ancillary services, it will have to comply with provision I.B.6, establishing robust information barriers or corporate 'firewalls' between CRA's analysts and personnel engaged in the sale or performance of the ancillary services.

These firewalls might include a physical segregation between the rating and ancillary activities where practical, in order to mitigate the risk of improper influence by personnel working for the non-rating business lines. In any case, analysts from different business units should conduct work separately from one another. For example, employees of the ancillary units should not take part in the analytical discussions regarding a rating action, nor sit in rating committees. In particular, employees of other business lines should be banned from suggesting to analysts to take into account in the rating process factors that are not relevant for the credit analysis (for example, the revenues the CRA derives from the provision of ancillary services to the issuer being assessed). Finally, CRAs should also prohibit their analysts from conditioning the assignment of a favourable credit rating to the purchase of ancillary services provided by the CRA or from recommending such services.

Allowing Employees to own Financial Instruments Issued by Rated Entities or Having other Ownership Interests in Entities Rated by the CRA

The Regulation, as discussed above, only prohibits the CRA from issuing a rating if the analytical staff involved in the determination of the rating, or the CRA itself, owns securities issued by the rated entity. If a CRA allows its employees to own securities issued by an issuer rated by the CRA, even if they are not directly involved in the rating or monitoring process with respect to that issuer, there is the risk that these employees might seek to influence the analysts directly involved in the rating of that issuer. As this conflict is not contemplated in the Regulation, there are no measures envisaged to handle it.

Notwithstanding, in addition to the general organizational measures to address conflicts imposed by the Regulation, it would be prudent if CRAs disclose whether they allow their employees to own securities of the entities rated by the CRA or have other ownership interests in them, as required by the SEC's rules.

Rating an Entity in which the Parent Company of the CRA or a Fellow Subsidiary has a Financial Stake or any other Ownership Interests

This conflict is not referred to in the Regulation but is envisaged in the SEC's rules. As described previously, the prohibition in Annex I.B.3 (a) only refers to financial interests of a CRA or its analysts, employees, and other natural persons, but not to cases where it is the parent company or a fellow subsidiary the owner of the financial instruments issued by the rated entity. If the parent company holds, for example, a significant equity participation in a rated entity, the parent would be favourably or adversely affected by the rating actions of the CRA with respect to the rated entity. Specific measures to address this conflict are left to the CRA's own policies and procedures.[58]

Allowing Employees to have a Business Relationship with Entities Rated by the CRA

The SEC considers this situation as a conflict when the business relationship 'is more than an ordinary course business relationship', and cites as an example a loan extended by the rated issuer to its assigned analyst that has an interest rate far below market rates. Employees having these sort of significant business relationships with rated entities might be influenced to provide more favourable opinions than warranted. Even if the employees having the business relationship with the rated entity do not participate in the rating activities related to that entity, they could try to exert undue influence on the analysts determining the rating.

The Regulation does not include any specific measure to handle this potential conflict. Therefore, CRAs have flexibility in determining when the business relationship would be sufficiently material for the employee as to give rise to a conflict of interest and in designing policies and procedures to manage it.

3.8.3.5 *Rules on Analysts and Other Persons Directly Involved in Rating Activities*

Prohibition to Buy or Sell Securities of the Rated Issuer

Annex I.C.1 of the Regulation imposes a prohibition on analysts and any persons associated with them to buy or sell the securities of an issuer they have rated or are

---

[58] CRAs might also consider the need to disclose the possible conflict that would arise when the rated entity is linked by control to any shareholder of the CRA owning a significant portion (for example, 5%) of the voting rights of the CRA.

monitoring. This rule draws from provision 2.14 of the IOSCO Code. Analysts' access to confidential information is itself a potential conflict of interest, insofar as they may be tempted to use the information to trade securities on their own account. Therefore, the Regulation states that:

> Rating analysts, employees of the credit rating agency as well as any other natural person whose services are placed at the disposal or under the control of the credit rating agency and who is directly involved in credit rating activities, and persons closely associated with them within the meaning of Article 1(2) of Directive 2004/72/EC,[59] shall not buy or sell or engage in any transaction in any financial instrument issued, guaranteed, or otherwise supported by any rated entity within their area of primary analytical responsibility other than holdings in diversified collective investment schemes, including managed funds such as pension funds or life insurance.

According to Article 1.2 of Directive 2004/72/EC, 'persons closely associated' with CRA's employees involved in credit rating activities would be the following:

- the spouse or any partner considered by national law as equivalent to the spouse;
- according to national law, dependent children;
- other relatives who have shared the same household for at least one year on the date of the transaction concerned; and
- any legal person, trust, or partnership, whose managerial responsibilities are discharged by the CRA's employee involved in rating activities or by any of the persons mentioned in the preceding points, or which is directly or indirectly controlled by the CRA's employee, or that is set up for the benefit of this employee, or whose economic interests are substantially equivalent to those of such employee.

Prohibition to Participate in the Determination of a Rating in Case of Conflict

Annex I.C.2 provides that the employees of a CRA should not participate in a rating of an issuer or obligation if the employee owns securities of that issuer or any related entity, or if the employee used to work or had any other relationship with the rated entity. These rules are inspired by provision 2.13 of the IOSCO Code. Actually, Annex I.C.2 constitutes a duplication of the prohibitions of the conflicts set out in Annex I.B.3, points (a) and (d), as discussed under the list of prohibited conflicts provided earlier in this section.

'Point 1' referred to in Annex I.C.2 below means Annex I.C.1. Therefore, according to that point C.2, no analyst, employee, or any other individual involved in the credit rating activities of a CRA shall participate in or otherwise influence the determination of a credit rating of any particular rated entity if that person (or a closely associated person):

---

[59] EC Directive 2004/72/EC of 29 April 2004 implementing Directive 2003/6/EC of the European Parliament and of the Council as regards accepted market practices, the definition of inside information in relation to derivatives on commodities, the drawing up of lists of insiders, the notification of managers' transactions and the notification of suspicious transactions (*Official Journal* L 162, 30.4.2004: p. 70).

(a) owns financial instruments of the rated entity, other than holdings in diversified collective investment schemes;

(b) owns financial instruments of any entity related to a rated entity, the ownership of which may cause or may be generally perceived as causing a conflict of interest, other than holdings in diversified collective investment schemes;

(c) has had a recent employment, business or other relationship with the rated entity that may cause or may be generally perceived as causing a conflict of interest.

In order to monitor compliance with this provision, CRAs should require their employees to notify to the compliance function any securities they buy or sell as soon as they enter into the transaction.

3.8.3.6 Termination of Employment

Review of the Past Work of Analysts that Leave the CRA and Join a Rated Issuer

This issue is regulated by Annex I.C.6, which matches provision 2.17 of the IOSCO Code:

> Where a rating analyst terminates his or her employment and joins a rated entity, which he or she has been involved in rating, or a financial firm, with which he or she has had dealings as part of his or her duties at the credit rating agency, the credit rating agency shall review the relevant work of the rating analyst over two years preceding his or her departure.

The purpose of this 'look-back' requirement is to determine whether any rating action developed by a member of the staff that now works at an issuer was subject to undue influence from that issuer and to take action if appropriate. Although the provision refers only to 'rating analysts', it seems that the review of work after leaving the company should be carried out not only with respect to the persons defined as 'rating analysts' by Article 3.1.(d) but also in relation to any member of the analytical staff having direct involvement in the credit rating activities of the CRA. Otherwise the tasks performed by an employee in its capacity of lead analyst or person approving ratings would be left outside the review.

The 'financial firm' referred to in Annex I.C.6 in addition to the rated entities could be, for example, an underwriter that has solicited a rating or a bank or investment firm that has acted as a related party to the rated entity in structured finance transactions.

Finally, if the review shows that rating actions with the participation of the employee were conflicted—and therefore the objectivity of the CRA was compromised—the CRA should disclose the conflict and put these ratings on the watch list in order to assess whether they should be revised. As soon as practicable, the CRA should, as appropriate, either publish a revised rating or confirm (affirm) the rating. This is the approach followed by the SEC proposed rules for NRSROs of May 2011.

Prohibition to Take up a Key Management Position with the Rated Entity

According to Annex I.C.7, a person referred to in point 1 of Annex I.C.7 'shall not take up a key management position with the rated entity or its related third party within six months of the credit rating'. The provision refers exclusively to rated entities or their related third parties that are within the employee's area of primary analytical responsibility. Regarding the trigger of the cooling-off period, it would be any rating action relating to those entities (assignment of the rating, confirmation, modification, or withdrawal).

Although Annex III.I.36 of the Regulation envisages supervisory measures or fines against a CRA for the infringement of this requirement, it is doubtful that a CRA can do much to prevent an employee from leaving the company, apart from making all new hires aware of this requirement and obliging them to sign a statement undertaking to comply with it.

3.8.3.7 Disclosures on Conflicts of Interest in the Application

As provided by ESMA's guidance on registration, applicants have to submit to ESMA as part of their application for registration an inventory of conflicts of interest relevant to the CRA and an explanation of how they are eliminated or managed and disclosed and a copy of the current policies and procedures for the identification, prevention, disclosure, and mitigation of conflicts of interest.

The inventory of potential conflicts of interest should include those with related third parties to the rated issuer and, where the applicant is part of a group of CRAs, the conflicts at the group of CRAs level. As already indicated, applicants also have to include the identity of their main clients—rated entities and related third parties that account for more than 3% of their revenues.

The policies and procedures to handle conflicts of interest should encompass those with respect to ancillary services, compensation from rated entities, discussions related to fees, trading by employees in securities rated by the CRA, and publication of the names of the rated entities accounting for more than 5% of the CRA's annual revenue. The application will describe the method used by the CRA to ensure that the relevant individuals are aware of those policies and procedures.

3.8.3.8 Treatment of Confidential Information

General

CRAs that do not rely exclusively on publicly available information to develop their ratings regularly contact the senior management of the issuer to obtain information about its operations, management, and financial situation. In the course of these contacts, issuers might provide a CRA's analysts with non-public information, such as strategic plans, planned business transactions, or profit forecasts. According to the Market Abuse Directive, issuers may communicate this sort of inside information to CRAs without triggering the obligation to simultaneously disclose it to the public, as long as the CRA is subject to a confidentiality agreement. The CRA then uses the confidential information for developing its opinion about the creditworthiness of the issuer or its debt instruments. It will subsequently publish a credit rating or other opinion regarding the issuer or a particular financial instrument which incorporates confidential information without specifically disclosing it.

Nevertheless, rated entities would be reluctant to share with CRAs non-public material information if they were concerned that the information would not be kept confidential or would be used for a purpose that was different from the determination of a rating. In order to encourage issuers' cooperation with CRAs during the rating process, the Regulation requires CRAs to implement policies and procedures to protect non-public information from premature disclosure or use in ways unrelated to a CRA's rating activities. Before analysing the policies required by the Regulation, it is relevant to describe the general framework on the treatment of issuer's inside information established by the Market Abuse Directive, which also applies to CRAs and their staff.

Market Abuse Directive

Article 1.1 of the Market Abuse Directive defines inside information as non-public information of a precise nature, relating to an issuer of a financial instrument or to a financial instrument which, if it were made public, would be likely to have a significant effect on the prices of the financial instrument.

The Market Abuse Directive requires issuers whose securities are admitted to trading on a regulated market to disclose inside information as soon as possible (Article 6). It also sets out a few situations in which an issuer may delay the disclosure of inside information, provided that the issuer can keep the information confidential. Therefore, there will only be limited circumstances in which an issuer can legitimately be in possession of inside information that is not widely known by the market. Only in these exceptional situations will it be possible for a CRA to have access to non-public information that amounts to 'inside information'. In addition, there can also be other confidential information which is not required to be disclosed according to the Market Abuse Directive.

CRAs may legitimately have access to inside information because the Market Abuse Directive explicitly allows issuers to disclose such information to third parties in the normal course of their activities if the recipient is bound by a confidentiality agreement. Otherwise, disclosure of inside information would amount to an offense against the Market Abuse Directive. ESMA has explicitly considered CRAs as possible recipients of inside information, requiring issuers to include CRAs' employees that have had access to inside information in their insiders' lists.[60]

The Regulation does not refer to 'inside information' and uses instead the language of the IOSCO Code—'confidential information'—which is the source of most of the rules on confidential information included in the Regulation. The term 'confidential information' is not defined in the Regulation and there are no explanations in the recitals on how it should be understood; therefore, for the purposes of the Regulation it would encompass any material non-public information that an issuer holds that might or might not amount to inside information as defined by the Market Abuse Directive. In any case, confidential information

---

[60] CESR (May 2009), *Market Abuse Directive Level 3—Third set of CESR guidance and information on the common operation of the Directive to the market (Ref. CESR/09-219)* (paragraph 15).

about a rated issuer that does not have securities admitted to trading on a regulated market could not constitute inside information.

Measures Required by the Regulation

In addition to the framework on inside information established by the Market Abuse Directive, the Regulation imposes several safeguards to prevent disclosure of confidential information and to ensure its proper use. Annex I.C.3 requires CRAs to adopt four specific procedures designed to achieve those objectives. These measures are based on provisions 3.13, 3.16, 3.17, and 3.18 of the IOSCO Code.

Annex I.C.3 of the Regulation requires CRAs to ensure that rating analysts, employees of the CRA, as well as any other natural person whose services are placed at the disposal or under the control of the CRA and who is directly involved in credit rating activities, and persons closely associated with them within the meaning of Article 1.2 of Directive 2004/72/EC, comply with the obligations set out below.

ESMA's guidance on registration requires applicants to include in their application a copy of any policies and procedures with respect to the control of confidential information and a description of the process used to ensure that the relevant individuals are aware of these policies.

MEASURES TO PROTECT CONFIDENTIAL INFORMATION. The persons referred to in Annex I.C.3 must 'take all reasonable measures to protect property and records in possession of the credit rating agency from fraud, theft or misuse, taking into account the nature, scale and complexity of their business and the nature and range of their credit rating activities' (according to point (a) of Annex I.C.3).

A CRA should have in place policies requiring its employees to safeguard the confidential information they possess and, as discussed above, to share it only with those other employees that need to know the information to perform credit rating activities. These policies will typically include measures on how to store files containing non-public information in places that are not accessible to other persons or how to avoid conversations where confidential information is discussed that can be overheard.

PROHIBITION TO DISCLOSE CONFIDENTIAL INFORMATION OUTSIDE THE CRA. In accordance with point (b) of Annex I.C.3, the persons referred to in that provision must 'not disclose any information about credit ratings or possible future credit ratings of the credit rating agency, except to the rated entity or its related third party'. This provision requires a CRA to have policies and procedures in place designed to prevent the inappropriate dissemination of confidential information to persons outside the CRA.

Notwithstanding, it is worth noting that a CRA might be allowed to disclose confidential information that does not amount to inside information if permitted by the confidentiality agreement with the issuer. This has been confirmed by ESMA's Q&A. Conversely, disclosure by the CRA of inside information to third parties, even if permitted by the issuer, would constitute an offense against the Market Abuse Directive.

Although the requirement refers to 'any information', it should be understood as referring to any material confidential information with respect to credit ratings already published or pending rating actions. In fact, two scenarios are addressed:

1. Credit rating actions already issued:

the CRA's policies should ensure that confidential information that has been used to form the basis of a rating opinion is neither publicly disclosed nor selectively disclosed to certain persons outside the CRA (such as investors or subscribers). Provision 3.11 of the IOSCO Code states that 'the CRA and its employees should not disclose confidential information in press releases, through research conferences, to future employers, or in conversations with investors, other issuers, other persons, or otherwise'.

In particular, some market participants have expressed concerns regarding the access to confidential information obtained during the rating process that subscribers to a CRA's services may have. Possible ways for subscribers to access inside information are the detailed reports they receive which explain the basis for a rating action, or direct conversations with the CRA's analysts.

The framework established under the Market Abuse Directive permitting issuers to disclose inside information to others who owe a duty of confidentiality does not apply to these persons and therefore does not permit the widespread circulation of inside information from one entity or individual to another. Hence, CRAs and their staff are prohibited from passing on inside information to subscribers or anyone else. Any such disclosure of inside information would constitute an offence under the Market Abuse Directive.

2. Pending credit rating actions:

a rating action that has not been published yet is confidential information and might constitute in itself inside information as defined by the Market Abuse Directive. One reason why rating actions are themselves likely to influence the prices of the rated instruments is because of the inside information factored into the rating decision. But even rating actions compiled purely on the basis of publicly available information might have an impact on prices, given the influence CRAs have on market participants' investment decisions.

This is why CRAs should have policies in place designed to prevent the selective disclosure to third parties of a pending rating action, or any internal deliberations conducted to form it, before the rating is made publicly available on the Internet (or made available to subscribers, in the case of CRAs operating under this model).

PROHIBITION TO DISCLOSE CONFIDENTIAL INFORMATION INSIDE THE CRA. According to Annex I.C.3.(c) employees of the CRA are also prohibited from sharing confidential information entrusted to the credit rating agency with rating analysts and employees of any person directly or indirectly linked to it by control, as well as with any other natural person whose services are placed at the disposal or under the control of any person directly or indirectly linked to it by control, and who is not directly involved in the credit rating activities.

Analysts may use confidential information received from an issuer to form a rating opinion, but they must not reveal the confidential information to anyone outside the CRA, as discussed above, or to any other members of the CRA's staff, unless this is strictly necessary for the elaboration of a specific rating (ESMA Q&A).

ESMA has therefore provided a restrictive interpretation of this provision, in the sense that analysts should be prohibited not only from sharing non-public information with any employee working for the ancillary business lines of the CRA or related third parties, but also with other analytical staff working for the rating business lines of the CRA, except where, in this latter case, the confidential information is needed for the development of a rating.

It is important to note that CRAs have to keep a record related to each rating action identifying all the employees in possession of confidential information—including those to whom the information was passed on a need-to-know basis (see Section 3.8.2).

PROHIBITION TO USE CONFIDENTIAL INFORMATION. Finally, the persons referred to in Annex I.C.3 must not use or share confidential information for the purpose of trading financial instruments, or for any other purpose except the conduct of the credit rating activities, according to point (d) of Annex I.C.3. CRAs must ban their employees from using any confidential information obtained during the course of their work except for the developing of a credit rating. This prohibition will address the risk that employees in possession of confidential information may trade securities on the information or may tip others who could trade on the inside information. Any employees of the CRA that deal on the basis of inside information they are given will also be committing an offence under the Market Abuse Directive.

Provision 3.15 of the IOSCO Code prescribes that 'CRA employees should familiarize themselves with the internal securities trading policies maintained by their employer, and periodically certify their compliance as required by such policies'.

In general, it should be the task of the compliance function to adopt the measures that will ensure employees' awareness of the obligations laid down in Annex I.C.3.

3.8.4 Methodologies, Models, and Key Assumptions

3.8.4.1 Rating Methodology

The primary objective of a methodology is to describe as clearly as possible the quantitative and qualitative factors that a CRA should consider when determining an entity's creditworthiness. A methodology will not typically contain the macroeconomic (such as unemployment rate) or transaction-specific (such as recovery rate) assumptions to be applied to a given rating, but rather identifies that these factors should be considered, where applicable, in the rating process.

The application of predefined methodologies facilitates consistency in the approach by analysts and rating committees within the agency, as they should capture all the relevant inputs that have to be considered in the process of elaborating a rating. This, however, does not mean that the same methodology applied by different rating committees to identical transactions would always lead to identical ratings. The model embedded in the methodology will produce the same output if fed with the same data for two different transactions; but the mathematical model is only one part of the methodology employed to determine a rating. Ultimately, ratings are just opinions that reflect the majority view of the rating committee's members. If two different rating committees have different views about, for example, the volatility levels of the recovery rate or the interest rates environment, they might arrive at different opinions about the credit risk of a transaction.

CRAs do not have a single credit assessment methodology. Typically, they publish different criteria for different sectors or asset classes (such as corporates, financial institutions, insurance companies, public finance, or structured finance), for different sub-classes (for example, RMBS or CMBS within the structured finance sector) and for different geographical regions (US RMBS, European RMBS). Additionally, CRAs may have other criteria that affect multiple sectors (for example, regarding counterparties in structured finance transactions that would apply across RMBS, CMBS and other sub-classes within structured finance). This means that a CRA might end up having many methodologies and a number of them might be applicable to a particular rating.

3.8.4.2 *Principle of Non-interference of Public Authorities in Methodologies*

An overarching and internationally accepted principle of the CRA industry is the protection of CRAs' independence. CRAs' independence from issuers, investors, other CRAs, and governments is of paramount importance to the role these entities play in the market. Thus, market participants welcomed the categorical and explicit statement in Article 23 of the Regulation that requires ESMA, the EC, and any public authorities of Member States and their competent authorities to respect CRAs' independence and to avoid intruding upon CRAs' opinion formation process, including the development of their models, methodologies, or procedures.

This article states that 'in carrying out their duties under this Regulation, ESMA, the Commission or any public authorities of a Member State shall not interfere with the content of credit ratings or methodologies'.

Certainly, the international consensus is that quality and integrity in the rating process can be achieved by using different methodologies or techniques to determine credit ratings. As concluded by IOSCO,[61] the CRA legal frameworks of the USA, Japan, and the EU have provisions that prohibit the competent authorities from regulating the substance of credit ratings or credit rating methodologies. Instead, the objective of these regulatory programmes focuses on controls and processes designed to ensure that whatever methodology a CRA employs to determine ratings (such as a qualitative assessment of relevant factors, a quantitative model using relevant inputs, or a combination of both) is employed in a systematic and consistent manner by competent analysts and that the results can be reviewed to assess whether the methodology produces ratings that enhance the ability of market participants to assess relative creditworthiness.

Consistent with the principle of non-interference, the Regulation does not regulate the content of CRA's methodologies. Rather, it sets a number of principles, drawn from the IOSCO Code, that CRAs should follow in the design of their methodologies and requires that the methodologies are adequately disclosed and kept up to date.

---

[61] IOSCO (February 2011), *Report on regulatory implementation of the statement of principles regarding the activities of credit rating agencies in the different jurisdictions.*

3.8.4.3 *Transparency of Methodologies*

Article 8.1 stipulates that 'a credit rating agency shall disclose to the public the methodologies, models and key rating assumptions it uses in its credit rating activities as defined in point 5 of Part I of Section E of Annex I'. According to Annex I, this requirement also applies to any material changes to the methodologies, models, and assumptions.

The purpose of this requirement is to allow all potential users of ratings to understand how a rating was arrived at by the CRA. Therefore, the Regulation—Annex I.D.2.(b)—requires that each rating announcement has to indicate the principal methodology that was used in determining the rating and a reference to its comprehensive description. This is a principle taken from provisions 3.3 and 3.5 of the IOSCO Code.

ESMA is not required by the Regulation to issue guidance on how CRAs should comply with this provision or, in particular, guidelines on the level of detail about the methodologies that should be published. However, Recital 25 of the Regulation gives an indication when stating that the level of detail 'should be such as to give adequate information to the users of credit ratings in order to perform their own due diligence when assessing whether to rely or not on those credit ratings'.

CRAs must keep a record of their methodologies (see Section 3.8.2), but they do not have to publish them; a comprehensive description of each of their credit assessment methodologies in an easily understandable way is sufficient. The retained record will assist ESMA in determining whether the description of the methodologies made available to the public is adequate to enable market participants to understand the key criteria the CRA is going to consider in its analysis of credit risk and the qualitative and quantitative treatment of the information it is going to assess before reaching its rating opinion. Recital 34 adds that the description of the methodologies is to be 'published in a manner permitting comprehensive review'.

Examples of significant qualitative and quantitative rating factors that CRAs typically assess when developing a rating are provided in Section 1.4. In addition to describing those criteria, the methodology will address the degree to which the weighting of some factors will vary depending on the specifics of the analysis.

The Regulation gives flexibility to CRAs in determining the level of detail of their public descriptions of methodologies. Only Annex I.D.I.2.(c) of the Regulation—regarding presentation of credit ratings—mandates two specific disclosures about methodologies that CRAs will have to make public. These are the meaning of each rating category and the definition of default or recovery, both also specifically required by provision 3.5 of the IOSCO Code.

Regarding the method of publication, clearly the most accessible way would be the public area of the CRA's website. Access to the information should be free of charge, according to ESMA's Q&A, and continuous until the methodology is withdrawn. This would happen when the criteria are no longer in use and the CRA does not have any outstanding ratings based on that methodology.

Finally, it is worth noting that some of the procedures and methodologies established by the CRA may involve the use of proprietary models. This is why the Regulation, in its Recital 25, permits CRAs not to disclose information concerning models that could reveal sensitive business information or seriously impede innovation.

3.8.4.4 *Information Used to Produce Ratings*

Information to be Analysed

The first subparagraph of Article 8.2 of the Regulation draws on the language in provisions 1.1 and 1.4 of the IOSCO Code. It states that 'a credit rating agency shall adopt, implement and enforce adequate measures to ensure that the credit ratings it issues are based on a thorough analysis of all the information that is available to it and that is relevant to its analysis according to its rating methodologies'. The purpose of this principle is to guarantee that ratings are issued only after a full analysis of all the information that the CRA has to consider according to the applicable methodology.

This provision only requires CRAs to analyse the information that is relevant according to their methodologies, so what is basically required is that CRAs apply their methodologies when issuing ratings. Concerning the information that they have to use, this paragraph does not add much to the obligation of having methodologies that fulfil the requirements of Article 8.3. CRAs are free to decide which criteria are relevant for their analysis, so they only have to state in the applicable methodology the information they are going to use.

Additionally, Article 8.2 clarifies that the information that CRAs have to consider is only that available to them. Therefore, CRAs are not expected to make an active search for all existing information and, for example, if the issuer does not participate in the rating process, the CRA is only required to analyse the public information that is relevant.

Quality of the Information

The second subparagraph of Article 8.2 obliges a CRA to 'adopt all necessary measures so that the information it uses in assigning a credit rating is of sufficient quality and from reliable sources'. The language of this requirement is based on provision 1.7 of the IOSCO Code. But here again EU legislators went beyond the international consensus by adding that the information used by the CRA should be 'from reliable sources'.

In the context of the subprime market turmoil, some market participants believed that in certain cases CRAs relied on information that was questionable or of dubious quality. CRAs have traditionally argued that they are not auditors and therefore they do not, and cannot, conduct due diligence on the data provided to them from any third party, including the rated entity. Whilst regulators and investors concur that CRAs cannot perform the same type of confirmation expected of independent auditors, they expect CRAs to take reasonable steps to ensure that the information they use is of sufficient quality to support a credit rating.

However, Annex I.D.I.4 of the Regulation sets a clear limit in its second paragraph when prohibiting CRAs to issue a rating when the information available is deficient or refers to a new complex financial instrument which would be difficult to rate (the provision refers in particular to new structured finance instruments):

> In a case where the lack of reliable data or the complexity of the structure of a new type of financial instrument or the quality of information available is not satisfactory or raises serious questions as to whether a credit rating agency can provide a credible credit rating, the credit rating agency shall refrain from issuing a credit rating or withdraw an existing rating.

The ultimate decision about the adequacy of the information rests with the rating committee, taking into account the recommendation of the lead rating analyst. ESMA's guidance on methodologies leaves to the CRAs the design of the appropriate policies to ensure that the analytical teams have sufficient reliable information to develop a rating. It prescribes that a CRA must have 'written procedures on how the CRA assesses if it has sufficiently reliable data to provide a credible credit rating or if it is the case to refrain from issuing a rating or to withdraw an existing rating'.

Among the policies a CRA might adopt to ensure that the information it uses is reliable, Recital 35 sets out the following:

1. Reliance on independently audited financial statements and public disclosures. The verification provided by the auditor will enable the CRA to rely on the financial statements of the company. Regulated information filed with market supervisors in accordance with the applicable legislation (such as prospectuses or interim financial reports) can also be relied upon. On the contrary, if the issuer fails to submit the required disclosures within the timeframe set, it might be an indication that the information available on the issuer should be subject to further investigation by the CRA.

2. Verification by reputable third parties. The CRA should have processes to evaluate which third parties can be relied upon by analysts.

3. Contractual provisions clearly stipulating liability for the rated entity or its related third parties, if the information provided under the contract is knowingly materially false or misleading or if the rated entity or its related third parties fail to conduct reasonable due diligence regarding the accuracy of the information as specified under the terms of the contract. Even in the absence of such contractual provisions, CRAs could be able to rely on information provided by issuers that have a history of providing reliable information.

4. Random sampling examination of the information received. Where the information necessary to conduct the credit analysis does not belong to any of the categories indicated above, the CRA may evaluate the quality of the information using an established random sampling methodology.

In any case, the type of investigation conducted by a CRA on the information relied upon by it in accordance with its methodology will vary depending on the specifics of each individual situation. Among these circumstances are the type of rated securities (the information necessary to rate structured finance instruments is of a different nature than that used for rating corporates), the type of issuers, the legislation and practices of the jurisdiction where the issuer is based, and the availability of any of the information or mechanisms laid down in the first three items of the above mentioned list.

Finally, it is worth noting that, according to Annex I.D.I.4, the publication of a rating must be accompanied by a prominent disclosure from the CRA stating 'whether it considers satisfactory the quality of information available on the rated entity and to what extent it has verified information provided to it by the rated entity or its related third party'.

3.8.4.5 *Requirements on Methodologies*

Article 8.3 provides that 'a credit rating agency shall use methodologies that are rigorous, systematic, continuous and subject to validation based on historical experience, including back-testing'.

The purpose of this provision, as analysed in more detail below, is to ensure that the CRA's methodologies produce informed and well-founded opinions about the credit risk of the rated instruments and entities. The wording of the Regulation is based on the technical criteria set out in the CRD for the recognition of ECAIs. In particular, one of the standards eligible ECAIs have to satisfy in order to be recognized by competent authorities is objectivity, as defined in Annex VI, part 2 of the CRD: 'competent authorities shall verify that the methodology for assigning credit assessments is rigorous, systematic, continuous and subject to validation based on historical experience'.

In turn, the CRD's requirements on methodologies are based on provision 1.2 of the IOSCO Code although the language is not exactly the same. On top of the IOSCO standards, the CRD and the CRA Regulation require the methodologies to be 'continuous', as explained below.

Rigorous

From ESMA and EBA's guidelines on ECAIs, it can be concluded that a CRA uses rigorous methodologies if it devotes sufficient resources and appropriate procedures to their development and review. And it is critical that these procedures allow the CRA to identify and assess factors driving creditworthiness and ensure that these factors are incorporated into the methodologies.

The CRA's staff responsible for preparing, approving, and monitoring ratings should be a core resource in understanding credit risk analysis. It is therefore critical that these analysts are involved in the process of developing a methodology relevant to their area of expertise. In particular, analysts should be expected to identify aspects of a methodology that should be reviewed or new methodologies that should be issued in response to new developments in their analytical areas. Therefore, business lines are in the best place to initiate the process of developing a methodology by issuing recommendations for the relevant CRA's body to consider.

The approval process of the proposals made by the rating teams would depend on the materiality of the proposal to issue a new methodology or to change an existing one. For example, it seems appropriate that the development of new methodologies addressing a new sector or asset class is approved by the CRA's review function. As prescribed by the Regulation (Annex I.A.9), the review function must be independent of the business lines that are responsible for rating activities and shall report to the CRA's board. This independence ensures a further review of the recommendation issued by the rating teams. In case of non-material proposals, such as a minor adjustment to an existing methodology, the responsibility for approval could rest with the relevant rating departments of the CRA.

In general, it seems that significant proposals that should be approved by the review function would include cases where a change in an existing methodology or the implementation of a new one would affect a significant number of outstanding ratings, materially impact several classes or sub-classes of ratings, or where the adoption of the change would imply inconsistencies with other existing methodologies.

Finally, as discussed in the analysis of Article 8.5 dealing with the review of the methodologies, CRAs should also ensure that the comments or insights provided by the analysts monitoring rated entities and financial instruments are appropriately fed into the process of reviewing the methodologies.

Systematic and Continuous

ESMA's guidance on methodologies requires CRAs to have internal controls in order to ensure that analysts consistently apply a given methodology in the formulation of all ratings belonging to the same asset class and that the methodology is also consistently applied over time. A way of ensuring that all lines of business in the agency apply the methodologies consistently is, for example, to have members of the review function in every rating committee. Also internal control and compliance functions should periodically conduct tests to monitor this requirement. If a rating committee has diverged from the predefined methodology, the CRA should keep appropriate records of the reasons for the departure.

ESMA also expects CRAs to have 'written procedures and policies concerning decisions to amend, withdraw or suspend a rating methodology and associated ratings'. It is not very clear what a suspension of a methodology is. Ratings will have to be produced according to the relevant methodology as disclosed by the CRA (and if the CRA comes to the conclusion that an existing methodology is no longer appropriate, it should stop using it and replace it following a due process). So it seems that when the guidance talks about suspension, in fact it is referring to the situation where, due to the circumstances of the case, the CRA disapplies a particular feature of the applicable methodology or adds another risk characteristic not captured by the existing criteria. Therefore, whilst it is sensible to require procedures regarding the development, amendment, and withdrawal of methodologies, the suspension of a methodology might be more appropriately considered and managed on a case-by-case basis. When deviation from a particular feature of the methodology becomes the usual practice, then the analysts should trigger the process for reviewing the methodology.

Subject to Validation Based on Historical Experience

This requirement stems from the IOSCO Code, although its provision 1.2 only requires validation based on historical experience 'where possible'. The CRA Regulation and the CRD have strengthened the IOSCO principle by requiring validation of all CRA's methodologies. The purpose of the validation requirement is to ensure that the CRA's methodologies and their outputs remain appropriate over time and through different market conditions.

ESMA's guidance on methodologies[62] further develops what 'validation of methodologies' means: 'methodologies and underlying assumptions are consistently reviewed against actual performance, new data and changes to underlying macroeconomic assumptions'.

ESMA's guidance requires CRAs to have well documented validation policies and procedures that they adhere to; these will describe the content of the validation process and in particular how this activity is related to possible changes in methodologies, for each asset type. ESMA also states that CRAs must devote sufficiently knowledgeable and independent employees to this function and shall identify its ultimate responsible.

A key aspect of the validation process is back-testing. EBA defines 'back-testing' as an analysis of outcomes vis-à-vis rated entities/issues designed to assess the performance—that is, the discriminatory power—of the ratings. Thus, EBA considers that back-testing is the process of validating the methodologies based on historical experience, rather than just a specific part of the validation process. However, back-testing is dependent on the nature of the methodology employed and the type of assets covered. It might happen that for some methodologies CRAs will lack sufficient historical data to derive the ratings that would have been assigned if the methodology had been in place in prior years.

Regarding the frequency of back-testing, the CRD requires eligible ECAIs to demonstrate to competent authorities that they have established back-testing for at least one year. The CRA Regulation does not impose a minimum frequency and ESMA has therefore retained some flexibility in its guidance; the frequency will depend on the nature of the credit rating methodology and the assets covered, the specific risk to which it is exposed, and changes in market conditions, among other factors. This implies a change in the approach for ECAIs that are registered according to the CRA Regulation. As discussed earlier in the book, the CRD criteria on methodologies do not apply to applicants for ECAI recognition that have been registered according to the CRA Regulation.

Finally, it seems that back-testing should be carried out for each of the market segments that the CRA has included in its application for registration. According to ESMA's guidance, each of those market segments should have a basic methodology that should be validated.

3.8.4.6 *Organizational Requirements Concerning Methodologies*

The importance attributed by the CRA Regulation to the methodologies, models, and assumptions used by CRAs is also reflected in the organizational requirements imposed on the agencies. There are two governance requirements that are directly aimed at ensuring sound processes for the development and review of the CRA's methodologies: the review function and the independent directors of the board. The former requirement has been drawn from the IOSCO Code (provisions 1.7-1 and

---

[62] CESR (August 2010), *Guidance on common standards for assessment of compliance of credit rating methodologies with the requirements set out in Article 8.3. (Ref. CESR/10-945).*

1.7-2); the latter is a specific European feature without matching provisions in the IOSCO Code.

Review Function

METHODOLOGIES DEVELOPMENT AND REVIEW. Annex I.A.9 provides that:

> A credit rating agency shall establish a review function responsible for periodically reviewing its methodologies, models and key rating assumptions, such as mathematical or correlation assumptions, and any significant changes or modifications thereto as well as the appropriateness of those methodologies, models and key rating assumptions where they are used or intended to be used for the assessment of new financial instruments.

CRAs are required by Article 8.5 of the Regulation to review their methodologies on an ongoing basis and at least annually. And Recital 37 provides that CRAs should 'establish proper procedures for the regular review of methodologies, models and key rating assumptions used by the credit rating agency in order to be able to properly reflect the changing conditions in the underlying asset markets'.

The responsibility for reviewing the CRA's methodologies rests with the review function. Small CRAs may not be exempted from the requirement to set up this department. ESMA's guidance clarifies that the review function 'is deemed to review methodology development and update as well as the staff that develops them'. Therefore, it does not have the task of reviewing the work of the analysts who apply the methodologies in producing ratings, although, as already discussed, the CRA should have other controls in place to ensure that the methodologies are applied appropriately. The objective of the review function is to assess periodically whether the methodologies incorporate all the key factors driving credit risk and whether any changes should be adopted.

ESMA's guidance also prescribes how CRAs should staff this function: it should be 'managed by a credit risk officer, or a person with similar responsibilities, with sufficient knowledge, experience and the relevant background to understand the complexities of rating methodologies'. And the staff should have 'appropriate qualifications and/or appropriate experience and expertise'. In line with the language used by Article 7 of the Regulation (which requires in general that the staff has 'appropriate knowledge and experience'), ESMA does not mandate any specific qualifications of analysts developing and reviewing methodologies.

According to Annex I.A.9, second paragraph, 'the review function shall be independent of the business lines which are responsible for credit rating activities' and report to the independent members of the board. However, the review function does not perform its tasks in isolation. Feedback from the rating teams that apply the methodology on a day-to-day basis should be a key element in its ongoing review. Also, analysts conducting the monitoring of the ratings will provide a valuable input, as they will be the first to see whether the securities are performing according to the CRA's predictions.

As previously discussed, normally the initiative for a change to an existing methodology or for the development of a new one is taken by the rating teams when they identify the need for a revision. Moreover, CRAs may adopt non-significant changes to their methodologies without the need for involving their review function. Those non-material changes could be vetted by the relevant body within the business lines. Normally, CRAs should have in place an escalation procedure that would determine the relevant committee or body to approve such changes, depending on the significance of the revision.

Where the importance of the proposed change warrants the intervention of the review function, the rating team that identified the need for the amendment prepares a draft recommendation that goes through that department. The person or body within the review function that signs off the amendment to the methodology depends on the significance of the proposed change. It seems that the Regulation does not prevent analytical staff from participating in such bodies, but the CRA needs to consider the appropriateness of the balance of staff (control versus analytical) in order to ensure that the independence of the review function is not compromised. In any case, the personnel of the review function must control the process.

Apart from the reviews triggered by the business lines, the review function typically performs its own regular checks. Among them are research on the historical performance of the ratings, analysis of alternative methodologies by other market participants, and comparison with market opinions as inferred from credit spreads. Significant changes to a methodology should not occur frequently. Therefore, the main task of the CRA's review function should be, under normal circumstances, the annual review of all credit rating methodologies. This task should include the regular verification of the coding accuracy of any models embedded in the methodologies, with the aim of reducing model risk to the minimum possible.

It is clear that performance data should be a relevant factor in the review process, such as default data and transition matrices for securities belonging to the same sector or category (ESMA's guidance on methodologies). If, for example, the volatility of the ratings or the rate of defaults or impairments is abnormally high, the CRA should investigate further. Such performances could indicate a significant change in economic trends—and therefore the assumptions should be checked—or that the methodology is not incorporating all relevant factors.

The Regulation specifically requires CRAs to incorporate in their rating processes the macroeconomic and financial market conditions. They should have in place personnel tasked with the monitoring of the economy and markets and making macroeconomic forecasts for use by analysts in the rating process. Significant changes in the underlying macroeconomic phenomena should also be taken into account in the review of the methodologies.

Finally, if the outcome of the annual review is that the methodology remains appropriate, the review function should produce a report including a set of suggestions or concerns for the business units to consider. In the extreme cases where the review finds that the methodology is unsound, the agency should stop issuing ratings based on such methodology and appropriate changes should be implemented as soon as practicable (as explained further when analysing Article 8.6).

CONSULTATION AND PUBLICATION OF MODIFICATIONS TO METHODOLOGIES. Material changes to methodologies have to be published according to Annex I.E.I.5. With a view to ensuring transparency, Recital 37 indicates that 'disclosure of any material modification to the methodologies and practices, procedures and processes of credit rating agencies should be made prior to their coming into effect, unless extreme market conditions require an immediate change in the credit rating'.

Although not required by the Regulation, it is desirable that CRAs seek input from market participants before adopting significant changes to methodologies or issuing new ones. This might improve the features of the methodology and alerts the market of a possible change so it is not caught by surprise when the modification is implemented. CRAs normally, when feasible, consult on any proposed material changes to methodologies. Nonetheless, what constitutes a material change is not always a straightforward issue and, as the AMF noted in its 2007 report,[63] some issuers felt in the past that the agencies failed to consult them before introducing changes with a major market or sector impact.

As required by ESMA's guidance on registration, once a material change to a methodology has been adopted, the CRA will notify ESMA. This requirement is intended to enable ESMA to assess whether the methodologies continue to meet the criteria set out in Article 8.3 of the Regulation on an ongoing basis.

ASSESSMENT OF APPROPRIATENESS OF EXISTING METHODOLOGIES TO NEW FINANCIAL INSTRUMENTS. Also, in addition to methodologies development and review, the review function is assigned the task of considering the appropriateness of methodologies, models, and key rating assumptions where they are used or intended to be used for the assessment of new financial instruments. A new financial instrument for this purpose would be a complex product having unusual structural features or a structure consisting of a new asset class. In the light of the experience drawn from the last financial crisis, it seems that structured products lacking robust data on the underlying assets should also be included in this category.

OUTSOURCING OF THE REVIEW FUNCTION. ESMA has addressed the issue of whether the tasks of the review function must be always carried out in-house or whether it is permissible that they are performed by another entity within the group. Doubts arise because the Regulation indicates that each CRA must have an independent review function to assess the methodologies and models used in ratings determined by that particular CRA. (Actually, as discussed earlier, all the requirements of the Regulation are imposed on individual CRAs, not on the groups to which they might belong.)

The conclusion provided by ESMA's Q&A focuses only on reviews conducted within the EU group, stating that this could be considered acceptable if subject to appropriate outsourcing arrangements. Actually, despite ESMA's silence regarding reviews in third countries, there should be no impediment for EU CRAs to outsource the review function to the parent company or to other subsidiaries within the group located outside the EU. After all, as also acknowledged by ESMA in its Q&A, a key aspect of the usefulness of ratings to market participants is the consistency in approach to assessment of credit risk. And this consistency must be understood globally, not only within the EU borders.

Independent Members of the Board

The independent directors of the CRA are assigned the task of monitoring the methodologies employed in the credit rating activities (Annex I.A.2). They do not

---

[63] AMF (January 2008), *2007 Report on rating agencies: credit rating of corporate issuers.*

need to have a direct involvement in the development of the methodologies but rather have the task of monitoring that development. To that end, as indicated earlier in this section, the review function reports to them.

3.8.4.7 Ongoing Review of Ratings and Methodologies

According to Article 8.5 of the Regulation:

> A credit rating agency shall monitor credit ratings and review its credit ratings and methodologies on an ongoing basis and at least annually, in particular where material changes occur that could have an impact on a credit rating. A credit rating agency shall establish internal arrangements to monitor the impact of changes in macroeconomic or financial market conditions on credit ratings.

This paragraph imposes two key requirements on CRAs: reviewing their methodologies and reviewing their ratings. The first has already been analysed in the section devoted to the review function.

Review of Ratings

An existing credit rating might be changed as a result of a modification of the methodology that was used to determine it or due to new developments that materially affect the creditworthiness of the issuer.

REVIEW FOLLOWING A METHODOLOGY CHANGE. When methodologies, models, or key rating assumptions are changed, paragraph 6 of Article 8 requires CRAs to:

(a) immediately, using the same means of communication as used for the distribution of the affected credit ratings, disclose the likely scope of credit ratings to be affected;

(b) review the affected credit ratings as soon as possible and no later than six months after the change, in the meantime placing those ratings under observation; and

(c) re-rate all credit ratings that have been based on those methodologies, models or key rating assumptions if, following the review, the overall combined effect of the changes affects those credit ratings.

The CRA has to identify the credit ratings that used the prior version of the methodology and determine if the changes are likely to impact those ratings. The potential scope of the ratings likely to be affected will be published and the CRA will indicate the timeframe for the review of those ratings; in any case, the review must be completed not later than six months after the change to the methodology.

If the CRA does not re-rate the impacted ratings at the same time that it announces the methodology change, it has to place them under observation until the review is completed. In the terminology commonly used by CRAs, this means to put the likely affected ratings on the watch list (see Section 3.3.1).

REVIEW FOLLOWING THE MONITORING PROCESS. Apart from the reviews of ratings that result from methodology changes, CRAs are required by Article 8.5 to have in place policies and procedures for the ongoing surveillance of all their outstanding credit ratings that are under the scope of the Regulation (private ratings are outside the scope and thus CRAs will monitor them or not according to the terms of the contract). The purpose of this requirement is to keep ratings timely and credible. As a result of the surveillance activity, the CRA might decide that a rating change is warranted.

CRAs must have processes in place to detect material changes to the rated entity's operations or financial situation or to the macroeconomic or market conditions that could potentially change the CRA's opinion regarding its creditworthiness. Identification of these changes should trigger another process for the review of the rating.

The monitoring processes vary, depending on the type of ratings: corporate and sovereign/public finance ratings on the one hand and structured finance ratings on the other (see Section 1.4). One thing both types of monitoring procedures have in common is the maximum period for the review: according to the Regulation it should take place at least every 12 months—and this period is reset each time the rating is reviewed, as ESMA's Q&A clarifies. Nonetheless, the actual timing of the review will obviously depend on the occurrence of material changes (specific to the issuer, its sector, or the wider economic environment) that might impact the rating. In fact, Article 8.5 requires an ongoing assessment of the ratings and this seems to be a more effective requirement than that of performing annual formal reviews. However, although it is not clear in the Regulation what process the CRA should follow in order to perform the annual review, it seems that the added value of this requirement would be to force CRAs to go through a similar process as that followed for the determination of the initial rating, which would imply the participation of a rating committee and the publication of the outcome of the review—confirmation or change of the rating. The fact that the annual review of ratings and their ongoing monitoring are different processes can also be inferred from Recital 23 of the CRA Regulation: 'the requirement that credit rating agencies review credit ratings at least annually should not compromise the obligation on credit rating agencies to monitor credit ratings on a continuous basis and review credit ratings as necessary'.

It is interesting to mention that the European Commission proposed in its November 2010 consultation the idea of reducing the maximum time period after which sovereign debt ratings should be reviewed. In particular, the Commission suggested reducing the review period to six months, after which CRAs would have to provide a full review of the sovereign debt rating. It is doubtful that an obligation to conduct more frequent formal reviews would enhance ratings quality, and in particular it is questionable that sovereign ratings should be treated differently to corporate ratings.

3.8.4.8 Possible Anti-competitive Practices on Structured Finance Ratings

Article 8.4 of the Regulation provides that:

> Where a credit rating agency is using an existing credit rating prepared by another credit rating agency with respect to underlying assets or structured finance instruments, it shall not refuse to issue a credit rating of an entity or a financial instrument because a portion of the entity or the financial instrument had been previously rated by another credit rating agency.
>
> A credit rating agency shall record all instances where in its credit rating process it departs from existing credit ratings prepared by another credit rating agency with

respect to underlying assets or structured finance instruments providing a justification for the differing assessment.

This provision has been included in the article that deals with the CRA's methodologies because it relates to the procedures and methodologies employed by CRAs when determining credit ratings for structured products. It addresses some practices that have been questioned by some market participants, including some CRAs, on the grounds that they might be anti-competitive. These practices relate to instances where the CRA that has been mandated to issue a rating of a structured product has not rated the securities or assets that underlie that structured product and some or all of these underlying securities or assets have been rated by another CRA.

The SEC has explained the different ways in which CRAs might treat the ratings from another CRA on the underlying assets of a structured product as a condition of issuing the rating of the structured instrument.[64] The contracted CRA might require that it issues a public or private rating on those assets underlying the structured product and request a fee for the extra work. Another practice is to require an internal credit analysis of another person related to the transaction, such as the sponsor or manager of the structured product. Finally, the mandated CRA can also incorporate the ratings of another CRA into the credit rating of a structured product but only after having lowered them following a mapping methodology. This practice is commonly known in the market as 'notching' or 'notching down' (see Section 2.1.5).

Some market participants have argued that these practices have a negative effect on competition and, furthermore, could have occurred for anti-competitive purposes. They claim that these practices should be prohibited and that CRAs should rely on the ratings of another CRA without employing any mapping methodology to reduce those ratings. However, other experts consider that CRAs should not be forced to blindly rely on the ratings issued by other competitors because such a requirement would unduly interfere with their methodologies for issuing ratings. According to the latter position, CRAs would not be able to properly opine on the creditworthiness of the securities they rate if they do not carry out their own analysis in order to fully understand the credit quality of the underlying assets.

The SEC came up in 2007 with a twofold solution. The above-mentioned practices are prohibited when such practices are engaged in by the CRA for an anti-competitive purpose. In particular, the SEC prohibits the following practices: issuing or threatening to issue a lower credit rating, lowering or threatening to lower an existing credit rating, refusing to issue a credit rating, and withdrawing or threatening to withdraw a credit rating unless all or a portion of the underlying assets are also rated by a CRA that rates the structured product.

This prohibition is coupled with three record-keeping requirements. First, CRAs are required to retain internal documents related to their methodologies and procedures to treat the ratings of another CRA. Second, they have to make a record of all the structured finance products and their corresponding ratings where the CRA, in determining these ratings, treated underlying assets it had

---

[64] SEC Release No. 34-55857; File No. S7-04-07. Final rule issued on June 2007 to implement provisions of the Credit Rating Agency Reform Act of 2006.

not rated. Third, the CRA must retain a record describing the treatment for each of the securities where the CRA, when determining the rating, incorporated a rating on the underlying assets issued by another CRA.

The US regime in this area seems more comprehensive than the European one. First, the SEC prohibits a range of practices when having an anti-competitive purpose whilst in the EU the only practice that is banned is the refusal to issue a credit rating when a portion of the underlying assets have been previously rated by another CRA—this seems to be the only plausible explanation of the confusing language used in Article 8.4. For example, notching down in the EU would not be unlawful, even when it is done for anti-competitive purposes.

Regarding the record-keeping regime, Article 8.4 does not require CRAs to retain the procedures and methodologies used to treat the ratings of another CRA. However, ESMA expects to receive this information as part of the CRA's disclosures accompanying its application for registration. ESMA's guidance on registration states that the procedures for the issuance of credit ratings should include a collation, analysis, and assessment of information used to determine a rating, including (where applicable) reliance on analysis by another CRA or third parties.

The records required under the US regime should assist the SEC in understanding whether the above-mentioned practices are employed with the intent of ensuring the quality of the ratings or as pretexts for anti-competitive behaviour. In the latter case, the SEC could consider that the practice falls under the prohibition of anti-competitive behaviour established by its rules. Under the EU Regulation, the records will enable ESMA to determine whether the CRA is adhering to its disclosed procedures and methodologies.

3.8.4.9 EU Authorities' Supervision of Methodologies

Supervision by ESMA

As discussed above, when carrying out its ongoing supervision, ESMA will assess whether a CRA has publicly disclosed sufficient information about its procedures and methodologies and also whether the CRA is adhering to them when issuing ratings. ESMA's guidance on methodologies sets out the information that CRAs have to submit in order to enable it to assess whether the controls and processes in place are adequate; and this information will supplement the description of the procedures and methodologies used to issue and review credit ratings that CRAs have to provide in its application for registration (according to ESMA's guidance on registration).

According to this framework, the key elements of the reporting to ESMA are:

- Policies, procedures, and responsibilities for rating methodology development and review, and for disclosing the description of methodologies, models, and key rating assumptions; size, skills, and experience of CRAs' quantitative teams responsible for developing and reviewing methodologies and models.

- For each asset type, a high-level description of the range of core models and methodologies used to determine credit ratings, including the qualitative and quantitative inputs, and their related weightings. This should also include a description of the interrelationship between macroeconomic data and the key assumptions and between the assumptions and the volatility of ratings over time.

- Procedures in place that ensure that methodologies are implemented and applied consistently across ratings classes and different CRAs within a group; among them, the CRA should provide those for reviewing situations when ratings diverge from the pre-defined methodology.
- Details on how the rating and performance reviews feed into the revision of rating methodologies.
- Policies, procedures, and responsibilities for the issuance of credit ratings. These would include the processes for determining which CRA within a group is responsible for assigning the rating; determination of which methodology to use; role and responsibilities of lead analysts, support analysts, and persons approving the ratings; skills and experience of the rating teams; assessment of minimum information requirements and process for its review; description of any review performed on internal and external data input into rating models; and procedures for notifying the rated entity and for disclosing the rating decision.
- Policies, procedures, and responsibilities for the monitoring of ratings. In particular, the CRA should explain whether different methodologies are used for ratings surveillance than for determining initial ratings. The processes will include those for deciding when a rating should be formally reviewed or withdrawn, including reviews resulting from an amendment to the related methodology.
- Quantitative evidence of the discriminatory power of the credit assessment methodology using statistical techniques, comparing, for example, actual defaults with probabilities of default set out in the transition matrices, to demonstrate the robustness and predictive power of credit assessment over time and across different asset classes.
- Written policies and procedures describing the content of the validation process and in particular how this activity is related to possible changes of methodologies, for each asset type. At the time of the application for registration, applicants have to provide ESMA with historic information on validation and back-testing of methodologies and models; this information should be provided for the past three years where quantitative data is available. As part of its ongoing supervision of CRAs, ESMA has to examine regularly their compliance with the back-testing obligation. In particular, the CRA Regulation (Article 22a as incorporated in CRA Regulation II) specifically requires ESMA, in the framework of such ongoing supervision, to verify the execution of back-testing by CRAs, to analyse its results, and to verify that the CRAs have processes in place to take into account the results of the back-testing into their rating methodologies.

Finally, CRAs are required to fully document their methodologies and procedures for issuing and monitoring ratings (see Section 3.8.2).

Supervision by Banking Authorities

As regards supervision of ECAIs' methodologies under the CRD, prudential supervisors have to be satisfied at the time the ECAI is recognized that its methodologies meet the objectivity criteria set out in the CRD. And, as discussed above, they also have to assess on an ongoing basis whether recognized ECAIs continue to meet the criteria that led to their initial recognition. As already mentioned, registered CRAs applying for ECAI recognition are considered to be compliant with the CRD's criteria on methodologies (see Section 3.5.3). Therefore, it is logical that banking authorities do not supervise those criteria on an ongoing basis—they rely on ESMA's supervision of methodologies.

An overarching principle also in this area is that competent authorities, when assessing an ECAI's methodology, will avoid making any judgement as to whether an ECAI's methodology is objectively correct—as stated in EBA's guidelines on ECAIs.

Instead, the oversight conducted by banking and investment firm authorities focuses on three areas. First, they assess whether the ECAI has processes in place to ensure that its methodologies incorporate all factors relevant in determining an entity's creditworthiness. Second, the ECAI will have to demonstrate that these methodologies are applied consistently when issuing ratings. And third, the key aspect of the supervision is the assessment of the discriminatory power of the ECAI's methodologies. Competent authorities will perform this analysis employing quantitative methods such as default and transition studies when the ECAI has sufficient data available. In case there is less quantitative evidence to prove the consistency and predictive power of the ECAI's credit assessments, EBA recommends authorities to undertake a greater assessment of the entity's processes.

In essence, EBA considers that competent authorities should be satisfied that 'the credit assessment drivers used in the ECAI's methodology are sensible predictors of creditworthiness'. It might be challenging for banking authorities to assess the inputs of the methodological process without making any judgement as to whether an ECAI's methodology is objectively correct (the principle of non-intrusion in the ECAI's methodologies). Certainly, this seems to go beyond the role of competent authorities under the CRA Regulation, which basically consists of ensuring that CRAs publish the way they rate products and that afterwards they adhere to the published methodologies when reaching their rating conclusions. In other words, authorities do not have the power to pass judgement on the appropriateness of the factors considered in the methodology.

3.8.4.10 US Approach on Methodologies

The US system is similar to the European one. Its key elements are public disclosure of the procedures and methodologies used by the NRSRO to determine credit ratings; need to assess the effectiveness of the methodologies on an ongoing basis (Dodd–Frank Act requirement that NRSROs establish an internal control structure governing the implementation of, and adherence to, credit rating methodologies); and supervision by the SEC of the appropriateness of the NRSRO's public disclosures and its adherence to the disclosed methodologies when determining ratings (without interference with the actual content of methodologies).

3.8.5 Disclosure and Presentation of Ratings

3.8.5.1 *Scope for Disclosure and Presentation Requirements*

Article 10 and Annex I.D of the Regulation impose disclosure and presentation requirements on 'credit ratings'. It seems logical to understand these requirements as referring not only to the initial assignment of a credit rating, but also to any subsequent confirmation or change in a rating (upgrade or downgrade) and to any withdrawal of a rating. They do not apply to rating statuses such as placing a rating on the watch list, or taking it off the list, or outlook actions.

The Regulation does not prescribe a form for the inclusion of all required disclosures. The mandatory information should accompany the disclosure of any of the above rating actions, whatever the name used by the CRA to designate the publication (announcement, press release, report, etc.).

3.8.5.2 *Transparency of Policies and Procedures*

Applicants for registration must submit to ESMA their policies and procedures with respect to the disclosure requirements analysed in this section and evidence of how the applicant meets or intends to meet these disclosure requirements in practice (for example, in the form of a copy of credit rating reports or a snapshot of the website). Also, for each type of credit rating, the applicant must provide ESMA with sample templates of letters communicating the rating to the issuer.

It is also worthwhile noting that Annex I.E.I requires CRAs to publicly disclose their policies concerning the publication of credit ratings and other related communications.

3.8.5.3 *Disclosure of Ratings*

Article 10.1 of the CRA Regulation incorporates into the EU framework the principle of transparency and timeliness of ratings disclosure imposed by provision 3.1 of the IOSCO Code. According to said article:

> A credit rating agency shall disclose any credit rating, as well as any decision to discontinue a credit rating, on a non-selective basis and in a timely manner. In the event of a decision to discontinue a credit rating, the information disclosed shall include full reasons for the decision.
>
> The first subparagraph shall also apply to credit ratings that are distributed by subscription.

The obligation of disclosing any credit ratings does not apply to private ratings because they are outside the scope of the Regulation.

Distribution on a Non-selective Basis

Article 10.1 imposes on CRAs the obligation to distribute their ratings on a non-selective basis. CRAs use different methods of distribution depending on their business models. CRAs operating under the issuer-pays model will publish their ratings free of charge on their website. Once the rating is publicly available on the Internet the requirement of distribution on a non-selective basis is complied with.

CRAs that permit only paying subscribers to access their credit ratings should make the complete range of its credit ratings available to all subscribers at equivalent terms. This is the language used by the CRD that could serve as guidance to construe Article 10.1. The CRD sets out a number of requirements for eligible ECAIs; one of them is the transparency of their credit assessments, which intends to create a level playing field by ensuring that all institutions 'having a legitimate interest' in an ECAI's credit assessments have equal and timely access to them (see Section 3.5.3). Institutions 'having a legitimate interest' are those banks that use the standardized approach and the securitization ratings-based approach to calculate their regulatory capital requirements, and that intend to use the credit assessments of the respective ECAI for risk weighting purposes. EBA's guidance on ECAIs has interpreted the meaning of the expression 'at equivalent terms': a CRA should not make undue price discrimination among credit institutions that are under the same economic circumstances.

Timeliness of Distribution

In conformity with the IOSCO Code, Article 10 prescribes that a CRA should disclose rating actions 'in a timely manner'. CRAs therefore have flexibility in determining the most suitable time to release their rating actions.

According to IOSCO,[65] some financial regulators in certain jurisdictions have expressed concern regarding the moment when rating decisions are made public. The concern is that rating actions made public during trading hours may contribute to intra-day volatility in the market, as investors will trade on the rated instrument without having had time to fully analyse the implications of the released rating action. Following this line of thinking, the EC consultation on CRAs November 2010 proposed requiring CRAs to make their rating decisions public—although surprisingly only those related to sovereign bonds—only once the relevant market has closed.

On the other hand, concerns about volatility should be balanced against the possible effects that delaying the release of a rating may have on market transparency and efficiency. A restriction requiring that CRA's rating actions are made public only after the close of business of European trading venues might unduly favour either large EU institutions with international offices or non-EU investors trading in another time zone before the EU markets open again. This would be against the interests of less sophisticated institutions and EU retail investors. Additionally, there is a risk that volatility at the opening of EU markets would increase.

For these reasons, it seems appropriate to leave to the CRAs' judgement the choice of the right timing for publication, taking into account the needs of market participants and the market abuse rules as discussed below.

12-Hour Rule

SCOPE. Annex I.D.I.3 provides that 'the credit rating agency shall inform the rated entity at least 12 hours before publication of the credit rating and of the

---

[65] IOSCO (September 2003), *Report on the activities of credit rating agencies.*

principal grounds on which the rating is based in order to give the entity an opportunity to draw attention of the credit rating agency to any factual errors'.

This rule is based on provision 3.7 of the IOSCO Code, although IOSCO only mandates CRAs to afford issuers the opportunity to clarify any factual misperceptions or other matters 'where feasible and appropriate' and does not indicate a minimum time period for the issuer's review.

During the rating process the issuer has the opportunity to provide to the CRA any relevant information and explanation. Therefore, once the rating committee has reached a rating decision, the Regulation enables issuers only to check the factual accuracy of the draft rating announcement. This is the stated objective of the provision, although it should also serve the purpose of avoiding inadvertent disclosure of non-public information in the rating release. Normally these should be the only issues that the rated entity should raise at this point.

The EU requirement fuelled discussions among regulators and CRAs; prior to the 12-hour rule coming into effect, CRAs used to provide considerably shorter periods for issuer's review—in accordance with the above-mentioned objectives of the notice. They feared a longer period could be understood as affording issuers a sort of negotiation process with the CRA. In addition, the change of practice raised market abuse concerns because, as discussed earlier in the book, a pending rating action might amount to inside information according to the Market Abuse Directive.

The Regulation requires a CRA to inform the rated entity 12 hours before 'publication'. By contrast, according to provision 3.7 of the IOSCO Code, the CRA should inform the issuer prior 'to issuing or revising' a rating. The question that arises is whether a CRA operating under the subscriber-pays model—and therefore not publishing its ratings—is also required to comply with the 12-hour rule. As the main purpose of the rule is to give issuers an opportunity to correct any factual inaccuracies that might have been relied upon in determining the rating, it seems that CRAs that do not publish their ratings should also comply with Annex I.D.I.3—ratings distributed to subscribers should also be factually correct and comply with the same quality standards as published ratings.

CRAs also have to consider how the 12-hour rule works in relation to unsolicited ratings, or, more precisely, in relation to ratings determined without participation of the issuer in the rating process. In a case where the rating has been developed without any interaction with the rated entity, CRAs could believe that there is no need to alert it 12 hours before publication of the rating. However, this understanding would not be consistent with the Regulation. 'Rated entity' is defined in Article 3 of the Regulation as the person whose creditworthiness is assessed, whether or not it has provided information for the determination of the rating. Therefore, an unsolicited draft rating or a rating developed without participation of the issuer should also be communicated to the issuer 12 hours before the final rating is disclosed. This interpretation is also in line with the above-mentioned objectives of the provision.

ISSUER'S FEEDBACK. It is doubtful that a CRA can shorten the 12-hour period by an early response or request from the issuer. On the one hand, if the CRA receives an issuer's written confirmation to proceed with the publication in less than 12 hours from the time it was notified, it would seem logical that the CRA publishes the rating action without still having to wait for the full 12 hours to elapse. Issuer and CRA should have an interest in having the rating action published as soon as possible in order to limit the risk that their employees trade on the information or pass it on to others and also considering the market needs to receive up-to-date information.

However, on the other hand, the language of the Regulation seems to suggest that a CRA must still wait for the full 12 hours even where it has received confirmation of the issuer. Only once 12 hours have elapsed, regardless of whether the issuer has replied, may the CRA distribute the rating. This would be the safest interpretation for CRAs in the absence of clarification of this issue by ESMA. ESMA's Q&A reiterates the wording of the Regulation—'a CRA must alert the rated entity at least 12 hours before publication'—and states that any concern a CRA might have over the handling of the draft rating by the issuer could be reported to the relevant competent authority; but the rule has to be respected in all cases.

In the event that the CRA receives feedback from the issuer, it should duly evaluate it and take reasonable efforts to correct any errors or remove any inadvertently included confidential information. If the rated entity brings to the attention of the CRA the fact that a material fact was omitted from the analysis and the lead analyst considers that the information is important, it would seem prudent to call the rating committee in order to ascertain whether the draft rating action should be modified accordingly. It is expected though that these cases would be exceptional. Any amendment to the draft announcement as a result of the issuer's feedback should be indicated in the final release of the rating action, according to Annex I.D.I.2.(a).

Finally, the Regulation does not require that the 12 hours are business hours. Nevertheless, it would seem appropriate that at least part of the review period coincides with the issuer's working hours.

RECORD-KEEPING. Although not explicitly required by the Regulation, CRAs should document in the record of the credit rating the time when the issuer was notified, the identification of the issuer's representative that received the notification, any answer received, any steps taken by the CRA to react to the issuer's comments, and the time of publication of the rating action. This would assist ESMA in assessing compliance with the 12-hour requirement.

Decision to Discontinue a Credit Rating

The CRA Regulation is using the term 'discontinuation' as a synonym of 'withdrawal'. The Regulation requires disclosure of a withdrawal in a similar way as the disclosure of a credit rating. Additionally, a CRA must explain the reasons for the decision to withdraw the rating; this explanation must be included in the press release announcing the withdrawal, as well as in the reporting of any withdrawal to CEREP.

Publication of Ratings on Traded Securities that have been Based on Confidential Information

Provision 3.4 of the IOSCO Code provides that:

> Except for 'private ratings' provided only to the issuer, the CRA should disclose to the public, on a non-selective basis and free of charge, any rating regarding publicly issued securities, or public securities themselves, as well as any subsequent decisions to discontinue such a rating, if the rating action is based in whole or in part on material non-public information.

This provision has not been incorporated into the CRA Regulation. As already discussed, CRAs operating under the issuer-pays model publish their ratings on their websites free of charge, therefore in compliance with provision 3.4 of the IOSCO Code. However, ratings issued by CRAs that derive their revenues from subscription fees are only available to the clients that subscribe to the CRAs' services. Nevertheless, this practice should not contravene the IOSCO Code because these agencies normally issue only unsolicited ratings, therefore no confidential information would be factored into the rating process.

Private ratings on listed companies communicated by the rated issuer to third parties (for example, to a bank that is financing the company) under a confidentiality agreement should be in conformity with the said IOSCO provision. If the confidential information shared by the issuer with the third party would constitute inside information according to the Market Abuse Directive, the rated issuer should take appropriate measures to protect the confidentiality of the information.

3.8.5.4 *General Rules on Presentation of Ratings*

Article 10.2 stipulates that CRAs 'shall ensure that credit ratings are presented and processed in accordance with the requirements set out in Section D of Annex I'. The information Annex I.D requires CRAs to disclose along with the rating must not be charged for according to ESMA's Q&A. ESMA bases its opinion on Article 13 of the Regulation: 'a credit rating agency shall not charge a fee for the information provided in accordance with Articles 8 to 12'. The information should remain available free of charge until the rating is withdrawn (for example, due to maturity or early redemption of the rated instrument).

Annex I.D.I contains the general obligations on presentation. These rules apply to all credit ratings (traditional ratings such as corporate and sovereign/public finance ratings, as well as structured finance ratings). As the disclosures required by Annex I.D.I. might be too extensive for inclusion in a press release, the Regulation allows CRAs to incorporate them by reference. According to the second paragraph of Annex I.D.I.5, where the information laid down in Annex I.D.I, points 1, 2, and 4 'would be disproportionate in relation to the length of the report distributed, it shall suffice to make clear and prominent reference in the report itself to the place where such disclosures can be directly and easily accessed, including a direct web link to the disclosure on an appropriate website of the credit rating agency'.

There is, however, one exception to this possibility: the key elements underlying the credit rating must always be included in the report or press release and therefore may not be linked to another place.

CRAs should ensure that the use of links to other sections of their websites is reasonable and does not compromise the accessibility of information by users of ratings. In the past market participants have raised the need to improve the navigability of the websites of the CRAs.

Lead Rating Analyst, Person Approving the Rating, and Office Elaborating the Rating in Case of Groups

Annex I.D.I.1 stipulates that a CRA 'shall ensure that any credit rating states clearly and prominently the name and job title of the lead rating analyst in a given credit rating activity and the name and position of the person primarily responsible for approving the credit rating'.

Credit ratings are assigned by a CRA and not by any individual analyst employed by the CRA. However, identification of the persons having more direct responsibility over the rating is valuable information for users of ratings, for example, should they wish to address any queries to the CRA about the rating.

Additionally, in order to enable users of ratings to know which CRA of a global group has issued a rating, ESMA's guidance on registration prescribes that 'the name and address of the office elaborating the rating and issuing it, including the member state in which the agency has issued the rating must accompany each credit rating at all times'. This is relevant information, because, according to the rules on endorsement, EU financial institutions might be banned from using for regulatory purposes the ratings issued by certain non-EU offices of a global CRA.

Material Sources

Annex I.D.I.2.(a) obliges CRAs to ensure that 'all substantially material sources, including the rated entity or, where appropriate, a related third party, which were used to prepare the credit rating are indicated together with an indication as to whether the credit rating has been disclosed to that rated entity or its related third party and amended following that disclosure before being issued'.

Disclosure of the sources used by the CRA, together with the information required by Annex I.D.I.4—reproduced further down this section—about the CRA's view regarding the quality of that information and any verification conducted, will enable users of ratings to make their own judgement about the completeness and accuracy of the information used by the CRA to develop the rating.

It is also mandatory to indicate any change to the draft rating decision following issuers' feedback. As discussed earlier, the main objective of the 12-hour procedure is to enable issuers to bring to the attention of the CRA factual errors or confidential information inadvertently included in the draft announcement of the rating action. Material changes to the draft rating or its accompanying explanations due to other reasons could be perceived by market participants as diminishing the impartiality of the CRA; hence the relevance of requiring CRAs not only to indicate, but also to explain, those changes.

Methodology Used

Annex I.D.I.2.(b) imposes the next disclosure on CRAs:

> The principal methodology or version of methodology that was used in determining the rating is clearly indicated, with a reference to its comprehensive description; where the credit rating is based on more than one methodology, or where reference only to the principal methodology might cause investors to overlook other important aspects of the credit rating, including any significant adjustments and deviations, the credit

rating agency shall explain this fact in the credit rating and indicate how the different methodologies or these other aspects are taken into account in the credit rating.

The description of the methodology may be incorporated by reference only when this would not diminish the accessibility to investors of all material information needed to understand how the rating was developed.

As already discussed, one of the key requirements of the Regulation on methodologies is that CRAs implement them and apply them consistently across classes of credit ratings and offices within the same group of CRAs. It is important that CRAs explain in their rating announcements any adjustments and deviations to the methodology (such as adjustments to the result implied by the model where a quantitative model is a substantial component in the rating process); this disclosure will enable users of ratings to determine whether the adjustments to the methodology were made by applying appropriate qualitative factors in accordance with the CRA's procedures or because of undue influence from the rated entity.

Meaning of Each Rating Category, Definition of Default or Recovery, and Risk Warnings

According to Annex I.D.I.2.(c), CRAs have to ensure that 'the meaning of each rating category, the definition of default or recovery and any appropriate risk warning, including a sensitivity analysis of the relevant key rating assumptions, such as mathematical or correlation assumptions, accompanied by worst-case scenario credit ratings as well as best-case scenario credit ratings are explained'.

Credit ratings express risk in relative rank order (see Section 3.3.1). For investors to understand the meaning of a rating, it is important to know the relative position of the rating within the rating scale and the meaning of each category. CRAs use different scales (for example, for long-term and short-term issuer's ratings) and different nomenclatures to label each category within a scale.

The definition of default or recovery used by the CRA is obviously a key element that users of ratings have to understand in order to judge how the CRA arrived at its opinion. For example, a broad definition of default would produce lower ratings than a narrow one. In practice, CRAs do have different approaches, hence the need for a specific disclosure about default or recovery accompanying the rating (see Section 3.3).

Finally, regarding sensitivity analysis, Recital 38 provides that 'the sensitivity analysis should explain how various market developments that move the parameters built into the model may influence the credit rating changes (for example volatility)'.

Date of Last Update

Annex I.D.I.2.(d) requires CRAs to indicate clearly and prominently 'the date at which the credit rating was first released for distribution and when it was last updated'. As credit ratings must be monitored on an ongoing basis and reviewed at least annually (Article 8.5), this disclosure will help users follow the history of the rating.

Warning About New Financial Instruments or Instruments Rated for the First Time

Annex I.D.I.2.(e) imposes on CRAs the obligation to give information 'as to whether the credit rating concerns a newly issued financial instrument and whether the credit rating agency is rating the financial instrument for the first time'.

The concern this provision is addressing is the limited historical data a CRA might have in those cases to build a rating. Also, if the rating refers to a type of structure that is materially different from the structures the CRA has rated so far, it must have ascertained the feasibility of providing such a credit rating (Annex I.A.9).

Attributes and Limitations

According to Annex I.D.I.4:

> A credit rating agency shall state clearly and prominently when disclosing credit ratings any attributes and limitations of the credit rating. In particular, a credit rating agency shall prominently state when disclosing any credit rating whether it considers satisfactory the quality of information available on the rated entity and to what extent it has verified information provided to it by the rated entity or its related third party. If a credit rating involves a type of entity or financial instrument for which historical data is limited, the credit rating agency shall make clear, in a prominent place, such limitations of the credit rating.

The objective of this provision is that CRAs assist investors in understanding better what a credit rating is and what are its limitations. CRAs' disclosures about limitations should not be limited to boilerplate language; rather, they should be specific to the rating action being issued.

One of those limitations is that CRAs do not generally confirm the validity of the information provided to them by issuers or related parties. Nevertheless, CRAs are expected to take reasonable steps to ensure that the information they use is of sufficient quality to support a rating (see Section 3.8.4). As prescribed by the above provision, a CRA has to disclose what measures it has taken in order to be in a position to state that the quality of the information available on the rated entity is satisfactory.

Regarding the understanding of what a credit rating is, one of the valuable lessons drawn from the subprime market turmoil is that credit risk is not the same as liquidity risk or volatility risk. Traditionally, it was assumed that holders of instruments having the highest ratings would not have difficulties in quickly finding buyers in the market; also, these high-rated securities were associated with low volatility. The crisis highlighted these common misconceptions.

Finally, the crisis also drew attention to another important limitation, especially regarding the rating process of structured finance products, which rely heavily on models. CRA's probabilistic modelling of the underlying pools is based on the assumption that the assets will perform according to the past behaviour of similar assets. When the economic and financial circumstances change dramatically, these assumptions might not withstand, even for the ratings in the highest categories of the scale. The limitations of the models are also evident when the assumptions are based on limited historical data on some of the underlying assets.

Key Elements Underlying the Credit Rating

According to Annex I.D.I.5, 'when announcing a credit rating, a credit rating agency shall explain in its press releases or reports the key elements underlying the credit rating'. Investors should be able to understand clearly how the rating opinion was formed. To achieve this aim, the key factors or criteria and the key assumptions underlying the rating should be listed and explained in detail, not in general terms. It is also important that facts are clearly separated from interpretations and assumptions.

Finally, it is interesting to note that the Dodd–Frank Act requires NRSROs to identify in their press releases announcing rating actions the five most important assumptions in the rating process.

Information about Conflicts of Interests

There is one particular disclosure on conflicts that the Regulation does explicitly require: Annex I.B.4 states that a CRA shall disclose in the final ratings reports any ancillary services provided for the rated entity or any related third party.

In addition, although not specifically required under the rules on presentation of credit ratings, following Annex I.B.1, a CRA should disclose in the announcement accompanying the publication of the rating any conflict of interest related to the rating action being issued and how the CRA has addressed the conflict (for instance, if it derives more than 5% of its annual revenue from the rated entity or if a rating is changed as a result of the look-back requirement following the termination of employment of the analyst).

Unsolicited Ratings

CRAs that use a subscription fee-based business model will normally issue only unsolicited ratings because they do not charge fees to rated entities. CRAs that are paid by issuers might also issue unsolicited ratings in order to incorporate them into the rating process on other entities or financial instruments. And, as already mentioned, these ratings might help new CRAs to increase their coverage and to gain market credibility.

As discussed below, unsolicited ratings in the past gave rise to several concerns, leading some regulators to even consider the prohibition of this practice. However, legislators are also aware that new CRAs frequently rely on unsolicited ratings in order to build their reputations; a blanket prohibition of unsolicited ratings would constitute a barrier to new entrants.

For these reasons, EU legislators decided to deal with the issues posed by unsolicited ratings through disclosure. The rules of the Regulation are contained in paragraphs 4 and 5 of Article 10, both based on provision 3.9 of the IOSCO Code.

CRA'S ACCESS TO CONFIDENTIAL INFORMATION. According to Article 10.5, 'when a credit rating agency issues an unsolicited credit rating, it shall state prominently in the credit rating whether or not the rated entity or related third party participated in the credit rating process and whether the credit rating agency had access to the accounts and other relevant internal documents of the rated entity or a related third party'.

A CRA developing an unsolicited rating may lack the type of issuer's input, such as access to confidential information, which a solicited rating may incorporate. Nevertheless, issuers may participate in the rating process even if they did not hire the CRA to issue the rating. Information on whether issuers or obligors cooperated with the CRA and provided non-public information is relevant for market participants because it will help them understand the methodology used to build the rating and the amount and kind of information factored into the rating.

ABUSIVE PRACTICES. Some issuers have argued in the past that CRAs operating under the issuer-pays model could coerce issuers into paying for those ratings. For this reason, Article 10.4 of the Regulation requires CRAs to 'disclose its policies and procedures regarding unsolicited credit ratings'. Apart from imposing transparency to unsolicited ratings, the Regulation does not prescribe any particular measures to address said concern. To avoid putting pressure on issuers, CRAs could, for example, adopt the practice of informing issuers not seeking a rating that the agency is not going to request any payment for the assignment of the rating.

A rating that was initially solicited might become unsolicited if the rated entity requests the CRA to withdraw the existing credit rating—or simply ceases to pay the rating fees—and the CRA decides to continue monitoring the rating. In these cases, the agency will have to designate the credit rating as unsolicited in any subsequent announcement of actions regarding that rating and disclose whether the issuer or obligor is participating in the rating process.

Endorsed Ratings

According to Article 4.2 of the Regulation, CRAs have to clearly identify endorsed credit ratings. ESMA's guidance on registration expects endorsing CRAs to state in the press release or report accompanying the rating that the rating has been endorsed and also give identification of the foreign CRA within the group that has issued the rating.

3.8.5.5 *Additional Obligations for Structured Finance Ratings*

The role of CRAs in structured finance has been a source of debate for some time. But concerns were exacerbated as a result of the US subprime mortgage-driven crisis. As discussed previously, the questions about the independence and quality of structured finance ratings led international securities regulators such as IOSCO and ESMA to make a number of proposals to address the regulatory issues in this market.

Some of them (such as the prohibition to advise issuers on how to design the deals) have already been analysed. The following describes the requirements on presentation of structured finance ratings that were adopted in the aftermath of the market turmoil.

Structured Finance Indicator

Article 10.3 of the Regulation states that 'when a credit rating agency issues credit ratings for structured finance instruments, it shall ensure that rating categories that are attributed to structured finance instruments are clearly differentiated using an additional symbol which distinguishes them from rating categories used for any other entities, financial instruments or financial obligations'.

The IOSCO Code, as amended in 2008, also requires CRAs to differentiate ratings of structured finance products from traditional corporate bond ratings, preferably through a different rating symbology. The Code goes on to require CRAs to disclose how the differentiation works and apply it consistently (provision 3.5.b).

As many market participants experienced during the last financial crisis, structured finance may be more volatile and less liquid under stress conditions than traditional corporate bonds. If even under normal conditions, trading of structured finance instruments in the secondary markets is very thin, under a stress situation the market might dry up completely. This lack of trading might be due to different factors, such as the complexity and opacity of the structures or the buy-and-hold strategies followed by many investors. One the objectives of this provision is to alert investors of the possible liquidity and volatility risk of structured finance—although, as already noted, credit ratings address only credit risk and not other types of risks.

This explanation is consistent with the wording of Recital 40 of the Regulation: 'under certain circumstances structured finance instruments may have effects which are different from traditional corporate debt instruments. It could be misleading for investors to apply the same rating categories to both types of instruments without further explanation.'

Additionally, a clear difference between the ratings of structured finance instruments and the ratings of corporate bonds is the different rating process used to determine the rating, as already explained. This means, for example, using different sources and types of information and more reliance on quantitative models in the case of structured finance. The structured finance indicator might be useful to make investors aware of the specificities of the structured finance products in relation to traditional ones (Recital 40).

Nevertheless, the separate symbol approach has been criticized by some market participants, arguing that it does not add value and might even be confusing for investors, as default risks for structured finance products are essentially the same as for other types of debt instruments.

Finally, ESMA's Q&A left the decision on how to implement the requirement to CRAs' discretion. DBRS, Fitch, Moody's, and S&P chose an SF suffix.

Annex I.D.II sets out below the additional obligations on presentation of structured finance ratings.

Loss and Cash-flow Analysis

Annex I.D.II.1 provides that 'where a credit rating agency rates a structured finance instrument, it shall provide in the credit rating all information about loss and cash-flow analysis it has performed or is relying upon and an indication of any expected change in the credit rating'.

The first task in the rating process of a structured finance instrument is to analyse the loans in the pool to develop predictions as to how many loans will default under stresses of different severity. This loss analysis will also predict how much principal of the loans would be recovered in the event of default. The CRA will then inform the issuer of the credit enhancement required for assigning the desired rating to each tranche of securities.

Once the sponsor or issuer determines the structure of the transaction, the CRA will perform a cash-flow analysis on the principal and interest payments expected to be received from the loans and determine whether these funds will be sufficient to service any payments due and payable on the securities.

Due Diligence on the Underlying Assets

The obligation to disclose to what extent the CRA has verified the information used to determine the rating is imposed by the general rules on presentation that have been analysed before. However, EU legislators wanted to ensure that CRAs make specific disclosures about the level of due diligence carried out on the assets underlying structured finance instruments. As CRAs base their analysis on the data on the pool of loans provided by originators, they should take reasonable steps to deal with the risk that the information supplied is inaccurate or misleading. According to Annex I.D.II.2:

> A credit rating agency shall state what level of assessment it has performed concerning the due diligence processes carried out at the level of underlying financial instruments or other assets of structured finance instruments. The credit rating agency shall disclose whether it has undertaken any assessment of such due diligence processes or whether it has relied on a third party assessment, indicating how the outcome of such assessment impacts on the credit rating.

Explanation of Assumptions, Parameters, Limits, and Uncertainties

Annex I.D.II.3 provides that:

> Where a credit rating agency issues credit ratings of structured finance instruments, it shall accompany the disclosure of methodologies, models and key rating assumptions with guidance which explains assumptions, parameters, limits and uncertainties surrounding the models and rating methodologies used in such credit ratings, including simulations of stress scenarios undertaken by the agencies when establishing the ratings. Such guidance shall be clear and easily comprehensible.

A key issue for investors is to understand the main assumptions used within the methodologies and their relative impact on the rating (such as asset default assumptions and recovery rate). A CRA has to make a number of subjective judgements to build the rating; transparency about those assumptions will allow investors to assess whether the CRA's expectations are aligned with their own.

Underlying assumptions that prove wrong might have a dramatic impact on the rating. In order to ensure that the rating category assigned to each tranche can withstand adverse macroeconomic conditions, CRAs run stress scenarios of different severity to determine the credit enhancement needed for each rating category. For example, the most severe stress is run to determine the level of credit enhancement required for an AAA or Aaa rating, the next most severe scenario is run to determine the credit enhancement of the AA or Aa tranche, and so on. Information on the level of stress testing carried out during the rating process will assist investors in assessing rating actions.

Rating Shopping

Recital 41 of the Regulation states that 'credit rating agencies should take measures to avoid situations where issuers request the preliminary rating assessment of the structured finance instrument concerned from a number of credit rating agencies in order to identify the one offering the best credit rating for the proposed structure. Issuers should also avoid applying such practices.'

Market participants have raised the concern that sponsors or issuers can present a transaction to a number of CRAs in order to pick up the one that would assign the highest rating to the proposed pool of assets. This practice is possible because there is no obligation to issue a final public rating and CRAs might not even charge for the analytical work conducted if the issuer decides not to proceed with the rating. It should be noted though that some issuers possess and are able to run CRAs' models, so they can determine themselves which one would be more favourable to their interests.

With the aim of discouraging ratings shopping, Annex I.D.II.4 states that 'a credit rating agency shall disclose, on an ongoing basis, information about all structured finance products submitted to it for their initial review or for preliminary rating. Such disclosure shall be made whether or not issuers contract with the credit rating agency for a final rating.'

Whilst this measure is welcomed, the details of its implementation by the CRAs are very important to ensure that this information assists market participants in determining whether issuers or sponsors are rating shopping. The provision does not require CRAs to identify the deals where the issuer did not hire the CRA for a final rating; but even if CRAs provided such information, it would be difficult for market participants to match a 'failed' or non-issued rating in a CRA's list with a final rating issued by another CRA. This is because the fields to identify the transaction submitted for initial review are not standardized and also because the issuer might just make some slight variations to the structure or asset pool in order to have a 'different' product rated by another CRA.

Finally, neither the Regulation nor ESMA have specified the time frame for the reporting of rating applications. The Regulation requires disclosure 'on an ongoing basis' which seems to suggest that CRAs must update the list of request for structured finance ratings as soon as they receive a new application. Only this immediate update will help prospective investors in the search for possible shopped transactions before purchasing the securities.

A more effective measure to combat rating shopping could be to ensure that CRAs are compensated for their initial reviews of the loan pools, regardless of whether they are ultimately selected to rate the transaction (the New York attorney general agreed this measure in 2008 with the three principal CRAs, Fitch, Moody's, and S&P).[66]

---

[66] Office of the Attorney General, State of New York, June 2008. Announcement of agreements between Attorney General Cuomo with the three principal credit rating agencies: *Standard & Poor's, Moody's, and Fitch agree to change fee structures, obtain due diligence information for the first time, and create due diligence and lender standards for residential mortgage-backed securities.*

3.8.5.6 *Rating Agency Data Room*

SEC Rule 240 17g-5

On 4 December 2009, the SEC adopted several amendments to its rules on NRSROs with the aim of addressing, through disclosure, the conflict that arises when an agency is paid by an issuer or sponsor to rate a structured finance instrument and with the objective of promoting the issuance of credit ratings by non-mandated NRSROs.

Amended Rule 240 17g-5 requires an NRSRO that is hired by an arranger (defined as an issuer, sponsor, or underwriter) to determine an initial rating for a structured finance product to take certain steps designed to allow non-mandated NRSROs to nonetheless determine an initial rating—and subsequently monitor that credit rating—for the structured finance product.

In essence, each NRSRO has to maintain a password-protected website detailing all structured finance transactions where the agency has been mandated to determine an initial credit rating and to identify the website address where the arranger is hosting the information provided to the hired NRSRO, both for assigning the initial rating and for ongoing surveillance.

This information includes the characteristics of the underlying assets and the legal structure of the transaction and all the data provided to the NRSRO for the purpose of monitoring the rating, including the performance of the assets. When the arranger hires an NRSRO to rate a structured finance product, it has to provide it with a written compromise that it will make this information available on a password-protected website. Such protected websites will be accessible to the non-hired NRSROs, provided they satisfy certain conditions. A NRSRO cannot rate a structured finance instrument if the above requirements are not complied with.

The SEC's rules apply to registered NRSROs, therefore including non-US subsidiaries that are included in the registration. The extraterritorial application of the rule raised concerns in foreign jurisdictions—such as Europe—about potential disruptions of local securitization markets. In response to these concerns, the SEC exempted, until 2 December 2012, NRSROs from compliance with the rule where the issuer of the structured finance product is a non-US person and the NRSRO can reasonably expect that the securities will be offered and sold outside the US.

Recital 5 of CRA Regulation II

The EC proposal CRA Regulation II put forward an amendment with similar objectives. According to the EC's proposed amendment, issuers of structured finance instruments would be required to give access to the information they give to the hired CRA for the purpose of issuing a structured finance rating to competing CRAs. Nevertheless, the provision was not endorsed by the EU governments and Parliament and, therefore, the EC had to withdraw it from the final text. The proposed EC's rule would have imposed obligations on entities other than credit rating agencies, and market participants expressed doubts over whether this proposal would actually achieve its aims or would simply impose an unnecessary cost on the financial services industry. For example, a widespread criticism was that CRAs would not make use of the information as they would not be paid for producing any ratings derived from the information and would assume reputational and regulatory risk.

The above explains Recital 5 of the CRA Regulation II, which mandates the EC to explore the possibility of imposing transparency of the information underlying the ratings of all financial instruments, in order to promote unsolicited ratings issued by non-hired CRAs. Therefore, the deal reached by EU legislators was the deletion of the initial EC's proposal on structured finance ratings in exchange for a mandate to the EC to put forward legislative proposals regarding the availability to non-mandated CRAs of the information necessary to rate any financial instrument.

It is noteworthy that ESMA had already analysed the appropriateness of that idea in 2005.[67] ESMA advised against the establishment of a rating agency data room for all rating agencies to have access to the same information from companies. Paragraph 171 of ESMA's advice summarizes its rationale:

> The relationship between an issuer and a CRA is likely to vary considerably depending on the circumstances of the issuer and the reasons why a rating is being sought. For ratings sought by CRAs themselves and not by issuers, a level playing field in terms of the information available would be of benefit, particularly to smaller CRAs trying to increase their coverage, but there is a question as to whether it is appropriate to mandate that an issuer must provide the same information to a CRA it does not want to engage with that it has made available to a CRA that it has willingly co-operated with. We note that no similar requirement exists in the context of issuers' contacts with research analysts where similar demands to meet with senior management are often made.

At least in the area of structured finance, it seems that what the marketplace demands is enhanced public disclosure, enabling not only other CRAs but also investors, to have access to the same information on the underlying assets the mandated CRA receives (at the time of the determination of the initial rating and also regular information updates on the performance of the asset pool). Among the initiatives in this direction are the ECB proposals discussed in Section 3.5.4 or the new Article 122a of the CRD II, which requires sponsor and originator credit institutions to 'ensure that prospective investors have readily available access to all materially relevant data on the credit quality and performance of the individual underlying exposures, cash flows and collateral supporting a securitisation exposure as well as such information that is necessary to conduct comprehensive and well informed stress tests on the cash flows and collateral values supporting the underlying exposures'.

3.8.5.7 *Prohibition on Using ESMA's Name*

Article 10.6 of the Regulation states that 'a credit rating agency shall not use the name of ESMA or any competent authority in such a way that would indicate or suggest endorsement or approval by ESMA or any authority of the credit ratings or any credit rating activities of the credit rating agency'.

---

[67] CESR (March 2005), *Technical advice to the European Commission on possible measures concerning credit rating agencies (Ref. CESR/05-139b).*

This provision would apply to any indication that the activities of a CRA are recommended by the authorities made in regulatory disclosures or in any marketing materials made available by the CRA.

3.8.6 Transparency of Rating Agencies' Activities, Policies, and Procedures

3.8.6.1 *Categories of Required Disclosures*

Articles 11 and 12 of the Regulation and Annex I.E impose a number of disclosure requirements of different natures on CRAs. These disclosures are aimed at ensuring transparency about the credit rating activities of a CRA, its procedures, and the functioning of its internal processes, at making data on CRAs' performance available in a standardized manner, as well as at providing information to ESMA for the purposes of ongoing supervision.

These disclosure requirements are classified below into four categories:

- General disclosures to be published after registration and that must be kept up to date.
- Periodic disclosures to be published annually in the form of a 'transparency report'.
- Annual information to be submitted to ESMA for supervisory purposes (lists of clients and ratings).
- Performance data to be provided every six months to ESMA; this information is uploaded by ESMA into a public central repository.

The language regime for the disclosures imposed on CRAs has been analysed in Section 3.6.3.

3.8.6.2 *General Disclosures*

Scope

According to Article 11.1, 'a credit rating agency shall fully disclose to the public and update immediately information relating to the matters set out in Part I of Section E of Annex I'. Annex I.E.I requires a CRA to disclose the fact that it is registered in accordance with the Regulation and the following information:

1. any actual and potential conflicts of interest referred to in point 1 of Section B;
2. a list of its ancillary services;
3. the policy of the credit rating agency concerning the publication of credit ratings and other related communications;
4. the general nature of its compensation arrangements;
5. the methodologies, and descriptions of models and key rating assumptions such as mathematical or correlation assumptions used in its credit rating activities, as well as their material changes;
6. any material modification to its systems, resources or procedures; and
7. where relevant, its code of conduct.

As recommended by the IOSCO Code, CRAs are obliged to make certain disclosures on their actual and potential conflicts of interests, their methodologies, and their policies regarding distribution of ratings. The purpose of these disclosures has been analysed in the relevant sections of the book dealing with these matters. CRAs should also publish in a prominent position on its home webpage a link to their codes of conduct, as required by point 7 (which implements provision 4.3 of the IOSCO Code).

Finally, point 6 obliges CRAs to publish any material modification of its systems, resources, or procedures. As CRAs are not required to publish in the first place all their systems, resources, and procedures, it is not easy to understand a provision that requires them to publish any material modification of these. As already indicated in the book, a CRA in the EU provides ESMA, in its application for registration, with comprehensive information regarding its activities, resources, procedures, and processes. However, contrary to the US system, CRAs in the EU are not required to publish their applications for registration. It seems that pursuant to Annex I.E.I.6, a CRA should make public, at least, any modification to its systems, resources, or procedures that would amount to a material change to the conditions for initial registration according to Article 14.3.

Means of Publication

The Regulation only refers to the means of publication of the transparency report, but not to the method of publication of the general disclosures required under Article 11.1. Article 12 states that the transparency report should remain available on the agencies' website for at least five years.

ESMA's guidance on registration states that the CRA's website is the only place where the information could be easily accessible by investors and ESMA. Therefore, according to ESMA's guidance, general disclosures required under Article 11.1 should be published on the website of the CRA. In order to facilitate market participants' accessibility to the required disclosures, it seems reasonable that CRAs have a place in their websites where they provide at least a list of all general disclosures and the links to the other parts of the website where the full information can be found.

Timing

ESMA's guidance on registration considers that the CRA should publish the general disclosures on its website as soon as practicable after ESMA notifies its decision to register the agency. This publication should take place without undue delay, and after the initial publication any updates should be published immediately.

Information to be Provided in the Application for Registration

An applicant should submit to ESMA its policies and procedures with respect to the general disclosure requirements and evidence of how it meets or intends to meet these requirements in practice (such as copy of credit rating reports or a snapshot of the CRA's website).

3.8.6.3 *Periodic Disclosures: Transparency Report*

Scope

Article 12 of the CRA Regulation stipulates that

> A credit rating agency shall publish annually a transparency report which includes information on matters set out in Part III of Section E of Annex I. The credit rating agency shall publish its transparency report at the latest three months after the end of each financial year and shall ensure that it remains available on the website of the agency for at least five years.

An applicant should submit to ESMA its policies and procedures with respect to the production of the transparency report.

Annex I.E.III sets out the content of the transparency report:

1. Detailed information on legal structure and ownership of the credit rating agency, including information on holdings within the meaning of Articles 9 and 10 of Directive 2004/109/EC of the European Parliament and of the Council of 15 December 2004 on the harmonization of transparency requirements in relation to information about issuers whose securities are admitted to trading on a regulated market.
2. A description of the internal control mechanisms ensuring the quality of its credit rating activities.
3. Statistics on the allocation of its staff to new credit ratings, credit rating reviews, methodology or model appraisal, and senior management.
4. A description of its record-keeping policy.
5. The outcome of the annual internal review of its independent compliance function.
6. A description of its management and rating analyst rotation policy.
7. Financial information on the revenue of the credit rating agency divided into fees from credit rating and non-credit-rating activities with a comprehensive description of each.
8. A governance statement within the meaning of Article 46a (1) of Council Directive 78/660/EEC of 25 July 1978 on the annual accounts of certain types of companies. For the purposes of that statement, the information referred to in Article 46a (1)(d) of that Directive shall be provided by the credit rating agency irrespective of whether it is subject to Directive 2004/25/EC of the European Parliament and of the Council of 21 April 2004 on takeover bids.

This is a list of heterogeneous disclosures that can be grouped into the three categories below.

DISCLOSURES ON CRAS' INTERNAL PROCESSES AND PROCEDURES. Those disclosures that respond to the objective of providing transparency with respect to the functioning of the internal processes and procedures of the CRA (such as the internal control mechanisms, the record-keeping, or the rotation policies) would have been better placed under the general disclosures requirements. This would have avoided repetitions in successive transparency reports when the policies have not changed since the previous year and would have ensured that the CRA's disclosures are always up to date when changes occur.

DISCLOSURES ON LEGAL STRUCTURE, OWNERSHIP, AND CORPORATE GOVER-NANCE. The purpose of these disclosures is to enable market participants to assess whether a CRA is organized in a way that ensures the independence, objectivity, and reliability of its ratings.

A CRA has to provide ESMA with details about its legal structure and ownership in its application for registration (see Section 3.8.1). As this information will also be useful for users of ratings, CRAs might choose to disclose to the public similar information to that provided in their application for registration. Regarding information on significant shareholders, the reference in the first point of Annex I.E.III to the Transparency Directive means that the CRA has to identify its shareholders having 5% or more of the voting rights.

The governance statement indicated in point 8 is a Community legislation requirement for companies whose securities are admitted to trading on a regulated market. It has to be included in the annual report of the company and must contain a reference to the corporate governance code to which the company is subject or that it voluntarily applies and any additional corporate governance practices. It will also explain if the company departs from any provisions of its applicable code and the reasons for doing so.

Other aspects that CRAs have to include in their governance statements (in accordance with Directive 78/660/EEC) are a description of the main features of its internal control and risk management systems in relation to the financial reporting process; the operation of the shareholder meeting and its key powers and a description of shareholders' rights and how they can be exercised; and the composition and operation of the administrative, management and supervisory bodies, and their committees.

Finally, even if the CRA is not subject to the Directive on Takeover bids (because its securities are not admitted to trading on a regulated market), the Regulation requires it to disclose some information that listed companies have to provide according to that directive:

- significant direct and indirect shareholdings (including indirect shareholdings through pyramid structures and cross shareholdings) within the meaning of Article 85 of Directive 2001/34/EC;[68]

- the holders of any securities with special control rights and a description of those rights;

- any restrictions on voting rights, such as limitations of the voting rights of holders of a given percentage or number of votes, deadlines for exercising voting rights, or systems whereby, with the company's cooperation, the financial rights attaching to securities are separated from the holding of securities;

---

[68] *Official Journal*, L 184, 6.7.2001: p. 1–66.

- the rules governing the appointment and replacement of board members and the amendment of the articles of association; and

- the powers of board members, and in particular the power to issue or buy back shares.

OTHER DISCLOSURES ON THE ACTIVITIES OF THE CRA. The compliance officer has to report regularly about the activities and findings of the department to the senior management and independent directors (see Section 3.8.1). The CRA will have to publish the outcome of its annual review.

Finally, disclosures on the allocation of staff to the different rating activities and the breakdown of revenues will enable market participants to assess whether the CRA is devoting appropriate resources to the issuance and monitoring of the classes of ratings it covers.

Timing

Article 12 defines the publication deadline for the transparency report. It must be published at the latest three months after the end of each financial year. Concerning the first transparency report, ESMA's guidance on registration clarified that it should be published three months after registration if the date of registration is more than four months away from the end of the financial year.

Transparency Report of Groups of CRAs

ESMA's approach to this issue is that groups of CRAs are able to publish a single transparency report prepared at EU-wide level (ESMA's Q&A). However, this report would 'have to include the information of each credit rating agency in a format that allowed to be identified as coming separately from each particular CRA'.

More generally, ESMA also concludes that 'disclosures expected of a CRA under the Regulation will need to be provided at a CRA subsidiary level'. In addition, another question addressed by ESMA in its Q&A, indicates that 'CRAs are expected to provide information on revenues at a subsidiary level, and where applicable, at branch level'.

3.8.6.4 *Annual Information to be Submitted to ESMA*

Scope

Article 11.3 stipulates that 'a credit rating agency shall provide annually, by 31 March, to ESMA information relating to matters set out in point 2 of Part II of Section E of Annex I'. According to this provision, this information is the following:

(a) a list of the largest 20 clients of the credit rating agency by revenue generated from them;

(b) a list of those clients of the credit rating agency whose contribution to the growth rate in the generation of revenue of the credit rating agency in the previous financial year exceeded the growth rate in the total revenues of the credit rating agency in that year by a factor of more than 1.5 times. Any such client shall be included on the list only where, in that year, it accounted for more than 0.25% of the worldwide total revenues of the credit rating agency at global level; and

(c) a list of credit ratings issued during the year, indicating the proportion of unsolicited credit ratings among them.

For the purposes of this point, 'client' means an entity, its subsidiaries, and associated entities in which the entity has holdings of more than 20%, as well as any other entities in respect of which it has negotiated the structuring of a debt issue on behalf of a client and where a fee was paid, directly or indirectly, to the credit rating agency for the rating of that debt issue.

The disclosure to ESMA on an annual basis of a list of the largest 20 clients and a list of those clients whose contribution to the growth rate of the revenues has exceeded the growth rate of the revenues by more than 1.5 times will enable ESMA to focus its supervisory activities. Important clients might be in a position to exert undue influence on a CRA's rating activities.

ESMA has considered that the definition of 'client' provided by Annex I.E.II.2 also applies to structured finance ratings. Regarding these types of deals, CRAs asked ESMA whether 'client' for the purposes of reporting the revenue information would be either the arranger, originator/sponsor, or collateral manager, depending upon which one has, in the CRA's assessment, the greatest economic benefit from the transaction. ESMA provided a rather confusing answer in its Q&A, stating that CRAs should 'monitor the related third parties to the transaction (as defined in Article 3 of the Regulation) and consider them as clients and reflect this in disclosures on revenues'. This seems to mean that all related third parties will be considered clients and, therefore, the CRA will have to assign each of them all the revenues generated by the deal.

Another question analysed by ESMA is the application of the requirement under Annex I.E.II. (b) in years where there is no overall growth in a CRA's revenue. ESMA considered that the required disclosure would be on 'any entity from which the CRA increased its revenue generation and that made up greater than 0.25% of the global revenue'.

Finally, the requirement under letter (c) was introduced by the CRA Regulation II. As discussed below under the analysis of ESMA's central repository, this provision overlaps to some extent the obligation CRAs have to report to ESMA their ratings active at the beginning and at the end of every semester. The list of ratings issued during the year should help ESMA in its monitoring role, especially in order to identify trends in the CRA's activities. For example, a significant growth in one class of ratings might lead to a more focused examination to analyse if the CRA is devoting sufficient resources to those ratings and is managing adequately any possible conflicts of interest arising from that business line. ESMA is required by the CRA Regulation to draw up regulatory technical standards regarding the content and format of these periodic reports on ratings data.

Timing

The annual disclosures required by Article 11.3 are linked to the revenues of the CRAs. Therefore, it makes sense that CRAs provide this information to ESMA three months after the end of the financial year at the latest. This is the language used by Article 12 of the Regulation regarding the transparency report (that also contains certain disclosures related to the revenues and other information included in the CRA's annual report). However, Article 11.3 obliges CRAs to submit the information 'by 31 March', which could create difficulties for CRAs whose reporting year does not coincide with the calendar year.

3.8.6.5 *Information on Historical Performance Data: ESMA's Central Repository*

Objectives of the Regulation

The research conducted by ESMA[69] prior to releasing its guidelines on the EU CRAs central repository evidenced that major CRAs are used to publish voluntarily historic performance data. The core metrics agencies disclosed were default rates, cumulative default rates, ratings upgrades and downgrades, transition matrices, and accuracy ratios. However, CRAs varied in the names, time horizons, and definitions of these metrics, causing difficulties for investors trying to compare among CRAs. Another frequent complaint from market participants was the lack of completeness of the data provided.

With the aim of enhancing transparency and facilitating performance comparisons between CRAs, the Regulation mandated ESMA to set up a central repository (CEREP) that would provide information on the past performance of CRAs and on the credit ratings issued in the past.

The information published by ESMA should contribute to reduce the costs for investors of searching and processing the data. Facilitating the ability of individual comparisons of CRAs' ratings performance, the disclosure of ratings history through the CEREP should enable market participants to generate their own statistics about CRAs' performance by compiling and processing the information. This could even encourage market participants to develop performance measurement statistics that would supplement those published by the CRAs themselves and by the CEREP.

In addition, the disclosure of ratings history and performance statistics should make CRAs' track record more transparent to the marketplace and should enable market participants to conduct a more accurate analysis of CRAs' performance. It would highlight those agencies that do better work assessing creditworthiness and this might lead users of ratings to give greater weight to ratings of those CRAs that have a better history of credit rating performance than their peers. Moreover, to the extent this can improve the quality of credit ratings, users of ratings would have better information to base their decisions and, therefore, the CEREP would contribute to the protection of investors. Finally, the central repository might help market participants get to know the smaller agencies, which could promote competition in the market.

Recital 39 of the Regulation outlines the key elements of the design of the CEREP. CRAs should provide information to the repository in a standardized form; ESMA 'should make that information available to the public and should, annually, publish summary information on the main developments observed'. These elements are discussed in the next paragraphs.

---

[69] CESR (July 2009), *Consultation paper, CRAs central repository (Ref. CESR/09-579).*

Information to be Reported to ESMA

LEGAL PROVISIONS. The only provisions in the Regulation dealing with the CEREP are Article 11.2 and Annex I.E.II.1.

According to Article 11.2, 'a credit rating agency shall make available in a central repository established by ESMA information on its historical performance data including the ratings transition frequency and information about credit ratings issued in the past and on their changes. A credit rating agency shall provide information to that repository on a standard form as provided for by ESMA'.

Annex I.E.II.1 further specifies that a CRA shall disclose 'every six months, data about the historical default rates of its rating categories, distinguishing between the main geographical areas of the issuers and whether the default rates of these categories have changed over time'.

RAW DATA CONCEPT. Having in mind the objectives pursued by the Regulation, ESMA had to define the standardized form in which CRAs have to provide information to the CEREP. ESMA had to consider the trade-off between, on the one hand, the need to introduce new and common methodologies to classify the ratings information—in order to ensure comparability—and, on the other hand, the use of existing historical information and statistics produced by CRAs—in order to avoid interference with CRAs' processes and methodologies and reduce costs.

ESMA balanced these arguments and finally opted for a system that requires CRAs to supply 'raw data' (data files on individual ratings) instead of 'statistical data'. Based on the ratings reported, ESMA will compile and publish its own statistics for each CRA and for different periods. This approach minimizes costs for CRAs and facilitates possible future adjustments to the system. In addition, as discussed below, ESMA defined certain reporting standards in order to ensure a satisfactory degree of comparability.

Based on ESMA's guidelines on CEREP, the following paragraphs explain the types of data reported by CRAs and the statistics ESMA calculates and publishes on the basis of the data collected.

CRAS SUBJECT TO REPORTING REQUIREMENTS. The CEREP system centrally collects data on credit ratings issued by registered CRAs (including endorsed ratings) and by certified CRAs. In addition, CEREP will collect credit ratings issued in a third country by CRAs not certified or registered but belonging to the same group of a registered CRA if these ratings are voluntarily provided to the CEREP. Only CRAs with a minimum of one year of rating activity are subject to the reporting requirements.

RATING TYPES. Ratings to be reported are those that were active at the beginning or at the end of the relevant period. The requirement covers both solicited and unsolicited ratings. Regarding the reporting asset classes, ESMA has defined three broad categories that have been broken down into the following segments:

- corporate ratings: financial institutions—including banks, brokers, and dealers—insurances, other corporate issuers;

- structured finance ratings: asset-backed securities (ABS), residential mortgage-backed securities (RMBS), commercial mortgage-backed securities (CMBS), collateralized debt obligations (CDO), asset-backed commercial papers (ABCP), and other structured finance securities that cannot be categorized into the other five major sectors;

- sovereign and public finance ratings: sovereign, other local governments (for example, states or regions), and municipalities, supranational organizations, and public entities (such as public administration and defence; compulsory social security, education).

For corporate and public ratings CRAs report data for both short- and long-term ratings, if available. For structured finance products only long-term issue ratings are supplied (with the exception of ABCP, for which only short-term ratings are reported).

REPORTING OF DEFAULTS. The Regulation in its Recital 38 highlights the relevance that comparable historical performance information, in particular in relation to defaults, has for investors:

> The credit rating agency should ensure that the information on historical default rates of its rating categories is verifiable and quantifiable and provides a sufficient basis for interested parties to understand the historical performance of each rating category and if and how rating categories have changed. If the nature of the credit rating or other circumstances makes a historical default rate inappropriate, statistically invalid, or otherwise likely to mislead the users of the credit rating, the credit rating agency should provide appropriate clarification. That information should, to the extent possible, be comparable with any existing industry patterns in order to assist investors in drawing performance comparisons between different credit rating agencies.

As discussed earlier, when developing the common reporting standards ESMA tried to the extent possible not to interfere with CRAs' methodologies. For example, ESMA did not attempt to harmonize CRAs' rating categories. However, ESMA considered that some minimum harmonized standards were necessary in order to generate comparable statistics.

As emphasized by Recital 38, one of the metrics that could have a greater impact upon comparability is the default of the rated issuer. And, as ESMA noted in its consultation paper on the CEREP, CRAs' definitions of default varied significantly. This is why ESMA tried to achieve a common standard of reporting, considering a default to have happened, if:

- the rating indicates that a default (according to the CRA's definition of default) has occurred;

- the rating has been withdrawn due to bankruptcy of the rated entity or due to debt restructuring; or

- any other instance in which a CRA considers a rated entity or security as materially impaired (or equivalent).

Notwithstanding, it is doubtful that this standard definition of default will achieve meaningful standardization across CRAs. ESMA's definition is actually based on CRA's own definitions of default, debt restructuring, or material impairment.

Determination of when these events have occurred is inherently subjective and CRAs are likely to differ in their approaches.

TREATMENT OF RATING WITHDRAWALS. ESMA's research on CRAs' perfor-mance reports prior to the CRA Regulation found that major CRAs did not disclose the reasons for withdrawals of ratings. There is a risk that a CRA could withdraw a rating to make its transition or default statistics appear more favour-able. For this reason, ESMA considers that this is useful information for market participants and accordingly requires CRAs to report ratings withdrawn and the reason for the withdrawal according to one of the following categories:

- incorrect or insufficient information provided;
- bankruptcy of rated entity or debt restructuring;
- reorganization of rated entity (including merger or acquisition of rated entity);
- maturity of the debt obligation;
- automatic invalidity of rating due to business model of CRA in case of a subscription based rating model; or
- end of rating due to other reasons.

REPORTING AND STATISTICAL PERIODS. In accordance with Annex I.E.II.1, CRAs have to report data every six months. The first reporting period is from 1 January to 30 June and the second one from 1 July to 31 December. The data must be reported during the three months following the end of each reporting period.

It is important to note that in their first report, CRAs have to submit data covering at least the past ten years before the entry into force of the Regulation (or the shortest period covering their rating activities if they were created less than ten years ago).

Although CRAs report biannually, the minimum statistical period of the CEREP is twelve months (covering two consecutive six-month periods). In addition, CEREP will display multi-year statistics, covering multiple twelve-month periods.

Statistics Produced by ESMA

Article 11.2 states that ESMA shall make the information collected from the agencies 'accessible to the public and shall publish summary information on the main developments observed on an annual basis'.

The raw data reported by the CRAs is not published by the CEREP. ESMA computes the data in order to provide several statistics which are displayed for each type of rating issued by each CRA (corporate, sovereign and public finance, structured finance) including different time horizons (short-term or long-term) where available. If available, users are able to select further segregation of the data in terms of geographic area and industry or asset class. In addition, the CEREP publishes some qualitative information provided by the CRAs, such as their methodologies or definitions of default.

The CEREP provides rating data as absolute figures and as a percentage, where applicable. The figures, to be published annually, include the number of ratings at the beginning and at the end of the year, the number of rating changes (upgrades and downgrades), the number of withdrawals, the reasons for withdrawals, and the average number of notches for upgrades and downgrades.

In addition, the public have access to information on CRAs' historical performance. These reports are one-year default statistics (presented both as absolute numbers of defaults and as a percentage of the number of ratings at the beginning of the period) and CRAs' one-year transition matrices. A transition matrix illustrates how ratings change during a defined period. The matrix compares the number of issuers with a certain rating category at the beginning of the period with the distribution of the rating categories of these same issuers at the end of the period.

The CEREP provides also multi-year default rates and multi-year rating transition matrices. These statistics cover the latest three, five, seven, ten, twenty, and thirty years, where applicable.

SEC Rules

Important steps have been made in the past couple of years in the USA to enhance the transparency of ratings performance. In fact, the USA is moving towards a system close to that of the CEREP, although the information required refers only to rating activity (it does not include default rates or transition matrices) and does not have to be provided to a central repository but is to be published individually by each CRA.

In February 2009, the SEC introduced the obligation (paragraph (d) of Rule 17g–2) to disclose rating actions histories, in eXtensible Business Reporting Language ('XBRL') format, for 10% of the ratings in each class for which the NRSRO had registered and for which it has issued 500 or more issuer-paid ratings. This rule, sometimes referred to as the '10% requirement', required disclosure of a new rating action to be made no later than six months after the rating action was taken.

In November 2009, with a compliance date of June 2010, the SEC adopted an amendment that applies to all NRSROs regardless of their business model (issuer-pays ratings, subscriber-pays ratings, or unsolicited credit ratings). According to this rule, NRSROs have to disclose rating actions histories for all ratings initially determined on or after 26 June 2007 in an interactive data file that uses a machine-readable format, until the SEC develops the XBRL format for this (the '100% requirement'). In the case of issuer-paid credit ratings, each new rating action has to be added to the publicly disclosed histories no later than twelve months after it is taken, while in the case of rating actions that are not issuer-paid, each new rating action has to be reflected no later than twenty-four months after it is taken.

With the Dodd–Frank Act, an additional step is given to harmonize the disclosure of rating histories. In a specific section entitled *Transparency of ratings performance* the Act requests the SEC to set a rule to require 'that each nationally recognized statistical rating organization publicly disclose information on the initial credit ratings determined by the nationally recognized statistical rating organization for each type of obligor, security, and money market instrument, and any subsequent changes to such credit ratings, for the purpose of allowing users of credit ratings to evaluate the accuracy of ratings and compare the performance of ratings by different nationally recognized statistical rating organizations'.

Moreover, the Act specifies some minimum requirements that the SEC rules have to include: the information has to be published and made freely available by the NRSROs on an easily accessible portion of its website; the disclosures should be clear and informative to all kinds of investors and comparable among NRSROs to allow users of ratings to compare the performance of credit ratings; the information has to include performance data over a range of years and for a variety of types of credit ratings, including ratings withdrawn; and the requirements have to be appropriate to the business model of the NRSROs. The SEC proposed rules for NRSROs May 2011 have opted for enhancing transparency to the maximum (see Appendix 4).

3.8.6.6 *Communication with Market Participants*

Although not required by the CRA Regulation, it is noteworthy that the IOSCO Code recommends CRAs establish a function 'charged with communicating with market participants and the public about any questions, concerns or complaints that the CRA may receive'. Its provision 4.2 stipulates that 'the objective of this function should help ensure that the CRA's officers and management are informed of those issues that the CRA's officers and management would want to be made aware of when setting the organization's policies'.

4

Use of Non-EU Ratings in the EU

As a result of the financial crisis, a strong international consensus emerged that regulation and supervision over CRAs was needed. In this respect, the G-20 declaration of April 2009 stated, among other things, that 'all CRAs whose ratings are used for regulatory purposes should be subject to a regulatory monitoring regime that includes registration and is consistent with the IOSCO CRA Code' (see Section 2.2.2).

Following the G-20 declaration, national and regional initiatives are going on to strengthen the monitoring of CRAs taking the IOSCO Code as a basis. At the time of writing, some countries already have regimes in place (for example, the USA, Japan, Argentina, India, and Mexico) and others are in the process of developing one (such as Canada, Hong Kong, and Singapore). A detailed analysis of the US legislation on CRAs is provided in Appendix 4 and of the Japanese regulatory framework in Appendix 5. In addition, a brief overview of some of the current regulatory initiatives on CRAs is provided in the following paragraphs.[1]

In Mexico, CRAs have been regulated and supervised by the National Banking and Securities Commission since July 1993 and authorization of CRAs has been required since December 1999. In the past couple of years, Mexico has been working on a new regulatory framework to improve the quality, transparency, and integrity of the rating process and avoid conflicts of interest, while developing guidelines for rating structured products.

Canada is developing an oversight regime for CRAs that wish to have their ratings eligible for use in securities legislation. The Canadian securities authorities published revised proposals for consultation in March 2011. The aim of the Canadian authorities is to develop a regulatory regime that is consistent with international standards, in particular with the EU CRA Regulation. For this reason, the initial proposals have been amended in order to require mandatory compliance with the IOSCO Code and to add a number of additional requirements on corporate governance and on disclosures in ratings reports. In addition, legislative amendments are proposed to grant supervisory powers to the securities regulatory authorities.

Hong Kong is also developing a compatible regulatory regime with that of the EU. Hence, an amendment to the current regulatory regime has been proposed in

---

[1] Report of the Financial Stability Board to G-20 Finance Ministers and Governors in April 2010 and IOSCO (February 2011), *Report on regulatory implementation of the statement of principles regarding the activities of credit rating agencies in the different jurisdictions.*

order to require CRAs to be registered with the Hong Kong Securities and Futures Commission. Once registered, the CRAs will be required to comply with a code of conduct based on the IOSCO Code and with other requirements applicable to the licensed persons of other types of regulated activities. A number of the new requirements have been taken from the EU CRA Regulation.

In Australia, in January 2010 a new legislation revoked previously existing licensing relief for the three largest CRAs operating in the country. Since CRAs give financial advice,[2] they are from January 2010 covered by the existing Australian licensing regime for all financial services providers and consequently CRAs operating in Australia are required to hold an Australian Financial Services license. In addition, compliance with the IOSCO Code is a mandatory licensing condition from July 2010.

In South Korea, the revision of CRA regulations took effect in October 2009, making it mandatory for CRAs to establish processes to ensure rating accuracy and prevent conflict of interest; to disclose rating methodology and rating process on structured products; and to disclose ratings performance data.

The introduction of monitoring regimes in foreign countries is important for the EU as the import of non-EU ratings is based, according to the CRA Regulation, on the existence of a regulatory framework in those countries. The following sections will analyse the use of non-EU ratings in the EU as envisaged in CRA Regulation.

4.1 PROCEDURES SET OUT BY THE CRA REGULATION

One aspect subject to considerable debate during negotiations on the Regulation in the European Council and Parliament was the use in the EU of ratings issued by agencies from third countries.[3] The EC proposal CRA Regulation did not establish any mechanisms allowing for the use for regulatory purposes of these ratings, therefore imposing an obligation on agencies from third countries to establish a subsidiary in Europe in order to be able to issue ratings that could be used for regulatory purposes in the EU. The EU Council and Parliament, in order to meet the needs of global agencies and European-supervised entities, modified the EC's proposal in order to allow the use of ratings issued by agencies from third countries for regulatory purposes in the European Union. The mechanism used is twofold: an endorsement procedure and another of certification based on equivalence.

Nevertheless, the reluctance of the EC and some Member States to allow the use of foreign credit ratings in the EU left its mark on the text of the Regulation. The treatment of ratings issued by CRAs established in third countries is massively over-complicated and this problem is compounded by the restrictive interpretation of the requirements on endorsement that the EC and ESMA are adopting.

---

[2] Defined under the Australian legislation to include opinions or reports that could reasonably be regarded as intended to influence a person in making a decision in relation to a financial product.

[3] García Alcubilla, Raquel and Ruiz del Pozo, Javier (2009), Credit rating agencies: Analysis of the proposal for European Parliament and Council Regulation. *CNMV Bulletin*, Quarter II.

As mentioned when discussing the scope of the CRA Regulation, agencies from third countries do not need to be registered in order to issue ratings on EU issuers, or on securities issued by EU issuers, or offered to EU residents, but these ratings may not be used for regulatory purposes by EU-supervised entities if they do not follow one of the two procedures set out by the Regulation.

The Regulation considers, for all purposes, the ratings of agencies of third countries issued following any of these two procedures to be ratings issued by a registered agency. Consequently, the Regulation establishes safeguards in both mechanisms to ensure that the issue of ratings in third countries respects requirements as stringent as those set out in the Regulation.

4.1.1 Systemic Importance

The notion which determines the possibility of accessing one procedure or another is that of 'systemic importance to the financial stability or integrity of financial markets of one or more Member States'. Consequently, interpretation of this concept is fundamental. ESMA's guidance on registration considered that Fitch, Moody's, and S&P groups are systematically important and, therefore, not eligible for certification. As for other CRAs, from ESMA's guidance it can be inferred that this is a matter to be assessed by competent authorities and that ESMA, before making a decision, should ask the competent authorities of all Member States whether the CRAs' activities are of systemic importance in their respective jurisdictions.

In particular, it must be examined whether an agency from a third country which has been recognized as ECAI for the purposes of the CRD previously mentioned, would be by definition 'important' for any EU Member State and therefore would not fulfil the requirements to proceed by the certification procedure. It should be noted, though, that Japan Credit Rating Agency, Ltd is recognized as ECAI in a number of EU countries and this has not been an impediment for this agency to be certified in accordance with the Regulation.

4.2 ENDORSEMENT

4.2.1 Scope

Endorsement is provided in Article 4.3 of the CRA Regulation for agencies whose ratings have systemic importance for the financial stability or integrity of financial markets of one or more Member States.

The endorsement system allows agencies established in the EU and registered in accordance with the Regulation to authorize the validity in Europe of a rating issued by an entity in its group established in a third country (for example, Moody's Madrid may endorse the ratings issued by Moody's New York), provided that a series of conditions are fulfilled. The Regulation also permits the endorsement of ratings issued by an agency which does not belong to the group of the endorsing agency, provided that the activities leading to the issue of the rating have been carried out in whole or in part by the endorsing agency.

4.2.2 Conditions

Endorsement of a rating is only possible when there is an objective reason for this rating to be made in a third country and when the activities which give rise to the rating fulfil the following conditions:

- the endorsing agency has verified and is able to demonstrate on an ongoing basis to ESMA that the conduct of rating activities by the agency of the third country complies with requirements at least as stringent as those contained in the substantive requirements of the Regulation (Articles 6 to 12);
- the ability of ESMA to evaluate and supervise compliance by the third country agency of the requirements referred to in the previous paragraph is not limited;
- the endorsing CRA makes available on request to ESMA all the information necessary to enable ESMA to supervise on an ongoing basis compliance with the requirements of the Regulation;
- the foreign agency is authorized or registered and is subject to supervision in its country;
- the legislation of the third country prevents the interference by the competent authorities and other public authorities with the content of methodologies and ratings; and
- there is an appropriate cooperation agreement between ESMA and the competent authority of the third country agency.

4.2.3 Responsibility of the Endorsing CRA

The agency which has endorsed ratings issued in a third country will be responsible for the ratings endorsed and for complying with the conditions established in the Regulation. In this respect, all the supervisory measures and pecuniary sanctions envisaged in the Regulation (see Section 3.7), will be applicable to the endorsing registered CRA. In fact, Annex III includes two specific infringements in relation to endorsement:

- When the CRA endorses 'a credit rating issued in a third country without complying with the conditions set out in Article 4(3)(a) to (h), unless the reason for that infringement is outside the credit rating agency's knowledge or control'. Inevitably, interpretative issues will arise in relation to the reference to the conditions in Article 4.3.(b) (the foreign CRA fulfils requirements as stringent as those set out in Articles 6 to 12).
- When the CRA uses 'the endorsement of a credit rating issued in a third country with the intention of avoiding the requirements of this Regulation'.

Article 4.2 requires CRAs to clearly identify the credit ratings that have been endorsed. According to ESMA's guidance on registration such identification does not necessarily require a separate 'identifier' as appropriate disclosure could be made in ratings publications. The guidance requires that in the disclosure CRAs also include an indication of the third country CRA that issued the endorsed rating. This identification might be useful for ESMA's supervisory purposes.

4.2.4 Application for Endorsement

As the Regulation is silent on the procedure that authorities should follow to allow endorsement, ESMA in its guidance on registration considered that that they should use the procedure laid down in the Regulation for registration and has provided additional clarity in relation to the steps that EU CRAs intending to endorse ratings of foreign CRAs have to follow.

At the time of the application for registration the CRA should inform ESMA that it intends to endorse ratings of a foreign CRA; as part of the application pack, the EU CRA would be expected to submit 'documents and detailed information related to the expected use of endorsement' (Annex II.16 of the CRA Regulation). In particular, it should submit the following documents so that ESMA can check that all the conditions set out in Article 4.3 are complied with.

4.2.4.1 *Legal Information on the Third Country CRA*

For each third country CRA involved in the process of issuing ratings for which endorsement is envisaged, the applicant has to provide:

- Full name.
- Legal status, including details of company registration (such as excerpt from the relevant commercial or court register), or other form of evidence, current as of the application date, of the place of incorporation, and scope of business activity.
- Country of establishment.
- Details of the types of credit rating which the applicant expects to endorse and according to the classifications of corporate (financial institutions, insurance, and corporate issuers), public/sovereign, and structured finance instruments.
- An organizational ownership chart of each CRA, subsidiary, fellow subsidiary, branch, and parent involved in the process of issuing ratings for which endorsement is envisaged. The chart will include legal status, full name, and address of all entities within the ownership structure of the relevant CRAs.

4.2.4.2 *Assessment on Requirements Being 'as Stringent as'*

The CRA has to provide a reasoned assessment on how the conduct of the rating activities of the third country CRA resulting in the issuing of credit ratings, for which an application for endorsement has been submitted, fulfils requirements which are at least as stringent as the requirements set out in Articles 6 to 12 of the Regulation.

In this respect, ESMA expects the applicant to provide detailed information, structured analysis, and reasoning for each requirement set out in Articles 6 to 12, for example in the form of a tabular analysis of each requirement. From this it can be inferred that ESMA does not take at face value the analysis provided by the CRA and makes its own assessment on the 'as stringent as' test on the basis of the information supplied by the agency. It seems that ESMA's approach is that CRAs should use the same methodology employed by ESMA when assessing the equivalency of a foreign framework with that of the EU. Therefore, this would imply that in its application for registration, the CRA should provide the information that demonstrates that it has carried out the same tests conducted by ESMA when assessing the equivalency of third countries' frameworks. ESMA's methodology to assess equivalence is set out in its advices to the EC on the equivalence between the EU and the US and Japanese frameworks.[4] An overview of ESMA's methodology for assessing equivalence is provided in Section 4.3.5.

Moreover, CRAs have to also provide the procedures put in place by the endorsing EU CRA to monitor that the third country CRA fulfils de facto such requirements, as well as any potential concerns identified by the endorsing EU CRA with respect to the fulfillment of such requirements.

4.2.4.3 Non-Avoidance Justification

The application has to include information that justifies that ratings are not produced in a third country to avoid being subject to the CRA Regulation. In particular, the CRA should provide objective reasons for ratings to be developed in a specific third country (for example, expertise of analysts, nationalities of rated entities, organizational structure of the group of CRAs) and the number of analysts working for each of the CRAs based in third countries which contribute to the issuance of ratings for which an application to be endorsed has been submitted.

ESMA has provided, in its Q&A, a few non-exhaustive examples as to what can be considered an objective reason for a rating to be determined in a non-EU country for the purposes of the endorsement regime:

1) The CRA has only recently opened an EU office and the staff that have the experience rating the EU entities that they cover are based outside the EU—immediately transferring the rating of these entities to the new EU office may lead to a decline in the quality of the rating.

2) Corporate action (for example a takeover/merger) means the rating activity does not reflect new corporate structures.

---

[4] CESR (May 2010), *Technical advice to the European Commission on the equivalence between the US regulatory and supervisory framework and the EU regulatory regime for credit rating agencies. (Ref. CESR/10–332)* and CESR (June 2010), *Technical advice to the European Commission on the equivalence between the Japanese regulatory and supervisory framework and the EU regulatory regime for credit rating agencies (Ref. CESR/10–333).*

Moreover, it has also considered that it would, in principle, not be acceptable that the rating activity relating to an issuer or security that had traditionally been carried out by analysts based in the EU could be moved without an objective reason.

ESMA seems to consider that ratings on issuers domiciled in the EU, or on the securities they issue, should in principle be determined by EU CRAs (in the case of global groups, by any of the subsidiaries based in the EU). Actually, global CRAs try to establish, where possible, offices in significant national markets to meet the business needs of issuers established in these countries or regions. Having local presence brings many advantages to the CRAs and the markets where they are located. Local analysts may have specific national industry expertise, which is relevant not only for the analysis of credit risk in the local market, but also for the development of methodologies tailored to national specificities. In addition, they operate in the same time zone as the issuers they rate and speak the same language. Finally, local offices reduce the time and costs associated with international travel to the markets they cover.

Notwithstanding the above arguments, CRAs should have flexibility to manage globally the availability of their resources. There could be situations where it might be appropriate to allocate analytical work relating to an issuer domiciled in the EU to analysts located elsewhere in the group. The way to manage this according to the Regulation is through outsourcing arrangements (with other EU CRAs or third country CRAs) or endorsement (in case the analytical resource is based outside the EU).

4.2.4.4 Registration and Supervision in the Country of Origin

The applicant has to indicate that the CRA established in the third country is authorized or registered and is subject to supervision in the relevant jurisdiction, together with the relevant reference to the law and/or regulation in the third country which provides for the authorization or registration and supervision. In addition, the CRA should provide an excerpt from the relevant commercial or court register, or other form of evidence, current as of the application date, of the place of incorporation and scope of business activity.

Finally, the applicant has to submit a copy of relevant legislation in place demonstrating that public authorities are not entitled to interfere with the content of ratings and methodologies used by CRAs incorporated in the relevant jurisdiction.

4.2.5 Approval of Endorsement and Endorsing Activity

Once it has analysed all the relevant documentation, ESMA will notify the applicant in its registration decision whether the expected use of endorsement has been approved or not. As endorsement is an activity that is voluntary for the CRA that applies for registration, ESMA considered in its guidance on registration that the applicant CRA should be registered if it complies with all the conditions for registration, even if those required for endorsement are not met. This would mean that the registered CRA would not be able to endorse any ratings until it demonstrates to ESMA full compliance with all the conditions under Article 4.3.

In case a CRA that has already been registered decides afterwards to endorse ratings from other foreign CRAs, ESMA's guidance on registration considered that the registration procedure would also be used (when applicable) to determine all procedural issues (such as format of application, deadlines, language, or notifications). The CRA should supply the same information and ESMA should conduct the same checks as if the request had been submitted at the time of the initial application for registration.

However, it must be noted that such a case would constitute a material change to the conditions for initial registration that must be notified to ESMA according to Article 14.3 of the Regulation. As discussed in Section 3.6.6, neither the Regulation nor ESMA have clarified the procedure to be carried out by ESMA when receiving such notifications.

Once ESMA is satisfied, following the procedure mentioned above, that the CRA that expects to endorse ratings complies with the requirements set out in Article 4.3, the EU CRA should be able to start endorsing ratings without the need for having any actual endorsement of individual ratings previously approved by ESMA (therefore supervision would take place ex post). This seems to be the only practical way to make endorsement work in practice, as it would be a very burdensome process if ESMA had to check beforehand every rating that is going to be endorsed. However, the CRA should be in a position to prove at any time, ex post and upon the request of ESMA, that all the endorsements it has issued comply with the requirements of the Regulation.

4.2.6 Changes to Endorsing Regime

ESMA understood that Article 14.3 of the Regulation which states that a registered CRA shall comply at all times with the conditions for initial registration, should be applied also to the conditions for endorsement. Moreover, as expressly mentioned in Recital 52, 'significant changes in the endorsement regime . . . should, inter alia, be considered as material changes to the conditions for initial registration of a credit rating agency'.

4.3 CERTIFICATION BASED ON EQUIVALENCE

4.3.1 Scope

This system is intended for small CRAs of third countries which do not have subsidiaries in the EU, on condition that they are not of systemic importance to the financial stability or integrity of the financial markets of one or more EU Member States. Consequently, the advantage of certification with respect to endorsement is that certified agencies would not be obliged to establish a subsidiary in the EU. In fact, Recital 14 mentions that the certification regime has been introduced for those cases where 'it may be necessary to adjust the requirement of physical presence in the Community . . . , notably as regards smaller credit rating agencies from third countries with no presence or affiliation in the Community'.

An additional condition in the Regulation for the use of the certification regime is that it is only permitted in respect of ratings related to instruments issued in a third country or to issuers domiciled in a third country. Consequently, ratings by a certified CRA of issuers domiciled in the EU or of instruments issued in the EU may not benefit from certification and consequently may not be used by European entities for regulatory purposes.

4.3.2 Process

The system of certification takes place in two consecutive stages, as explained below.

4.3.2.1 Determination of Equivalence

Certification requires that the EC has previously determined, on prior advice from ESMA, the equivalence of the legal and supervisory framework of the home country of the agency which applies for certification with respect to the requirements set out in the CRA Regulation. For the legal and supervisory framework of a third country to be considered equivalent, at least the following conditions must be fulfilled:

- the third country agencies must be subject to a system of authorization or registration and to supervision and control of effective compliance on an ongoing basis;
- the third country agencies must be subject to legally binding rules equivalent to those set out in the substantive requirements under the Regulation (Articles 6 to 12 and Annex I); and
- the legislation of the third country must prevent the interference by supervisory authorities and other public authorities with the methods used by the agencies and their ratings.

The equivalence mechanism does not constitute automatic access to the Community for agencies of the third country considered equivalent, but is a prior requirement which permits agencies of that third country to be individually assessed.

4.3.2.2 Certification Decision

The application for certification must be examined by ESMA following a process similar to that established for an application for registration. In order to obtain certification the following conditions must be met:

- the applying agency must be authorized and registered and be subject to supervision in the third country; and

- there must be an appropriate cooperation agreement of ESMA with the competent authority of the third country agency.

ESMA will certify the applicant once it is satisfied that the above conditions are fulfilled and that the CRA has submitted the information that must accompany the application, as discussed in the following paragraphs. Finally, it is noteworthy that ESMA may withdraw a certification decision under the same circumstances envisaged in the CRA Regulation for the withdrawal of registration (Article 5.8).

4.3.3 Application for Certification

ESMA's guidance on registration sets out the information that ESMA would expect to receive as part of an application for certification by a CRA: general information about the CRA, business activities, class/type of credit rating, ownership structure, organizational structure, and financial resources.

Therefore, the level of information required from foreign CRAs applying for certification is less comprehensive than that required from EU CRAs seeking registration. ESMA only requires for certification those items of information from the registration procedure that are necessary for a good understanding of the operations of the foreign CRA. The level of detail to be provided under each of those items is in general the same required in the application for registration; notwithstanding, under the heading on ownership structure a foreign CRA has to include an additional disclosure on whether it holds or intends to hold ECAI status and under the heading on financial resources no information is required at group level.

Apart from the items of information taken from the registration procedure, there are three additional disclosures described below that are specific to the certification procedure and are therefore only required to foreign CRAs.

4.3.3.1 Information on Domestic Supervision of the CRA

The applicant must indicate that the CRA established in the third country is authorized or registered and is subject to supervision in the relevant jurisdiction, together with the relevant part of the law and/or regulation in the third country which provides for the authorization or registration and supervision and an excerpt from the relevant commercial or court register, or other form of evidence, current as of the application date, of the place of incorporation and scope of business activity.

4.3.3.2 Information on Systemic Importance of the CRA

The application must provide information on the volume of outstanding ratings the applicant has issued (including a breakdown between corporate, sovereign, and structured finance). This information will enable ESMA and the Member State's competent authorities to decide whether or not the CRA is systemically important.

4.3.3.3 Exemptions

When applying for certification, the CRA may also apply to be granted an exemption in respect of some of the organizational requirements applicable to CRAs active in the EU. In particular, according to Article 5.4 the CRA can apply to be exempted:

1. On a case-by-case basis from complying with some or all of the require-ments laid down in Annex I.A and Article 7.4 if the CRA is able to demonstrate that the requirements are not proportionate in view of the nature, scale and complexity of its business and the nature and range of its issuing of credit ratings.

    According to ESMA's guidance, where an applicant requests an exemp-tion of some, or all, of the requirements set out in Annex I.A and Article 7.4 it should provide a detailed description of the relevant requirement of the Regulation from which it is requesting an exemption and the reasons why it considers the requirement not to be proportionate.

    It is difficult to understand why these exemptions have been included, taking into account that certification requires a previous positive decision by the EC regarding the equivalency of the foreign legislation with that of the EU (that will imply equivalence with the requirements included in Annex I.A and in Article 7.4).

2. From the requirement of physical presence in the EU where such a require-ment would be too burdensome and disproportionate in view of the nature, scale, and complexity of its business and the nature and range of the ratings it issues.

    The exemption of the requirement of physical presence in the EU also poses questions of interpretation because, as explained before, the whole process of certification has been structured for those CRA that are not based in the EU—Article 5.1 refers to 'a credit rating agency established in a third country'. This means that there is no requirement to be exempted from. Forcing the foreign CRA to set up a subsidiary in the EU would not make sense because this subsidiary would be an EU CRA and, therefore, obliged to register in the EU. The only plausible explanation is that EU legislators wanted to give ESMA the power to require the foreign CRA to establish a branch in the EU for supervi-sory purposes. However, it seems that this requirement would not be justified either because the certification regime relies on the supervision carried out by the third country authority.

4.3.4 Sanctioning Regime

A key aspect of certification is the application of the sanctioning regime of ESMA to certified CRAs. In relation to the supervisory measures envisaged in Article 24, Article 5.8 of the Regulation expressly states that these provisions 'shall apply *mutatis mutandis* to certified credit rating agencies and to credit ratings issued by them'. Therefore, ESMA is able to impose any supervisory measure directly on the certified CRA.

However, the Regulation does not include any provision to allow ESMA to impose pecuniary sanctions on certified CRAs and, consequently, ESMA is not able to impose fines or periodic penalty payments on them. In fact, as explained when analysing the provisions on pecuniary sanctions, enforcement of these sanctions is done through national competent authorities and follows the rules of civil procedure of the Member State in which the CRA is located. In the case of certified CRAs, as they do not have physical presence in the EU, the enforcement of pecuniary sanctions would have been complicated to articulate.

In principle, this situation should be solved by the joint combination of the provisions of Article 5: the requirement that the certified CRA is subject to registration and supervision in its country, the need for an equivalence decision by the EC in relation to the supervisory and enforcement framework of the third country, and the establishment of cooperation agreements between ESMA and the competent authority of the certified CRA.

Theoretically, it could be argued that an infringement by a certified CRA of a provision of the Regulation could also imply a breach of its national rules (as they should be equivalent to the EU Regulation) and, thus, lead to a sanction by the competent authority of its country. Moreover, through the cooperation arrangements, ESMA could inform and insist on the need for such sanction. However, equivalence does not mean that the provisions of the foreign legislation are the same or similar to those of the CRA Regulation; the EU requirement breached by the certified CRA might not have a matching requirement in the third country framework.

Consequently, it could happen that an infringement of a provision of the EU Regulation, that if committed by a registered CRA would have led to a pecuniary sanction, is not sanctioned if committed by a certified agency. Nevertheless, ESMA always has the possibility of addressing these undesirable circumstances through the imposition of supervisory measures.

4.3.5 ESMA's Methodology to Assess Equivalence

4.3.5.1 Holistic Approach

As indicated above, prior to adopting a decision on equivalence, the EC requires ESMA's advice. ESMA has published its approach to assessing equivalence in its reports regarding the US and Japanese frameworks, quoted above. ESMA recognizes that, in contrast to other legal and supervisory frameworks, the EU CRA Regulation is very prescriptive and detailed. Nevertheless, ESMA's approach to equivalence is holistic, and, therefore, it should take a high level look at the overall foreign framework, the powers of the authorities entrusted to enforce it, and their overall approach to supervision.

This approach is consistent with the objectives set out by the EC in its mandates to ESMA regarding equivalence. According to the EC, 'the priority should lie in assuring that users of ratings in the EU would benefit from equivalent protections in terms of CRA's integrity, transparency, good governance and reliability of the credit rating activities'. Therefore, to achieve equivalence it is not necessary that all the EU requirements are adopted in the foreign framework in an identical manner. What is important is that the same regulatory objectives are achieved.

4.3.5.2 Steps

The steps followed by ESMA in its assessments of equivalence are set out below.

Drafting a Questionnaire for Self-Assessment

ESMA has drafted a questionnaire covering all aspects of the EU Regulation. The third country authority is asked to fill in the questionnaire and to explain how it considers it meets the same objectives of the EU requirements. ESMA also asks the third country regulator to provide the relevant rules and regulations translated into English.

Establishing Conditions for Objectively Assessing Equivalence

Pure self-regulatory regimes are insufficient for an equivalence assessment. The third country regime must be based on laws and regulations that are binding. Where only draft laws or regulations exist, an equivalent assessment can only be made on condition that the draft laws and regulations are likely to come into force as proposed. Finally, the scope of the foreign regime should be in line with that of the EU Regulation; there needs to be clarity regarding what a credit rating agency is and what are the activities covered by the regulatory and supervisory framework.

Assessing the Third Country's Framework Against the Conditions

ESMA reviews the responses to the questionnaire and identifies the similarities and differences on a provision-by-provision basis. Where the provisions differ, ESMA analyses how the objective of the EU rule is achieved either by other types of provisions or through supervisory practice.

Establishing the Global Assessment of Equivalence

Once the assessment of all the provisions has been completed, the third country's framework is looked at as a whole and ESMA makes its global assessment of equivalence, according to the objectives indicated above.

4.3.6 ESMA's Advice on the Equivalence Between the US and EU Frameworks

ESMA published in May 2010 its technical advice in relation to the equivalence between the US legal and supervisory framework and the CRA Regulation,[5] in accordance with the EC's mandate received in June 2009. ESMA's advice to the EC was that, 'overall, the US legal and supervisory framework is broadly equivalent to the EU regulatory regime for credit rating agencies in terms of achieving what CESR considers to be the overall objective of assuring that users of ratings in the US would benefit from equivalent protections ... '.

In coming to its conclusion, ESMA grouped the requirements of the CRA Regulation into seven areas: scope of the framework; corporate governance;

---

[5] See footnote 4.

conflicts of interest; organizational requirements; quality of methodologies and quality of ratings; disclosure; and supervision and enforcement. In its final assessment, ESMA considered that, overall, the US framework does not achieve the objectives of the EU CRA Regulation in relation to two of those areas, namely, the quality of methodologies and of ratings and the disclosure of credit ratings. This led ESMA to qualify its statement on the equivalence of the US framework, considering it only to be 'broadly' equivalent.

ESMA further recommended 'the identified differences be addressed to allow for further convergence between both regimes' and considered that 'reducing the difference may be achieved by future regulatory amendments to the Securities and Exchange Commission's (SEC) rules'.

At the time of writing, over a year has elapsed since the submission and publication of ESMA's advice and the EC has not yet taken its decision. Presumably the strategy of the EC has been to wait and see if the changes introduced by the Dodd–Frank Act could bridge the gaps identified in ESMA's advice. However, whilst there are some self-executing provisions in the Act, there are other areas where rules have to be issued by the SEC. This means that the EC would have to wait until those rules are adopted in order to be able to conclude that the differences identified by ESMA have been fully addressed (see Appendix 4).

In any case, whilst it is clear that the Dodd–Frank Act strengthens the US regime in a number of areas, and in particular in one that ESMA considered problematic—rating disclosures requirements—, regarding quality of methodologies and quality of ratings it might be more difficult for the EC to conclude that the Dodd–Frank Act has addressed the differences highlighted in ESMA's advice, at least if the EC follows ESMA's methodology for making that judgement. Notwithstanding, the EC can obviously take other considerations into account and decide that the US framework is equivalent to the EU CRA Regulation.

Actually we do not consider that EU investors have less protection when using ratings produced in the USA. The differences between the US and the EU framework, as clearly explained in ESMA's advice (paragraphs 224–238), result from the different philosophy of approach. The US system relies heavily on the public disclosure of CRAs' applications, the market passing judgement on this information, and the ex post supervision by the SEC; in Europe there is more reliance on ex ante supervision and more detailed requirements in certain areas, such as methodologies to produce ratings. The SEC takes a strict approach to the concept of non-interference with credit rating methodologies and the content of ratings, which means that the SEC does not regulate the content of procedures and methodologies to determine ratings. These different philosophies do not imply that one framework is better or worse than the other. And in addition, it is important to note that the authorities' supervision and enforcement is at least as important as the rules. As we can see in Appendix 4, the US regulatory framework has been built and is being amended continuously on the basis of the experience gained from the SEC's supervisory activity.

4.3.7 European Commission's Equivalence Decision on Japan

In September 2010, following ESMA's advice,[6] the EC concluded that the Japanese framework provides for equivalent protection in terms of integrity, transparency, good governance of credit rating agencies, and reliability of the credit rating activities. Consequently, its Decision[7] stated that 'for the purposes of Article 5 of Regulation (EC) No 1060/2009, the Japanese legal and supervisory framework for credit rating agencies shall be considered as equivalent to the requirements of Regulation (EC) No 1060/2009'.

4.4 RELATIONSHIP BETWEEN ENDORSEMENT AND CERTIFICATION BASED ON EQUIVALENCE

The relationship between the two different systems included in the Regulation for the use of ratings of third countries has raised interesting debates between the authorities, the EC, and CRAs. The main discussions have concentrated on the interpretation of the requirements for endorsement that the third country CRA has to fulfil according to Article 4.3.(b): 'the conduct of credit rating activities by the third country credit rating agency resulting in the issuing of the credit rating to be endorsed fulfils requirements which are at least as stringent as the requirements set out in Articles 6 to 12'.

Market participants and the main CRAs understand that those requirements have to be based on the behaviour of the third country CRA ('conduct'), whilst the Commission's services (in an informal position provided to ESMA and not published) consider that the requirements should be based on the legislation of the third country.

We consider that the agreement among legislators as reflected in the Regulation requires that the conduct of business and not the legislation of the third country CRA provides for requirements as stringent as those set out in the EU Regulation.

This interpretation was supported by several Member States in the course of the discussions in the autumn of 2010 to amend the CRA Regulation. In particular, a joint declaration was submitted to the EU Council[8] by the UK, Spain, the Netherlands, Sweden, Austria, Finland, Hungary, and Ireland, welcoming the fact that ESMA should issue and update guidelines on the application of the endorsement regime and stating that these guidelines are necessary to clarify:

> that endorsement can take place if the third country's regulatory regime or, in the absence of such regulatory requirements, the credit rating agency itself applies

---

[6] See footnote 4.

[7] EC (September 2010), *Decision on the recognition of the legal and supervisory framework of Japan as equivalent to the requirements of Regulation (EC) No 1060/2009 of the European Parliament and of the Council on credit rating agencies.*

[8] Council of the European Union: 2344th meeting of the Permanent Representatives Committee held in Brussels on 8, 10, and 13 December 2010, Addendum to the Public Summary Record.

requirements which are at least as stringent as the requirements set out in articles 6-12 of Regulation 1060/2009. The endorsing credit rating agency shall remain responsible to ESMA for compliance with such requirements, in accordance with paragraph 5 of Article 4 of Regulation 1060/2009.

Also, the European Parliament in its resolution of June 2011:[9]

'reiterates that Regulation (EC) No 1060/2009 devises two systems to deal with external credit ratings from third countries and that the intention behind the endorsement regime was to allow external credit ratings from third countries deemed non-equivalent to be used in the European Union if clear responsibility was attached to an endorsing CRA' (paragraph 14).

As recognized in the European Parliament's resolution, the endorsement mechanism was designed to be materially distinct from the equivalence regime. If the requirements in Article 4.3.(b) were to be based on local regulations to be assessed by ESMA, then this would effectively be duplication of the equivalence regime, but with one significant difference: it would be ESMA deciding whether a foreign framework was equivalent, as opposed to the EC. ESMA would assess and decide on the equivalency of the third country framework when deciding on an application for endorsement or ratings issued by a foreign CRA.

In addition, the wording in Recital 13 of the Regulation which indicates that 'credit rating agencies should determine and monitor, on an ongoing basis whether the credit rating activities resulting in the issuing of such a credit rating comply with . . .' places emphasis on the conduct of the CRA ('activities') and not on the foreign legislation. Therefore, the wording in the Regulation always refers to 'conduct' or 'activities' when establishing the endorsement regime whilst, in contrast, it refers to 'legally binding rules' (Article 5.6.(b)) and 'legal and supervisory framework' (Article 5.1.(b)) when regulating the certification regime.

As explained below, this interpretation would mean that Article 4.3.(b) does not entail voluntary compliance with the requirements of the EU Regulation, in any way imply that the ratings would not be subject to adequate monitoring, or mean that ESMA would have no legal basis for taking action.

According to the Regulation, the EU-based endorsing CRA retains responsibility for the issuance of an endorsed rating as the Regulation clearly indicates that endorsed ratings shall be considered as ratings issued by the endorsing EU CRA (Articles 4.2, 4.4, and 4.5). Therefore the EU CRA is fully accountable for the ratings that it endorses for use in the EU and for ensuring that these ratings are produced in accordance with Article 4.3.(b).

The Regulation also requires that ESMA is able to 'assess and monitor the compliance' of the third country CRA with the requirements referred to in Article 4.3.(b) (Article 4.3.(c)). Moreover, the endorsing CRA has to make available on request all information necessary for this assessment by ESMA to enable it to supervise on an ongoing basis its compliance (Article 4.3.(d)).

The conclusion that can be drawn from this is that there is both legal accountability for the conduct of the third country CRA and an appropriate ability to

[9] European Parliament (June 2011), *Resolution on credit rating agencies: future perspectives (2010/2302(INI))*.

monitor compliance with EU requirements if the endorsement regime is based on an assessment of the conduct of the CRA in the third country rather than on the third country regulatory regime.

However, despite the concluding arguments from the industry mentioned above, ESMA's guidance on registration opted to follow the Commission's services informal non-public view, understanding that the Article 4.3.(b) should be interpreted as requiring local legal and regulatory systems to impose requirements as stringent as those found in Articles 6 to 12 of the EU Regulation.

The ESMA's position, that does not sit well with either the wording nor with the intent of the CRA Regulation, caused considerable concern in the market and led EU legislators to require ESMA—in cooperation with EBA and EIOPA—to issue and update guidelines on the application of the endorsement regime (Article 21.3 of the CRA Regulation as amended by the CRA Regulation II). Accordingly, in March 2011 ESMA published a consultation paper[10] in order to seek views from market participants on this issue and published in May 2011 its final guidance[11] that confirmed ESMA's previous interpretation. ESMA also considered that the transitional arrangements envisaged in Article 24.2 of the CRA Regulation would apply. At the time of writing, it is unclear how this will work in practice.

The main consequence of this interpretation is that, in practice, it would not be possible for an EU CRA to endorse ratings from a third country CRA if the legislation in that third country is not equivalent to the EU Regulation. As, at the time of writing, only Japan has been considered by the EC as equivalent, ratings issued by CRAs from the rest of the world (or foreign subsidiaries of the major CRAs), could not be used by European entities for regulatory purposes. This could cause significant difficulties to European institutions bearing in mind that, until the Regulation entered into force, they used ratings issued by third countries CRAs without limitations (and in many cases, not even taking into account the entity within the group that had 'issued' the rating).

As only a limited number of countries are likely to pass the 'as stringent as EU Regulation' test (at least in the short term), a massive number of outstanding ratings would be effectively withdrawn from the EU market, as EU institutions would no longer be able to use them for regulatory purposes. Respondents to ESMA's call for evidence on endorsement published on January 2011[12] and to ESMA's consultation in March raised a number of unintended consequences associated with the interpretation held by ESMA and the Commission's services and asked for mitigating actions if this interpretation was not modified.

At a time when banks are already struggling to meet higher capital requirements as a result of the forthcoming Basel III Framework and other regulatory initiatives, that interpretation could generate a significant rise in the financial institutions' regulatory capital, as they would not be able to use many foreign

---

[10] ESMA (March 2011), *Consultation paper, Guidelines on the application of the endorsement regime under Article 4 (3) of the Credit Rating Regulation 1060/2009 (Ref. ESMA/2011/97).*

[11] ESMA (March 2011), *Guidelines on the application of the endorsement regime under Article 4 (3) of the Credit Rating Regulation 1060/2009 (Ref. ESMA/2011/139).*

[12] ESMA (January 2011), *Call for evidence on the criteria for endorsement (Article 21 (2) (a) of the draft amended CRA Regulation (Ref. ESMA/2011/0005).*

ratings for portfolios in the standardized approach and for securitization exposures. Also, the already battered securitization market would be severely hit as the risk weight for an AAA rated instrument would increase from 7% to 1250% (or full deduction from regulatory capital). This would force institutions to sell securitization positions and might cause a sharp decline in the valuation of other market participant's portfolios. In addition, the inability to endorse foreign ratings would hinder the management of liquidity in Europe and increase concentration risks across the market.

Finally, in order to assess the impact of the ESMA's guidance on the EU banking sector, it is obviously critical to know whether ratings issued in the USA could be endorsed by EU CRAs (see Appendix 4).

4.5 COOPERATION ARRANGEMENTS

In both processes of endorsement and certification, the CRA Regulation requires that there are cooperation arrangements between ESMA and the competent authorities of the foreign CRAs involved. Such arrangements shall specify at least the mechanism for the exchange of information between the competent authorities concerned and the procedures concerning the coordination of supervisory activities.

In the course of 2010 and 2011, ESMA engaged in negotiations for the establishment of cooperation arrangements with third country regulators in order to serve the purposes of the endorsement and certification regimes.[13] The first cooperation arrangement was signed on 1 June 2011 between ESMA and the Financial Services Agency of Japan.

---

[13] CESR (December 2010), *Annual report according to Article 21 of Regulation (EC) 1060/2009 on credit rating agencies (Ref. CESR/10–1424).*

5

Future Developments

The previous chapters of the book have aimed at providing a thorough and structured analysis of the historic and current role of ratings in financial markets, the deficiencies in the activities of the CRAs detected following the subprime crisis, the different initiatives undertaken at global level to address those failures, and, more specifically, at analysing in depth the EU regulatory framework for CRAs.

As we have seen in the previous pages, during the past few years CRAs have been in the spotlight constantly and policy-makers and regulators all over the world have incorporated CRAs into their regulatory agenda, mainly through the G-20 agreements. This has led to a situation in which new studies, recommendations, and regulatory initiatives are being produced at an enormously fast speed in this area.

The vertiginous rate that we have seen in the past will continue in the future as it seems that CRAs will not jump off the regulatory agenda, at least for the next couple of years. The Dodd–Frank Act enacted in August 2010, has clearly signalled US legislators' willingness to improve the oversight regime on CRAs. And, in Europe, it has been the European sovereign debt crisis that has stirred up, even further, the debate on the role that CRAs play during crises and the interdependence between different financial markets.

The effect of the current phase of the economic cycle on the creditworthiness of some EU sovereigns has highlighted the relevance of sovereign debt and the impact of its ratings in interconnected markets. The general perception in the market is that sovereign ratings have important, and on many occasions unintended, consequences in financial markets, as downgrades make a country's borrowing more expensive. In fact, downgrades have resulted in significant widening of sovereign bond and credit default swap (CDS) spreads, and have exerted significant pressure on stock markets. This has led major EU policy-makers (heads of states, EC, ECB) to publicly express their growing unease with the excessive impact of CRAs' decisions on the stability of the EU economy.

The spillover effect of sovereign ratings is supported by some studies such as the one published in March 2011 in the IMF Working Paper 11/68 entitled *Sovereign rating news and financial markets spillovers: evidence from the European debt crisis.*[1] This study analyses the effects of sovereign rating actions on European financial markets during the period 2007–2010 using daily data on sovereign CDS

---

[1] Arezki, Rabah, Candelon, Bertrand, and Sy, Amadou N.R. (March 2011), *Sovereign rating news and financial markets spillovers: evidence from the European debt crisis.* IMF Working Paper 11/68.

spreads and stock market indices for banking and insurance. The main conclusion of the study is that:

> Sovereign rating downgrades have statistically and economically significant spillover effects both across countries and financial markets. The sign and magnitude of the spillover effects depend both on the type of announcements, the source country experiencing the downgrade and the rating agency from which the announcement originates. However, we also find evidence that downgrades to near speculative grade ratings for relatively large economies such as Greece have a systematic spillover effect across Euro zone countries. Rating based triggers used in banking regulation, CDS contracts, and investment mandates may help explain these results.

The aftermath of the financial crisis for the CRAs industry could be entitled 'from structured finance ratings to sovereign ratings'. Back in 2008, the first tangible reaction from regulators was the strengthening of the IOSCO Code with a number of new provisions on structured finance ratings. Three years after the IOSCO Code review, the EU sovereign crisis led the EC to come up with a set of proposals exclusively addressed at sovereign ratings. In addition to the treatment of sovereign debt ratings, other key aspects of the rating industry are being reopened. Some of the issues are being debated at international level, whilst others are more specific to Europe, at least for the time being.

As CRAs say, it is not easy to foresee the future; but we will try to provide in the next pages an indication of the themes that will keep policy-makers and supervisors busy in the near future and our views on some of the ideas being discussed.[2]

5.1 RETHINKING BUSINESS MODELS

Of the ten CRAs registered as NRSROs, seven operate predominantly under the issuer-pays model,[3] whilst the remaining three operate mainly under the subscriber-pays model.[4] Moreover, the CRAs operating under the issuer-pays model have determined approximately 99% of the total currently outstanding ratings issued by NRSROs.[5] The data provided for the USA can be directly extrapolated to Europe and also to the world's rating industry.

The issuer-pays model is clearly the prevailing business model in the CRA industry and, as we have discussed in different sections of the book, this model gives rise to questions of conflict of interest. In fact, one of the weaknesses highlighted by supervisors and market participants during the crisis was the potentially distorting influence of a fee-paying issuer over the determination of ratings, mainly in the structured finance area. However, although this perception

---

[2] The topics have been selected taking into account the views of the IMF as included in its Global Financial Stability Report (October 2010), the contributions to the SEC's roundtable to examine oversight of credit rating agencies (April 2009), the responses to the EC consultation on CRAs November 2010 and the EP Resolution on CRAs (June 2011).

[3] A.M. Best., DBRS, Fitch, Japan Credit Rating Agency, Moody's, Rating and Investment Information, and S&P.

[4] Egan-Jones Rating Company, LACE Financial Corp., Realpoint LLC.

[5] SEC (January 2011), *Annual report on nationally recognized statistical rating organisations*.

has been analysed by a number of studies, there is no hard evidence that the issuer-pays model leads to more optimistic ratings.

Nevertheless, the potential conflict has generated a lively debate among policy-makers and market participants on the convenience of promoting alternative business models. Academics and market participants are coming up with many creative ideas. The main models suggested are discussed below.

5.1.1 Investor-Pays Model

The subscriber-pays or investor-pays approach is conceived as the most feasible alternative to the issuer-pays model as it was the model followed by the main CRAs until the 1970s. Also, the fact that it is currently used by a few smaller CRAs shows that it is a viable model, that there is demand in the market for these services, and that subscriber-pays CRAs are a valuable complement to the issuer-pays CRAs (for example, they serve niche markets).

Under the investor-pays model, CRAs generate their revenues by charging subscribers for access to their rating assessments. Therefore, ratings issued by subscription-based CRAs are only available to defined people (the subscribers).

The investor-pays model's strength is that it aligns the interests of CRAs with those of investors. Since investors desire accurate ratings, (in principle) having an investor-pays model should strengthen a CRA's incentives to provide independent ratings. However, market participants have also highlighted important drawbacks to this alternative that are analysed below.

5.1.1.1 Conflicts of Interest

The issuer-pays model does not eliminate conflicts of interest but instead shifts them from issuers to investors, who may also have motivations to influence ratings so they are assigned (or maintained) in a manner that is most beneficial to their interests; and these interests may often be conflicted with the goal of having objective ratings. This risk is particularly acute if the CRA's customer base is not adequately diversified and if a group of relevant investors coordinate to put pressure on CRAs to achieve a desired rating. Some examples of situations where conflicts of interests might arise under this model are provided below:

- A subscriber may hold a securities position (long or short) that could potentially be advantaged by upgrades or downgrades in the rating as such action can cause the market value of the security to increase or decrease. For example, this might be the case for short sellers, such as hedge funds, that take a significant short position on a particular company.

- An investor/subscriber may want to hold a particular security in an investment portfolio but may be constrained from doing so because its rating is lower than the legislation (or its internal investment guidelines) allows. An upgrade of the security by the CRAs could remove this impediment to invest in the security,[6]

---

[6] See footnote 5.

thus the subscriber might be tempted to exert influence on the CRA or the CRA might take this fact into account when taking a rating action.

- Long-term investors are also interested in the outcome of rating actions. Before they purchase a security they may prefer lower ratings to obtain higher yields; once they hold the security, they are likely to prefer to have ratings maintained or raised to avoid, for example, valuation mark-downs or forced sales.[7]

In addition, the shifting of the paying entity may not always prevent issuers from using other means to try to influence ratings, such as litigation to coerce higher ratings.

5.1.1.2 Free Rider Problem

This expression refers to the practice of those who consume more than their fair share of a resource, or shoulder less than a fair share of the costs of its production.

The subscriber-pays model relies heavily on the ability to enforce property rights to information that is very easy to disseminate. In fact, the change in the 1970s from the investor-pays to the issuer-pays model was largely motivated by the advances in reproduction and distribution technologies that increased simultaneously the free rider problem. At that moment in time, technology had advanced to the point where it was too easy to transmit both research and the ratings, so it was very hard to get subscribers to pay for the ratings (considering that others could have access to the information quite easily for free). Nowadays, the technological possibilities for easily transmitting information have multiplied and, thus, the free rider problem is even more difficult to handle.

5.1.1.3 Economic Sustainability of the Model and Risk of Reduced Coverage

The move from the investor-pays to the issuer-pays model in the 1970s was driven by the free rider problem but also by the increasing size and complexity of the markets that demanded a model through which additional resources could be funded. New markets required more specialization, more qualified and higher paid analysts, lawyers and compliance officers, the opening of offices in regional areas, and so on. And the increased costs associated with the production of ratings of quality could not be funded just by subscribers.

Nowadays, issuer-pays CRAs not only derive their revenues from issuers, they also have revenues from subscribers that pay to get more in-depth analysis that supports the ratings. However, moving to a system of revenues coming only from subscribers could potentially undermine CRAs' revenue, and thus the quality and the coverage of ratings. Most investors are unlikely to be willing to pay the substantial subscription fees necessary to generate the revenue stream that would allow CRAs to continue rating as many entities and issuances as they do

---

[7] Moody's (January 2011), *Moody's response to the European Commission public consultation on CRAs*.

currently. As a result, this model would probably result in substantially fewer offerings receiving ratings, to the detriment of smaller issuers and less liquid issues.

Finally, it is also worth noting that if issuers do not pay for the ratings they might be less willing to provide confidential information to CRAs, thereby leading to ratings of lesser quality or to reduced coverage by CRAs if the agencies consider that they do not have sufficient information to support a rating.

5.1.1.4 Public Policy Considerations

The principal social benefit of the issuer-pays model is that all ratings are released to the market simultaneously and at no cost to investors. The general public has access to this information and larger investors have no advantage over smaller investors. Conversely, the investor-pays model does not allow for public and broad disclosure of ratings; rather, the model involves selective disclosure of information via subscription because, if ratings are made public, investors would not be willing to pay for them. Therefore, the basis of the model is to charge fees in return for selective access to information for those investors who can afford the subscription fees.

Regulators consider that ratings on publicly offered securities are a public good. Therefore, promoting a system in which ratings are disclosed publicly to the market is beneficial to potential investors (besides subscribers) and in general to other stakeholders (such as shareholders or suppliers) and, therefore, useful to finance companies, and, more broadly, the economy.

5.1.2 Public Utility Model

The public utility model is based on the idea that a CRA is a public utility and thus should be funded with government revenues. Therefore, this alternative would imply a government-created and managed rating agency that would be designed to somehow check the ratings issued by the private CRAs. It would not have the exclusivity to rate, but investors could compare ratings issued by private CRAs with the ratings of the public CRA.

This idea has been mainly debated in Europe, where key policy-makers have publicly supported the establishment of a European CRA. In addition, the EC consultation on CRAs in November 2010 expressly included several public alternatives as possible means to enhance competition in the market that implied entrusting the ECB, national central banks, or even a new European credit rating agency with the task of issuing ratings (for example, to be used for regulatory purposes by European institutions). In particular, the consultation stated the following:

A new independent European Credit Rating Agency could be set up in a public/private structure such as an Institution 'd'utilité publique', a Public Interest Company, a European foundation or a public-private partnership. The costs of establishing a new EU credit rating agency could be wholly or partially covered by the private sector. In order to ensure professional autonomy of its management and staff and, consequently its credibility, such entity should be independent. Public authorities' main role should be to ensure that the capital spending is assigned for the purposes for which it was created. Subsidies could be provided through existing mechanisms by the European Investment Bank, the European Commission and Member States. Any initial public investment could then be phased out, ultimately allowing the new credit rating agency to become a purely private entity. Alternatively, a new EU credit rating agency could conceivably be operated as a not for profit organisation, relying on revenues generated by its rating activities.

The public utility model, in its different versions, would face the following problems.[8]

5.1.2.1 Conflict of Interest

The involvement of public entities could create a conflict of interest with their core objectives and threaten their independence and credibility. For example, in the case of central banks, they could decide that monetary and financial stability objectives are to be preserved to the detriment of accurate ratings. In addition, a European credit rating agency could be subject to heavy political pressure. Governments, faced with competing financial market and social policy objectives, may seek to have ratings 'protect' nationally, systemically, or politically important issuers such as large industrial employers, banks, or governments themselves.[9] This is especially relevant in situations when downgrading an institution might lead to the government having to provide support to the entity.

5.1.2.2 Market Acceptance

Ratings produced by CRAs supported or established by EU or national funding could be viewed as biased by investors. The risk of government interference with ratings (real or perceived) is embedded in the public utility models and, if the agency is seen as having been set up to be more likely to be influenced by issuers or by governments in the region, it would not be credible to investors or for the role ratings may play in regulation.

5.1.2.3 Further Over-Reliance on Ratings

The ratings issued by public sector entities may be relied on even more heavily than is the case for private sector CRAs' ratings. Its official status could mislead market participants to assume that the public CRA provides a quality stamp, thus replacing the current over-reliance on ratings issued by the big CRAs with a reliance on ratings issued by a public agency.

5.1.2.4 Further Barriers to Entry

The public utility model can crowd out the private sector. It is likely that the public CRA would become another dominant player, thus making it even more difficult for other new and smaller entities to capture market share. In fact, the

[8] United Kingdom authorities' response to the EC consultation on CRAs November 2010.
[9] See footnote 7.

provision of ratings by a public entity would be a further barrier to entry for new competitors, since investors would tend to use the more 'official ratings'.

5.1.2.5 *Quality of Ratings and Costs*

The public CRAs should be subject to the same regulatory requirements and standards as private sector CRAs, but there is no reason to believe that such a public structure would issue more accurate and timely ratings than the current private CRAs. Private CRAs operating today in the market already have well-developed business structures and a high level of expertise gained through many years of providing ratings. To ensure that a newly created public CRA can provide ratings of quality, a significant amount of public money (from taxpayers) would be required.

5.1.3 Payment-Upon-Results Model

This model envisages that the performance of ratings over time could be used to determine the level of fees that the CRAs may charge. An important part of the fees could be put into a fund, against which the CRAs could borrow to finance their operations.

Theoretically, this model could hold CRAs more accountable for the quality of their ratings. It could align financial interests of the CRA with the interest to produce a rating of high quality, as the payment would depend on the accuracy of the rating, which can only be evaluated over time. However, the model raises a key concern over how 'results' would be assessed and by whom. The metric or criteria for assessing performance could introduce perverse incentives, as CRAs might decide to alter their methodology to ensure they achieve the desired 'result'. This would probably drive convergence in ratings, rather than a diversity of opinions.

Another difficulty that this model could have is that, if not properly organized, it might lead to another barrier to entry for smaller CRAs in the industry. The only CRAs that could afford to wait the period needed to determine ratings performance (minimum of two or three years) to get paid for their work would be those that have accumulated sufficient reserves and cash from prior work to survive during the waiting period.

5.1.4 Hiring Agent Model

This model will be subject to a considerable level of analysis in the USA as the Dodd–Frank Act requires the SEC to submit a study to the US Congress and Senate, 24 months after the date of enactment of the Act, on:

> The feasibility of establishing a system in which a public or private utility or a self-regulatory organization assigns nationally recognized statistical rating organizations to determine the credit ratings of structured finance products, including—
>
> (A) an assessment of potential mechanisms for determining fees for the nationally recognized statistical rating organizations;

(B) appropriate methods for paying fees to the nationally recognized statistical rating organizations;

(C) the extent to which the creation of such a system would be viewed as the creation of moral hazard by the Federal Government; and

(D) any constitutional or other issues concerning the establishment of such a system.

More specifically, the Act sets a 'fallback system' that shall be implemented unless the SEC proposes an alternative. In this system, an issuer that seeks an initial credit rating for a structured finance product would be required to submit a request for the initial rating to the CRA Board (a self-regulatory organization). The CRA Board would select a qualified NRSRO to provide the initial rating to the issuer (although the NRSRO might refuse the request). The qualified NRSROs would be able to determine fees unless the CRA Board deems it necessary to issue rules on fees. The CRA Board would prescribe rules to evaluate the performance of each qualified NRSRO (including the accuracy of the ratings as compared to the other NRSROs).

In May 2011, the SEC published a document for comments to assist it in carrying out the study to prepare the report to the Congress and Senate. This report will also include a description of the rating process for structured finance products and the conflicts of interest associated with the issuer-pays and the subscriber-pays models; an analysis of the range of metrics that can be used to determine the accuracy of ratings for structured finance products; and a study of alternative means for compensating NRSROs that would create incentives for accurate ratings for structured finance products.

In addition, the EC consultation on CRAs in November 2010 has also included the hiring agent model among the different alternatives being proposed, taking the Dodd–Frank Act as a reference. Under the EC's proposal, the selection of the CRA could be undertaken by an independent agency:

> An independent 'Credit Rating Agencies Board' composed of supervisors, representatives of issuers, subscribers/investors and credit rating agencies could be empowered to select a credit rating agency either at random or on the basis of objectively defined criteria to rate an issuer's structured finance instruments. The issuer would remain free to (1) secure no rating from selected agency at all, or (2) hire additional credit rating agencies if it wished.

This model could prevent rating shopping, as the rated entity would be rated by the CRA assigned by the independent hiring agent (and not exclusively by the one chosen by the issuer on the basis of its likely rating).

However, its success would critically depend on the criteria used by the hiring agency in matching issuers to CRAs. If CRAs are allocated to issuers on a random basis, CRAs would win business even if they were not responding to the needs of investors, which would be against the objective of enhancing rating quality. If the hiring agency uses some specific metric to measure the performance of the rating agencies to decide on the assignation of business, it could result in perverse incentives, as explained when discussing the payment-upon-results model.

In addition, this model puts a heavy burden on the hiring agency, which could be susceptible to lobbying, and direct involvement of government in the matching process could give rise to moral hazards. Furthermore, the hiring agency might choose a CRA that investors do not value as providing robust ratings, to the detriment of the rated issuer.

5.2 OVER-RELIANCE

Reducing over-reliance on ratings is a clear objective of policy-makers all over the world. There is a broad consensus, reflected on the G-20 endorsement of the FSB's *Principles for reducing reliance on CRA ratings*, on the need to take action for reducing reliance on ratings in standards, laws, and regulations. In Europe, the recent Euro debt crisis has renewed concerns that financial institutions and institutional investors may still be relying too much on ratings and that ratings have discouraged investors from making independent judgements of risks and performing their own due diligence.

As explained in Section 2.2.5, it will not be easy to eliminate over-reliance on ratings in the near term as ratings are embedded not only at a regulatory level but also at investor level (in private investment contract or guidelines). Additionally, it is not easy to find alternative instruments to measure credit risk. However, the FSB principles set the right path to reduce, in the medium term, the key role that ratings play in financial markets and to break the blind reliance that markets have shown on them.

Two paths are to be followed: authorities need to assess reference to ratings in regulations and eliminate them, where possible; and firms have to make their own credit assessments. According to Basel III, 'banks should assess exposures, regardless of whether they are rated or unrated, and determine whether the risk weights applied to such exposures, under the Standardised Approach, are appropriate for their inherent risk'.

To facilitate the latter process, increased disclosure by issuers, especially in the area of structured finance instruments, should be promoted to allow investors to carry out their own additional due diligence on a well-informed basis. In this respect, markets have welcomed the ECB's ABS loan-level initiative, which establishes specific loan-by-loan public disclosure requirements for asset-backed securities accepted as collateral in Eurosystem credit operations. The aim of the ECB is to increase transparency and make available more timely information on the underlying loans and their performance to market participants in a standardized format (see Section 3.5.4).

Nevertheless, although reducing regulatory references to ratings will diminish some of the reliance on ratings and could spur a decline in the use of ratings in private contracts as well, ratings are still likely to continue to serve an important role given the substantial existing information and analytical capacity asymmetries, in particular for smaller investors and illiquid instruments.[10]

The problem of over-reliance is inextricably linked with the next aspect we are going to discuss: lack of competition. This is because market participants have relied excessively only on the ratings widely used in the markets; that is, the

---

[10] IMF (October 2010), *Global financial stability report: sovereigns, funding, and systemic liquidity.*

ratings issued by the major global CRAs. Regulators face the same problem they have with the global accounting firms: if one of them was to fail (for example, due to litigation or to supervisory action) the consequences would be systemic. The same considerations apply to the CRA industry. In order for the withdrawal of registration to be a credible supervisory measure, the reliance of the markets on the major CRAs must be reduced.

5.3 COMPETITION

As discussed in Section 2.1.5, many players have pointed to the limited scope of competition in the CRA industry as one of the factors that could have contributed to the incorrect functioning of the CRAs during the subprime crisis. However, there are also some studies that shed doubts as to whether increased competition would be beneficial for the rating industry and point to the risk that more competition could lead to deteriorating standards employed to attract more customers, partly due to enhanced opportunities for rating shopping ('race to the bottom').

The lack of competition in the CRA industry has been one of the frequent issues of the regulatory debates and will continue to be on the regulatory agenda in the near future. In fact, the SEC is required by the CRA Reform Act to submit an annual report to the US Congress and Senate that specifies the SEC's views on the state of competition.

In the EU, the CRA Regulation[11] also requires the EC to prepare a report to be submitted to the European Council and Parliament by December 2012, analysing, among other issues, the impact of the Regulation on the level of concentration in the credit rating market and including the assessment of the creation of a public EU CRA. To address this issue, the EC consultation on CRAs in November 2010 proposes the creation of such a European CRA and puts forward other ideas such as entrusting the ECB (or national central banks) with the task of issuing ratings to be used for regulatory purposes or promoting a network of European small and medium-sized CRAs.

As in any industry, for new players to enter the market there has to be a potential for high profit and no excessively high barriers to entry. In the CRA sector, barriers to entry are an important factor in the high concentration of market.

There are some barriers to entry that are, to a certain extent, inevitable and even beneficial for investors, as they are likely to lead to high quality in ratings. Economies of scale favour larger CRAs as they can allocate the high fixed costs of analytical software and general functions (administrative, legal, compliance, and marketing staff) across a wider number of ratings. In addition, CRAs have important sink costs as the development of rating methodologies and procedures is a key aspect for the success of the company. Finally, the relevance of reputation in this sector is another aspect that creates barriers to entry. As it is difficult to evaluate the quality of a rating at the moment of purchase (the accuracy of a rating can only be evaluated over an extended period of time), issuers and investors tend

---

[11] Article 39 and Recital 73.

to use the quality of prior ratings (historic rating performances) to decide which CRA to trust. This complicates the entrance of new CRAs. Moreover, if the markets positively value the quality of the ratings of the incumbent CRAs, additional credit assessments by new entrants will add less value for market participants, whilst the cost of supervision of the industry will increase.

However, the main barrier to entry has been driven by the use of ratings in legislation (and also in private contracts), that has created a captive market for the CRAs and has led to concentration in the industry. The fact that regulatory requirements use ratings, in many instances of specific recognized agencies, has promoted a certain 'quality stamp' for the main CRAs, making it more complicated for smaller firms to be seen as providing reliable ratings.

Increasing competition in the CRA industry would not automatically imply better quality of ratings and, therefore, the focus of regulators should be placed on enhancing the quality of the ratings, rather than increasing the number of players. Regulators and policy-makers cannot help new entrants earn their reputation. This is something CRAs should do on their own by providing high-quality services. What regulators should do is to mandate transparency of CRAs' performance in order to enable the comparability of the different CRAs and to ensure that regulation does not give a special advantage to the big firms or create unnecessary barriers to entering the market.

Finally, despite its best intention, we believe that direct public intervention by, for example, establishing a public CRA, could hurt competition as it could have, as discussed in the previous section, a spillover effect on private CRAs (and would induce more over-reliance on ratings). The idea of imposing two obligatory ratings, either paid both by the issuer[12] or one by the issuer and another by the investor,[13] does not seem the right way to solve competition issues either. This would lead to an increase in costs for market participants that would not necessarily entail better quality ratings and would reinforce reliance on ratings. The ECB has recently introduced the requirement of a second AAA rating in order to accept structured finance instruments as collateral. Given the limited number of CRAs that have the capability to rate securitizations, it seems that this move will contribute to increasing the grip of the big three on the market and, at most, might help DBRS to build its reputation in EU.

5.4 CIVIL LIABILITY

Regulators will also need to decide how to treat CRA liability issues. This debate has been prompted mainly by the change introduced in the USA by the Dodd–Frank Act and, to a certain extent, by the lack of understanding of the different national civil liability rules (for example, in the different EU countries) and how these are, or can be, applied to CRAs' actions.

---

[12] European Parliament (June 2011), *Resolution on credit rating agencies: future perspectives.*
[13] EC consultation on CRAs November 2010.

Currently, CRAs are subject to legal measures that provide issuers and investors with legal tools to take criminal and civil actions.[14] However, some voices propose moving towards a more stringent and specific regime whereby CRAs are assimilated to other 'gatekeepers', such as auditors.

Key institutions, such as the European Parliament, are advocating exposing CRAs to civil liability in the event of gross negligence or misconduct, arguing the ratings cannot be classified as mere opinions.

In addition, the Dodd–Frank Act has also moved a step forward by removing the previously existing exemption for NRSROs that related to the inclusion of ratings in registration statements and prospectuses of securities registered under the Securities Act of 1933. As a result of the repeal of that exemption, ratings that are included in the registration statements with the CRA's consent are considered 'expert opinions' and have the attached liability associated with providing such opinions. In reaction, NRSROs have refused to consent to the inclusion of their ratings in registration statements, thereby temporarily freezing the US ABS market. To deal with this situation, the SEC issued a no-action letter providing that the SEC staff would not recommend enforcement if ABS issuers omitted ratings information from registration statements for offerings until January 2011. In December 2010, the SEC indefinitely extended their initial six-month no-action relief to consider how the new ABS disclosure requirements might be affected.

Imposing civil liability on CRAs gives rise to a number of technical difficulties. First, the regime would have to determine the required standard of liability. It is clear that this can not be the 'incorrectness' of the rating, as ratings are only opinions about the future, therefore incorporating a number of subjective judgements.[15] A standard based on intent would be impracticable due to the difficulties in proving it. For these reasons, proponents of civil liability suggest in general to base it on CRA's negligence. But here the proof would also be problematic, because of the subjective nature of the ratings. Some market participants have proposed that CRAs should be held liable for significant failures in the rating process. However, requiring liability in the case of lack of compliance with the applicable rules would be tricky too, because a breach of the Regulation does not necessarily mean that the rating was 'incorrect' and led to investors' losses. And this leads us to the key issue a liability regime should sort out: how to link an infringement committed intentionally or negligently with an investor's loss, especially when investors are being told that they must carry out their own assessments and use ratings as only one of their sources of credit analysis, if at all.

A civil liability regime might not only bring back a high dose of reliance on ratings. As seen in the reaction of CRAs to the Dodd–Frank Act requirement, it might have other unintended consequences, as increased exposure to litigation could induce CRAs to respond in one or more of the following ways:[16]

---

[14] For example, although the EU CRA Regulation does not regulate civil liability itself, it states that any claim against CRAs in relation to any infringement of its provisions should be made in accordance with the applicable national law on civil liability (Recital 69).

[15] CRAs, unlike auditors that give opinions on statements regarding historic facts, are 'forward-focused'; they use their own non-standardized methodologies to predict the likelihood of future events.

[16] Moody's, S&P, and DBRS responses to the EC consultation on CRAs November 2010.

- Convergence: the risk of litigation could give rise to a convergence of ratings in the market as CRAs would abstain from issuing controversial opinions and would strive to reflect prevailing market sentiment. Moreover, the fear of litigation might result in disincentives for analytical innovation.

- Limit availability of public ratings: as many ratings are available to all market users, there is a huge number of potential plaintiffs who might not agree with a rating. Therefore, CRAs could attempt to mitigate their potential exposure through contract, providing ratings only to specific users and limiting public disclosure of its ratings (as in the case of the Dodd–Frank Act provision). This could have the effect of reducing or eliminating the free, public availability of ratings.

- Reduced rating coverage: CRAs could narrow the range of issuers and offerings they rate. CRAs might decide to withdraw from rating certain types of issuers or securities that are regarded as particularly high risk or which have a limited track record (for example, smaller issuers, emerging markets, or new products).

- Erosion of independence: CRAs could be exposed to more pressure from issuers who might use the threat of legal action to try to impact on a rating or delay the production of ratings they find unfavourable.

In addition, an increase in the liability standard for CRAs could discourage new entrants to the ratings market, thereby undermining competition. If every rating published was vulnerable to a suit, the resources needed to face all possible litigation costs (and possible compensation) would be quite high. Therefore, there is a chance that many CRAs would not be able to survive and new entrants would not be induced to compete in such market conditions. In addition, those capable of surviving might increase the fees they charge for their services to finance the necessary resources to face litigation risks, thus making ratings more expensive for issuers and, consequently, for investors.

Finally, as already mentioned, the proposal to increase liability for CRAs is inconsistent with the aim of reducing reliance on ratings, as it is likely to encourage investors to rely inappropriately on ratings, discouraging them from doing their own evaluation of the security (as they could recur to civil liability allegations if they incurred losses). With significant regulatory reliance on ratings, investors could have an argument that legal recourse for rating inaccuracy is needed. However, this will become less important if the objective of reducing regulatory reliance on ratings is achieved.

5.5 SOVEREIGN RATINGS

The issue of sovereign ratings has a special relevance in Europe. As explained in the EC consultation on CRAs in November 2010, 'in the context of the recent Euro debt crisis, credit rating agencies have been criticized for having adapted the credit ratings of certain Eurozone Member States too slowly to the deterioration of their public finances and, subsequently, for having overreacted in the downgrading actions, without for instance taking due account of supportive measures of the Eurozone Member States'.

In particular, these critical voices have shed doubts on the following aspects in relation to ratings of sovereign debt: the appropriateness of the methodologies and models used by CRAs; the level of qualification and expertise of CRA's staff; the effectiveness of the monitoring of these ratings; and the timing of rating publications.

As mentioned previously, sovereign debt ratings play a crucial role for the rated countries, since a downgrade has the immediate effect in many cases of making a country's borrowing more expensive, not only for sovereigns but also for the large majority of entities located in the country, as sovereign ratings usually cap the ratings of those entities. In addition, downgrades of certain countries have contaminated the market perception of the solvency of other countries in the Eurozone.

The spillover effect of sovereign downgrades has alerted policy-makers and has placed this issue at the top of the regulatory agenda in Europe. For the time being, the proposals go along the line of requiring further measures to improve transparency, monitoring, methodologies, and the process of sovereign debt ratings. More specifically, the European Parliament resolution[17] also suggests requiring CRAs to explain deviation from the forecasts of the main international financial institutions.

Actually, solving the problem of excessive reliance on ratings, and in particular on sovereign ratings, would be a good way to avoid the spillover effect and reduce market overreaction to downgrades. In fact, this is one of the possible actions to address the risks from the spillover effect proposed by the IMF Working Paper 11/68 mentioned previously, along with another two:

> First, as soon as other countries are downgraded, policy makers should act preventively by communicating effectively to dissipate concerns regarding what market participants perceive as weaknesses. Second, since spillover effects go beyond sovereign debt markets, policy makers should be prepared to address possible instability in the banking, insurance, and non-financial sector by preparing a contingency plan. Third, as financial instability may stem from the existence of ratings-based regulations, policy makers should review the appropriateness of using credit ratings in financial markets regulation.

5.6 GLOBAL CONSISTENCY IN REGULATION AND OVERSIGHT OF RATING AGENCIES

5.6.1 Regulatory Consistency

The regulatory and oversight programmes that have emerged worldwide as a result of the financial crisis have a degree of convergence that is quite unique in financial regulation. One of the reasons for this convergence is that major

---

[17] See footnote 12.

financial centres started drafting their legislations only very recently, following the G-20 declaration of April 2009.[18] And regulations were developed on the basis of the previous international consensus formed in 2003 with the IOSCO Principles and further enhanced with the IOSCO Code (that had also been the benchmark for the previous prevalent self-regulation by CRAs).

The consensus represented by the IOSCO Principles and the IOSCO Code was possible because regulators were aware of the international nature of the major CRAs. By providing a universal measure for expressing credit risk, global CRAs facilitate the flow of capital worldwide. If the ratings issued by these global CRAs did not mean the same (because they were produced following different procedures and methodologies) the efficient cross-border flow of capital could be hindered. In this context, securities regulators were minded not to hamper the comparability of ratings worldwide when they agreed the IOSCO Principles in 2003.

Unfortunately, the recent regulatory frenzy is putting at risk such comparability. Whilst the newly established regimes have respected the high-level IOSCO Principles, some of the details included in these frameworks might force global CRAs to operate differently, depending on the jurisdictions where they issue ratings. It is too early to judge whether these differences in implementation are only making CRAs' global operations more complex or whether, in addition, they could affect the global meaning and comparability of ratings. As an example, some market participants argue that the EC's proposals on sovereign ratings could erode the independence of EU sovereign ratings, thereby leading to the perception that these ratings are tainted.

The EU CRA Regulation is based on the IOSCO Principles and on the IOSCO Code and, in addition, took elements from the US CRA Reform Act and the SEC rules issued in 2007—in turn, the Dodd–Frank Act has taken into account measures included in the CRA Regulation. Notwithstanding this, as discussed earlier in the book, a key aspect of the CRA Regulation that has caused concern is the treatment of ratings issued by CRAs established in foreign countries. Effectively, the CRA Regulation, as interpreted by the EC, requires that a foreign jurisdiction has adopted the EU regulatory standards in order for ratings issued out of that country to be eligible for regulatory use by EU institutions.

The failure by a third country to obtain an equivalency determination from the EC, and the consequent inability of CRAs based in that country to follow the endorsement or certification procedures in the CRA Regulation, would have a negative impact on these CRAs. The issuers that such CRAs rate might also be adversely impacted to the extent that those ratings are used for regulatory purposes in the EU. For these reasons, as discussed in Chapter 4, many countries that are in the process of developing or amending their regulatory oversight frameworks are incorporating into their regimes the additional requirements imposed by the EU CRA Regulation (on top of the IOSCO Code) in order to obtain an equivalency decision from the EC. This has been the case of the newly proposed regimes in Canada and Hong Kong.

---

[18] Prior to the G-20 declaration, CRAs were only regulated and supervised in Mexico (since July 1993) and in the USA (since June 2007), when the SEC adopted final rules to implement the registration and oversight programme established by the CRA Reform Act.

Whilst this can be regarded as a way to promote further convergence, the EU solutions might not always fit into a third country framework, thereby creating the risk of fragmentation of CRAs' operations, if the differences with the non-EU regime lead the EU to consider it non-equivalent.

One of the tasks of the IOSCO Standing Committee on CRAs is to 'regularly discuss, evaluate, and consider regulatory and policy initiatives vis-à-vis credit rating agency activities and oversight in an effort to seek cross border regulatory consensus through such means as the IOSCO CRA Code'. This forum should help legislators and regulators seeking new national solutions to ensure that any new measures proposed are consistent with one another and with the IOSCO Code.

5.6.2 Oversight Coordination

Concerning the surveillance of CRAs' operations, the EU made a big step in the right direction when the CRA Regulation II transferred registration and monitoring powers from colleges of national supervisors to ESMA. The authority has been granted extensive monitoring and sanctioning powers that it should use to provide additional safety and soundness in the market. The most effective mechanism to achieve the aim of enhancing the quality of ratings is for ESMA to oversee and supervise the implementation of the Regulation, holding CRAs responsible for breaches. The EU Regulation has already created a framework that will be able to meet both preventive and disciplinary objectives. Europe should now concentrate efforts on implementing an effective supervisory model.

Important challenges lie ahead for the EU. ESMA was only created in January 2011, with little time to prepare for taking over supervisory powers from national authorities. At the time of writing, ESMA is in the process of setting its internal structure and, according to its website, counts only five people devoted to CRA monitoring. It is critical that national EU authorities match market expectations and provide ESMA with adequate resources.

Finally, the global operations of the largest CRAs can complicate ESMA's monitoring efforts, hence the need for international coordination. IOSCO also provides the right avenue for cooperation. The IOSCO Standing Committee on CRAs has the mandate to 'facilitate regular dialogue between securities regulators and the credit rating industry'. This should allow supervisors to share experience from CRAs examinations—allowing them to gain more insight into the CRAs' global operations—and also to share information obtained through enforcement actions. Another important role of IOSCO is also to serve as a point of dialogue between supervisors and the CRA industry.

5.7 OVERALL CONCLUSIONS

In a short period of time, the world has moved from a system of self-regulation by CRAs to a regime of registration and oversight by public authorities. Now, the main challenge policy-makers face is to find an adequate way of reducing regulatory and investors' over-reliance on ratings.

In Europe, the CRA industry has experienced a drastic move from a self-regulatory framework to a very prescriptive legislation, in which a centralized authority in charge of supervising CRAs has been created almost from scratch. Clearly, the main challenge for the EU is to ensure that its new authority performs its supervisory role appropriately and with credibility. However, even before the registration of existing CRAs has concluded and the newly established authority starts its job, a new set of regulatory interventions has been proposed by the EC.

It would seem prudent that further amendments to the EU new brand regime are only adopted once there has been sufficient time to reflect upon the impact of the new framework. Actually, beyond political considerations, as discussed in the following paragraphs, we consider that the EU Regulation as it stands, and if properly enforced, already provides adequate means to address the issues currently under debate.

All CRAs' business models suffer from conflicts of interest and have important drawbacks. There seems to be broad agreement at the moment that the subscriber-pays model is less conflict-prone than the issuer-pays system and could be a feasible option bearing in mind that it is already used by some CRAs. However, we agree with the IMF's conclusion that 'there seem to be few viable alternative compensation models to an issuer-pay business model in the foreseeable future. In particular, it is not realistic to return to a general investor-pay subscription model.'[19]

Furthermore, prohibiting CRAs from receiving compensation from issuers is not only unrealistic but undesirable too. We believe that it is healthy to have various payment models in the CRA industry, as the market is diverse, with different investors having distinct needs. Therefore, we are not convinced that there is a benefit in mandating one business model over the others (or introducing public intervention). The way forward should be to ensure an appropriate level of regulatory monitoring and accountability for all CRAs operating in the market, regardless of the way they generate revenues. In particular, as discussed in Section 3.8.3, the EU CRA Regulation envisages a number of measures in order to ensure that CRAs manage the conflicts that are inherent in the issuer-pays model (or in any other model used). It should be ESMA's job to ensure that these provisions are complied with.

Regarding the current oligopolistic nature of the market, in our view the way forward to promote competition, avoiding a 'race to the bottom', is to combine measures that eliminate references to ratings in legislation (reducing mechanistic reliance on ratings), with public disclosure of CRAs' performance statistics that would facilitate new CRAs demonstrating that their ratings are reliable and, consequently, enhance their reputation (for example, through ESMA's central repository, discussed in Section 3.8.6).

Another of the topical themes in Europe and elsewhere is civil liability. In our view, accountability of CRAs is already being achieved by the introduction in the CRA Regulation of requirements on transparency and disclosure, independence, and integrity of the ratings process that promote the issuance of high-quality ratings. Moreover, ESMA has been given effective tools to enforce compliance of

---

[19] IMF (October 2010), *Global financial stability report: sovereigns, funding, and systemic liquidity*.

CRAs with those requirements, including sanctioning powers. Therefore, we consider that there is no need at this stage to introduce higher civil liability standards, which could be counterproductive to reduce reliance on ratings and impact negatively on competition. It should be up to regulatory authorities to supervise CRAs' activities and make them responsible for any infringement they commit. Further research and more time to judge existing enforcement provisions in the CRA Regulation at the least would be needed before an EU civil liability regime can be considered.

The last key issue in the EU regulatory agenda is the rating of sovereign debt. Whilst recognizing the unique significance of sovereign ratings and understanding the politicians' will to reduce the power of CRAs in EU markets, we note that, from a technical perspective, the existing regulatory framework in the EU already provides the legislative infrastructure to facilitate appropriate control over to sovereign ratings. As analysed throughout Chapter 3 of the book, the EU Regulation has introduced many transparency and disclosure obligations and requires CRAs to significantly improve their rating process and development of methodologies.

To sum up, in our view, the only significant weakness of the current EU legal framework remains the over-reliance of regulatory bodies and investors on CRAs' ratings. The already adopted measures to supervise CRAs' activities should now be complemented with measures to reduce market participants' absolute faith on CRAs assessments (as has been the case in the EU sovereign debt crisis). Hence we welcome the EC's willingness to promote a more diverse system of analytical sources, in line with the G-20 recommendations. On other issues, proposing new rules, without leaving time for assessing the impact of the existing legislation, can entail the risk of over-regulating the CRA industry without adding any substantial improvements to the framework.[20]

The focus should now move to supervision and enforcement of the existing rules. And a critical element in this monitoring must be ensuring that ESMA is adequately resourced to perform its responsibilities correctly. In addition, it is essential to promote global coordination of the regulatory and supervisory activities of ESMA, the SEC, and other authorities through IOSCO.

EU policy-makers should let ESMA gain experience and be confident that the enforcement and supervisory powers given to ESMA will be sufficient to address the concerns relating to the CRAs' activities. Therefore, for the time being, new legislative interventions in Europe should be limited to those necessary to reduce over-reliance on ratings. Whatever the final design of this new framework is, we think that CRAs, with their critical mass of expertise and resources, will still provide a crucial analytical resource for market participants and supervisors.

---

[20] Actually, the EU has already over-regulated in some areas, especially regarding the treatment of non-EU ratings (see Chapter 4).

APPENDIX 1

The European System of Financial Supervisors

Overview

The effects of the subprime crisis in Europe highlighted weaknesses in the EU supervisory framework. The crisis exposed the dangers of the existing fragmented European system of supervision with as many as 80 national and sectoral supervisors being responsible for EU-wide cross-border financial operators and products. Against this background, in November 2008, the EC mandated a High Level Group chaired by Mr Jacques de Larosière to make recommendations on how to strengthen European supervisory arrangements with a view to establishing a more efficient, integrated, and sustainable supervisory framework.

The key recommendations of the *de Larosière Report*, published in February 2009, that suggested the need to make relevant changes at micro- and macro-prudential supervision level, were broadly endorsed in March 2009 by the EC and the European Council. Following this endorsement, the EC published in May 2009 a *Communication on financial supervision in the EU*,[1] describing in detail how de Larosière's recommendations could be put into effect. The European Council of 18 and 19 June 2009 confirmed that the May EC Communication established the way forward in setting the new framework and requested the EC to present all necessary proposals by early autumn 2009 at the latest so that the new framework would be fully in place in the course of 2010.

In September 2009, the EC brought forward proposals to replace the EU existing supervisory architecture with a European System of Financial Supervisors (ESFS) in order to 'help restore confidence, contribute to the development of a single rulebook, solve problems with cross-border firms and prevent the build-up of risks that threaten the stability of the overall financial system'.

On 22 September 2010, the European Parliament—following agreement by all Member States—voted through the new supervisory framework proposed by the EC. This was confirmed by the ECOFIN Council on 17 November 2010, and the final texts were published in the Official Journal of the European Union on 15 December 2010.[2]

The new ESFS, in place since 1 January 2011, has been established to bring together the actors of financial supervision at national level and at the level of the EU. The ESFS is composed by the supervisory authorities of the Member States and four new bodies, as discussed below.

---

[1] EC (May 2009), *Communication on European financial supervision COM (2009) 252 final.*
[2] Regulation (EU) No 1092/2010 of the European Parliament and of the Council of 24 November 2010 on European Union macro-prudential oversight of the financial system and establishing a European Systemic Risk Board; Regulation (EU) No 1093/2010 of the European Parliament and of the Council of 24 November 2010 Establishing a European Supervisory Authority (European Banking Authority), amending Decision No 716/2009/EC and repealing Commission Decision 2009/78/EC; Regulation (EU) No 1094/2010 of the European Parliament and of the Council of 24 November 2010 Establishing a European Supervisory Authority (European Insurance and Occupational Pensions Authority), amending Decision No 716/2009/EC and repealing Commission Decision 2009/79/EC; Regulation (EU) No 1095/2010 of the European Parliament and of the Council of 24 November 2010 establishing a European Supervisory Authority (European Securities and Markets Authority), amending Decision No 716/2009/EC and repealing Commission Decision 2009/77/EC.

The European Systemic Risk Board

The European Systemic Risk Board (ESRB) has been tasked to provide macro-prudential monitoring of the financial system to assess potential threats to the stability of the financial system.

The board's general council of the ESRB is composed of the president and vice-president of the ECB, the governors of the central banks of the Member States, the chairpersons of the three European Supervisory Authorities (ESAs), a member of the EC, chairpersons and vice-chairpersons of two advisory committees, and (as non-voting members) the president of the Economic and Financial Committee and representatives of each of the national supervisory authorities.

To fulfil its role, the ESRB can issue warnings and, where necessary, recommendations either of a general or a specific nature, which can be addressed to the EU as a whole or to one or more Member States, or to one or more of the ESAs, or to one or more of the national supervisory authorities, with a specified timeline for the relevant policy response.

The ESRB monitors compliance with its warnings and recommendations, based on reports from addressees, in order to ensure that recommendations are effectively followed. Addressees of recommendations should follow them and, in case of inaction, they should provide an adequate justification ('act or explain' mechanism).

If the ESRB considers that the reaction is inadequate, it should inform, subject to strict confidentiality rules, the addressees, the European Council and, where appropriate, the ESA concerned. On a case-by-case basis, the ESRB can decide to make its recommendations public (after informing the Council) as a way to foster compliance with the recommendations.

Three New European Supervisory Authorities

The ESAs have been created on the basis of the Lamfalussy Level 3 committees (CEBS, CEIOPS, and CESR), at micro-financial level: European Banking Authority (EBA), European Insurance and Occupational Pensions Authority (EIOPA), and the European Securities and Markets Authority (ESMA). ESAs comprise high-level representatives of all of the Member States' supervisory authorities under permanent chairmanships.

In addition, a Joint Committee has been set up to ensure cooperation and to coordinate the sharing of information between the ESAs and the ESRB.

National authorities remain responsible for the day-to-day supervision of individual firms, whilst the ESAs are to be responsible for ensuring that a single set of harmonized rules and consistent supervisory practices are applied by all national supervisory authorities.

The new ESAs took over all of the functions of the former Level 3 committees, and in addition have certain extra competences, including the following: to draw up specific rules for national authorities and financial institutions; to develop technical standards, guidelines and recommendations towards a 'single rule book'; to monitor how rules are being enforced by national supervisory authorities; to take actions in emergency situations, including the banning of certain products; to mediate and settle disputes between national supervisors; to ensure the consistent application of EU laws; and, where necessary, to have the possibility of settling disagreements between national authorities, in particular in areas that require cooperation, coordination, or joint decision-making by supervisory authorities from more than one Member State.

In addition, the ESAs will be able to address decisions directly to national authorities in three areas: in cases where they are mediating between national authorities involved in the supervision of a cross-border group and where they need to agree or coordinate their position; in cases where a national authority is incorrectly applying EU Regulations; and when an emergency situation is declared by the European Council.

In these three cases, and only where there is EU legislation directly applicable, the ESAs will be able to take decisions directly applicable to financial institutions or market participants as a last resort where the ESA has addressed a decision to the national supervisor but the national supervisor has not complied with it.

ESMA's Governance Structure and Resources

Governance Structure

There are two main bodies in ESMA's governance structure: the Board of Supervisors, which brings together the head of the national competent authorities, and the Management Board.

The Board of Supervisors is composed of the heads of 27 EU national authorities and, as observers, a representative of the following organizations: the EC, EBA, EIOPA, and the ESRB. The heads of the competent authorities of Norway, Iceland, and Liechtenstein are also permanent observers.

The main role of the Board of Supervisors is to take all relevant decisions of ESMA, such as decision on the compliance by national competent authorities with community legislation, interpretation of community legislation, decisions in crisis situations, approval of draft technical standards, guidelines, peer reviews, and approval of reports. The Board of Supervisors also takes the final decision on ESMA's budget.

According to ESMA Regulation, the Board of Supervisors has to meet at least twice a year (in practice, it meets more regularly) and decisions are taken on a simple majority basis for all matters except guidelines and technical standards, where voting is done by qualified majority, as set out under the EU Treaty.

The Management Board is composed of six members selected by the Board of Supervisors among its members. There is also one representative from the EC and the Executive Director attending as non-voting participants. The Management Board focuses on the management aspects of ESMA, such as the development of a multi-annual work programme, the budget, and staff resources.

Budget

ESMA's revenues consist of a combination of contributions from the national authorities competent for the supervision of financial market participants (that are represented in ESMA's Board of Supervisors); a subsidy from the budget of the EU; and any fees paid to ESMA in the cases specified in Union law.

ESMA's main source of funding will come from the EU funds and competent authorities' contributions. At least in its first year, 40% of the funding for ESMA will come from the Union budget and 60% from its members (that will be allocated according to the weighted voting rights established under the Union Treaties). The costs of implementing the CRA Regulation will be financed via industry fees and levies from 2012.

Human Resources

ESMA has a full-time independent Chair to lead the organization, together with the Executive Director. The Chair is responsible for preparing the work of the Board of Supervisors and chairs both the meetings of the Board of Supervisors and the Managing Board. The Chair is responsible for the accountability of ESMA to the European Parliament, the EU Council, and to the EC. The Executive Director is responsible for preparing the work of the Management Board, for implementing the annual work programme, and for managing staff matters.

The day-to-day work in ESMA will be mainly carried out by the Standing Committees established under ESMA that are normally chaired by senior national representatives and bring together the national experts with support from ESMA's staff. Even in the area of CRAs where all the supervisory powers have been transferred to ESMA, the authority will have to rely heavily on the resources of its members. In fact, national competent authorities still have a key role in relation to CRAs. The national supervisors remain deeply involved in the decision-making process within ESMA, acting as members of ESMA's Board of Supervisors, and technical staff participate in internal ESMA panels or committees (Recital 6 of CRA Regulation II).

However, ESMA stills needs to be adequately staffed with its own personnel to ensure that it can discharge its new functions effectively. In this respect, the ESMA Regulation has set some transitional measures to facilitate those people working for ESMA at the end of 2010 to become ESMA's staff (Article 77). In addition, according to the information published in its website, ESMA intends to increase its staff substantially in the near future. The target is to reach around 120 staff in total in 2014.

The area of CRAs is specially relevant as ESMA will have direct supervisory powers over these entities: 'it is anticipated that there will be 15 staff dedicated to the supervision of CRAs of which five are currently in place, nine of these will be temporary agents and six will be seconded national experts in 2011'.

ESMA's staff conditions are regulated, according to Article 68 of ESMA Regulation, by the *Staff Regulations, the Conditions of Employment of Other Servants of the European Communities*. These rules and Article 70 of ESMA Regulation set the obligation of professional secrecy for ESMA's staff. In addition, Article 32.1 of CRA Regulation insists on the obligation of professional secrecy that is further broadened to encompass other people besides ESMA's staff:

> The obligation of professional secrecy shall apply to ESMA, the competent authorities, and all persons who work or who have worked for ESMA, for the competent authorities or for any other person to whom ESMA has delegated tasks, including auditors and experts contracted by ESMA. Information covered by professional secrecy shall not be disclosed to another person or authority except where such disclosure is necessary for legal proceedings.

APPENDIX 3

Mapping Factors Under CRD

Mapping Factors for Credit assessments of Exposures Other than Securitization Positions

In order to comply with the principles of objectivity and consistency, quantitative data must form the basis of the mapping process. Additionally, qualitative factors will be used by competent authorities to ensure comparability between the data provided by the different ECAIs.

Quantitative Factors

The CRD requires competent authorities to consider 'quantitative factors such as the long-term default rate associated with all items assigned the same credit assessment'.

In particular, in order to differentiate between the relative degrees of risk expressed by each credit assessment, the CRD states that supervisors shall 'compare default rates experienced for each credit assessment of a particular ECAI and compare them with a benchmark built on the basis of default rates experienced by other ECAIs on a population of issuers that the competent authorities believes to present an equivalent level of credit risk'.

According to the benchmark and monitoring guidance of the BCBS, the key variable to conduct the mapping is the 'cumulative default rate' (CDR) measured over a three-year period. This three-year CDR is defined by EBA as the sum of all defaults that have occurred in a given three-year period for all rated items belonging to the same bucket.

The BCBS proposes two separate measures of CDRs associated with each risk rating contained in the standardized approach. The benchmarks were derived using the default experience of the major global rating agencies.[1] It is worthwhile noting that the performance of all ECAIs—even that of those major ECAIs that were used to create the benchmarks—should be compared with the BCBS's benchmarks, as clarified in its guidance. When mapping these global CRAs, authorities will be comparing their individual default frequencies with the aggregate international default experience.

First, to have a sense of the long-run default experience over time, competent authorities should evaluate the ten-year average of the three-year CDR when this set of data is available. For ECAIs lacking ten years of default data, authorities would ask the agencies to make their own estimate of what their ten-year average of the three-year CDR would be. Second, supervisors should consider the two most recent three-year CDRs, where available.

The CRD indicates the action authorities might take as a result of comparing an ECAI's performance with the benchmarks (when conducting the initial mapping or when carrying out ongoing reviews). If the default rates experienced for an ECAI's credit assessments are materially and systematically higher than the benchmark, competent authorities shall assign a higher credit quality step in the credit quality assessment scale to the ECAI's credit assessment. If after such an increase the ECAI is able to demonstrate that its default rates are no longer materially and systematically higher than the benchmark, authorities may

---

[1] Actually, as these global CRAs employ different methodologies to determine their ratings, the fact that their default experience is very similar seems rather surprising.

decide to restore the original credit quality step in the scale. The way authorities apply the CRD's provisions on the basis of the BCBS's and EBA's guidance is described below.

ECAIs are expected to have three-year CDR data. This will enable competent authorities to compare the CDR measures mentioned above (the ten-year average and the two most recent CDRs) with the following BCBS's reference and benchmark values of CDRs:

1. Ten-year average of the three-year.

For each step in the rating scale, the most recent ten-year average of the three-year CDR will be compared with the long-run 'reference' three-year CDR (see Table Appendix 3.1) that represents a sense of the long-run international default experience of risk assessments based on the BCBS's observations of the default experience reported by major rating agencies internationally.

The benchmarks in Table Appendix 3.1 have been produced by the BCBS as guidance for supervisors and therefore it is not expected that ECAI's ten-year CDRs will exactly match these references. The percentages for each category in the ECAI's scale are considered mid-point rates. If the ECAI's historical performance shows that the ten-year average CDR of its ratings exceeds the reference levels, supervisors will analyse the reasons and consider whether the differences are within acceptable bounds.

2. Two most recent three-year CDRs.

In the same way, for each step in the ECAI's rating scale, competent authorities will monitor the two most recent three-year CDRs with two benchmarks set by the BCBS: the 'monitoring level' benchmark and the 'trigger level' benchmark as set out in Table Appendix 3.2.

In this case, both benchmarks are considered upper limits. The BCBS has explained how supervisors should apply them.

Exceeding the monitoring CDR benchmark implies that an ECAI current default experience for a particular rating grade is markedly worse than the international historical default experience. Authorities should be expected to investigate the reasons for the deviation; in case it is attributable to weaker standards for assessing credit risk, supervisors should assign a higher risk weight to the ECAI's assessment category that exceeds the BCBS's benchmark.

Exceeding the trigger CDR benchmark means that the historical performance of a particular rating grade is considerably above the international default experience. Therefore, there is a presumption that the ECAI's standards for assessing credit risk are either too

Table Appendix 3.1. BCBS proposed long-run 'reference' three-year CDRs

S&P assessment (Moody's)	AAA-AA (Aaa-Aa)	A (A)	BBB (Baa)	BB (Ba)	B (B)
20-year average of 3-year CDR	0.10%	0.25%	1.00%	7.50%	20.00%

Table Appendix 3.2. BCBS proposed three-year CDR benchmarks

S&P assessment (Moody's)	AAA-AA (Aaa-Aa)	A (A)	BBB (Baa)	BB (Ba)	B (B)
Monitoring level	0.8%	1.0%	2.4%	11.0%	28.6%
Trigger level	1.2%	1.3%	3.0%	12.4%	35.0%

weak or not applied appropriately. Thus, if the trigger level is exceeded in two consecutive years, supervisors should increase the risk weight associated with the assessment category. However, authorities can rebut the presumption and keep the original risk weight if, for example, they find out that the cause of the bad performance is a temporary phenomenon and not attributable to weaker standards.

In line with the BCBS's guidance, EBA states that for recently established ECAIs and those that have compiled only a short record of default data, supervisors will ask ECAIs for their two most recent CDRs and a projection of what they believe the ten-year average of the three-year CDR would be for each risk rating. Supervisors will analyse with caution these estimates from less experienced ECAIs and, therefore, they are likely to incorporate an appropriate degree of conservatism in the final mapping.

Qualitative Factors

The CRD requires competent authorities to consider qualitative factors such as the pool of issuers that the ECAI covers; the ranges of credit assessments that the ECAI assigns; each credit assessment meaning; and the ECAI's definition of default.

As indicated by EBA, these parameters are important in the analysis of the transition and default data submitted by the ECAIs and the comparison of their performance with the BCBS's benchmarks. For example, a stricter definition of default than that used for producing the benchmark would lead to more defaults of the reporting ECAI and the opposite if the definition is less stringent. The sample size used by the ECAI is also very important, as a small one can lead to more volatile CDRs.

Finally, EBA recommends competent authorities to consider additional qualitative factors such as the variable used to weight default events, the geographic coverage of the performance data, and the dynamic properties and characteristics of the methodology (a 'point-in-time' rating system or a 'through the cycle' system).

Mapping Factors for Credit Assessments of Securitization Positions

The CRD requires a separate mapping of credit assessments of securitization positions. The securitization mapping has to follow the same principles of objectivity and consistency. There are, however, important differences compared to the mapping of other credit assessments. Neither the BCBS's guidance nor the CRD require competent authorities to create a benchmark for default rate comparison. The fact that the BCBS has not developed yet such a benchmark reflects the difficulties of the task. It is, however, desirable that the BCBS provides such a benchmark for the ongoing monitoring by supervisory authorities. Otherwise, it is difficult to justify the initial mapping and why it is changed or not during the ongoing reviews.

The CRD requires competent authorities to consider 'quantitative factors, such as default and/or loss rates, and qualitative factors such as the range of transactions assessed by the ECAI and the meaning of the credit assessment'.

In the absence of complete recovery rate data, EBA requires authorities to consider data relating to the default/impairment rates associated with different credit assessments. EBA hopes that the amount of loss data available will grow and improve over time in order for authorities to be able to incorporate an analysis of loss data into the mapping process.

EBA provides a number of factors that supervisors should take into account. For example, it recommends the use of a 'cohort' approach (incorporating the effect of ratings migration in the analysis of the performance of the rating). Also, authorities need to consider the approach of the ECAI to the repayment of missed payments and withdrawn credit assessments and how these factors affect the ECAI's performance studies. And, obviously, a key parameter will be the number of years covered by the performance data (for example three years versus five years).

Finally, EBA also considers qualitative factors, such as market participants' views regarding the degree to which the assessments of an ECAI are seen as an equivalent indicator of creditworthiness to those of its peers.

APPENDIX 4

US Legislation on CRAs

NRSRO No-action Letter Process

It was in the 1970s, when the largest rating agencies began the practice of charging issuers as well as investors for rating services, that the term Nationally Recognized Statistical Rating Organizations ('NRSRO') was first used by the SEC. In 1975 the SEC adopted the broker-dealer net capital rule, where the term NRSRO was used to classify debt instruments in terms of the amount they would be haircut for regulatory capital purposes, depending on the rating of a NRSRO. However, before the SEC adopted this rule the New York Stock Exchange already used the term NRSRO in its net capital rule, which distinguished between investment grade and non-investment grade instruments.

Despite the use of the NRSRO term in its rules, the SEC had no explicit authority to regulate CRAs as such. Therefore, the designation process of CRAs as NRSROs was done through the SEC staff's no-action letter process. In that process, the staff reviewed information and documents submitted by the CRAs, including how broadly their ratings were used in the securities markets, to determine whether the agency had achieved broad market acceptance for ratings. If it was considered that there was a broad acceptance, the staff would issue a letter stating that it would not recommend enforcement action against broker-dealers who used the agency's ratings for purposes of complying with the net capital rule. Although the no-action letters only referred to the SEC's net capital rule, they effectively conferred NRSRO status for the purposes of all US statutes and regulations using that term. In the 1970s the three largest rating agencies (Fitch, S&P, and Moody's) received no-action letters as NRSROs through this process.

Over time, the NRSRO concept was incorporated into additional SEC's rules, and into laws and regulations from the USA and other countries.

NRSRO Legislation

In September 2006, the US Congress enacted the Credit Rating Agency Reform Act of 2006 to 'improve the ratings quality for the protection of investors and in the public interest by fostering accountability, transparency and competition in the CRA industry'.

The CRA Reform Act substituted the staff no-action letter process, which lacked transparency, for a voluntary registration system for CRAs and provided the SEC with broad authority to oversee NRSROs. In particular, it provided the SEC with authority to prescribe the form of the application (including requiring the submission of additional information); the records the NRSRO must make and retain; the financial reports a NRSRO must provide to the SEC on a periodic basis; the specific procedures the NRSRO must implement to manage the handling of material non-public information; the conflicts of interest an NRSRO must manage or avoid; and the practices that an NRSRO must not engage in if the SEC determines they are unfair, coercive, or abusive. In addition, the Act provided the SEC with the authority to examine all books and records of an NRSRO and to bring enforcement action against NRSROs for violations of the US federal securities laws.

The operative provisions of the CRA Reform Act became applicable upon the SEC's adoption in June 2007 of a series of rules implementing a registration and supervision regime for CRAs that register as NRSROs.

As envisaged in the CRA Reform Act, the rules on registration prescribe, among other things, the application form a CRA has to submit in order to be registered with the SEC, the minimum information the applicant has to include in its form, and the obligation to keep its registration updated. These rules are very detailed and provide clarity regarding the basis upon which the application for registration is to be accepted and the grounds upon which the SEC could reject it.

Once a NRSRO is registered, it has to make its application form publicly available, together with most of the exhibits that accompany the application. The public disclosures include, among other things, organizational information, ratings performance statistics, ratings methodologies, conflicts of interest, and analysts' experience. This upfront disclosure enables market participants to make their own assessment regarding the NRSRO's integrity and quality of ratings and, together with the extensive records NRSROs are required to retain, form the basis of the SEC's examinations. The rules also include annual financial reports that NRSROs have to submit on a confidential basis.

Combined with the extensive disclosure requirements, the other pillars of the 2007 rules are the detailed requirements on conflicts of interest (those that are prohibited and those that the NRSRO is required to identify, manage, and disclose) and the provisions requiring procedures to prevent the misuse of material non-public information.

Since the CRA Reform Act became effective in June 2007, ten CRAs have registered as NRSROs under the US legislative framework: A.M. Best Company, Inc., DBRS Ltd, Fitch, Inc., Japan Credit Rating Agency, Ltd, Moody's Investors Service, Inc., Rating and Investment Information, Inc., Standard & Poor's Ratings Services, LACE Financial Corp, Realpoint LLC, and Egan-Jones Rating Company.

According to the CRA Reform Act, the SEC has to provide an annual report to the US Congress. Until now the SEC has provided and published three reports in 2008, 2009, and January 2011, which are available at the SEC's website.[1]

SEC's NRSRO Monitoring

Following the global market turmoil, in September 2007, the SEC used its new monitoring authority to initiate examinations of the three largest NRSROs, Fitch, Moody's, and S&P. These examinations focused on their compliance with the law and rules regarding the integrity of the credit rating processes, the policies and controls the CRAs adopted to address conflicts of interest in these processes, and the quality and soundness of their compliance control systems. In particular, the SEC staff reviewed the CRAs processes for rating subprime RMBS and CDOs.

The period reviewed by the examination generally covered January 2004 through July 2008. The SEC staff's examinations highlighted many of the market failures that have been described in Section 2.1 and, given the global nature of the NRSROs investigated, the conclusions of the report were extremely relevant for policy-makers and supervisors in other jurisdictions. In particular, the main findings of the SEC staff can be summarized as follows:

- Increased deal volume and complexity: there was a substantial increase in the number and complexity of RMBS and CDO deals beginning in 2002 and some of the NRSROs appeared to struggle with the growth due to the lack of sufficient staff and resources to manage the increasing volume of business.

[1] SEC's Annual Reports to Congress under Section 6 of the Credit Rating Agency Reform Act of 2006.

- Disclosure of ratings process: significant aspects of the ratings process were not always disclosed (for example, relevant ratings criteria). In addition, the NRSROs made 'out-of-model adjustments' without documenting the rationale for such adjustments.

- Documentation of ratings policies and procedures: the NRSROs' policies and procedures for rating RMBS and CDOs could be better documented as none of the CRAs examined had consolidated and comprehensive written procedures for rating these products. The SEC staff also found that the NRSROs did not appear to have specific policies and procedures to identify or address errors in their models or methodologies.

- Documentation of the ratings process: NRSROs did not always document significant participants and steps in the ratings process and there was also a lack of documentation of rating committee's actions and decisions.

- Surveillance processes: the surveillance processes appeared to be less robust than their initial ratings processes, there was poor documentation of the monitoring conducted, and the lack of resources appeared to impact the timeliness of the surveillance efforts.

- Management of conflicts of interest: while each NRSRO had policies and procedures restricting analysts from participating in fee discussions with issuers, the policies still allowed key participants in the ratings process to take part in these discussions. In addition, the NRSROs did not appear to take steps to prevent the possibility that considerations of market share and other business interests could influence ratings. Moreover, although the NRSROs had policies prohibiting employees from owning securities that were subject to a rating by them, the NRSROs varied in how rigorously they monitored or prevented prohibited transactions from occurring.

- Internal audits: the internal audits of the ratings processes of two NRSROs appeared to be inadequate. For example, at one NRSRO, the internal audits of its RMBS and CDO groups constituted a one-page checklist limited in scope to evaluate the completeness of deal files.

- Due diligence practices: NRSROs did not engage in any due diligence or otherwise seek to verify the accuracy or quality of the loan data underlying the RMBS pools they rated during the review period. They relied on the information provided to them by the sponsor of the RMBS.

Amendments to NRSRO Rules

The findings from these initial examinations informed a round of rule amendments, which the SEC proposed in June 2008 and adopted in February 2009. The amended rules required NRSROs to make additional public disclosures about their methodologies for determining structured finance ratings, to publicly disclose the histories of their ratings, and to hold more internal records and submit additional information to the SEC in order to assist staff's examinations of NRSROs. The amendments also prohibited NRSROs and their analysts from engaging in certain activities that could impair their objectivity, such as recommending how to obtain a desired rating and then rating the resulting security.

In November 2009, the SEC adopted additional amendments. The new rules required a broader disclosure of credit ratings history information, such as the initial rating and any actions subsequently taken, including downgrades, upgrades, confirmations, and placements on watch. The rules required a NRSRO to disclose, on a delayed basis, ratings history information in a downloadable format for all ratings initially determined on or after 26 June 2007 ('100% requirement'). This new disclosure requirement, as explained in Section 3.8.6—under the analysis of ESMA's central repository—is designed to foster greater transparency of ratings quality and accountability among NRSROs, by making it easier for investors to analyse the actual performance of ratings.

Also in November 2009, a new rule (amended rule 240 17g-5) was adopted in order to enable competing CRAs to offer unsolicited ratings for structured finance products, by granting them access to the necessary underlying data of the transactions (see Section 3.8.5).

Dodd–Frank Act

In August 2010 the Dodd–Frank Wall Street Reform and Consumer Protection Act was passed. As a response to the financial crisis, this complex piece of legislation reforms a number of areas of the US financial services framework. Its provisions, among other things, address systemic risk; regulate advisers to hedge funds; establish a Federal Insurance Office and seek to reform insurance regulation; regulate over-the-counter derivatives markets; reform the transaction clearing and settlement process; and strengthen investor protection and improve a number of areas of the securities regulation. Among the reforms in the last area mentioned are the improvements to the regulation of CRAs included in Title IX, Subtitle C of the Act. The following paragraphs summarize the key provisions and requirements of the Dodd–Frank Act that relate to CRAs.[2]

New Office of Credit Ratings at the SEC

The Act creates an Office of Credit Ratings at the SEC with its own director and compliance staff, composed of people with 'knowledge of and expertise in corporate, municipal, and structured debt finance'. The mission of the Office is to protect the users of ratings, promote accuracy in credit ratings issued by NRSROs, and ensure that such ratings are not unduly influenced by conflicts of interest. The Office is required to examine NRSROs at least once a year and make key findings public. In connection with its annual examinations, the Office will review the following aspects of the NRSRO's operations: whether the NRSRO is conducting business in accordance with its policies, procedures, and rating methodologies; the management of conflicts; the implementation of ethics policies; the internal supervisory controls; the governance; the processing of complaints; and the policies governing the post-employment activities of former staff of the NRSRO.

The Office will have authority to establish rules necessary to enforce the new regulations and be able to establish fines and other penalties for violation of the regulations.

Disclosure and Internal Control Requirements

The Act creates new requirements for the development and maintenance of internal controls in NRSROs and increases the amount of disclosure required by NRSROs.

Internal Controls

Each NRSRO must establish an effective internal control structure governing the implementation of and adherence to policies, procedures, and methodologies for determining ratings. Each NRSRO must submit to the SEC an annual internal control report that is attested by the chief executive officer and that describes the responsibility of management in establishing and maintaining controls and assessing the effectiveness of the internal control structure of the NRSRO.

Disclosure of Rating Methodologies

The SEC has to prescribe rules to ensure that ratings are produced in accordance with procedures and methodologies that have been approved by the NRSRO's board. The

---

[2] Bowden, Bruce, Patel, Neal A. and Loveman, John A. (2010), *U.S. Financial Reform: Credit Rating Agencies*.

NRSRO must disclose the reasons for any material change in rating procedures and methodologies and the changes must be applied consistently to all ratings to which the changed procedures and methodologies apply. The NRSRO must notify the users of the following: the methodology used with respect to a particular rating; any material change made to a procedure or methodology; any significant error that is identified in a procedure or methodology that may result in rating changes; and the likelihood that a material change in procedure or methodology would result in a change in current ratings.

Form for Disclosure
The SEC will prescribe rules to require NRSROs to publish with each rating a form (in paper or electronic format) including a number of disclosures. In particular, the form must discuss: the main assumptions underlying the rating; potential limitations of the rating; information on the uncertainty of ratings; whether and to what extent third party due diligence reports have been used; data about the issuer used in determining the rating; the NRSRO's assessment of the quality of data available and considered; and information related to conflicts of interest and other information that the SEC may require.

Third Party Due Diligence Services for Structured Finance Products
Issuers of asset-backed securities must make public the findings and conclusions of any due diligence report obtained by the issuer. Third party due diligence services must certify (in a form and content to be established by the SEC) that they have conducted a thorough review of data, documentation, and other relevant information necessary for the NRSRO to provide an accurate rating. NRSROs shall make such certifications public, in order to allow market participants to determine the adequacy of third party due diligence services.

Transparency of Performance
The SEC has to issue rules that require each NRSRO to 'publicly disclose information on the initial credit ratings determined by the [NRSRO] for each type of obligor, security, and money market instrument, and any subsequent changes to such credit ratings'.

Corporate Governance and Management of Conflicts of Interests
The Dodd–Frank Act also contains provisions related to the corporate governance of NRSROs to ensure that conflicts of interest are minimized in the rating process.

Independent Directors and Duties of the Board
Each NRSRO must have a board of directors, and at least half the members of the board (but not fewer than two directors) must be independent. Independent directors may receive compensation, but such compensation cannot be linked to the business performance of the NRSRO. The term of the independent director is required to be for a non-renewable fixed term not to exceed five years. Provisions concerning the board's role stipulate that, in addition to their overall responsibilities, the board of directors is required to oversee the policies and procedures for determining ratings and for addressing, managing, and disclosing conflicts of interest; the effectiveness of the internal control system; and the compensation and promotion policies and practices of the NRSRO.

Conflicts of Interest
The SEC has to prescribe rules to prevent the sales and marketing considerations of NRSROs from influencing the production of ratings. Such rules will provide exceptions for small NRSROs.

Employees
There is a new requirement for NRSROs to conduct a one-year look-back review when an employee goes to work for an issuer, obligor, or underwriter of a security that has been

rated by that NRSRO. The NRSRO is also required to report to the SEC when certain employees are hired by an entity that the NRSRO has rated in the previous 12 months.

Independent Information
In developing a rating, an NRSRO must consider information from a source other than the rated issuer that the NRSRO finds credible and potentially significant to a rating decision.

Enforcement and Liability
The Dodd–Frank Act also contains several provisions that allow for greater enforcement of violations by NRSROs and provides the SEC with the right to revoke an NRSRO's status under certain circumstances.

Private Actions
The Act amends the Securities Exchange Act of 1934 to allow investors to bring private actions against NRSROs for a knowing or reckless failure to conduct a reasonable investigation of the rated security with respect to factual elements relied upon by its own methodology or to obtain reasonable verification of such factual elements from other sources that are reliable and independent of the issuer. Additionally, NRSROs will now be subject to 'expert liability' through the nullification of the rule which previously provided an exemption for credit ratings provided by NRSROs from being considered a part of a registration statement. In this context, NRSROs will now face the same type of liability in private securities actions faced by registered public accounting firms or securities analysts.

Right to Deregister
The Act authorizes the SEC to revoke a CRA's NRSRO status for a particular class of securities when an NRSRO has insufficient financial and managerial resources to consistently produce accurate ratings.

NRSROs are Required to Refer Tips to Authorities
The Act provides that each NRSRO must refer to law-enforcement or regulatory authorities credible information that it receives that alleges that an issuer of securities rated by the NRSRO has committed a material violation of law.

Other Provisions
Testing and Education
The Act directs the SEC to issue rules to ensure that any person employed by an NRSRO to perform ratings meets standards of training, experience, and competence necessary to produce accurate ratings, and is tested for knowledge of the rating process.

Universal Rating Symbols
NRSROs are required to clearly define any symbols used to denote a credit rating, and apply those symbols in a consistent manner to all types of securities. However, there is no restriction on NRSROs using distinct sets of symbols to denote credit ratings for different types of securities (such as the structured finance indicator in the EU).

Reduce Reliance on Ratings
Effective as of two years after the date of enactment of the Act, various statutory references to ratings will be removed.

SEC Implementation of the Dodd–Frank Act
The Act directs the SEC to issue within one year the final rules required by the Act. At the time of writing the SEC has undertaken some relevant actions.

Credit Rating Standardization Study
In December 2010, the SEC requested comments for the preparation of the Credit Rating Standardization Study. These comments will help inform the SEC study pursuant to the Dodd–Frank Act on the feasibility and desirability of 'standardizing credit ratings terminology, so that all credit rating agencies issue credit ratings using identical terms; standardizing the market stress conditions under which ratings are evaluated; requiring a quantitative correspondence between credit ratings and a range of default probabilities and loss expectations under standardized conditions of economic stress; and standardizing credit rating terminology across asset classes, so that named ratings correspond to a standard range of default probabilities and expected losses independent of asset class and issuing entity'.

Removal of References to Ratings in Legislation
During the first semester of 2011, the SEC proposed revisions to the rules that contain references to credit ratings. In particular, the SEC proposed to: change existing rules related to money market funds that allow such funds to only invest in securities that have received one of the two highest categories of short-term credit ratings; to remove references to ratings from broker-dealer capital and other financial responsibility rules and, where necessary, substitute alternative standards of creditworthiness; and to remove ratings as one of the conditions for companies seeking to use short form registration when registering securities for public sale.

Study on a System to Assign NRSROs to Determine Ratings
for Structure Finance Products
In May 2011, the SEC published for comment a document to assist it in carrying out the study requested by the Dodd–Frank Act on the feasibility of establishing a system in which a public or private utility or a self-regulatory organization assigns NRSROs to determine credit ratings for structured finance products (see Section 5.1.4).

Detailed Implementing Rules
In May 2011, the SEC published a set of proposed rules to implement a number of provisions of the Dodd–Frank Act (SEC proposed rules for NRSROs May 2011). Basically, the proposed rules analyse the provisions of the Act dealing with disclosure and internal control requirements and employees, as explained before, and, in some cases, propose more detailed requirements. For example, in relation to the provision on transparency of the performance, the SEC proposes to standardize the way an NRSRO calculates and presents aggregate information about how its ratings change over time and how often a rated entity or product subsequently defaulted. In addition, it proposes to enhance the so-called '100% Requirement' to require that the disclosures include any credit ratings that were outstanding as of 26 June 2007, and any subsequent rating actions taken with respect to those ratings.

At the time of writing, the SEC has not yet published the final rules. If adopted along the lines proposed, this reform will be a mayor step towards strengthening the US monitoring of CRAs.

APPENDIX 5

Japanese Legislation on CRAs

Background

Following the G-20 mandate, Japan introduced new legislation in 2009 to establish a registration and supervisory regime for CRAs. Before, and for nearly 20 years previously, a designated rating agencies system that did not imply regulation or supervision over CRAs was in place in Japan. Under this system the Commissioner of the Financial Services Agency of Japan (JFSA) recognized certain CRAs as Designated Rating Agencies ('DRA') in order to allow the ratings of these CRAs to be used for a number of regulatory purposes. Among others, ratings assigned by DRAs were, and are, used for the following purposes:[1]

- calculation of capital adequacy ratios by banks (External Credit Assessment Institutions);

- determination of market risks and counterparty risks for the purposes of calculating the capital adequacy ratios for investment firms;

- to ban security dealers from being lead managers for the security that its parent or subsidiary company issues unless the security is rated by a DRA;

- calculation of the solvency margin ratios by insurance companies when estimating credit risks: there is also a restriction on insurance companies investing in assets without ratings issued by DRAs;

- prospectus eligibility: ratings issued by DRAs must be disclosed in securities registration statements and prospectuses;

- authorization to the Banks Shareholding Purchase Cooperation to purchase only the stocks of issuers with ratings issued by DRAs; and

- issuance of specific short-term securities, promissory notes, and short-term investment corporate bonds: a rating issued by a DRA is required for these instruments.

When conferring a CRA the status of DRA the JFSA took into account the following aspects: ratings performance; human resources; organization; rating methodologies; capital structure; and independence from issuers. The following entities were recognized as DRAs: Rating and Investment Information, Inc. (R&I); Japan Credit Rating Agency, Ltd (JCR); Moody's Investments Securities, Inc. (Moody's); Standard and Poor's Credit Market Securities (S&P); and Fitch Ratings Limited (Fitch).

New Regulatory Framework for CRAs in 2009

In June 2009, the Japanese Parliament passed legislation introducing a new regulatory framework for CRAs, which was followed by the release in December 2009 of Cabinet Orders and Cabinet Office Ordinances laying out the details of this framework,[2] which

---

[1] In accordance with the latest developments in international forums, Japan has the intention of reviewing the references to ratings in its regulations.

[2] The Japanese legal and supervisory framework for credit rating agencies consists of the Financial Instruments and Exchange Act (Act No. 25 of 1948) related to the Regulation of Credit Ratings

became effective in April 2010. The aim of the new rules is to ensure the independence of CRAs by preventing conflicts of interest, to improve the quality and fairness of the rating process, and to increase transparency for market participants.

The new legislation sets a registration regime whereby CRAs are required to be registered with the JFSA in order for their ratings to be used for regulatory purposes in Japan. The JFSA is in charge of the supervision of CRAs on an ongoing basis and is endowed with a wide range of powers, including the ability to impose sanctions against CRAs for breach of the provisions of the regulations.

The Japanese legislation differentiates between the use of ratings for regulatory purposes that requires registration of the CRA with the JFSA as a precondition, and ratings that are used for non-regulatory purposes. The registration system is voluntary, as CRAs have choice of whether to register or not.

Non-registered CRAs

Credit ratings issued by entities not registered as CRAs with the JFSA cannot be used for regulatory purposes but can be used for non-regulatory purposes. In this case, there are additional disclosure obligations imposed on broker-dealers and other persons offering financial instruments rated by non-registered CRAs. In particular, the JFSA has the power to take action against those offering financial contracts in the event that the following information is not provided to the clients:

- a statement that the rating has been determined by an entity that has not been registered with the JFSA;
- information regarding the importance of registered status;
- a summary of the policies and methodology adopted for the determination of such rating; and
- assumptions, significance, and limitations of the credit rating.

Registered CRAs

Registration is a requirement for those CRAs that want their ratings to be used for regulatory purposes. Under the new registration regime and as of the time of writing, the JFSA has registered the following five entities and placed them in the list of licensed (registered) financial institutions: Japan Credit Rating Agency, Ltd; Moody's Japan K.K.; Moody's SF Japan K.K.; Standard & Poor's Ratings Japan K.K.; and Rating and Investment Information, Inc.

Once a CRA decides to register, it is subject to all the provisions of the registration status irrespective of whether or not its credit ratings are used for regulatory purposes. There are four basic principles at the core of the legal and supervisory framework for CRAs.

Duty of Good Faith
This principle requires CRAs to conduct operations with fairness and integrity as independent entities.

Agencies; the Cabinet Office Ordinance on Financial Instruments Business (Ordinance No 52 of 2007) related to the Regulation of Credit Rating Agencies; the Cabinet Office Ordinance on Definitions under Article 2 of the Exchange Act (Ordinance of the Ministry of Finance No 14 of 1993) related to the Regulation of Credit Rating Agencies, as well as the Comprehensive Guidelines for Supervision of Financial Instruments Business Operators (Supplement) and the Guidelines for Supervision of Credit Rating Agencies. It is available in English at the JFSA website.

Control Systems
CRAs are obliged to develop control systems for the purpose of conducting their credit rating business fairly and appropriately. Among others, the following requirements are set:

- Quality control in the rating process: CRAs must employ sufficient staff with expertise and skills; ensure the quality of the information used in the rating activities; examine the validity and effectiveness of rating policies; and review and update existing ratings.
- Procedures to ensure the independence and fairness of ratings: requires ratings to be determined by rating committees and regular rotation of analysts.
- Prevention of conflicts of interest: requires CRAs to specify situations of conflicts and publish measures for preventing them; review past ratings of analysts who became employees of a rated entity.
- Organizational controls: establishment of a supervisory committee that is responsible for the operational control systems.

Prohibited Acts
The Japanese legislation prohibits a CRA and its employees from carrying out any of the following acts with regard to the rating activities:

- the provision of a rating where there is a close relationship between the CRA or its employees and the rated entity;
- the provision of advice by the CRA or its employees to the rated entity where this may have a material influence on the rating;
- acts, specified in the regulations, which result in insufficient protection of investors or cause a loss of confidence in the credit rating business; and
- CRA lending its name to another person to engage in rating business under its name.

Duty to Record and Disclose Information
The Japanese legislation sets requirements relating to timely disclosure and presentation of ratings (for example, provision of ratings without delay and list of items to be published in a rating report), to periodic disclosure (such as requirements to publish annually information on the historical performance data), and to record keeping.

Japan- and non-Japan-related Ratings

The Japanese legislation differentiates between Japan- and non-Japan-related ratings. Those credit ratings that are classifiable as 'non-Japan-related ratings' are outside the scope of the regulatory and supervisory regime and, therefore, do not need to meet the requirements that apply to Japan-related ratings that are within the scope of the Japanese regime.

To be classifiable as a non-Japan-related rating, the rating determined at an overseas location by a foreign CRA has to satisfy the following criteria:[3]

- the rating is not a credit rating of a financial instrument offered to Japanese residents;
- the rated entity is not domiciled in Japan; and
- in respect of structured finance transactions, the main part of the underlying assets are not located in Japan.

[3] As an example of what a non-Japan related rating is in practice, this would be a Fitch rating issued from London on a Spanish bank bond which is solely sold to EU investors.

It is up to each foreign CRA to assess whether or not the use of its ratings produced at an overseas location falls within any of the three criteria. Therefore, the differentiation between Japan- and non-Japan-related ratings needs to be determined by the foreign CRA on a rating by rating basis.

The Japanese legislation, therefore, requires that if the ratings are to be used in Japan, they have to be issued by a CRA registered in Japan and, in order to be registered, the agency has to have an office (physical presence) in Japan. It is noteworthy that in the future Japan could have a similar system in place to that of the EU in respect of credit ratings that are issued outside of Japan where there is no form of physical presence in Japan, but where such credit ratings can be used if the CRA is considered to be subject to equivalent supervision in the third country.

Amendment to the Rules on CRAs January 2011

In January 2011, an amendment to the Japanese CRA regulations entered into force. The change was introduced to deal with situations where multiple entities comprise a group of CRAs that provide ratings using a common rating methodology (mainly global CRAs). In these cases, the amendment requires the registered CRA to also provide further information in relation to unregistered CRAs that belong to its group. In particular, 'methods of obtaining the outline of policies and methods for providing credit ratings from the unregistered entity'.[4]

---

[4] *JFSA Newsletter* No. 88. 2010.

Glossary

Basel II Framework:	BCBS (June 2004), *International Convergence of Capital Measurement and Capital Standards. A revised framework.*
Basel III Framework:	BCBS (December 2010), *A global regulatory framework for more resilient banks and banking system* and BCBS, (December 2010), *International framework for liquidity risk measurement, standards and monitoring.*
CRA Reform Act:	US Credit Rating Agency Reform Act of 2006.
CRA Regulation:	Regulation (EC) No 1060/2009 of the European Parliament and of the Council of 16 September 2009 on credit rating agencies (OJ L302 17.11.2009), as amended by CRA Regulation II.
CRA Regulation II:	Regulation (EC) No 513/2011 of the European Parliament and of the Council of 11 May 2011 amending Regulation (EC) No 1060/2009 on credit rating agencies.
CRD (Capital Requirement Directives):	Directive 2006/48/EC of the European Parliament and the Council of 14 June 2006 relating to the taking up and pursuit of the business of credit institutions (recast) (OJ L 177, 30.6.2006); and Directive 2006/49/EC of the European Parliament and the Council of 14 June 2006 on the capital adequacy of investment firms and credit institutions (recast) (OJ L 177, 30.6.2006).
CRD II:	Directive 2009/111/EC of the European Parliament and of the Council of 16 September 2009 amending Directives 2006/48/EC, 2006/49/EC, and 2007/64/EC as regards banks affiliated to central institutions, certain own funds items, large exposures, supervisory arrangements, and crisis management.
Dodd–Frank Act:	Dodd–Frank Wall Street Reform and Consumer Protection Act.
EBA's guidelines on ECAIs:	CEBS (November 2010), *Revised guidelines on the recognition of External Credit Assessment Institutions.*
EC impact assessment CRA Regulation:	European Commission (November 2008), *Commission staff working document accompanying the Proposal for a Regulation of the European Parliament and of the Council on credit rating agencies, Impact assessment [COM(2008) 704] [SEC (2008) 2746].*
EC impact assessment CRA Regulation II:	European Commission (June 2010), *Commission staff working document accompanying the Proposal for a Regulation of the European Parliament and of the Council amending Regulation (EC) No 1060/2009 on credit rating agencies, Impact assessment [COM(2010) 289 final] [SEC (2010) 679].*

EC consultation on CRAs November 2010:	European Commission (November 2010), *Consultation on Credit Rating Agencies (CRAs), new initiatives.*
EC proposal CRA Regulation:	European Commission (November 2008), *Commission staff working document accompanying the Proposal for a Regulation of the European Parliament and of the Council on credit rating agencies, Impact assessment [COM(2008) 704] [SEC(2008) 2746].*
EC proposal CRA Regulation II:	European Commission (June 2010), *European Commission's proposal for a Regulation of the European Parliament and of the Council on amending Regulation (EC) No 1060/ 2009 on credit rating agencies (COM(2010) 289 final) (SEC (2010) 678}{SEC(2010) 679}).*
ESMA's Q&A:	CESR (June 2010), *Frequently asked questions regarding the EU Regulation on credit rating agencies: common positions agreed by CESR members (Ref. CESR/10-521).*
ESMA's consultation on registration:	CESR (October 2009), *Consultation paper, guidance on registration process, functioning of colleges, mediation protocol, information set out in Annex II, information set for the application for certification and for the assessment of CRAs systemic importance (Ref. CESR/09-955).*
ESMA's guidance on registration:	CESR (June 2010), *Guidance on registration process, functioning of colleges, mediation protocol, information set out in Annex II, information set for the application for certification and for the assessment of CRAs systemic importance (Ref. CESR/10-347).*
ESMA's guidance on enforcement:	CESR (August 2010), *Guidance on the enforcement practices and activities to be conducted under Article 21.3(a) of the Regulation (Ref. CESR/10-944).*
ESMA's consultation on CEREP:	CESR (July 2009), *Consultation paper, CRAs Central Repository (Ref. CESR/09-579).*
ESMA's guidelines on CEREP:	CESR (June 2010), *Guidelines for the implementation of the Central Repository (CEREP) (Ref. CESR/10-331).*
ESMA's guidance on methodologies:	CESR (August 2010), *Guidance on common standards for assessment of compliance of credit rating methodologies with the requirements set out in Article 8.3. (Ref. CESR/10-945).*
ESMA Regulation:	Regulation (EU) No 1095/2010 of the European Parliament and of the Council of 24 November 2010 establishing a European Supervisory Authority (European Securities and Markets Authority), amending Decision No 716/2009/EC and repealing Commission Decision 2009/77/EC.
IOSCO Code:	IOSCO (October 2004), *Code of conduct fundamentals for credit rating agencies,* as revised in May 2008.
IOSCO Principles:	IOSCO (September 2003), *Statement of principles regarding the activities of credit rating agencies.*

Market Abuse Directive:	Directive 2003/6/EC of the European Parliament and of the Council of 28 January 2003 on insider dealing and market manipulation (market abuse) (OJ L 96, 12.4.2003).
MiFID (Markets in Financial Instruments Directive):	Directive 2004/39/EC of the European Parliament and of the Council of 21 April 2004 on markets in financial instruments amending Council Directives 85/611/EEC and 93/6/EEC and Directive 2000/12/EC of the European Parliament and of the Council and repealing Council Directive 93/22/EEC.
Prospectus Directive:	Directive 2003/71/EC of the European Parliament and of the Council of 4 November 2003 on the prospectus to be published when securities are offered to the public or admitted to trading and amending Directive 2001/34/EC as amended by Directive 2010/73/EU.
Prospectus Regulation:	Commission Regulation (EC) No 809/2004 of 29 April 2004 implementing Directive 2003/71/EC of the European Parliament and of the Council as regards information contained in prospectuses as well as the format, incorporation by reference and publication of such prospectuses and dissemination of advertisements.
SEC staff's examinations:	SEC (July 2008), *Summary report of issues identified in the commission staff's examinations of select credit rating agencies.*
SEC proposed rules for NRSROs May 2011:	SEC (May 2011), Proposed rules for Nationally Recognized Statistical Rating Organizations. Release No. 34-64514; File No. S7-18-11.
Takeover Bids Directive:	Directive 2004/25/EC of the European Parliament and of the Council of 21 April 2004 on takeover bids (OJ L 142/12 30.4.2004).
Transparency Directive:	Directive 2004/109/EC of the European Parliament and of the Council of 15 December 2004 on the harmonisation of transparency requirements in relation to information about issuers whose securities are admitted to trading on a regulated market and amending Directive 2001/34/EC (OJ L 390/38 31.12.2004).

Bibliography

Amato, Jeffery D. and Furfine, Craig H. (2003), *Are credit ratings procyclical?* BIS Working Papers No 129.

AMF (January 2008), *2007 Report on rating agencies: credit rating of corporate issuers.*

—— (July 2010), *2009 Report on rating agencies.*

Arezki, Rabah, Candelon, Bertrand, and Sy, Amadou N.R. (March 2011), *Sovereign rating news and financial markets spillovers: evidence from the European debt crisis.* IMF Working Paper 11/68.

Bank of England (2007), *Financial stability report,* October, Issue No 22.

BCBS (July 1988), *International convergence of capital measurement and capital standards.*

—— (August 2000), *Credit ratings and complementary sources of credit quality information.* Working papers no. 3.

—— (June 2004), *International convergence of capital measurement and capital standards. A revised framework.*

—— (December 2010), *A global regulatory framework for more resilient banks and banking system.*

—— (December 2010), *International framework for liquidity risk measurement, standards and monitoring.*

Becker, Bo and Milbourn, Todd (September 2010), *How did increased competition affect credit ratings?* NBER Working Paper Series 16404.

Bongaerts, Dion, Cremers, K.J. Martijn, and Goetzmann, William N. (2009), *Multiple ratings and credit spreads.* NBER Working Paper Series 15331.

Bowden, Bruce, Patel, Neal A., and Loveman, John A. (2010), *U.S. Financial Reform: Credit Rating Agencies.* Duane Morris LLP Overview.

Cantor, Richard, and Mann, C. (2009), *Are Corporate Bond Ratings Procyclical? An update.* Moody's Investor Services, Moody's Global Credit Policy, Special Comment.

CEBS (2006), *Guidelines on outsourcing.*

—— (October 2010), *Consultation paper CP43 on CEBS's advice to the European Commission on the non-eligibility of entities producing only credit scores for ECAI recognition.*

—— (November 2010), *Revised Guidelines on the recognition of External Credit Assessment Institutions.*

—— (December 2010), *Advice to the European Commission on the non-eligibility of entities only producing credit scores for ECAI recognition.*

CEIOPS (2009), *Advice for level 2 implementing measures on Solvency II: system of governance.*

CESR (January 2005), *Recommendations for the consistent implementation of the European Commission's Regulation on Prospectuses n° 809/2004 (Ref. CESR/05-054b).*

—— (March 2005), *Technical advice to the European Commission on possible measures concerning credit rating agencies (Ref. CESR/05-139b).*

—— (December 2006), *Report to the European Commission on the compliance of credit rating agencies with the IOSCO Code (Ref. CESR/06-545).*

—— (May 2008), *Second report to the European Commission on the compliance of credit rating agencies with the IOSCO Code and the role of credit rating agencies in structured finance (Ref. CESR/08-277).*

—— (May 2009), *Market Abuse Directive Level 3—Third set of CESR guidance and information on the common operation of the directive to the market (Ref. CESR/09-219).*

—— (May 2009), *Report on compliance of EU-based credit rating agencies with the 2008 IOSCO Code of Conduct (Ref. CESR/09-417).*

—— (July 2009), *Consultation paper CRAs central repository (Ref. CESR/09-579).*

—— (October 2009), *Consultation paper, Guidance on registration process, functioning of colleges, mediation protocol, information set out in Annex II, information set for the application for certification and for the assessment of CRAs systemic importance (Ref. CESR/09-955).*

—— (May 2010), *Technical advice to the European Commission on the equivalence between the US Regulatory and Supervisory Framework and the EU Regulatory Regime for Credit Rating Agencies (Ref. CESR/10-332).*

—— (June 2010), *Frequently asked questions regarding the EU Regulation on credit rating agencies: common positions agreed by CESR members (Ref. CESR/10-521).*

—— (June 2010), *Guidance on registration process, functioning of colleges, mediation protocol, information set out in Annex II, information set for the application for certification and for the assessment of CRAs systemic importance (Ref. CESR/10-347).*

—— (June 2010), *Guidelines for the implementation of the Central Repository (CEREP) (Ref. CESR/10-331).*

—— (June 2010), *Technical advice to the European Commission on the equivalence between the Japanese Regulatory and Supervisory Framework and the EU Regulatory Regime for Credit Rating Agencies (Ref. CESR/10-333).*

—— (August 2010), *Guidance on common standards for assessment of compliance of credit rating methodologies with the requirements set out in Article 8.3. (Ref. CESR/10-945).*

—— (August 2010), *Guidance on the enforcement practices and activities to be conducted under Article 21.3(a) of the Regulation (Ref. CESR/10-944).*

—— (December 2010), *Annual report according to Article 21 of Regulation (EC) 1060/2009 on credit rating agencies (Ref. CESR/10-1424).*

CGFS (January 2005), *The role of ratings in structured finance: issues and implications.* Report produced by a CGFS Working Group available at CGFS's website.

—— (July 2008), *Ratings in structured finance: what went wrong and what can be done to address shortcomings?* CGFS Publications No 32.

Council of the European Union (September 2010), *Press release 16452/10 17 November 2010 and Financial Supervision Package—frequently asked questions MEMO/10/434.*

De Larosière Group, (2009), *Report of The High-Level Group on Financial Supervision in the EU,* chaired by Jacques de Larosière.

Dun & Bradstreet, *History of Dun & Bradstreet.* Available at Dun & Bradstreet's website.

ECB (2000), *Guidelines of the European Central Bank on monetary policy instruments and procedures for the Eurosystem.*

ESMA (January 2011), *Call for evidence on the criteria for endorsement (Article 21 (2) (a) of the draft amended CRA Regulation (Ref. ESMA/2011/0005).*

—— (January 2011), *Frequently asked questions about ESMA (Ref. ESMA/2011/009).*

—— (March 2011), *Consultation paper, Guidelines on the application of the endorsement regime under Article 4 (3) of the Credit Rating Regulation 1060/2009 (Ref. ESMA/2011/97).*

—— (May 2011), *Guidelines on the application of the endorsement regime under Article 4 (3) of the Credit Rating Regulation 1060/2009 (Ref. ESMA/2011/139).*

—— (May 2011), *Technical advice to the Commission on fees for CRAs (Ref. ESMA/2011/144).*

European Commission (March 2006), *Communication on credit rating agencies, (2006/C 59/02 OJ C59, 11.3.2006).*

—— (July 2008), *Consultation document on policy options to address the problem of excessive reliance on ratings.*

—— (November 2008), *Commission staff working document accompanying the proposal for a Regulation of the European Parliament and of the Council on credit rating agencies, Impact assessment [COM(2008) 704] [SEC(2008) 2746].*

—— (November 2008), *European Commission's proposal for a Regulation of the European Parliament and of the Council on credit rating agencies (COM(2008) 704 final) (SEC 2008) 2745) {SEC(2008) 2746}).*

European Commission (July 2009), *Commission Services Staff working document: Possible further changes to the capital requirements directive.*

—— (July 2009), *Proposal for a Directive of the European Parliament and of the Council amending Directives 2006/48/EC and 2006/49/EC as regards capital requirements for the trading book and for re-securitisations, and the supervisory review of remuneration policies. [SEC(2009) 974 final; SEC(2009) 975 final].*

—— (February 2010), *Commission Services Staff working document: Possible further changes to the capital requirements directive.*

—— (June 2010), *Commission Staff working document accompanying the proposal for a Regulation of the European Parliament and of the Council amending Regulation (EC) No 1060/2009 on credit rating agencies, Impact assessment [COM(2010) 289 final] [SEC (2010) 679].*

—— (June 2010), *European Commission's proposal for a Regulation of the European Parliament and of the Council on amending Regulation (EC) No 1060/2009 on credit rating agencies (COM(2010) 289 final) (SEC(2010) 678}{SEC(2010) 679}).*

—— (September 2010), *Decision on the recognition of the legal and supervisory framework of Japan as equivalent to the requirements of Regulation (EC) No 1060/2009 of the European Parliament and of the Council on credit rating agencies.*

—— (November 2010), *Consultation on Credit Rating Agencies (CRAs), new initiatives.*

European Parliament (January 2004), *Resolution on Role and methods of rating agencies (2003/2081(INI)).*

—— (June 2011), *Resolution on credit rating agencies: future perspectives (2010/2302(INI).*

European Securities Markets Expert Group (2008), *Report to the European Commission on the role of credit rating agencies.*

Fitch, *The history of Fitch Ratings.* Available at Fitch's website.

—— (November 2002), *Fitch's views provided on SEC hearings on the current role and function of credit rating agencies in the operation of the securities markets.*

—— (November 2007), *The impact of poor underwriting practices and fraud in subprime RMBS performance.*

FSB (April 2010), *Report to G20 finance ministers and governors.*

—— (October 2010), *Principles for reducing reliance on CRA ratings.*

FSF (April 2008), *Report on enhancing market and institutional resilience.*

—— (October 2008), *Report on enhancing market and institutional resilience: update on implementation.*

—— (April 2009), *Report on enhancing market and institutional resilience: update on implementation.*

G-20, Summits declarations. Available at G-20's website.

García Alcubilla, Raquel and Ruiz del Pozo, Javier (2008), Credit rating agencies: the debate on future European legislation. *CNMV Bulletin,* Quarter III.

—— (2009), Credit rating agencies: Analysis of the proposal for European Parliament and Council Regulation. *CNMV Bulletin,* Quarter II.

González, Fernando, Haas, François, Johannes, Ronald, Persson, Mattias, Toledo, Liliana, Violi, Roberto, Wieland, Martin, and Zins, Carmen (June 2004), *Market dynamics associated with credit ratings, a literature review.* Occasional Paper Series, n.º 16, ECB.

IMF (October 2010), *Global financial stability report: sovereigns, funding, and systemic liquidity.*

IOSCO (September 2003), *Report on the activities of credit rating agencies.*

—— (September 2003), *Statement of principles regarding the activities of credit rating agencies.*

—— (October 2004), *Code of conduct fundamentals for credit rating agencies.*

—— (2005), *Principles on outsourcing of financial services for market intermediaries.*

—— (February 2007), *Review of implementation of the IOSCO fundamentals of a code of conduct for credit rating agencies. Consultation report.*

—— (March 2008), *Consultation report. The role of credit rating agencies in structured finance markets.*

—— (May 2008), *Code of conduct fundamentals for credit rating agencies. Revised May 2008.*

—— (May 2008), *The role of credit rating agencies in structured finance markets. Final report.*

—— (March 2009), *A review of implementation of the IOSCO code of conduct fundamentals for credit rating agencies.*

—— (March 2009), *Note on international cooperation in oversight of credit rating agencies.*

—— (April 2010), *Disclosure principles for public offerings and listings of asset-backed securities.*

—— (May 2010), *Consultation report. Regulatory implementation of the statement of principles regarding the activities of credit rating agencies.*

—— (July 2010), *Transparency of structured finance products, final report.*

—— (February 2011), *Report on regulatory implementation of the statement of principles regarding the activities of credit rating agencies in the different jurisdictions.*

Joint Forum (June 2009), *Stocktaking on the use of credit ratings.*

Moody's, *Moody's History.* Available at Moody's website.

—— (July 2002), *Moody's analysis of US corporate rating triggers heightens need for increased disclosure,* Special comment.

—— (September 2002), *Rating triggers in Europe: limited awareness but widely used among corporate issuers.* Special comment.

—— (January 2011), *Moody's response to the European Commission public consultation on CRAs.*

Norris, James D (1978), *R.G. Dun & Co., 1841–1900: The Development of Credit Reporting in the Nineteenth Century.* Westport, CT: Greenwood Press.

Olegario, Rowena (2002), *Credit-reporting agencies: their historical roots, current status, and role in market development.* Background document for the World Development Report 2002.

Partnoy, Frank (1999), The Siskel and Ebert of financial markets? Two thumbs down for the credit rating agencies. *Washington University Law Quarterly,* 77, October.

SEC (July 2008), *Summary report of issues identified in the Commission staff's examinations of select credit rating agencies.*

—— (December 2010), *Requested comment for credit rating standardization study.*

—— (January 2011), *Annual report on nationally recognized statistical rating organisations.*

—— (February 2011), *Proposed revisions to rules that contain references to credit ratings.*

—— (March 2011), *Proposed revisions to rules that rely on credit ratings as an assessment of credit worthiness, and replace them with alternative criteria.*

—— (May 2011), *Proposed rules for nationally recognized statistical rating organizations. Release No. 34-64514; File No. S7-18-11.*

S&P, *Standard and Poor's Company History.* Available at Standard and Poor's website.

Sy, Amadou N.R., (2009), *The systemic regulation of credit rating agencies and rated markets.* IMF Working Paper 09/129.

Sylla, Richard (2002), *An Historical Primer on the Business of Credit Rating.* The New York University Salomon Center Series on Financial Markets and Institutions, Kluwer Academic Publishers, Boston.

White, Lawrence J (2001), *The credit rating industry: an industrial organization analysis.* Paper presented at a conference at the Stern School of Business.

—— (2010), Markets: The credit rating agencies. *Journal of Economic Perspectives,* 24(2): 211–26.

Index

Haircut - diff bet.

Market value of asset used as loan collateral

& amount of loan - amount of haircut reflects lender's perceived risk of loss from asset falling in value / sold in fire sale.

fire sale - selling goods & assets at heavily discounted prices

---

RATING TRIGGER : provision in loan agreement / bond indenture allowing one party / other to take a certain action if the borrower's CR changes for any reason - eg. if bond issuer's CR falls, a rating trigger may release bond holders from certain obligations specified in the indenture.

eg. downgrade in firm's CR may set off accelerated debt repayment in a backup credit line.

PG&E - importance of rating trigger in PG&E's subsequent bankruptcy caused one CRA to indicate it wd consider negative consequences of triggers in evaluating if company be able to survive ~~a~~ downgrade. Some cos. began to reconsider inclusion of rating triggers in borrowing agreements when they discovered CRAs wd consider such triggers in eval. credit quality of corporate debt.